The *Sams Teach Yourself in 24 Hours* Series

Sams Teach Yourself in 24 Hours books provide quick and easy answers in a proven step-by-step approach that works for you. In just 24 sessions of one hour or less, you will tackle every task you need to get the results you want. Let our experienced authors present the most accurate information to get you reliable answers—fast!

Using the Workshop Applets

Figures in a book are fine. However, they don't do anything; they just sit there. It would be nice if they could be more like a video, changing to show the different steps in a process. That's what the Workshop applets in this book do. Every time you push a button, you see a different step being executed. For example, bars in a bar chart are rearranged and data appears and disappears in a tree, all under your control. The applets make it easy to see how data structures and algorithms work.

To use the Workshop applets, you'll need a Web browser. One is supplied on the CD that accompanies this book. Read Appendix B, "How to Run the Workshop Applets and Sample Programs," and the readme file on the CD, to see how the supplied browser works. Or use your own browser. When you start an applet, you'll see a picture and several buttons. This chart summarizes what the buttons do.

An operation is carried out by clicking a particular button multiple times. After each click, a message tells you what is happening.

> Always keep clicking the button until the operation is complete. A completed operation is signaled by the message Push any button. For example, when inserting an item, continue to click the Ins button until the insertion is complete and Push any button appears.

Applets That Demonstrate General-Purpose Data Structures

The following buttons are used in the Array, Ordered, LinkList, Hash, HashDouble, and HashChain Workshop applets:

- New—Resets the applet and allows you to specify the size of the data structure (within limits).
- Fill—Fills the number of data items you specify into the structure. (This happens all at once, unlike Ins.)
- Ins—Inserts a single item, whose key value you specify, into t   Each click of the button shows one step in the insertion proc
- Find—Searches for an item whose key you specify. Each click shows one step in the search process.
- Del—Deletes an item whose key you specify. Each click of the button shows one step in the deletion process.

SAMS

Teach Yourself

Data Structures and Algorithms

in 24 Hours

D1294471

Applets That Demonstrate Trees

The following buttons are used in the Tree, RBTree, and Tree234 Workshop applets. These applets also use many of the buttons described in "Applets That Demonstrate General-Purpose Data Structures."

- Trav—(Tree only) Traverses a tree in one of the three orders you specify. A red arrow moves from node to node.
- Start—(RBTree only) Starts a new tree, which is empty except for a root with the key 50.
- Flip—(RBTree only) Exchanges the color of a parent with the color of its children (from red to black or black to red). Click on the parent before this operation.
- RoL—(RBTree only) Rotates part of the tree to the left. Click on the top node before this operation.
- RoR—(RBTree only) Rotates part of the tree to the right. Click on the top node before this operation.
- R/B—(RBTree only) Changes the color of a single node. Click on the node before this operation.
- Zoom—(Tree234 only) Toggles between the zoomed-in view, in which all data items in a node are shown but not all the nodes are visible at once, and the zoomed-out view, in which all the nodes are shown but not the data.

Applets That Demonstrate Sorting Algorithms

The following buttons are used in the bubbleSort, insertSort, mergeSort, Partition, quickSort1, and quickSort2 Workshop applets:

- New—Resets the bars to their unsorted order. Toggles between a random and an inversely sorted configuration.
- Size—Toggles between 10 or 12 bars and 100 bars.
- Draw—Redraws the picture. Clicking this button is sometimes necessary in Run mode, if the display becomes corrupted. This button stops the run, so after clicking Draw, click Run again.
- Run—Starts the sorting process running by itself. Most useful when 100 bars are being sorted. Clicking Run during a run stops the sort; clicking it again restarts the run.
- Step—Carries out one step of the sorting process.

Specialized Applets

The following buttons are used in the Stack, Queue, PriorityQ, and Towers Workshop applets:

- Push—(Stack only) Inserts one data item.
- Pop—(Stack only) Removes one data item.
- Peek—(Stack, Queue, and PriorityQ only) Returns the value of an item without removing it.
- Ins—(Queue and PriorityQ only) Inserts an item.
- Rem—(Queue and PriorityQ only) Removes an item.
- Step—(Towers only) Carries out one step in the puzzle solution.
- Run—(Towers only) Runs the puzzle solution at full speed.

SAMS

Robert Lafore

SAMS
Teach Yourself
Data Structures and Algorithms
in 24 Hours

SAMS

201 West 103rd St., Indianapolis, Indiana, 46290 USA

Sams Teach Yourself Data Structures and Algorithms in 24 Hours

Copyright © 1999 by Sams Publishing

All rights reserved. No part of this book shall be reproduced, stored in a retrieval system, or transmitted by any means, electronic, mechanical, photo-copying, recording, or otherwise, without written permission from the publisher. No patent liability is assumed with respect to the use of the information contained herein. Although every precaution has been taken in the preparation of this book, the publisher and author assume no responsibility for errors or omissions. Neither is any liability assumed for damages resulting from the use of the information contained herein.

International Standard Book Number: 0-672-31633-1

Library of Congress Catalog Card Number: 98-83221

Printed in the United States of America

First Printing: May 1999

01 00 99   4 3 2 1

Trademarks

All terms mentioned in this book that are known to be trademarks or service marks have been appropriately capitalized. Sams Publishing cannot attest to the accuracy of this information. Use of a term in this book should not be regarded as affecting the validity of any trademark or service mark.

Warning and Disclaimer

Every effort has been made to make this book as complete and as accurate as possible, but no warranty or fitness is implied. The information provided is on an "as is" basis. The authors and the publisher shall have neither liability or responsibility to any person or entity with respect to any loss or damages arising from the information contained in this book or from the use of the CD-ROM or programs accompanying it.

EXECUTIVE EDITOR
Brian Gill

DEVELOPMENT EDITOR
Jeff Durham

MANAGING EDITOR
Jodi Jensen

PROJECT EDITOR
Tonya Simpson

COPY EDITOR
Mike Henry

INDEXER
Larry Sweazy

PROOFREADERS
Mona Brown
Jill Mazurczyk

TECHNICAL EDITOR
Richard Wright

SOFTWARE DEVELOPMENT SPECIALIST
Dan Scherf

INTERIOR DESIGN
Gary Adair

COVER DESIGN
Aren Howell

COPY WRITER
Eric Borgert

LAYOUT TECHNICIANS
Brian Borders
Susan Geiselman

Contents at a Glance

Table of Contents

About the Author

Robert Lafore has degrees in Electrical Engineering and Mathematics, has worked as a systems analyst for the Lawrence Berkeley Laboratory, founded his own software company, and is a best-selling writer in the field of computer programming. Some of his current titles are *C++ Interactive Course*, *Object-Oriented Programming in C++*, and *Data Structures and Algorithms in Java by all Waite Group Press*. Earlier best-selling titles include *Assembly Language Primer for the IBM PC* and (back at the beginning of the computer revolution) *Soul of CP/M*.

Dedication

This book is dedicated to Laurie Cameron, a friend since the Paleolithic era,
and our English teacher Mrs. Mathews. Rule 22! Semicolons separate independent clauses!

Acknowledgments

My primary thanks go to my executive editor at Sams Publishing, Brian Gill, who conceived this book idea and ably shepherded it to completion. My development editor, Jeff Durham, performed his usual masterful job of expunging inconsistencies, lacunae, and downright blunders while readying the manuscript for production. Tonya Simpson, the project editor, did a masterful job of making sure that everyone else's work fit together into a coherent whole. Mike Henry handled the copy editing very professionally, ensuring that may was always might. Richard Wright, the tech editor, went through everything with a fine-tooth comb and caught a few whoppers that one else could have. Dan Scherf put the CD together in his usual competent way. My thanks to you all.

Tell Us What You Think!

As the reader of this book, *you* are our most important critic and commentator. We value your opinion and want to know what we're doing right, what we could do better, what areas you'd like to see us publish in, and any other words of wisdom you're willing to pass our way.

As an Associate Publisher for Sams Publishing, I welcome your comments. You can fax, email, or write me directly to let me know what you did or didn't like about this book—as well as what we can do to make our books stronger.

Please note that I cannot help you with technical problems related to the topic of this book, and that due to the high volume of mail I receive, I might not be able to reply to every message.

When you write, please be sure to include this book's title and author as well as your name and phone or fax number. I will carefully review your comments and share them with the author and editors who worked on the book.

Fax: 317-581-4770

Email: bjones@mcp.com

Mail: Bradley L. Jones
           Associate Publisher
           Sams Publishing
           201 West 103rd Street
           Indianapolis, IN 46290 USA

Introduction

This introduction tells you briefly

- What this book is about
- Why it's different
- Who might want to read it
- What you need to know before you read it
- The software and equipment you need to use it
- How this book is organized

What This Book Is About

This book is about data structures and algorithms as used in computer programming. Data structures are ways in which data is arranged in your computer's memory (or stored on disk). Algorithms are the procedures a software program uses to manipulate the data in these structures.

Almost every computer program, even a simple one, uses data structures and algorithms. For example, consider a program that prints address labels. The program might use an array containing the addresses to be printed, and a simple for loop to step through the array, printing each address.

The array in this example is a data structure, and the for loop, used for sequential access to the array, executes a simple algorithm. For uncomplicated programs with small amounts of data, such a simple approach might be all you need. However, for programs that handle even moderately large amounts of data, or which solve problems that are slightly out of the ordinary, more sophisticated techniques are necessary. Simply knowing the syntax of a computer language such as C++ isn't enough.

This book is about what you need to know *after* you've learned a programming language. The material we cover here is typically taught in colleges and universities as a second-year course in computer science, after a student has mastered the fundamentals of programming.

What's Different About This Book

There are dozens of books on data structures and algorithms. What's different about this one? Three things:

- Our primary goal in writing this book is to make the topics we cover easy to understand.
- Demonstration programs called *Workshop applets* bring to life the topics we cover, showing you step by step, with "moving pictures," how data structures and algorithms work.
- The sample code is written as clearly and concisely as possible, using C++.

Let's look at these features in more detail.

Easy to Understand

Typical computer science textbooks are full of theory, mathematical formulas, and abstruse examples of computer code. This book, on the other hand, concentrates on simple explanations of techniques that can be applied to real-world problems. We avoid complex proofs and heavy math. There are lots of figures to augment the text.

Many books on data structures and algorithms include considerable material on software engineering. Software engineering is a body of study concerned with designing and implementing large and complex software projects.

However, it's our belief that data structures and algorithms are complicated enough without involving this additional discipline, so we have deliberately de-emphasized software engineering in this book. (We'll discuss the relationship of data structures and algorithms to software engineering in Hour 1, "Overview of Data Structures and Alogorithms.")

Of course we use an object-oriented approach, and we discuss various aspects of object-oriented design as we go along, including a mini-tutorial on OOP in Hour 1. Our primary emphasis, however, is on the data structures and algorithms themselves.

Workshop Applets

The CD-ROM that accompanies this book includes demonstration programs, in the form of Java applets, that cover the topics we discuss. These applets, which we call *Workshop applets*, will run on most computer systems, using a Web browser. A Web browser for Microsoft Windows systems is included with the CD-ROM that accompanies this book. (See the `readme` file on the CD-ROM for more details on software compatibility.)

The Workshop applets create graphic images that show you in "slow motion" how an algorithm works.

For example, in one Workshop applet, each time you push a button, a bar chart shows you one step in the process of sorting the bars into ascending order. The values of variables used in the sorting algorithm are also shown, so you can see exactly how the computer code works when executing the algorithm. Text displayed in the chart explains what's happening.

Another applet models a binary tree. Arrows move up and down the tree, so you can follow the steps involved in inserting or deleting a node from the tree. There is at least one Workshop applet for each of the major topics in the book.

These Workshop applets make it far more obvious what a data structure really looks like, or what an algorithm is supposed to do, than a text description ever could. Of course, we provide a text description as well. The combination of Workshop applets, clear text, and illustrations should make things easy.

These Workshop applets are standalone graphics-based programs. You can use them as a learning tool that augments the material in the book. (Note that they're not the same as the C++ sample code found in the text of the book, which we'll discuss next.)

C++ Sample Code

C++ is the programming language most often used today for major software projects. Its predecessor, C, combined speed and versatility, making it the first higher-level language that could be used for systems programming. C++ retains these advantages and adds the capability for object-oriented programming (OOP).

OOP offers compelling advantages over the old-fashioned procedural approach, and is quickly supplanting it for serious program development. Don't be alarmed if you aren't familiar with OOP. It's not really that hard to understand. We'll explain the basics of OOP in Hour 1.

Who This Book Is For

This book can be used as a text in a data structures and algorithms course, typically taught in the second year of a computer science curriculum. However, it is also designed for professional programmers and for anyone else who needs to take the next step up from merely knowing a programming language. Because it's easy to understand, it is also appropriate as a supplemental text to a more formal course.

What You Need to Know Before You Read This Book

The only prerequisite for using this book is a knowledge of some programming language. Although the sample code is written in C++, you don't really need to know C++ to follow what's happening. The text and Workshop applets will give you the big picture.

If you know C++, you can also follow the coding details in the sample programs. C++ is not hard to understand, and we've tried to keep the syntax as general as possible, avoiding dense or obscure usages.

The Software You Need to Use This Book

There are two kinds of software associated with this book: Workshop applets and sample programs.

To run the Workshop applets you need a Web browser or an applet viewer utility. The CD-ROM that accompanies this book includes a Web browser that will work in a Microsoft Windows environment. If you're not running Windows, the browser on your system will probably work just as well.

Executable versions of the sample programs are provided on the CD-ROM in the form of .EXE files. To execute these files you can use the MS-DOS box built into Windows.

Source code for the sample programs is provided on the CD-ROM in the form of .CPP files. If you have a C++ compiler, you can compile the source code into an executable program. This allows you to modify the source code and experiment with it. Many manufacturers, including Microsoft and Borland, supply excellent C++ compilers.

Appendix B provides details on how to run the Workshop applets and sample programs. Also, see the readme file on the included CD-ROM for details on supported platforms and equipment requirements.

How This Book Is Organized

This section is intended for teachers and others who want a quick overview of the contents of the book. It assumes you're already familiar with the topics and terms involved in a study of data structures and algorithms.

The first three hours are intended to ease the reader into data structures and algorithms as painlessly as possible.

Hour 1 presents an overview of the topics to be discussed and introduces a small number of terms that will be needed later on. For readers unfamiliar with object-oriented programming, it summarizes those aspects of this discipline that will be needed in the balance of the book.

Hour 2, "Arrays," and Hour 3, "Ordered Arrays," focus on arrays. However, there are two subtexts: the use of classes to encapsulate data storage structures, and the class interface. Searching, insertion, and deletion in arrays and ordered arrays are covered. Linear searching and binary searching are explained. Workshop applets demonstrate these algorithms with unordered and ordered arrays.

In Hour 4, "The Bubble Sort," and Hour 5, "The Insertion Sort," we introduce basic sorting concepts with two simple (but slow) sorting techniques. Each sorting algorithm is demonstrated by a Workshop applet.

Hour 6, "Stacks," and Hour 7, "Queues and Priority Queues," cover three data structures that can be thought of as Abstract Data Types (ADTs): the stack, queue, and priority queue. Each is demonstrated by a Workshop applet. These structures will reappear later in the book, embedded in various algorithms.

Hour 8, "Linked Lists," introduces the concepts behind lists. A Workshop applet shows how insertion, searching, and deletion are carried out. Hour 9, "Abstract Data Types," uses implementations of stacks and queues with linked lists to demonstrate ADTs. Hour 10, "Specialized Lists," describes sorted lists and doubly linked lists.

In Hour 11, "Recursion," we explain recursion, and in Hour 12, "Applied Recursion," we explore several examples of recursion, including the Towers of Hanoi puzzle and the mergesort.

Hour 13, "Quicksort," delves into the most popular sorting technique: quicksort. Workshop applets demonstrate partitioning (the basis of quicksort), and a simple version of quicksort. Hour 14, "Improving Quicksort," focuses on some weaknesses of the simple version and how to improve them. Two more Workshop applets demonstrate how it works.

In Hour 15, "Binary Trees," we begin our exploration of trees. This hour covers the simplest popular tree structure: unbalanced binary search trees. A Workshop applet demonstrates insertion, deletion, and traversal. In Hour 16, "Traversing Binary Trees," we discuss traversal and show C++ code for a binary tree.

Hour 17, "Red-Black Trees," explains red-black trees, one of the most efficient balanced trees. The Workshop applet demonstrates the rotations and color switches necessary to balance the tree. Hour 18, "Red-Black Tree Insertions," shows how insertions are carried out using rotations and color changes.

In Hour 19, "2-3-4 Trees," we cover 2-3-4 trees as an example of multiway trees. A Workshop applet shows how they work. Hour 20, "Implementing 2-3-4 Trees," presents C++ code for a 2-3-4 tree and discusses the relationship of 2-3-4 trees to red-black trees.

Hour 21, "Hash Tables," introduces this data structure, focusing on linear probing. Hour 22, "Quadratic Probing," shows improvements that can be made to the linear probing scheme. Hour 23, "Separate Chaining," shows a different approach to hash tables. Workshops applets demonstrate all three approaches.

In Hour 24, "When to Use What," we summarize the various data structures described in earlier hours, with special attention to which structure is appropriate in a given situation.

Appendix B, explains how to Run the Workshop applets and sample programs. The `readme` file on the included CD-ROM has additional information on these topics.

Appendix C, "Further Reading," describes some books appropriate for further reading on data structures and other related topics.

Enjoy Yourself!

We hope we've made the learning process as painless as possible. Ideally, it should even be fun. Let us know if you think we've succeeded in reaching this ideal, or if not, where you think improvements might be made.

Conventions Used in This Book

This book uses different typefaces to differentiate between code and regular English, and also to help you identify important concepts.

Text that you type and text that should appear on your screen is presented in `monospace` type.

`It will look like this to mimic the way text looks on your screen.`

Placeholders for variables and expressions appear in `monospace italic` font. You should replace the placeholder with the specific value it represents.

This arrow (➡) at the beginning of a line of code means that a single line of code is too long to fit on the printed page. Continue typing all characters after the ➡ as though they were part of the preceding line.

A Note presents interesting pieces of information related to the surrounding discussion.

A Tip offers advice or teaches an easier way to do something.

A Caution advises you about potential problems and helps you steer clear of disaster.

NEW TERM New Term icons provide clear definitions of new, essential terms. The term appears in italic.

INPUT The Input icon identifies code that you can type in yourself. It usually appears next to a listing.

OUTPUT The Output icon highlights the output produced by running a program. It usually appears after a listing.

ANALYSIS The Analysis icon alerts you to the author's line-by-line analysis of a program.

 The CD-ROM icon alerts you to information or items that appear on the CD-ROM that accompanies this book.

 To Do tasks help you learn the topic by working hands-on. Follow these steps to create your own examples.

PART I

Introducing Data Structures and Algorithms

Hour

HOUR 1

Overview of Data Structures and Algorithms

Welcome to *Sams Teach Yourself Data Structures and Algorithms in 24 Hours*! In this first hour you will

- Find out why you need to know about data structures and algorithms
- Discover what data structures and algorithms are
- Learn some terminology we'll use in the rest of the book
- Review object-oriented programming

As you start this book, you might have some questions:

- What are data structures and algorithms?
- What good will it do me to know about them?
- Why can't I use simple program features like arrays and for loops to handle my data?
- When does it make sense to apply what I learn here?

In this first hour we'll attempt to answer these questions. We'll also introduce some terms you'll need to know and generally set the stage for the more detailed material to follow. Finally, for those of you who have not yet been exposed to object-oriented programming (OOP), we'll briefly explain just enough about it to get you started.

Some Uses for Data Structures and Algorithms

NEW TERM The subjects of this book are data structures and algorithms. A *data structure* is an arrangement of data in a computer's memory (or sometimes on a disk). Data structures include linked lists, stacks, binary trees, and hash tables, among others. *Algorithms* manipulate the data in these structures in various ways, such as inserting a new data item, searching for a particular item, or sorting the items. You can think of an algorithm as a recipe: a list of detailed instructions for carrying out an activity.

What sorts of problems can you solve with a knowledge of these topics? As a rough approximation, we might divide the situations in which they're useful into three categories:

- Real-world data storage
- Programmer's tools
- Modeling

These are not hard-and-fast categories, but they might help give you a feeling for the usefulness of this book's subject matter. You'll look at them in more detail in the following sections.

Real-World Data Storage

Many of the structures and techniques you'll learn are concerned with how to handle real-world data storage. By real-world data, we mean data that describes physical entities external to the computer. Some examples are a personnel record that describes an actual human being, an inventory record that describes an existing car part or grocery item, and a financial transaction record that describes, say, an actual check written to pay the grocery bill.

A non-computer example of real-world data storage is a stack of index cards. These cards can be used for a variety of purposes. If each card holds a person's name, address, and phone number, the result is an address book. If each card holds the name, location, and value of a household possession, the result is a home inventory.

Some operating systems come with a utility program that simulates a box of index cards. Previous versions of Microsoft Windows, for example, included the Cardfile program. Figure 1.1 shows how this program looked with data on the cards creating an address book.

FIGURE 1.1

The Cardfile program.

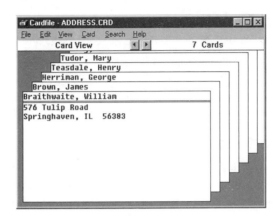

The filing cards are represented by rectangles. Above the double line is the card's title, called the *index line*. Below is the rest of the data. In this example a person's name is placed above the index line, with the address and phone number placed below.

You can find a card with a given name by selecting GoTo from the Search menu and typing the name, as it appears on the index line, into a text field. Also, by selecting Find from the Search menu, you can search for text other than that on the index line, and thus find a person's name if you know his phone number or address.

This is all very nice for the program's user, but suppose you wanted to write a card file program of your own. You might need to answer questions like this:

- How would you store the data in your computer's memory?
- Would your method work for a hundred file cards? A thousand? A million?
- Would your method permit quick insertion of new cards and deletion of old ones?
- Would it allow for fast searching for a specified card?
- Suppose you wanted to arrange the cards in alphabetical order. How would you sort them?

In this book, we will be focusing on data structures that might be used to implement the Cardfile program or solve similar problems.

As we noted, not all data-storage programs are as simple as the Cardfile program. Imagine the database the Department of Motor Vehicles uses to keep track of driver's licenses, or an airline reservation system that stores passenger and flight information. Such systems might include many data structures. Designing such complex systems requires the application of software engineering, which we'll mention toward the end of this hour. Now let's look at the second major use for data structures and algorithms.

Programmer's Tools

Not all data storage structures are used to store real-world data. Typically, real-world data is accessed more or less directly by a program's user. However, some data storage structures are not meant to be accessed by the user, but by the program itself. A programmer uses such structures as tools to facilitate some other operation. Stacks, queues, and priority queues are often used in this way. We'll see examples as we go along.

Real-World Modeling

The third use of data structures and algorithms is not as commonly used as the first two. Some data structures directly model a real-world situation. Stacks, queues, and priority queues are often used for this purpose. A queue, for example, can model customers waiting in line at a bank, whereas a priority queue can model messages waiting to be transmitted over a local area network.

Overview of Data Structures

Another way to look at data structures is to focus on their strengths and weaknesses. This section provides an overview, in the form of a table, of the major data storage structures discussed in this book. This is a bird's-eye view of a landscape that we'll be covering later at ground level, so don't be alarmed if it looks a bit mysterious. Table 1.1 shows the advantages and disadvantages of the various data structures described in this book.

TABLE 1.1 CHARACTERISTICS OF DATA STRUCTURES

Data Structure	Advantages	Disadvantages
Array	Quick insertion, very fast access if index known.	Slow search, slow deletion, fixed size.
Ordered array	Quicker search than unsorted array.	Slow insertion and deletion, fixed size.
Stack	Provides last-in, first-out access.	Slow access to other items.
Queue	Provides first-in, first-out access.	Slow access to other items.

Data Structure	Advantages	Disadvantages
Linked list	Quick insertion, quick deletion.	Slow search.
Binary tree	Quick search, insertion, deletion (if tree remains balanced).	Deletion algorithm is complex.
Red-black tree	Quick search, insertion, deletion. Tree always balanced.	Complex.
2-3-4 tree	Quick search, insertion, deletion. Tree always balanced. Similar trees good for disk storage.	Complex.
Hash table	Very fast access if key known. Fast insertion.	Slow deletion, access slow if key not known, inefficient memory usage.
Heap	Fast insertion, deletion, access to largest item.	Slow access to other items.

Overview of Algorithms

An algorithm can be thought of as the detailed instructions for carrying out some operation. In a computer program these instructions take the form of program statements. Many of the algorithms we'll discuss apply directly to specific data structures. For most data structures, you must know how to do the following:

- Insert a new data item.
- Search for a specified item.
- Delete a specified item.

NEW TERM You might also need to know how to *traverse* through all the items in a data structure, visiting each one in turn so as to display it or perform some other action on it.

NEW TERM Another important algorithm category is *sorting*. There are many ways to sort data, and we devote Hours 4, 5, 13, and 14 to this topic.

NEW TERM The concept of *recursion* is important in designing certain algorithms. Recursion involves a function calling itself. We'll look at recursion in Hours 11 and 12.

Some Initial Definitions

Before we move on to a more detailed look at data structures and algorithms in the chapters to come, let's look at a few terms that will be used throughout this book.

Datafile

NEW TERM We'll use the term *datafile* to refer to a collection of similar data items. As an example, if you create an address book using the Cardfile program, the collection of cards you've created constitutes a datafile. The word *file* should not be confused with the files stored on a computer's hard disk. A datafile refers to data in the real world, which might or might not be associated with a computer.

Record

NEW TERM *Records* are the units into which a datafile is divided. They provide a format for storing information. In the Cardfile program, each card represents a record. A record includes all the information about some entity, in a situation in which there are many such entities. A record might correspond to a person in a personnel file, a car part in an auto supply inventory, or a recipe in a cookbook file.

Field

NEW TERM A record is usually divided into several *fields*. A field holds a particular kind of data. In the Cardfile program there are really only two fields: the index line (above the double line) and the rest of the data (below the line); both fields hold text. Generally, each field holds a particular kind of data. In Figure 1.1, we show the index line field as holding a person's name.

More sophisticated database programs use records with more fields than Cardfile has. Figure 1.2 shows such a record, where each line represents a distinct field.

In a C++ program, records are usually represented by objects of an appropriate class. (In C, records would probably be represented by structures.) Individual data members within an object represent fields within a record. We'll return to this later in this hour.

Key

NEW TERM To search for a record within a datafile you must designate one of the record's fields as a *key*. You'll search for the record with a specific key. For example, in the Cardfile program you might search in the index-line field for the key Brown. When you find the record with that key, you'll be able to access all its fields, not just the key. We might say that the key *unlocks* the entire record.

FIGURE 1.2

A record with multiple fields.

Employee number:
Social security number:
Last name:
First name:
Street address:
City:
State:
Zip code:
Phone number:
Date of birth:
Date of first employment:
Salary:

In Cardfile you can also search for individual words or phrases in the rest of the data on the card, but this is actually all one field. The program searches through the text in the entire field even if all you're looking for is the phone number. This kind of text search isn't very efficient, but it's flexible because the user doesn't need to decide how to divide the card into fields.

In a more full-featured database program (Microsoft Access, for example), you can usually designate any field as the key. In Figure 1.2, for example, you could search by, say, zip code, and the program would find all employees who live in that zip code.

Search Key

NEW TERM Every record has a key. Often you have a key (a person's last name, for example) and you want the record containing that key. The key value you're looking for in a search is called the *search key*. The search key is compared with the key field of each record in turn. If there's a match, the record can be returned or displayed. If there's no match, the user can be informed of this fact.

That's all the definitions you'll need for a while. Now we'll briefly consider a topic that's not directly related to data structures and algorithms, but is related to modern programming practice.

A Quick Introduction to Object-Oriented Programming

This section is for those of you who have not yet been exposed to object-oriented programming. However, caveat emptor. We cannot, in a few pages, do justice to all the innovative new ideas associated with OOP. Our goal is merely to make it possible for you to understand the sample programs in the text of this book. What we say here won't transform you into an object-oriented C++ programmer, but it should make it possible for you to follow the sample programs. (If you know OOP, you can probably skip this section.)

If, after reading this section and examining some of the sample code in the following hours, you still find the whole OOP business as alien as quantum physics, you might need a more thorough exposure to OOP. See the reading list in Appendix C, "Further Reading," for suggestions.

Problems with Procedural Languages

OOP was invented because procedural languages, like C, Pascal, and BASIC, were found to be inadequate for large and complex programs. Why was this? The problems have to do with the overall organization of the program. Procedural programs are organized by dividing the code into functions (called procedures or subroutines in some languages). Groups of functions could form larger units called modules or files.

Crude Organizational Units

One difficulty with this kind of function-based organization was that it focused on functions at the expense of data. There weren't many options when it came to data. To simplify slightly, data could be local to a particular function, or it could be global—accessible to all functions. There was no way (at least not a flexible way) to specify that some functions could access a data item and others couldn't.

This caused problems when several functions needed to access the same data. To be available to more than one function, such variables had to be global, but global data could be accessed inadvertently by any function in the program. This led to frequent programming errors. What was needed was a way to fine-tune data accessibility, allowing variables to be available to functions with a need to access the data, but hiding it from others.

Poor Modeling of the Real World

It is also hard to conceptualize a real-world problem using procedural languages. Functions carry out a task, and data stores information, but most real-world objects do both these things. The thermostat on your furnace, for example, carries out tasks (turning the furnace on and off), but also stores information (the actual current temperature and the desired temperature).

If you wrote a thermostat control program, you might end up with two functions, `furnace_on()` and `furnace_off()`. But you might also end up with two global variables, `currentTemp` (supplied by a thermometer) and `desiredTemp` (set by the user). However, these functions and variables wouldn't form any sort of programming unit; there would be no unit in the program you could call `thermostat`. The only such unit would be in the programmer's mind.

For large programs, which might contain hundreds of entities like thermostats, this procedural approach made things chaotic, error-prone, and sometimes impossible to implement at all.

Objects in a Nutshell

The idea of objects arose in the programming community as a solution to the problems we just discussed with procedural languages. In this section, we'll discuss objects, classes, and several other topics.

Objects

Here's the amazing breakthrough that is the key to OOP: An object contains both functions and variables. A `Thermostat` object, for example, would contain not only `furnace_on()` and `furnace_off()` functions, but also `currentTemp` and `desiredTemp` variables.

This new entity, the object, solves several problems simultaneously. Not only does a programming object correspond more accurately to objects in the real world, it also solves the problem engendered by global data in the procedural model. The `furnace_on()` and `furnace_off()` functions can access `currentTemp` and `desiredTemp`. However, these variables are hidden from functions that are not part of `thermostat`, so they are less likely to be accidentally changed by a rogue function.

Incidentally, before going further we should note that functions within objects are called *member functions* in C++. (They're often called *methods* in other languages.) Variables within objects are called *data members*. (They're called *instance data* or *fields* in other languages.)

Classes

You might think that the idea of an object would be enough for one programming revolution, but there's more. Early on, it was realized that you might want to make several objects of the same type. Maybe you're writing a furnace control program for an entire apartment house, for example, and you need several dozen Thermostat objects in your program. It seems a shame to go to the trouble of specifying each one separately. Thus the idea of classes was born.

NEW TERM   A *class* is a specification—a blueprint—for one or more objects. Listing 1.1 shows how a Thermostat class, for example, might look in C++.

INPUT   **LISTING 1.1**   THE Thermostat CLASS

```
class Thermostat
    {
    private:
       float currentTemp();
       float desiredTemp();

    public:
    void furnace_on()
       {
       // function body goes here
       }

    void furnace_off()
       {
       // function body goes here
       }
    };  // end class Thermostat
```

The C++ keyword class introduces the class specification, followed by the name you want to give the class; here it's Thermostat. Enclosed in curly brackets are the data members and member functions (variables and functions) that make up the class. We've left out the body of the member functions; normally there would be many lines of program code for each one. C programmers will recognize this syntax as similar to that of a structure.

Object Creation

Specifying a class doesn't create any objects of that class. (In the same way specifying a structure in C doesn't create any variables.) To actually create objects in C++ you must define them as you do other variables. Here's how we might create two objects of class Thermostat:

```
Thermostat therm1, therm2;
```

 Incidentally, creating an object is also called *instantiating* it, and an object is often referred to as an *instance* of a class.

Accessing Object Member Functions

After you've specified a class and created some objects of that class, other parts of your program must interact with these objects. How do they do that? Typically, other parts of the program interact with an object's member functions, not with its data members. For example, to tell the therm2 object to turn on the furnace, we would say

```
therm2.furnace_on();
```

The dot operator is simply a period (.). It associates an object with one of its member functions (or occasionally with one of its data members).

At this point we've covered (rather briefly) several of the most important features of OOP. To summarize:

- Objects contain both member functions and data members (variables).
- A class is a specification for any number of objects.
- To create an object, you must define it as you would an ordinary variable.
- To invoke a member (usually a function) for a particular object, you use the dot operator.

These concepts are deep and far-reaching. It's almost impossible to assimilate them the first time you see them, so don't worry if you feel a bit confused. As you see more classes and what they do, the mist should start to clear.

A Runnable Object-Oriented Program

Let's look at an object-oriented program that runs and generates actual output. It features a class called BankAccount that models a checking account at a bank. The program creates an account with an opening balance, displays the balance, makes a deposit and a withdrawal, and then displays the new balance. Listing 1.2 is the code for bank.cpp.

```cpp
//bank.cpp
//demonstrates basic OOP syntax
#include <iostream>
using namespace std;
////////////////////////////////////////////////////////////////
class BankAccount
    {
    private:
        double balance;                    //account balance
    public:
//-------------------------------------------------------------
    BankAccount(double openingBalance) //constructor
        {
        balance = openingBalance;
        }
//-------------------------------------------------------------
    void deposit(double amount)        //makes deposit
        {
        balance = balance + amount;
        }
//-------------------------------------------------------------
    void withdraw(double amount)       //makes withdrawal
        {
        balance = balance - amount;
        }
//-------------------------------------------------------------
    void display()                     //displays balance
        {
        cout << "Balance=" << balance << endl;
        }
    };   //end class BankAccount
////////////////////////////////////////////////////////////////
int main()
    {
    BankAccount ba1(100.00);           //create account

    cout << "Before transactions, ";
    ba1.display();                     //display balance

    ba1.deposit(74.35);                //make deposit
    ba1.withdraw(20.00);               //make withdrawal

    cout << "After transactions,  ";
    ba1.display();                     //display balance
    return 0;
    }   //end main()
```

OUTPUT Here's the output from this program:

```
Before transactions, balance=100.00
After transactions,  balance=154.35
```

ANALYSIS There are two parts in bank.cpp: The first one is the declaration of the BankAccount class. It contains the member data and functions for our bank account. We'll examine it in detail in a moment. The second part is the function main(), where control goes when the program starts. The following sections describe each.

The main() Function

The main() function is not part of any class; it stands alone. It creates an object of class BankAccount, initialized to a value of 100.00, which is the opening balance, with this statement:

```
BankAccount ba1(100.00);   // create account
```

The BankAccount object displays its balance with the statement:

```
ba1.display();
```

The program then makes a deposit to, and a withdrawal from, the account by calling the BankAccount object's deposit() and withdraw() member functions:

```
ba1.deposit(74.35);
ba1.withdraw(20.00);
```

Finally, the program displays the new account balance and terminates.

The BankAccount Class

The only member data in the BankAccount class is the amount of money in the account, called balance. There are three member functions. The deposit() function adds an amount to the balance, withdrawal() subtracts an amount, and display() displays the balance.

Constructors

NEW TERM The BankAccount class also features a *constructor*. A constructor is a special member function that's called automatically whenever a new object is created. A constructor always has exactly the same name as the class, so this one is called BankAccount(). This constructor has one argument, which is used to set the opening balance when the account is created.

A constructor allows a new object to be initialized in a convenient way. Without the constructor in this program, you would have needed an additional call to deposit() to put the opening balance in the account.

Public and Private

NEW TERM Notice the keywords `public` and `private` in the `BankAccount` class. These keywords are *access modifiers* and determine what members of an object can be accessed by other parts of the program. The `balance` data member is preceded by `private`. A data member or member function that is private can only be accessed by member functions that are part of the same class. Thus, `balance` cannot be accessed by statements in `main()` because `main()` is not a member function of `BankAccount`.

However, all the member functions in `BankAccount` have the access modifier `public`, so they can be accessed by functions in other classes or `main()`. That's why statements in `main()` can call `deposit()`, `withdrawal()`, and `display()`.

Member data in a class is typically made private, whereas functions are made public. This protects the data; it can't be accidentally modified by functions in other classes. Any outside entity that needs to access data in a class must do so using a member function of the same class. Data is like a queen bee, kept hidden in the middle of the hive, fed and cared for by worker-bee member functions.

Inheritance and Polymorphism

For completeness we'll briefly mention two other key features of object-oriented programming: inheritance and polymorphism. We won't be using them in our program examples, but they are important in OOP.

NEW TERM *Inheritance* is the creation of one class, called the derived (or child) class, from another class called the *base* (or parent) class. The derived class has all the features of the base class, plus some additional features. For example, a `secretary` class might be derived from a more general `employee` class, and include a data member called `typingSpeed` that the `employee` class lacked.

Inheritance makes it easy to add features to an existing class and is an important aid in the design of programs with many related classes. Inheritance thus makes it easy to reuse classes for a slightly different purpose—a key benefit of OOP.

NEW TERM *Polymorphism* involves treating objects of different classes in the same way. For polymorphism to work, these different classes must be derived (inherited) from the same base class. In practice, polymorphism usually involves a function call that actually executes different member functions for objects of different classes.

For example, a call to `display()` for a `secretary` object would invoke a display function in the `secretary` class, whereas the exact same call for a `manager` object would invoke a different display function in the `manager` class. Polymorphism simplifies and clarifies program design and coding.

For those not familiar with them, inheritance and polymorphism involve significant additional complexity. To keep the focus on data structures and algorithms, we have avoided these features in our sample programs. Inheritance and polymorphism are important and powerful aspects of OOP, but are not necessary for the explanation of data structures and algorithms.

Now let's turn our attention to some newer features of C++.

New C++ Features

If you learned C++ some time ago, you might not be acquainted with its latest capabilities. This book uses several features that were introduced with Standard C++: the `string` class and the `vector` class from the Standard Template Library (STL). These features are a standard part of the C++ language specification, supported by all modern compilers. Using these features enables you to simplify our sample programs. They are fairly intuitive even if you're unfamiliar with them. In this section we'll mention a few details about these features, but for a full description you should consult Appendix C, or access the help system in your compiler.

The `string` Class

In pre-standard C++, strings were represented by arrays of type `char`. This created many inconveniences. For example, you couldn't compare strings using the comparison operators (<, >, and ==), and you couldn't set one string equal to another with the assignment operator (=). You also had to create the array yourself and manage its memory allocation. The `string` class in Standard C++ solves these problems.

To use the `string` class you must include the STRING file in your program:

```
#include <string>
```

It's easy to create objects of type `string`:

```
string str1, str2("George");
```

You can assign one string to another without worrying whether it's big enough; it will obtain the necessary memory automatically:

```
string str3;
str3 = "amanuensis";
```

You can use the `[]` operator to access specific characters in a string object, just as you can with an array (provided you use a valid index number):

```
char ch1 = str2[3];
```

The `string` class includes a variety of member functions. For example, `str1.size()` returns the number of characters in `str1`. In most other ways string objects behave similarly to basic C++ variables.

The `vector` Class

The STL is a group of data structures and algorithms implemented as templatized C++ classes. The data structures include lists, stacks, deques, and vectors. The algorithms allow you to perform almost any conceivable operation on the data structures.

We don't use the STL for examples of the data structures and algorithms described in this book. The source code for the STL is highly specialized and difficult for all but advanced programmers. Instead, we use homemade classes whose code is easy to understand. However, after you've learned about data structures and algorithms, you will certainly want to consider using the STL in your own programs. It is essentially as efficient as any code you write yourself, and of course far more convenient.

Although we don't use the STL to demonstrate concepts, we do use it as a handy improvement to C++. For example, we frequently use objects of the `vector` class instead of arrays. Among other advantages, this allows us to handle the sizing of the vector in the class constructor.

To use the vector class you'll need to include the VECTOR file:

```
#include <vector>
```

To create a vector you must use the template format, with the data type of the vector's contents placed in angle brackets and the vector's name in parentheses:

```
vector<double>(vect1);
```

From then on, you can treat the resulting vector much as you would an array, using bracket notation like the following to access individual elements in the vector:

```
vect1[13] = 3.14159;
```

The vector's member functions can be used for a variety of purposes. For example, `vect1.empty()` returns true if there is no data in a vector, and `vect1.size()` returns the number of elements currently in the vector.

Let's switch gears now from the details of C++ to a more theoretical topic.

Software Engineering

In recent years, it has become fashionable to begin a book on data structures and algorithms with a chapter on software engineering. We don't follow that approach, but let's briefly examine software engineering and see how it fits into the topics discussed in this book.

NEW TERM *Software engineering* is the study of how to create large and complex computer programs involving many programmers. It focuses on the overall design of the program and on the derivation of that design, beginning with the needs of the end users. Software engineering is concerned with the life cycle of a software project, which includes specification, design, verification, coding, testing, production, and maintenance.

It's not clear that mixing software engineering on one hand, and data structures and algorithms on the other, actually helps a student understand either topic. Software engineering is rather abstract and is difficult to grasp until you've been involved yourself in a large project. Data structures and algorithms, on the other hand, are nuts-and-bolts disciplines concerned with the details of coding and data storage.

Accordingly we focus on the nuts-and-bolts aspects of data structures and algorithms. How do they really work? What structure or algorithm is best in a particular situation? What do they look like translated into C++ code? As we noted, our intent is to make the material in this book as easy to understand as possible. For further reading, we mention some books on software engineering in Appendix C.

Summary

In this hour, you've learned the following:

- A data structure is the organization of data in a computer's memory (or in a disk file).
- The correct choice of data structure allows major improvements in program efficiency.
- Examples of data structures are arrays, stacks, and linked lists.
- An algorithm is a procedure for carrying out a particular task.
- Data structures can be used to build datafiles.
- A datafile is a collection of many similar records.
- Examples of datafiles are address books, recipe books, and inventory records.
- Data structures can also be used as programmer's tools: they help execute an algorithm.
- A record often represents a real-world object, like an employee or a car part.
- A record is divided into fields. Each field stores one characteristic of the object described by the record.

- A key is a field that's used to carry out some operation on the data. For example, personnel records might be sorted by a `LastName` field.
- A datafile can be searched for all records whose key field has a certain value. This value is called a search key.
- An object is a programming construct containing both functions and data.
- A class is a specification for many similar objects.
- Creating an object of a class is similar to creating a variable of a built-in type like `float`.
- Generally, an object's data is accessed by calling its member functions.

Q&A

Q Can I really learn object-oriented programming from the section in this chapter?

A Our aim is to teach just enough about OOP that someone who hasn't seen it before can follow the program examples. There's a lot more that we don't touch on, but what we've said should get you started.

Q There are a lot of new terms in this hour, like record, field, and key, but what is the big picture?

A The big picture is someone trying to store a lot of data in computer memory and then to access it efficiently. Don't worry if everything isn't clear at this point. In the next few hours you'll get a better idea what sorts of things we'll be talking about.

Workshop

The Workshop helps you solidify what you learned in this hour. See Appendix A, "Quiz Answers," for quiz answers.

Quiz

1. What is a data structure?
2. What is an algorithm?
3. Name two things you can use data structures for.
4. Name an algorithm commonly applied to stored data.
5. True or false: There is only one record in a data file.

6. What is one of the problems with procedural languages?

7. True or false: There is only one object of each class.

8. What is the most common use for the dot operator?

Exercise

Imagine a group of data you would like to put in a computer so it could be accessed and manipulated. For example, if you collect old comic books, you might want to catalog them so you could search for a particular author or a specific date.

HOUR 2

Arrays

An array is a number of data items of the same type arranged contiguously in memory. The array is the most commonly used data storage structure; it's built into most programming languages. Because they are so well-known, arrays offer a convenient jumping-off place for introducing data structures and for seeing how object-oriented programming and data structures relate to each other. In this hour we'll

- Show insertion, search, and deletion in arrays
- Demonstrate a simple, homemade array class
- Find out what a class interface is
- Improve the interface of your array class

The Array Workshop Applet

We'll start the hour with a Workshop applet that shows insertion, search, and deletion in an array. Later we'll show some sample C++ code that carries out these same operations.

Suppose that you're coaching kids-league baseball, and you want to keep track of which players are present at the practice field. What you need is an attendance-monitoring program for your laptop; a program that maintains a datafile of the players who have shown up for practice. You can use a simple data structure to hold this data. There are several actions you would like to be able to perform:

- Insert a player into the data structure when the player arrives at the field.
- Check to see if a particular player is present, by searching for their number in the structure.
- Delete a player from the data structure when the player goes home.

These three operations—insertion, search, and deletion—will be the fundamental operations in most of the data storage structures we'll study in this book.

In this book we'll often begin the discussion of a particular data structure by demonstrating it with a Workshop applet. This will give you a feeling for what the structure and its algorithms do, before we launch into a detailed discussion and demonstrate actual sample code. The Workshop applet called Array shows how an array can be used to implement insertion, search, and deletion. Start up this applet, as described in Appendix B, "How to Run the Workshop Applets and Sample Programs."

Figure 2.1 shows what you'll see. There's an array with 20 elements, 10 of which have items in them. You can think of these items as representing your baseball players. Imagine that each player has been issued a team shirt with the player's number on the back. To make things visually interesting, the shirts come in a variety of colors. You can see each player's number and shirt color in the array.

FIGURE 2.1

The Array Workshop applet.

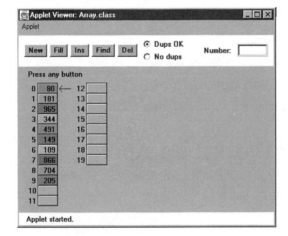

This applet demonstrates the three fundamental procedures mentioned above:

- The Ins button inserts a new data item.
- The Find button searches for a specified data item.
- The Del button deletes a specified data item.

Using the New button, you can create a new array of a size you specify. You can fill this array with as many data items as you want using the Fill button. Fill creates a set of items and randomly assigns them numbers and colors. The numbers are in the range 0 to 999. You can't create an array of more than 60 cells, and you can't, of course, fill more data items than there are array cells.

Also, when you create a new array, you'll need to decide whether duplicate items will be allowed; we'll return to this question in a moment. The default value is no duplicates and the No Dups radio button is selected to indicate this.

To Do: Insert Data into the Workshop Applet

1. Start with the default arrangement of 20 cells and 10 data items, and the No Dups button selected. You insert a baseball player's number into the array when the player arrives at the practice field, having been dropped off by a parent.

2. To insert a new item, press the Ins button once. You'll be prompted to enter the value of the item:

   `Enter key of item to insert`

3. Type a number, say 678, into the text field in the upper-right corner of the applet. (Yes, it is hard to get three digits on the back of a kid's shirt.)

4. Press Ins again and the applet will confirm your choice:

   `Will insert item with key 678`

5. A final press of the button will cause a data item, consisting of this value and a random color, to appear in the first empty cell in the array. The prompt will say something like this:

   `Inserted item with key 678 at index 10`

Each button press in a Workshop applet corresponds to a step that an algorithm carries out. The more steps required, the longer the algorithm takes. In the Array Workshop applet, the insertion process is very fast, requiring only a single step. This is because a new item is always inserted in the first vacant cell in the array, and the algorithm knows where this is because it knows how many items are already in the array. The new item is simply inserted in the next available space. Searching and deleting, however, are not so fast.

In no-duplicates mode you're on your honor not to insert an item with the same key as an existing item. If you do, the applet displays an error message, but it won't prevent the insertion. The assumption is made that you won't make this mistake.

To Do: Search for a Given Item

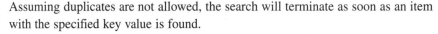

1. Click the Find button. You'll be prompted for the key number of the person you're looking for.

2. Pick a number that appears on an item somewhere in the middle of the array.

3. Type the number and repeatedly press the Find button. At each button press, one step in the algorithm is carried out. You'll see the red arrow start at cell 0 and move methodically down the cells, examining a new one each time you push the button. The index number in the following message will change as you go along:

   ```
   Checking next cell, index = 2
   ```

4. When you reach the specified item, you'll see the following message or whatever key value you typed:

   ```
   Have found item with key 505
   ```

   Assuming duplicates are not allowed, the search will terminate as soon as an item with the specified key value is found.

If you have selected a key number that is not in the array, the applet will examine every occupied cell in the array before telling you that it can't find that item.

Notice that (again assuming duplicates are not allowed) the search algorithm must look through an average of half the data items to find a specified item. Items close to the beginning of the array will be found sooner, and those toward the end will be found later. If N is the number of items, the average number of steps needed to find an item is N/2. In the worst-case scenario, the specified item is in the last occupied cell, and N steps will be required to find it.

As noted, the time an algorithm takes to execute is proportional to the number of steps, so searching takes much longer on the average (N/2 steps) than insertion (one step).

Deletion

To delete an item you must first find it. After you type the number of the item to be deleted, repeated button presses will cause the arrow to move, step by step, down the array until the item is located. The next button press deletes the item and the cell becomes empty. (Strictly speaking, this step isn't necessary because we're going to copy over this cell anyway, but deleting the item makes it clearer what's happening.)

NEW TERM Implicit in the deletion algorithm is the assumption that holes are not allowed in the array. A *hole* is one or more empty cells that have filled cells above them (at higher index numbers). If holes are allowed, all the algorithms become more complicated because they must check to see whether a cell is empty before examining its contents. Also, the algorithms become less efficient because they must waste time looking at unoccupied cells. For these reasons, occupied cells must be arranged contiguously: no holes allowed.

Therefore, after locating the specified item and deleting it, the applet must shift the contents of each subsequent cell down one space to fill in the hole. Figure 2.2 shows an example.

FIGURE 2.2

Deleting an item.

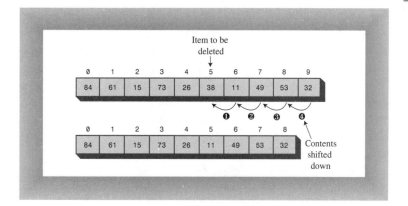

If the item in cell 5 (38, in the figure) is deleted, the item in cell 6 would shift into cell 5, the item in cell 7 would shift into cell 6, and so on to the last occupied cell. During the deletion process, after the item is located, the applet will shift down the contents of the higher-indexed cells as you continue to press the Del button.

A deletion requires (assuming no duplicates are allowed) searching through an average of N/2 elements, and then moving the remaining elements (an average of N/2 moves) to fill up the resulting hole. This is N steps in all.

The Duplicates Problem

When you design a data storage structure, you must decide whether items with duplicate keys will be allowed. If you're talking about a personnel file and the key is an employee number, duplicates don't make much sense; there's no point in assigning the same number to two employees. On the other hand, if the key value is last names, there's a distinct possibility several employees will have the same key value, so duplicates should be allowed.

Of course, for the baseball players, duplicate numbers should not be allowed. It would be hard to keep track of the players if more than one wore the same number.

The Array Workshop applet lets you select either option. When you use New to create a new array, you're prompted to specify both its size and whether duplicates are permitted. Use the radio button Dups OK or No Dups to make this selection.

If you're writing a data storage program in which duplicates are not allowed, you might need to guard against human error during an insertion by checking all the data items in the array to ensure that none of them already has the same key value as the item being inserted. This is inefficient, however, and increases the number of steps required for an insertion from one to N. For this reason, our applet does not perform this check.

Let's see how allowing duplicates affects our searching, insertion, and deletion algorithms.

Searching with Duplicates

Allowing duplicates complicates the search algorithm, as we noted. Even if it finds a match, it must continue looking for possible additional matches until the last occupied cell. This is one approach; you could also stop after the first match. It depends on whether the question is "Find me everyone with blue eyes" or "Find me someone with blue eyes."

When the Dups OK button is selected, the applet takes the first approach, finding all items matching the search key. This always requires N steps because the algorithm must go all the way to the last occupied cell.

Insertion with Duplicates

Insertion is the same with duplicates allowed as when they're not: a single step inserts the new item. But remember, if duplicates are not allowed, and there's a possibility the user will attempt to input the same key twice, you might need to check every existing item before an insertion.

Deletion with Duplicates

Deletion might be more complicated when duplicates are allowed, depending on exactly how "deletion" is defined. If it means to delete only the first item with a specified value, then, on the average, only N/2 comparisons and N/2 moves are necessary. This is the same as when no duplicates are allowed. However, if deletion means to delete every item with a specified key value, the same operation might require multiple deletions. This will require checking N cells and (probably) moving more than N/2 cells. The average depends on how the duplicates are distributed throughout the array.

The applet assumes the second meaning and deletes multiple items with the same key. This is complicated because each time an item is deleted, subsequent items must be shifted farther. For example, if three items are deleted, items beyond the last deletion must be shifted three spaces. To see how this works, set the applet to Dups OK and insert three or four items with the same key. Then try deleting them.

Table 2.1 shows the average number of comparisons and moves for the three operations, first when no duplicates are allowed, and then when they are allowed. N is the number of items in the array. Inserting a new item counts as one move.

TABLE 2.1   DUPLICATES OK VERSUS NO DUPLICATES

	No Duplicates	Duplicates OK
Search	N/2 comparisons	N comparisons
Insertion	No comparisons, one move	No comparisons, one move
Deletion	N/2 comparisons, N/2 moves	N comparisons, more than N/2 moves

You can explore these possibilities with the Array Workshop applet.

The difference between N and N/2 is not usually considered very significant, except when fine-tuning a program. Of more importance, as we'll discuss in the next hour, is whether an operation takes one step, N steps, log(N) steps, or N^2 steps.

Slow Array Algorithms

One of the significant things to notice when using the Array applet is the slow and methodical nature of the algorithms. With the exception of insertion, the algorithms involve stepping through some or all of the cells in the array. Different data structures offer much faster (but more complex) algorithms. We'll see one, the binary search on an ordered array, in the next hour, and others throughout this book.

An Array Example

Let's look at some sample programs that show how an array can be used. In case you're making the transition to OOP, we'll start with an old-fashioned procedural version, and then show the equivalent object-oriented approach. Listing 2.1 shows the old-fashioned version, called `array.cpp`.

```cpp
//array.cpp
//demonstrates arrays
#include <iostream>
using namespace std;
//////////////////////////////////////////////////////////////
int main()
   {
   int arr[100];                //array
   int nElems = 0;              //number of items
   int j;                       //loop counter
   int searchKey;               //key of item to search for
//-------------------------------------------------------------
   arr[0] = 77;                 //insert 10 items
   arr[1] = 99;
   arr[2] = 44;
   arr[3] = 55;
   arr[4] = 22;
   arr[5] = 88;
   arr[6] = 11;
   arr[7] = 00;
   arr[8] = 66;
   arr[9] = 33;
   nElems = 10;                 //now 10 items in array
//-------------------------------------------------------------
   for(j=0; j<nElems; j++)      //display items
      cout << arr[j] << " ";
   cout << endl;
//-------------------------------------------------------------
   searchKey = 66;              //find item with key 66
   for(j=0; j<nElems; j++)      //for each element,
      if(arr[j] == searchKey)   //found item?
         break;                 //yes, exit before end
   if(j == nElems)              //at the end?
      cout << "Can't find " << searchKey << endl; //yes
   else
      cout << "Found " << searchKey << endl;      //no
//-------------------------------------------------------------
   searchKey = 55;              //delete item with key 55
   cout << "Deleting " << searchKey << endl;
   for(j=0; j<nElems; j++)      //look for it
   if(arr[j] == searchKey)
      break;
   for(int k=j; k<nElems; k++)  //move higher ones down
      arr[k] = arr[k+1];
   nElems--;                    //decrement size
//-------------------------------------------------------------
   for(j=0; j<nElems; j++)      //display items
      cout << arr[j] << " ";
```

```
cout << endl;
return 0;
}   //end main()
```

ANALYSIS In this program, we create an array called arr, place 10 data items (kids' numbers) in it, search for the item with value 66 (the shortstop, Louisa), display all the items, remove the item with value 55 (Freddy, who had a dentist appointment), and then display the remaining nine items. The output of the program looks like this:

OUTPUT
```
77 99 44 55 22 88 11 0 66 33
Found 66
77 99 44 22 88 11 0 66 33
```

The data we're storing in this array is type int. We've chosen a basic type to simplify the coding. Generally the items stored in a data structure consist of several data members, so they are represented by objects rather than basic types. We'll see an example of this in the next hour.

Notice that the size of the array is fixed at 100 items. If the array holds fewer items, memory is wasted. If you try to insert more than 100 items, the program fails. This isn't very efficient or safe. We'll see in the next example how a vector provides a more flexible approach.

Inserting a New Item

Inserting an item into the array is easy; we use the normal array syntax

```
arr[0] = 77;
```

We also keep track of how many items we've inserted into the array with the nElems variable.

Searching for an Item

The searchKey variable holds the value we're looking for. To search for an item, step through the array, comparing searchKey with each element. If the loop variable j reaches the last occupied cell with no match being found, the value isn't in the array. Appropriate messages are displayed: Found 66 or Can't find 27.

Deleting an Item

Deletion begins with a search for the specified item. For simplicity we assume (perhaps rashly) that the item is present. When we find it, we move all the items with higher index values down one element to fill in the "hole" left by the deleted element, and we decrement nElems. In a real program, we would also take appropriate action if the item to be deleted could not be found.

Displaying the Array Contents

Displaying all the elements is straightforward: we step through the array, accessing each one with arr[j] and displaying it.

Program Organization

The organization of array.cpp leaves something to be desired. There are no classes; it's just an old-fashioned procedural program. Let's see if we can make it easier to understand (among other benefits) by making it more object-oriented.

We're going to provide a gradual introduction to an object-oriented approach, using two steps. In the first step, we'll separate the data storage structure (the array) from the rest of the program by making it into a separate class. The remaining part of the program (the main() function) will become a user of the structure. In the second step, we'll improve the communication between the storage structure and its user. We'll look at these steps in the next two sections.

Dividing a Program into Classes

The array.cpp program consisted of one big function. We can reap many benefits by dividing the program into several parts: The data storage structure itself is one candidate, and the part of the program that uses this data structure is another. The first part can be represented as a class, and the second by the special function main(). By dividing the program into these two parts we can clarify the functionality of the program, making it easier to design and understand (and, in real programs, easier to modify and maintain).

In array.cpp we used an array as a data storage structure, but we treated it simply as a language element. Now we'll encapsulate the array in a class, called LowArray. We'll also provide class member functions by which statements in main() can access the array. These member functions allow communication between LowArray and main().

Our first design of the LowArray class won't be entirely successful. It's an improvement on array.cpp, but it nevertheless demonstrates the need for an even better approach. The lowArray.cpp program in Listing 2.2 shows how it looks.

INPUT   **LISTING 2.2**   THE lowArray.cpp PROGRAM

```
//lowArray.cpp
//demonstrates array class with low-level interface
```

```cpp
#include <iostream>
#include <vector>
using namespace std;
/////////////////////////////////////////////////////////////////
class LowArray
    {
    private:
      vector<double> v;                   //vector holds doubles

    public:
//-------------------------------------------------------------
    LowArray(int max)                     //constructor
      { v.resize(max); }                  //size the vector
//-------------------------------------------------------------
    void setElem(int index, double value) //put element into
      { v[index] = value; }               //array, at index
//-------------------------------------------------------------
    double getElem(int index)             //get element from
      { return v[index]; }                //array, at index
//-------------------------------------------------------------
    };  //end class LowArray
/////////////////////////////////////////////////////////////////
int main()
    {
    LowArray arr(100);       //create a LowArray
    int nElems = 0;                       //number of items
    int j;                                //loop variable
//-------------------------------------------------------------
    arr.setElem(0, 77);                   //insert 10 items
    arr.setElem(1, 99);
    arr.setElem(2, 44);
    arr.setElem(3, 55);
    arr.setElem(4, 22);
    arr.setElem(5, 88);
    arr.setElem(6, 11);
    arr.setElem(7, 00);
    arr.setElem(8, 66);
    arr.setElem(9, 33);
    nElems = 10;                          //now 10 items in array
//-------------------------------------------------------------
    for(j=0; j<nElems; j++)               //display items
      cout << arr.getElem(j) << " ";
    cout << endl;
//-------------------------------------------------------------
    int searchKey = 26;                   //search for item
    for(j=0; j<nElems; j++)               //for each element,
      if(arr.getElem(j) == searchKey)     //found item?
        break;
    if(j == nElems)                       //no
```

continues

LISTING 2.2   CONTINUED

```
        cout << "Can't find " << searchKey << endl;
    else                                  //yes
        cout << "Found " << searchKey << endl;
//----------------------------------------------------------
    double deleteKey = 55;                //delete value 55
    cout << "Deleting element " << deleteKey << endl;
    for(j=0; j<nElems; j++)               //look for it
    if(arr.getElem(j) == deleteKey)
        break;
    for(int k=j; k<nElems; k++)           //higher ones down
        arr.setElem(k, arr.getElem(k+1) );
    nElems--;                             //decrement size
//----------------------------------------------------------
    for(j=0; j<nElems; j++)               //display items
        cout << arr.getElem(j) << " ";
    cout << endl;
    return 0;
    }  //end main()
```

OUTPUT   The output from this program is similar to that from `array.cpp`, except that we try to find a non-existent key value (26) before deleting the item with the key value 55.

```
77 99 44 55 22 88 11 0 66 33
Can't find 26
77 99 44 22 88 11 0 66 33
```

The `LowArray` Class and `main()`

ANALYSIS   In `lowArray.cpp`, we wrap the class `LowArray` around an ordinary C++ array. The array is hidden from the outside world inside the class; it's private, so only `LowArray` class member functions can access it. There are three such functions: `setElem()` and `getElem()`, which insert and retrieve an element, respectively; and a constructor, which creates an empty array of a specified size.

Notice that we use a vector to store the data instead of an array. It operates in most ways like an array, but allows us to specify the vector's size in the class constructor, using the `resize()` member function. This allows an object of class `LowArray` to hold any amount of data, unlike an array, which must always hold the same amount of data.

The `main()` function creates an object of the `LowArray` class and uses it to store and manipulate data. Think of `LowArray` as a tool, and `main()` as a user of the tool. We've divided the program into two parts with clearly defined roles. This is a valuable first step in making a program object-oriented.

> **NEW TERM** A class used to store data objects, as is LowArray in the lowArray.cpp program, is sometimes called a *container class*. Typically, a container class not only stores the data, but also provides member functions for accessing the data, and perhaps also sorting it and performing other complex actions on it.

The problem with the lowArray.cpp program is that main() must do too much work. In the next section we'll see how to fix this, and introduce the idea of interfaces.

Class Interfaces

We've seen how a program can be divided into separate parts. How do these parts interact with each other? Communication between classes and other parts of the program, and the division of responsibility between them, are important aspects of object-oriented programming. This is especially true when a class might have many different users. Typically a class can be used over and over by different users (or the same user) for different purposes. For example, it's possible that someone might use the LowArray class in some other program to store the serial numbers of her traveler's checks. The class can handle this just as well as it can store the numbers of baseball players.

If a class is used by many different programmers, the class should be designed so that it's easy to use. The way a class user relates to the class is called the class *interface*. Because class data members are typically private, when we talk about the interface we usually mean the class member functions: what they do and what their arguments are. It's by calling these member functions that a class user interacts with an object of the class. One of the important advantages conferred by object-oriented programming is that a class interface can be designed to be as convenient and efficient as possible. Figure 2.3 is a fanciful interpretation of the LowArray interface.

Making main()'s Job Easier

The interface to the LowArray class in lowArray.cpp is not particularly convenient. The member functions setElem() and getElem() operate on a low conceptual level, performing exactly the same tasks as the [] operator in an ordinary C++ array. The class user, represented by the main() function, ends up having to carry out the same low-level operations it did in the non-class version of an array in the array.cpp program. The only difference was that it used setElem() and getElem() instead of the [] operator. It's not clear that this is an improvement.

Also notice that there's no convenient way to display the contents of the array. Somewhat crudely, main() simply uses a for loop and the getElem() member function for this purpose. We could avoid repeated code by writing a separate function that main() could call to display the array contents, but isn't it really the responsibility of the LowArray class to provide this function?

FIGURE 2.3

The LowArray *inter-face.*

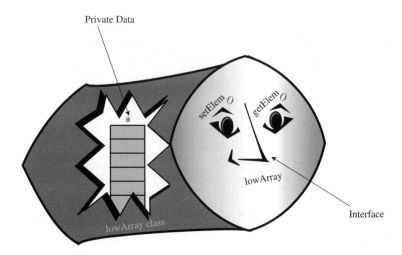

These questions suggest that we might redesign the interface between the class and main() to obtain more of the advantages of OOP.

Who's Responsible for What?

In the lowArray.cpp program, the main() routine, which is the user of the data storage structure LowArray, must keep track of the indices to the array. For some users of an array, who need random access to array elements and don't mind keeping track of the index numbers, this arrangement might make sense. For example, sorting an array, as we'll see in Hour 3, can make efficient use of this direct "hands-on" approach.

However, in a typical program, the user of the data storage device won't find access to the array indices to be helpful or relevant. In the Cardfile program in Hour 1, for example, if the card data were stored in an array and you wanted to insert a new card, it would be easier not to have to worry about exactly where in the array it is going to go.

The highArray.cpp Example

Our next sample program shows an improved interface for the storage structure class, called HighArray. Using this interface, the class user, main(), no longer needs to think about index numbers. The setElem() and getElem() member functions are gone; they are replaced by insert(), find(), and delete(). These new member functions don't require an index number as an argument because the class takes responsibility for handling index numbers. The user of the class is free to concentrate on the *what* instead of the *how*: what's going to be inserted, deleted, and accessed, instead of exactly how those activities are carried out.

Figure 2.4 shows the HighArray interface and Listing 2.3 shows the highArray.cpp program.

FIGURE 2.4

The HighArray interface.

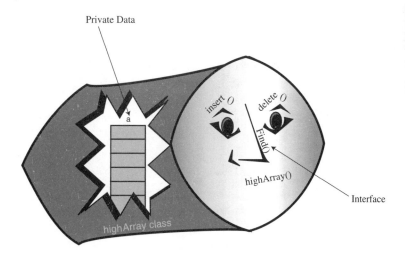

INPUT　**LISTING 2.3**　THE highArray.cpp PROGRAM

```cpp
//highArray.cpp
//demonstrates array class with high-level interface
#include <iostream>
#include <vector>
using namespace std;
////////////////////////////////////////////////////////////////
class HighArray
   {
   private:
      vector<double> v;                //vector v
      int nElems;                      //number of data items
   public:
//--------------------------------------------------------------
   HighArray() : nElems(0)             //default constructor
      {  }
//--------------------------------------------------------------
   HighArray(int max) : nElems(0)      //1-arg constructor
      { v.resize(max); }               //size the vector
//--------------------------------------------------------------
```

continues

LISTING 2.3   CONTINUED

```cpp
      bool find(double searchKey)        //find specified value
         {
         int j;
         for(j=0; j<nElems; j++)         //for each element,
            if(v[j] == searchKey)        //found item?
               break;                    //exit loop before end
         if(j == nElems)                 //gone to end?
            return false;                //yes, can't find it
         else
            return true;                 //no, found it
         }  //end find()
//---------------------------------------------------------------
      void insert(double value)          //put element into array
         {
         v[nElems] = value;              //insert it
         nElems++;                       //increment size
         }
//---------------------------------------------------------------
      bool remove(double value)          //remove element from array
         {
         int j;
         for(j=0; j<nElems; j++)         //look for it
            if( value == v[j] )
               break;
         if(j==nElems)                   //can't find it
            return false;
         else                            //found it
            {
            for(int k=j; k<nElems; k++)  //move higher ones down
               v[k] = v[k+1];
            nElems--;                    //decrement size
            return true;
            }
         }  //end delete()
//---------------------------------------------------------------
      void display()                     //displays array contents
         {
         for(int j=0; j<nElems; j++)     //for each element,
            cout << v[j] << " ";         //display it
         cout << endl;
         }
//---------------------------------------------------------------
      };  //end class HighArray
//////////////////////////////////////////////////////////////////
int main()
   {
   int maxSize = 100;                    //array size
   HighArray arr(maxSize);               //vector
```

```
arr.insert(77);                    //insert 10 items
arr.insert(99);
arr.insert(44);
arr.insert(55);
arr.insert(22);
arr.insert(88);
arr.insert(11);
arr.insert(0);
arr.insert(66);
arr.insert(33);

arr.display();                     //display items

int searchKey = 35;                //search for item
if( arr.find(searchKey) )
   cout << "Found " << searchKey << endl;
else
   cout << "Can't find " << searchKey << endl;

cout << "Deleting 0, 55, and 99" << endl;
arr.remove(0);                     //delete 3 items
arr.remove(55);
arr.remove(99);

arr.display();                     //display items again
return 0;
}   //end main()
```

ANALYSIS The HighArray class is now wrapped around the array (actually a vector). In main(), we create an object of this class and carry out almost the same operations as in the lowArray.cpp program: we insert 10 items, search for an item—one that isn't there—and display the array contents. Because it's so easy, we delete three items (0, 55, and 99) instead of one, and finally display the contents again. Here's the output:

OUTPUT
```
77 99 44 55 22 88 11 0 66 33
Can't find 35
Deleting 0, 55, and 99
77 44 22 88 11 66 33
```

Notice how short and simple main() is. The details that had to be handled by main() in lowArray.cpp are now handled by HighArray class member functions.

1. In the HighArray class, the find() member function looks through the array for the item whose key value was passed to it as an argument. It returns true or false, depending on whether it finds the item or not.

2. The insert() member function places a new data item in the next available space in the array. A data member called nElems keeps track of the number of array cells

that are actually filled with data items. The `main()` function no longer needs to worry about how many items are in the array.

3. The `delete()` member function searches for the element whose key value was passed to it as an argument, and when it finds that element, it shifts all the elements in higher index cells down one cell, thus writing over the deleted value; it then decrements `nElems`. We've also included a `display()` member function, which displays all the values stored in the array.

The User's Life Made Easier

In `lowArray.cpp`, the code in `main()` to search for an item took eight lines; in `highArray.cpp`, it takes only one. The class user, represented by `main()`, need not worry about index numbers or any other array details. Amazingly, the class user doesn't even need to know what kind of data structure the `HighArray` class is using to store the data. The structure is hidden behind the interface. In fact, in the next section, we'll see the same interface used with a somewhat different data structure.

Abstraction

The process of separating the *how* from the *what*—how an operation is performed inside a class, as opposed to what's visible to the class user—is called *abstraction*. Abstraction is an important aspect of software engineering. By abstracting class functionality we make it easier to design a program because we don't need to think about implementation details at too early a stage in the design process.

Summary

In this hour, you've learned the following:

- Unordered arrays offer fast insertion but slow searching and deletion.
- Wrapping an array in a class protects the array from being inadvertently altered.
- A class interface comprises the member functions (and occasionally data members) that the class user can access.
- A class interface can be designed to make things simpler for the class user (although possibly harder for the class designer).

Q&A

Q **Why should I wrap a class around an array? I've been using arrays for years without going to all this trouble.**

A This is our way of introducing the object-oriented approach to data structures. It might not seem to buy you much in these simple examples, but, as the data structures become more complicated in later hours, you'll see a payoff in the simplicity and robustness of the programming.

Q **Is all this talk about interfaces going to be important in understanding data structures and algorithms?**

A It's not central to how the data structures and algorithms work. However, if you're using object-oriented versions of data structures, you'll be using interfaces all the time, so it's helpful to be aware of the concept.

Workshop

The Workshop helps you solidify what you learned in this hour. See Appendix A, "Quiz Answers," for quiz answers.

Quiz

1. On average, how many items must be moved to insert a new item into an unsorted array with N items?

2. On average, how many items must be moved to delete an item from an unsorted array with N items?

3. On average, how many items must be examined to find a particular item in an unsorted array with N items?

4. What is a class interface?

5. Why is it important to make things easier for the class user than for the class designer?

6. What are the advantages of wrapping an array in a class?

7. What's an example of an operation that's easier to perform on an array that's in a class than on a simple array?

8. What is abstraction?

Exercise

Imagine ways to improve the interface between an array class and a user of the class such as the `main()` function. Dream up some new member functions to add to the class, such as a function that displays all data members with keys greater than a certain value. How many such functions would you need in a general-purpose array class? Would too many such functions become cumbersome?

Hour **3**

Ordered Arrays

In this hour we'll examine a special kind of array—the ordered array—in which the data is stored in ascending (or descending) key order. This arrangement makes possible a fast way of searching for a data item: the binary search. In this hour you will learn about

- Ordered arrays
- Binary searches
- Measuring the speed of binary searches
- Storing class objects in arrays
- Big O notation

The Ordered Workshop Applet

We'll start with a Workshop applet that demonstrates ordered arrays and binary searches.

 NEW TERM Imagine an array in which the data items are arranged in order of ascending key values; that is, with the smallest value at index 0, and each cell holding a value larger than the cell below it. Such an array is called an *ordered array*.

When we insert an item into this array, the correct location must be found for the insertion: just above a smaller value and just below a larger one. Then all the larger values must be moved up to make room. Why would we want to arrange data in order? One advantage is that we can speed up search times dramatically using a *binary search*.

Start the Ordered Workshop applet. You'll see an array; it's similar to the one in the Array Workshop applet, but the data is ordered. Figure 3.1 shows how this looks.

FIGURE 3.1

The Ordered Workshop applet.

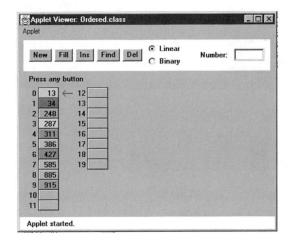

In the next sections we'll demonstrate the linear search and the binary search, a faster approach made possible by ordering the array. In the ordered array we've chosen to not allow duplicates. As we saw earlier, this speeds up searching somewhat but slows down insertion.

Demonstrating the Linear Search

Two search algorithms are available for the Ordered Workshop applet: linear and binary. Linear search is the default. Linear searches operate in much the same way as the searches in the unordered array in the Array applet: the red arrow steps along, looking for a match. The difference is that in the ordered array, the search quits if an item with a larger key is found.

Try this out. Make sure the Linear radio button is selected. Then use the Find button to search for a non-existent value that, if it were present, would fit somewhere in the middle of the array. In Figure 3.1, this might be 400. You'll see that the search terminates when the first item larger than 400 is reached; it's 427 in the figure. The algorithm knows there's no point looking further.

Try out the Ins and Del buttons as well. Use Ins to insert an item with a key value that will go somewhere in the middle of the existing items. You'll see that insertion requires moving all the items with key values larger than the item being inserted.

Use the Del button to delete an item from the middle of the array. Deletion works much the same as it did in the Array applet, shifting items with higher index numbers down to fill in the hole left by the deletion. In the ordered array, however, the deletion algorithm can quit partway through if it doesn't find the item, just as the search routine can.

Demonstrating the Binary Search

The payoff for using an ordered array comes when we use a binary search. This kind of search is much faster than a linear search, especially for large arrays. We'll start with an example of the binary search in a non-computer context.

The Guess-a-Number Game

A binary search uses the same approach you did as a kid (if you were smart) to guess a number in the well-known children's guessing game. In this game, a friend asks you to guess a number she's thinking of between 1 and 100. When you guess a number, she'll tell you one of three things: your guess is larger than the number she's thinking of, it's smaller, or you guessed correctly.

To find the number in the fewest guesses, you should always start by guessing the middle number of the unknown range, in this case, 50. If she says your guess is too low, you deduce the number is between 51 and 100, so your next guess should be 75 (halfway between 51 and 100). If she says it's too high, you deduce the number is between 1 and 49, so your next guess should be 25.

Each guess allows you to divide the range of possible values in half. Finally, the range is only one number long, and that's the answer.

Notice how few guesses are required to find the number. If you used a linear search—guessing first 1, and then 2, and then 3, and so on—on the average, it would take you 50 guesses to find the number. In a binary search each guess divides the range of possible values in half, so the number of guesses required is far fewer. Table 3.1 shows a game session when the number to be guessed is 33.

TABLE 3.1 GUESSING A NUMBER

Step Number	Number Guessed	Result	Range of Possible Values
0			1–100
1	50	Too high	1–49
2	25	Too low	26–49
3	37	Too high	26–36
4	31	Too low	32–36
5	34	Too high	32–33
6	32	Too low	33–33
7	33	Correct	

The correct number is identified in only seven guesses. This is the maximum. You might get lucky and guess the number before you've worked your way all the way down to a range of one. This would happen if the number to be guessed is 50, for example, or 34.

To Do: Perform a Binary Search in the Ordered Workshop Applet

1. To perform a binary search with the Ordered Workshop applet, you must use the New button to create a new array. After the first press you'll be asked to specify the size of the array (maximum 60) and which kind of searching scheme you want: linear or binary. Choose the binary scheme by clicking the Binary radio button.

2. After the array is created, use the Fill button to fill it with data items. When prompted, type the amount (not more than the size of the array). A few more presses fill in all the items.

3. After the array is filled, pick one of the values in the array and see how the Find button can be used to locate it. After a few preliminary presses, you'll see the red arrow pointing to the algorithm's current guess, and you'll see the range shown by a vertical blue line adjacent to the appropriate cells. Figure 3.2 depicts the situation when the range is the entire array.

At each press of the Find button the range is halved and a new guess is chosen in the middle of the range. Figure 3.3 shows the second range used in the process.

Even with a maximum array size of 60 items, six button presses suffice to locate any item.

Try using the binary search with different array sizes. Can you figure out, before you run the applet, how many steps are necessary for a search of a given size? This is an important question, and we'll return to it later in this hour.

FIGURE 3.2

The initial range in a binary search.

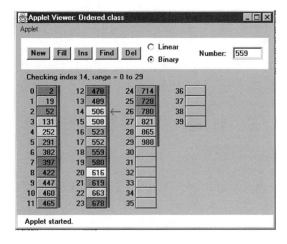

FIGURE 3.3

The second range of a binary search.

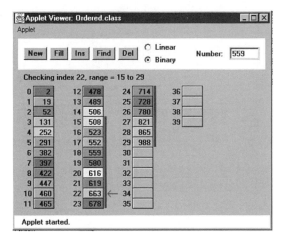

3

Notice that the insertion and deletion operations also employ the binary search (when it's selected). The place where an item should be inserted is found with a binary search, as is an item to be deleted. In this applet, items with duplicate keys are not permitted.

Now that we've seen how the Workshop applet handles algorithms in an ordered array, let's look at how C++ code performs these algorithms behind the scenes.

C++ Code for an Ordered Array

We'll use the OrdArray class to encapsulate the array and its algorithms. The heart of this class is the find() member function, which uses a binary search to locate a specified data item. We'll examine find() in detail before showing the complete program.

Conducting a Binary Search with the `find()` Member Function

The `find()` member function searches for a specified item by repeatedly dividing in half the range of array elements to be considered. Listing 3.1 shows how it looks:

LISTING 3.1   THE `find()` MEMBER FUNCTION

```
int find(double searchKey)
     {
     int lowerBound = 0;
     int upperBound = nElems-1;
     int curIn;

     while(true)
        {
        curIn = (lowerBound + upperBound ) / 2;
        if(v[curIn]==searchKey)
           return curIn;              //found it
        else if(lowerBound > upperBound)
           return nElems;             //can't find it
        else                          //divide range
           {
           if(v[curIn] < searchKey)
              lowerBound = curIn + 1; //it's in upper half
           else
              upperBound = curIn - 1; //it's in lower half
           } //end else divide range
        } //end while
     } //end find()
```

ANALYSIS   This member function begins by setting the `lowerBound` and `upperBound` variables to the first and last occupied cells in the array. This specifies the range where the item we're looking for, `searchKey`, might be found. Then, within the `while` loop, the current index, `curIn`, is set to the middle of this range.

If we're lucky, `curIn` might already be pointing to the desired item, so we first check whether this is true. If it is, we've found the item so we return with its index, `curIn`.

Each time through the loop we divide the range in half. Eventually it will get so small it can't be divided any more. We check for this in the next statement: If `lowerBound` is greater than `upperBound`, the range has ceased to exist. (When `lowerBound` equals `upperBound` the range is one and we need one more pass through the loop.) We can't continue the search without a valid range, but we haven't found the desired item, so we return `nElems`, the total number of items. This isn't a valid index because the last filled cell in the array is nElems-1. The class user interprets this value to mean that the item wasn't found.

If curIn is not pointing at the desired item, and the range is still big enough, we're ready to divide the range in half. We compare the value at the current index, a[curIn], which is in the middle of the range, with the value to be found, searchKey.

If searchKey is larger, we know we should look in the upper half of the range. Accordingly, we move lowerBound up to curIn. Actually we move it one cell beyond curIn because we've already checked curIn itself at the beginning of the loop.

If searchKey is smaller than a[curIn], we know we should look in the lower half of the range. So we move upperBound down to one cell below curIn. Figure 3.4 shows how the range is altered in these two situations.

FIGURE 3.4

Dividing the range in a binary search.

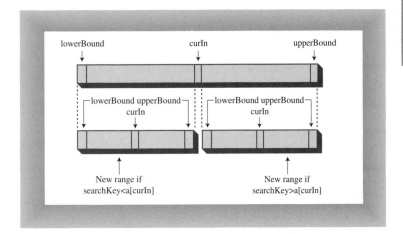

Investigating the OrdArray Class

In general, the orderedArray.cpp program is similar to highArray.cpp from Hour 2. The main difference is that find() uses a binary search, as we've seen.

We could have used a binary search to locate the position where a new item will be inserted. This involves a variation on the find() routine, but for simplicity we retain the linear search in insert(). The speed penalty might not be important because, as we've seen, an average of half the items must be moved anyway when an insertion is performed, so insertion will not be very fast even if we locate the item with a binary search. However, for the last

> ounce of speed, you could change the initial part of insert() to a binary
> search (as is done in the Ordered Workshop applet). Similarly, the delete()
> member function could call find() to figure out the location of the item to
> be deleted.

The OrdArray class includes a new getSize() member function, which returns the number of data items currently in the array. This is helpful for the class user, main(), when it calls find(). If find() returns nElems, which main() can discover with getSize(), the search was unsuccessful. Listing 3.2 shows the complete listing for the orderedArray.cpp program.

INPUT   **LISTING 3.2**   THE orderedArray.cpp PROGRAM

```cpp
//orderedArray.cpp
//demonstrates ordered array class
#include <iostream>
#include <vector>
using namespace std;
//////////////////////////////////////////////////////////////
class OrdArray
   {
   private:
      vector<double> v;                 //vector v
      int nElems;                       //number of data items
   public:
   //--------------------------------------------------------------
   OrdArray(int max) : nElems(0)        //constructor
      { v.resize(max); }                //size the vector
   //--------------------------------------------------------------
   int getSize()                        //return number of
      { return nElems; }                //elements
   //--------------------------------------------------------------
   int find(double searchKey)
      {
      int lowerBound = 0;
      int upperBound = nElems-1;
      int curIn;

      while(true)
         {
         curIn = (lowerBound + upperBound ) / 2;
         if(v[curIn]==searchKey)
            return curIn;               //found it
         else if(lowerBound > upperBound)
            return nElems;              //can't find it
         else                           //divide range
```

```
                  {
                  if(v[curIn] < searchKey)
                     lowerBound = curIn + 1;  //it's in upper half
                  else
                     upperBound = curIn - 1;  //it's in lower half
                  }   //end else divide range
               }   //end while
            }   //end find()
      //------------------------------------------------------------
      void insert(double value)              //put element into array
         {
         int j;
         for(j=0; j<nElems; j++)             //find where it goes
            if(v[j] > value)                 //(linear search)
               break;
         for(int k=nElems; k>j; k--)         //move bigger ones up
            v[k] = v[k-1];
         v[j] = value;                       //insert it
         nElems++;                           //increment size
         }   //end insert()
      //------------------------------------------------------------
      bool remove(double value)
         {
         int j = find(value);
         if(j==nElems)                       //can't find it
            return false;
         else                                //found it
            {
            for(int k=j; k<nElems; k++)      //move bigger ones down
               v[k] = v[k+1];
            nElems--;                        //decrement size
            return true;
            }
         }   //end remove()
      //------------------------------------------------------------
      void display()                         //displays array contents
         {
         for(int j=0; j<nElems; j++)         //for each element,
            cout << v[j] << " ";             //display it
         cout << endl;
         }
      //------------------------------------------------------------
   };   //end class OrdArray
//////////////////////////////////////////////////////////////////
int main()
   {
   int maxSize = 100;                        //array size
   OrdArray arr(maxSize);                    //create the array
```

continues

LISTING 3.2   CONTINUED

```
    arr.insert(77);                    //insert 10 items
    arr.insert(99);
    arr.insert(44);
    arr.insert(55);
    arr.insert(22);
    arr.insert(88);
    arr.insert(11);
    arr.insert(00);
    arr.insert(66);
    arr.insert(33);

    int searchKey = 55;                //search for item
    if( arr.find(searchKey) != arr.getSize() )
       cout << "Found " << searchKey << endl;
    else
       cout << "Can't find " << searchKey << endl;

    arr.display();                     //display items

    cout << "Deleting 0, 55, and 99" << endl;
    arr.remove(00);                    //delete 3 items
    arr.remove(55);
    arr.remove(99);

    arr.display();                     //display items again
    return 0;
    }  //end main()
```

The Advantages of Using Ordered Arrays

What have we gained by using an ordered array? The major advantage is that search times are much faster than in an unordered array. The disadvantage is that insertion takes longer because all the data items with a higher key value must be moved up to make room. Deletions are slow in both ordered and unordered arrays because items must be moved down to fill the hole left by the deleted item.

Ordered arrays are therefore useful in situations where searches are frequent, but insertions and deletions are not. An ordered array might be appropriate for a datafile of company employees, for example. Hiring new employees and laying off existing ones would probably be infrequent occurrences compared with accessing an existing employee's record for information, or updating it to reflect changes in salary, address, and so on.

A retail store inventory, on the other hand, would not be a good candidate for an ordered array because the frequent insertions and deletions—as items arrived in the store and were sold—would run slowly.

Now that we've seen how binary searches work, we'll shift gears and look at some of the mathematics that describe the process.

Logarithms

How many steps are necessary to perform a binary search on a given size array? In this section we'll explain how logarithms are used to calculate this number. If you're a math major, you can probably skip this section. If math makes you break out in a rash, you can also skip it, except for taking a long hard look at Table 3.2, which summarizes what you really need to know.

We've seen that a binary search provides a significant speed increase over a linear search. In the number guessing game, with a range from 1 to 100, it takes a maximum of seven guesses to identify any number using a binary search; just as in an array of 100 records, it takes seven comparisons to find a record with a specified key value. How about other ranges? Table 3.2 shows some representative ranges and the number of comparisons needed for a binary search.

TABLE 3.2 COMPARISONS NEEDED IN BINARY AND LINEAR SEARCHES

Range	Comparisons Needed in Binary Search	Comparisons Needed in Linear Search
10	4	5
100	7	50
1,000	10	500
10,000	14	5,000
100,000	17	50,000
1,000,000	20	500,000
10,000,000	24	5,000,000
100,000,000	27	50,000,000
1,000,000,000	30	500,000,000

Notice the differences between binary search times and linear search times. For very small numbers of items, the difference isn't dramatic. Searching 10 items would take an average of five comparisons with a linear search (N/2), and a maximum of four comparisons with a binary search. But the more items there are, the bigger the difference. With 100 items, there are 50 comparisons in a linear search, but only seven in a binary search. For 1,000 items, the numbers are 500 versus 10, and for 1,000,000 items, they're 500,000 versus 20. We can conclude that for all but very small arrays, the binary search is greatly superior.

An Equation Relating Range Size and Number of Steps

You can verify the results of Table 3.2 by repeatedly dividing a range (from the first column) in half until it's too small to divide further. The number of divisions this process requires is the number of comparisons shown in the second column.

Repeatedly dividing the range by two is an algorithmic approach to finding the number of comparisons. You might wonder whether you could also find the number using a simple equation. Of course there is such an equation, and it's worth exploring here because it pops up from time to time in the study of data structures. This formula involves logarithms. (Don't panic yet.)

The numbers in Table 3.2 leave out some interesting data. They don't answer questions like, "What is the exact size of the maximum range that can be searched in five steps?" To solve this, we must create a similar table, but one that starts at the beginning, with a range of one, and works up from there by multiplying the range by two each time. Table 3.3 shows how this looks for the first seven steps.

TABLE 3.3 POWERS OF TWO

Step s, Same as $log_2(r)$	Range r	Range Expressed as Power of 2 (2^s)
0	1	2^0
1	2	2^1
2	4	2^2
3	8	2^3
4	16	2^4
5	32	2^5
6	64	2^6
7	128	2^7
8	256	2^8
9	512	2^9
10	1024	2^{10}

For our original problem with a range of 100, we can see that six steps don't produce a range quite big enough (64), whereas seven steps cover it handily (128). Thus, the seven steps that are shown for 100 items in Table 3.2 are correct, as are the 10 steps for a range of 1000.

Doubling the range each time creates a series that's the same as raising two to a power, as shown in the third column of Table 3.3. We can express this as an equation. If s represents steps (the number of times you multiply by two—that is, the power to which two is raised)—and r represents the range, the equation is

$$r = 2^s$$

If you know s, the number of steps, this tells you r, the range. For example, if s is 6, the range is 2^6, or 64.

The Opposite of Raising Two to a Power

But our original question was the opposite: Given the range, we want to know how many comparisons it will take to complete a search. That is, given r, we want an equation that gives us s.

The inverse of raising something to a power is a logarithm. Here's the formula we want, expressed with a logarithm:

$$s = \log_2(r)$$

This says that the number of steps (comparisons) is equal to the logarithm to the base 2 of the range. What's a logarithm? The base-2 logarithm of a number r is the number of times you must multiply 2 by itself to get r. In Table 3.3, we show that the numbers in the first column, s, are equal to $\log_2(r)$.

How do you find the logarithm of a number without doing a lot of dividing? Pocket calculators and most computer languages have a log function. This is usually log to the base 10 (expressed $\log_{10}$), but you can convert easily to base 2 ($\log_2$) by multiplying by 3.322. For example, $\log_{10}(100) = 2$, so $\log_2(100) = 2$ times 3.322, or 6.644. Rounded up to the whole number 7, this is what appears in the column to the right of 100 in Table 3.3.

The key point here is to understand the relationship between a number and its logarithm. Look again at Table 3.2, which compares the number of items and the number of steps needed to find a particular item. Every time you multiply the number of items (the range) by a factor of 10, you add only three or four steps (actually 3.322, before rounding off to whole numbers) to the number needed to find a particular element. This is because as a number grows larger, its logarithm doesn't grow nearly as fast. We'll compare this logarithmic growth rate with that of other mathematical functions when we talk about Big O notation later in this hour.

3

Next we'll get away from math and see how objects relate to data structures and algorithms.

Storing Objects

In the C++ examples we've shown so far, we've stored primitive variables of type double in our data structures. This simplifies the program examples, but it's not representative of how you use data storage structures in the real world. Usually, the data items (records) you want to store are combinations of many fields. For a personnel record, you would store last name, first name, age, Social Security number, and possibly many other fields. For a stamp collection, you would store the name of the country that issued the stamp, its catalog number, condition, current value, and so on.

In our next C++ example, we'll show how objects, rather than variables of primitive types, can be stored.

Implementing the Person Class

In C++, a data record is usually represented by a class object. Let's examine a typical class used for storing personnel data. Listing 3.3 shows the code for the Person class:

INPUT   **LISTING 3.3**   THE Person CLASS

```
class Person
   {
   private:
      string lastName;
      string firstName;
      int age;
   public://-------------------------------------------------------
   Person(string last, string first, int a) :    //constructor
            lastName(last), firstName(first), age(a)
      {  }
//--------------------------------------------------------------
   void displayPerson()
      {
      cout << "   Last name: " << lastName;
      cout << ", First name: " << firstName;
      cout << ", Age: " << age << endl;
      }
//--------------------------------------------------------------
   string getLast()                        //get last name
      { return lastName; }
   };  //end class Person
```

ANALYSIS We show only three data members in this class, a person's last name, first name, and age. Of course, records for most applications would contain many additional fields.

A constructor enables a new `Person` object to be created and its data members initialized. The `displayPerson()` member function displays a `Person` object's data, and `getLast()` returns the `Person`'s last name; this is the key data member used for searches.

Examining the `classDataArray.cpp` Program

The program that makes use of the `Person` class is similar to the `highArray.cpp` program that stored items of type `double` in Hour 2, "Arrays." Only a few changes are necessary to adapt that program to handle `Person` objects. Here are the major changes:

- The type of the vector v is changed to `Person`.
- The key data member (the last name) is now a string object. The `getLast()` member function of `Person` obtains the last name.
- The `insert()` member function creates a new `Person` object and inserts it in the array, instead of inserting a `double` value.

The `main()` function has been modified slightly, mostly to handle the increased quantity of output. We still insert 10 items, display them, search for one, delete three items, and display them all again. Listing 3.4 shows `classDataArray.cpp`:

INPUT **LISTING 3.4** THE `classDataArray.cpp` PROGRAM

```
//classDataArray.cpp
//data items as class objects
#include <iostream>
#include <string>
#include <vector>
using namespace std;
////////////////////////////////////////////////////////////
class Person
   {
   private:
      string lastName;
      string firstName;
      int age;
   public:
//-------------------------------------------------------------
   Person(string last, string first, int a) :   //constructor
             lastName(last), firstName(first), age(a)
      { }
//-------------------------------------------------------------
```

continues

LISTING 3.4   CONTINUED

```cpp
   void displayPerson()
      {
      cout << "   Last name: " << lastName;
      cout << ", First name: " << firstName;
      cout << ", Age: " << age << endl;
      }
//-------------------------------------------------------------
   string getLast()                    //get last name
      { return lastName; }
   };   //end class Person
///////////////////////////////////////////////////////////////
class ClassDataArray
   {
   private:
      vector<Person*> v;               //vector of pointers
      int nElems;                      //number of data items
   public:
//-------------------------------------------------------------
   ClassDataArray(int max) : nElems(0) //constructor
      { v.resize(max); }               //create the array
//-------------------------------------------------------------
   ~ClassDataArray()                   //destructor
      {
      for(int j=0; j<nElems; j++)      //delete each element
         delete v[j];
      }
//-------------------------------------------------------------
   Person* find(string searchName)
      {                                //find specified value
      int j;
      for(j=0; j<nElems; j++)          //for each element,
         if( v[j]->getLast() == searchName )  //found item?
            break;                     //exit loop before end
      if(j == nElems)                  //gone to end?
         return NULL;                  //yes, can't find it
      else
         return v[j];                  //no, found it
      };   //end find()
//-------------------------------------------------------------
                                       //put person into array
   void insert(string last, string first, int age)
      {
      v[nElems] = new Person(last, first, age);
      nElems++;                        //increment size
      }
//-------------------------------------------------------------
   bool remove(string searchName)      //delete person from array
      {
```

```
        int j;
        for(j=0; j<nElems; j++)          //look for it
           if( v[j]->getLast() == searchName )
              break;
        if(j==nElems)                     //can't find it
           return false;
        else                              //found it
           {
           delete v[j];                   //delete Person object
           for(int k=j; k<nElems; k++)    //shift down
              v[k] = v[k+1];
           nElems--;                      //decrement size
           return true;
           }
        }  //end remove()
//-----------------------------------------------------------
   void displayA()                        //displays array contents
      {
      for(int j=0; j<nElems; j++)         //for each element,
         v[j]->displayPerson();           //display it
      }
//-----------------------------------------------------------
   };  //end class ClassDataArray
/////////////////////////////////////////////////////////////
int main()
   {
   int maxSize = 100;                     //array size
   ClassDataArray arr(maxSize);           //array

   arr.insert("Evans", "Patty", 24);      //insert 10 items
   arr.insert("Smith", "Lorraine", 37);
   arr.insert("Yee", "Tom", 43);
   arr.insert("Adams", "Henry", 63);
   arr.insert("Hashimoto", "Sato", 21);
   arr.insert("Stimson", "Henry", 29);
   arr.insert("Velasquez", "Jose", 72);
   arr.insert("Lamarque", "Henry", 54);
   arr.insert("Vang", "Minh", 22);
   arr.insert("Creswell", "Lucinda", 18);

   arr.displayA();                        //display items

   string searchKey = "Stimson";          //search for item
   cout << "Searching for Stimson" << endl;
   Person* found;
   found=arr.find(searchKey);
   if(found != NULL)
      {
      cout << "   Found ";
```

continues

LISTING 3.4 CONTINUED

```
        found->displayPerson();
        }
    else
        cout << "   Can't find " << searchKey << endl;

    cout << "Deleting Smith, Yee, and Creswell" << endl;
    arr.remove("Smith");                    //delete 3 items
    arr.remove("Yee");
    arr.remove("Creswell");

    arr.displayA();                         //display items again
    return 0;
    }  //end main()
```

OUTPUT   Here's the output of this program:

```
Last name: Evans, First name: Patty, Age: 24
    Last name: Smith, First name: Lorraine, Age: 37
    Last name: Yee, First name: Tom, Age: 43
    Last name: Adams, First name: Henry, Age: 63
    Last name: Hashimoto, First name: Sato, Age: 21
    Last name: Stimson, First name: Henry, Age: 29
    Last name: Velasquez, First name: Jose, Age: 72
    Last name: Lamarque, First name: Henry, Age: 54
    Last name: Vang, First name: Minh, Age: 22
    Last name: Creswell, First name: Lucinda, Age: 18
Searching for Stimson
    Found    Last name: Stimson, First name: Henry, Age: 29
Deleting Smith, Yee, and Creswell
    Last name: Evans, First name: Patty, Age: 24
    Last name: Adams, First name: Henry, Age: 63
    Last name: Hashimoto, First name: Sato, Age: 21
    Last name: Stimson, First name: Henry, Age: 29
    Last name: Velasquez, First name: Jose, Age: 72
    Last name: Lamarque, First name: Henry, Age: 54
    Last name: Vang, First name: Minh, Age: 22
```

ANALYSIS   This program shows that class objects can be handled by data storage structures in much the same way as primitive types. (Note that a program intended for public use, using the last name as a key would need to account for duplicate last names, which would complicate the programming, as discussed earlier.)

Now we'll move on to a key topic in the discussion of algorithms: a concise and useful way to describe algorithm efficiency.

Big O Notation

Automobiles are divided by size into several categories: subcompacts, compacts, mid-size, and so on. These categories provide a quick idea of what size car you're talking about, without mentioning actual dimensions. Similarly, it's useful to have a shorthand way to say how efficient a computer algorithm is. In computer science, this rough measure is called "Big O" notation.

You might think that in comparing algorithms you would say things like, "Algorithm A is twice as fast as algorithm B," but in fact this sort of statement isn't too meaningful. Why not? Because the proportion can change radically as the number of items changes. Perhaps you increase the number of items by 50%, and now A is three times as fast as B. Or you have half as many items, and A and B are now equal. What you need is a comparison that's related to the number of items. Let's see how this looks for the algorithms we've seen so far.

Inserting into an Unordered Array: Constant

Insertion into an unordered array is the only algorithm we've seen that doesn't depend on how many items are in the array. The new item is always placed in the next available position, at a[nElems], and nElems is then incremented. This requires the same amount of time no matter how big N—the number of items in the array—is. We can say that the time, T, to insert an item into an unsorted array is a constant K:

```
T = K
```

In a real situation, the actual time (in microseconds or some other unit of measure) required by the insertion is related to the speed of the microprocessor, how efficiently the compiler has generated the program code, and other factors. The constant K in the preceding equation is used to account for all such factors. To find out what K is in a real situation, you must measure how long an insertion took. (Software exists for this very purpose.) K would then be equal to that time.

Linear Searching: Proportional to N

We've seen that in a linear search of items in an array, the number of comparisons that must be made to find a specified item is, on the average, half of the total number of items. Thus, if N is the total number of items, the search time T is proportional to half of N:

```
T = K * N / 2
```

As with insertions, discovering the value of K in this equation would require timing a search for some (probably large) value of N, and then using the resulting value of T to calculate K. After you know K, you can calculate T for any other value of N.

For a handier formula, we can lump the 2 into the K. Our new K is equal to the old K divided by 2. Now we have

```
T = K * N
```

This says that average linear search times are proportional to the size of the array. If an array is twice as big, it will take twice as long to search.

Binary Searching: Proportional to log(N)

Similarly, we can concoct a formula relating T and N for a binary search:

$$T = K * \log_2(N)$$

As we saw in the section on Logarithms, the time is proportional to the base-2 logarithm of N. Actually, because any logarithm is related to any other logarithm by a constant (3.322 to go from base 2 to base 10), we can lump this constant into K as well. Then we don't need to specify the base:

```
T = K * log(N)
```

Eliminating the Constant K

Big O notation looks like the formulas we just examined, but it dispenses with the constant K. When comparing algorithms you don't really care about the particular microprocessor chip or compiler; all you want to compare is how T changes for different values of N, not what the actual numbers are. Therefore, the constant isn't needed.

Big O notation uses the uppercase letter O, which you can think of as meaning "order of." In Big O notation, we would say that a linear search takes O(N) time, and a binary search takes O(log N) time. Insertion into an unordered array takes O(1), or constant time. (That's the numeral 1 in the parentheses.)

Table 3.4 summarizes the running times of the algorithms we've discussed so far.

TABLE 3.4 RUNNING TIMES IN BIG O NOTATION

Algorithm	Running Time in Big O Notation
Linear search	O(N)
Binary search	O(log N)
Insertion in unordered array	O(1)

Algorithm	Running Time in Big O Notation
Insertion in ordered array	O(N)
Deletion in unordered array	O(N)
Deletion in ordered array	O(N)

Figure 3.5 graphs some Big O relationships between time and number of items. Based on this graph, we might rate the various Big O values (very subjectively) like this: O(1) is excellent, O(log N) is good, O(N) is fair, and O(N^2) is poor. O(N^2) occurs in certain sorting algorithms that we'll look at in Hours 4 and 5.

FIGURE 3.5

Graph of Big O times.

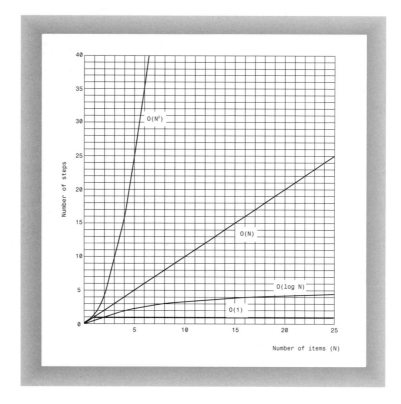

Remember: The idea in Big O notation isn't to give an actual figure for running time, but to convey how running times are affected by the number of items. This is the most meaningful way to compare algorithms, except perhaps actually measuring running times in a real installation.

Why Not Use Arrays for Everything?

We've looked at two different kinds of arrays used to store data. In the balance of this book we'll be looking at various other data structures. But what's wrong with arrays? Why not use them for everything?

We've already seen some of the disadvantages of arrays. In an unordered array you can insert items quickly, in O(1) time, but searching takes slow O(N) time. In an ordered array you can search quickly, in O(log N) time, but insertion takes O(N) time. For both kinds of arrays, deletion takes O(N) time because half the items (on the average) must be moved to fill in the hole.

It would be nice if there were data structures that could do everything—insertion, deletion, and searching—quickly, ideally in O(1) time, but if not that fast, then in O(log N) time. In the hours ahead, we'll see how closely this ideal can be approached, and the price that must be paid in complexity.

Summary

Today, you learned the following:

- A binary search can be applied to an ordered array.
- The logarithm to the base B of a number A is (roughly) the number of times you can divide A by B before the result is less than 1.
- Linear searches require time proportional to the number of items in an array.
- Binary searches require time proportional to the logarithm of the number of items.
- Big O notation provides a convenient way to compare the speed of algorithms.
- An algorithm that runs in O(1) time is the best, O(log N) is good, O(N) is fair, and O(N^2) is pretty bad.

Q&A

Q Do people actually use ordered arrays, or do they always use more sophisticated data structures?

A People actually use them, especially, as we noted, when search speed is important but insertion and deletion are infrequent.

Q I always confuse algorithms and logarithms. Can you help me?

A An *algorithm* is a sequence of instructions for carrying out an operation. A *logarithm* is a mathematical relationship between two numbers.

Q Is it important that I understand Big O notation?

A Yes. At the very least you should memorize the last point in the preceding summary. It gives you a quick way to compare algorithm efficiency.

Workshop

The Workshop helps you solidify what you learned in this hour. See Appendix A for quiz answers.

Quiz

1. Why is an ordered array better than an unordered array?

2. In one sentence, how does a binary search work?

3. What is the maximum number of comparisons necessary when performing a binary search of 100,000 items?

4. What is the equation that tells you how many steps a binary search will take if you already know the size of the range to be searched?

5. True or false: Only simple variables like int can be stored in a data structure.

6. What is the purpose of Big O notation?

7. Big O notation specifies a relationship between two variables. What are these variables?

Exercise

Think of other situations in real life that involve binary searches, or at least searches that use some of the same principles. For example, when you look up "potato" in a dictionary, you don't examine every word starting at "aardvark." Instead, you flip open the dictionary in a likely place, compare what's there with the word you're looking for, and then flip the dictionary open to another place you pick based on the comparison. As a human you can short-circuit such a search somewhat because you know "p" is closer to the end of the alphabet than the beginning, but the principle is similar.

HOUR 4

The Bubble Sort

In this hour we'll introduce the simplest way to sort data: the bubble sort. You'll learn

- How the bubble sort algorithm works.
- How to write code for the bubble sort in C++.
- How to measure the efficiency of the bubble sort.

Sorting

As soon as you create a significant collection of data, you'll probably think of reasons to sort it. You need to arrange names in alphabetical order, students by grade, customers by zip code, house sales by price, cities in order of increasing population, countries by GNP, stars by magnitude, and so on.

Sorting data may also be a preliminary step to searching it. As we saw in the last hour, a binary search, which can be applied only to sorted data, is much faster than a linear search.

Because sorting is so important and potentially so time-consuming, it has been the subject of extensive research in computer science, and some very sophisticated methods have been developed. However, in this hour we'll look at perhaps the simplest algorithm: the bubble sort. In Hour 5, "The Insertion Sort," we'll look at an improvement on the bubble sort. In Hour 12, "Applied Recursion," Hour 13, "Quicksort," and Hour 14, "Improving Quicksort," we'll examine more powerful sorts. All the sorting algorithms are demonstrated with their own Workshop applets.

The algorithms described in this and the next hour, although unsophisticated and comparatively slow, are nevertheless worth examining. Besides being easier to understand, they are actually better in some circumstances than more sophisticated algorithms. The insertion sort, for example, is preferable to quicksort for small files and for almost-sorted files. In fact, an insertion sort is commonly used as a part of a quicksort implementation.

The sample programs in this hour build on the array classes we developed in Hours 2, "Arrays," and 3, "Ordered Arrays." The sorting algorithms are implemented as member functions of similar array classes.

Be sure to try out the Workshop applets for the bubble sort and other sorting algorithms. They are more effective in explaining how the sorting algorithms work than prose and static pictures could ever be.

The bubble sort is notoriously slow, but it's conceptually the simplest of the sorting algorithms, and for that reason it is a good beginning for our exploration of sorting techniques.

Inventing Your Own Sorting Algorithm

How do you sort a collection of unsorted items? Imagine that your kids-league baseball team (mentioned in Hour 2) is lined up on the field, as shown in Figure 4.1. The regulation nine players, plus an extra, have shown up for practice. You want to arrange the players in order of increasing height (with the shortest player on the left) for the team picture. How would you go about this sorting process?

FIGURE 4.1

The unordered baseball team.

As a human being, you have advantages over a computer program. You can see all the kids at once, and you can pick out the tallest kid almost instantly; you don't need to laboriously measure and compare everyone. Also, the kids don't need to occupy particular places. They can jostle each other, push each other a little to make room, and stand behind or in front of each other. After some ad hoc rearranging, you would have no trouble in lining up all the kids, as shown in Figure 4.2.

FIGURE 4.2

The ordered baseball team.

A computer program isn't able to glance over the data in this way. It can only compare two players at once because that's how the C++ comparison operators work. This tunnel vision on the part of algorithms will be a recurring theme. Things might seem simple to us humans, but the algorithm can't see the big picture and must, therefore, concentrate on the details and follow some simple rules.

The algorithm in the bubble sort involves two steps, executed over and over until the data is sorted:

1. Compare two adjacent items.
2. If necessary, swap (exchange) them.

Bubble-Sorting the Baseball Players

Imagine that you're nearsighted (like a computer program) so that you can see only two of the baseball players at the same time, if they're next to each other and if you stand very close to them. Given this impediment, how would you sort them? Let's assume there are N players, and the positions they're standing in are numbered from 0 on the left to N–1 on the right.

To Do: Bubble-Sort the Baseball Players

1. You start at the left end of the line and compare the two kids in positions 0 and 1.
2. If the kid on the left (in position 0) is taller, you swap them. If the kid on the right (in position 1) is taller, you don't do anything.

▼ To Do

▼   3. Then you move over one position and compare the kids in positions 1 and 2.
       Again, if the kid on the left is taller, you swap them. This is shown in Figure 4.3.

FIGURE 4.3

Bubble sort: beginning of first pass.

▲

Here are the rules you're following:

1. Compare two players.

2. If the one on the left is taller, swap them.

3. Move one position right.

   You continue down the line this way until you reach the right end. You have by no means finished sorting the kids, but you do know that the tallest kid is on the right.

This must be true because as soon as you encounter the tallest kid, you'll end up swapping him every time you compare two kids, until eventually he (or she) will reach the right end of the line. This is why it's called the bubble sort: as the algorithm progresses, the biggest items "bubble up" to the top end of the array. Figure 4.4 shows the baseball players at the end of the first pass.

FIGURE 4.4

Bubble sort: end of first pass.

Sorted

After this first pass through all the data, you've made N–1 comparisons (where N is the number of players), and somewhere between 0 and N–1 swaps, depending on the initial arrangement of the players. The item at the end of the array is sorted and won't be moved again.

Now you go back and start another pass from the left end of the line, comparing the players at 0 and 1. Again you go toward the right, comparing and (if necessary) swapping. However, this time you can stop one player short of the end of the line, at position N–2 because you know the last position, at N–1, already contains the tallest player. This rule could be stated as step 4.

4. When you reach the first already-sorted player, start over at the left end of the line.

Continue this process until all the players are in order. This is all much harder to describe than it is to demonstrate, so let's watch the bubbleSort Workshop applet at work.

The bubbleSort Workshop Applet

Start the bubbleSort Workshop applet. You'll see something that looks like a bar graph, with the bar heights randomly arranged, as shown in Figure 4.5.

We'll now explain how to operate the applet.

FIGURE 4.5

*The bubbleSort
Workshop applet.*

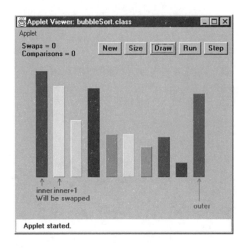

Sorting at Full Speed with the Run Button

This is a two-speed graph: you can either let it run by itself, or you can single-step
through the process. To get a quick idea what happens, click the Run button. The algorithm will bubble-sort the bars without pausing between steps. When it finishes, in 10
seconds or so, the bars will be sorted, as shown in Figure 4.6.

FIGURE 4.6

After the bubble sort.

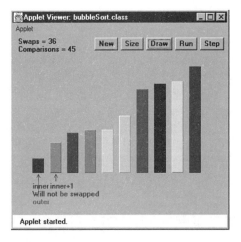

Starting a New Sort with the New Button

To do another sort, press the New button. New creates a new set of bars and initializes
the sorting routine. Repeated presses of New toggle between two arrangements of bars:

a random order as shown in Figure 4.5, and an inverse ordering where the bars are sorted backward. This inverse ordering provides an extra challenge for many sorting algorithms.

Single-Stepping with the Step Button

The real payoff for using the bubbleSort Workshop applet comes when you single-step through a sort. You'll be able to see exactly how the algorithm carries out each step.

To Do: Single-Step the Bubble Sort

1. Start by creating a new, randomly arranged graph with New. You'll see three arrows pointing at different bars. Two arrows, labeled inner and inner+1, are side-by-side on the left. Another arrow, outer, starts on the far right. (The names are chosen to correspond to the inner and outer loop variables in the nested loops used in the C++ code.)

2. Click once on the Step button. You'll see the inner and the inner+1 arrows move together one position to the right, swapping the bars if it's appropriate. These arrows correspond to the two players you compared, and possibly swapped, in the baseball scenario.

    A message under the arrows tells you whether the contents of inner and inner+1 will be swapped, but you know this just from comparing the bars: if the taller one is on the left, they'll be swapped. Messages at the top of the graph tell you how many swaps and comparisons have been carried out so far. (A complete sort of 10 bars requires 45 comparisons and, on the average, about 22 swaps.)

3. Continue pressing Step. Each time inner and inner+1 finish going all the way from 0 to outer, the outer pointer moves one position to the left. At all times during the sorting process, all the bars to the right of outer are sorted; those to the left of (and at) outer are not.

Changing the Array Size with the Size Button

The Size button toggles between 10 bars and 100 bars. Figure 4.7 shows what the 100 random bars look like. You probably don't want to single-step through the sorting process for 100 bars, unless you're unusually patient. Press Run instead, and watch how the blue inner and inner+1 pointers seem to find the tallest unsorted bar and carry it down the row to the right, inserting it just to the left of any previously sorted bars.

Figure 4.8 shows the situation partway through the sorting process. The bars to the right of the red (longest) arrow are sorted. The bars to the left are beginning to look sorted, but much work remains to be done.

FIGURE **4.7**

The bubbleSort applet with 100 bars.

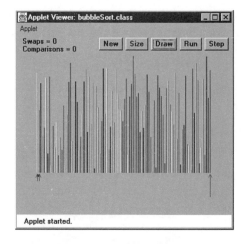

FIGURE **4.8**

100 partly sorted bars.

If you started a sort with Run and the arrows are whizzing around, you can freeze the process at any point by pressing the Step button. You can then single-step to watch the details of the operation, or press Run again to return to high-speed mode.

Fixing the Picture with the Draw Button

Sometimes while running the sorting algorithm at full speed, the computer takes time off to perform some other task. This can result in some bars not being drawn. If this happens, you can press the Draw button to redraw all the bars. Doing so pauses the run, so you'll need to press the Run button again to continue.

You can press Draw any time there seems to be a glitch in the display.

Now that we've seen what the bubble sort looks like with the Workshop applet, let's examine the details of some C++ code that does the same thing.

Implementing C++ Code for a Bubble Sort

In the bubbleSort.cpp program, shown in Listing 4.1, a class called ArrayBub encapsulates a vector v, which holds variables of type double.

In a more serious program, the data would probably consist of objects, but we use a primitive type for simplicity. (We'll see how objects are sorted in the objectSort.cpp program in the next hour.) Also, to reduce the size of the listing, we don't show find() and delete() member functions with the ArrayBub class, although they would normally be part of a such a class.

INPUT   **LISTING 4.1**   THE bubbleSort.cpp PROGRAM

```
//bubbleSort.cpp
//demonstrates bubble sort
#include <iostream>
#include <vector>
using namespace std;
//--------------------------------------------------------------
class ArrayBub
   {
   private:
      vector<double> v;              //vector v
      int nElems;                    //number of data items
//--------------------------------------------------------------
   void swap(int one, int two)       //private member function
      {
      double temp = v[one];
      v[one] = v[two];
      v[two] = temp;
      }
//--------------------------------------------------------------
   public:
//--------------------------------------------------------------
   ArrayBub(int max) : nElems(0)     //constructor
      {
      v.resize(max);                 //size the vector
```

continues

LISTING 4.1   CONTINUED

```cpp
      }
//-----------------------------------------------------------
   void insert(double value)       //put element into array
      {
      v[nElems] = value;           //insert it
      nElems++;                    //increment size
      }
//-----------------------------------------------------------
   void display()                  //displays array contents
      {
      for(int j=0; j<nElems; j++)  //for each element,
         cout << v[j] << " ";      //display it
      cout << endl;
      }
//-----------------------------------------------------------
   void bubbleSort()               //sorts the array
      {
      int out, in;

      for(out=nElems-1; out>1; out--)   //outer loop (backward)
         for(in=0; in<out; in++)        //inner loop (forward)
            if( v[in] > v[in+1] )        //out of order?
               swap(in, in+1);           //swap them
      }  //end bubbleSort()
//-----------------------------------------------------------
   };  //end class ArrayBub
////////////////////////////////////////////////////////////////
int main()
   {
   int maxSize = 100;              //array size
   ArrayBub arr(maxSize);          //create the array

   arr.insert(77);                 //insert 10 items
   arr.insert(99);
   arr.insert(44);
   arr.insert(55);
   arr.insert(22);
   arr.insert(88);
   arr.insert(11);
   arr.insert(00);
   arr.insert(66);
   arr.insert(33);

   arr.display();                  //display items
   arr.bubbleSort();               //bubble sort them
   arr.display();                  //display them again
   return 0;
   }  //end main()
```

ANALYSIS The constructor and the `insert()` and `display()` member functions of this class are similar to those we've seen before. However, there's a new member function: `bubbleSort()`. When this function is invoked from `main()`, the contents of the array are rearranged into sorted order.

OUTPUT The `main()` routine inserts 10 items into the array in random order, displays the array, calls `bubbleSort()` to sort it, and then displays it again. Here's the output:

```
77 99 44 55 22 88 11 0 66 33
0 11 22 33 44 55 66 77 88 99
```

The `bubbleSort()` member function is only a few lines long. Here it is, extracted from the listing:

```
void bubbleSort()                      //sorts the array
   {
   int out, in;

   for(out=nElems-1; out>1; out--)     //outer loop (backward)
      for(in=0; in<out; in++)          //inner loop (forward)
         if( v[in] > v[in+1] )         //out of order?
            swap(in, in+1);            //swap them
   } //end bubbleSort()
```

The idea is to put the smallest item at the beginning of the array (index 0) and the largest item at the end (index `nElems-1`). The loop counter `out` in the outer `for` loop starts at the end of the array (on the left), at `nElems-1`, and decrements itself each time through the loop. The items at indices greater than `out` are always completely sorted. The `out` variable moves left after each pass by `in` so items that are already sorted are no longer involved in the algorithm.

The inner loop counter, `in`, starts at the beginning of the array and increments itself each cycle of the inner loop, exiting when it reaches `out`. Within the inner loop, the two array cells pointed to by `in` and `in+1` are compared, and swapped if the value of `in` is larger than the value of `in+1`.

For clarity, we use a separate `swap()` member function to carry out the swap. It simply exchanges the two values in the two array cells, using a temporary variable to hold the value of the first cell while the first cell takes on the value in the second, and then setting the second cell to the temporary value. Actually, using a separate `swap()` function might not be a good idea in practice because the function call adds a small amount of overhead. If you're writing your own sorting routine, you might prefer to make the swap instructions "inline" to gain a slight increase in speed.

Let's look at a different sort of idea, one that will pop up in many places besides the bubble sort.

Invariants

NEW TERM In many algorithms there are conditions that remain unchanged as the algorithm proceeds. These conditions are called *invariants*. Recognizing invariants can be useful in understanding an algorithm. In certain situations they might also be helpful in debugging; you can repeatedly check that the invariant is true, and signal an error if it isn't.

In the bubbleSort.cpp program, there's one invariant: the data items to the right of outer are sorted. This remains true throughout the run of the algorithm. (On the first pass, nothing has been sorted yet, and there are no items to the right of outer because it starts on the rightmost element.)

Efficiency of the Bubble Sort

Typically, after we've examined an algorithm such as the bubble sort, we'll also investigate briefly how efficient it is. (Usually this means how fast.) We'll do that here and with other algorithms.

As you can see by watching the Workshop applet with 10 bars, the inner and inner+1 arrows make 9 comparisons on the first pass, 8 on the second, and so on, down to 1 comparison on the last pass. For 10 items this is

```
9 + 8 + 7 + 6 + 5 + 4 + 3 + 2 + 1 = 45
```

In general, where N is the number of items in the array, there are N–1 comparisons on the first pass, N–2 on the second, and so on. The formula for the sum of such a series is

```
(N-1) + (N-2) + (N-3) + ... + 1 = N*(N-1)/2
```

N*(N-1)/2 is 45 when N is 10.

Thus the algorithm makes about $N^2/2$ comparisons (ignoring the –1, which doesn't make much difference, especially if N is large).

There are fewer swaps than there are comparisons because two bars are swapped only if they need to be. If the data is random, a swap is necessary about half the time, so there will be about $N^2/4$ swaps. (Although in the worst case, with the initial data inversely sorted, a swap is necessary with every comparison.)

Both swaps and comparisons are proportional to N^2. Because constants don't count in Big O notation, we can ignore the divisors 2 and 4 and say that the bubble sort runs in $O(N^2)$ time. This is slow, as you can verify by running the Workshop applet with 100 bars.

Whenever you see nested loops such as those in the bubble sort, you can suspect that an algorithm runs in $O(N^2)$ time. The outer loop executes N times, and the inner loop executes N (or perhaps N divided by some constant) times for each cycle of the outer loop. This means you're doing something approximately N*N or N^2 times.

Summary

In this hour, you've learned the following:

- The sorting algorithm in this hour assumes an array as a data storage structure.
- Sorting involves comparing the keys of data items in the array and moving the items around until they're in sorted order.
- The bubble sort algorithm executes in $O(N^2)$ time.
- An invariant is a condition that remains unchanged while an algorithm runs.
- The bubble sort is the least efficient, but the simplest, sort.

Q&A

Q If the bubble sort is so slow, why are we learning about it?

A It's an easy way to ease into the various concepts involved in sorting. You've learned about comparisons, swaps, and seen some simple C++ code. Now you're ready for more complicated algorithms.

Q How much faster are the more powerful sorting algorithms you mention at the beginning of the hour?

A The fastest sort, quicksort, operates in $O(N*logN)$ time, which is much better than $O(N^2)$.

Workshop

The Workshop helps you solidify what you learned in this hour. See Appendix A, "Quiz Answers," for quiz answers.

Quiz

1. Describe the algorithm for carrying out the bubble sort.

2. How many statements does a C++ program need to carry out the bubble sort?

3. What's an invariant?

4. Why is the bubble sort so slow?

5. How many comparisons does a bubble sort perform in sorting N items?

6. In the `bubbleSort.cpp` program, why is the `bubbleSort()` function a member function of a class?

Exercise

Extract all the cards of one suit from a deck of cards. Shuffle them and then sort them. Pay close attention to how you sort them. Write down the steps you follow to carry out the sort. This is an algorithm. How does this algorithm differ from the bubble sort?

HOUR 5

The Insertion Sort

The bubble sort, described in Hour 4, "The Bubble Sort," is the easiest sort to understand, so it's a good starting place in our discussion of sorting. However, it's also the least sophisticated. We can improve it at the cost of some additional complexity. The result is the insertion sort. In this hour you will learn

- The insertion sort algorithm
- How to write C++ code for the insertion sort
- How to sort objects rather than simple variables

The insertion sort is substantially better than the bubble sort (and various other elementary sorts we don't describe here, such as the selection sort). It still executes in $O(N^2)$ time, but it's about twice as fast as the bubble sort. It's also not too complex, although it's slightly more involved than the bubble sort. It's often used as the final stage of more sophisticated sorts, such as quicksort.

Insertion Sort on the Baseball Players

Start with your baseball players lined up in random order. (They wanted to play a game, but clearly there's no time for that.) It's easier to think about the insertion sort if we begin in the middle of the process, when the team is partly sorted.

Demonstrating Partial Sorting

You'll need a marker to designate one player. Maybe you throw a red T-shirt on the ground in front of the player. The players to the left (not the right, as in the bubble sort) of this marker are *partially sorted* (or *internally sorted*). This means they are sorted among themselves; each one is taller than the person to his or her left. However, they aren't necessarily in their final positions because they might still need to be moved when previously unsorted players are inserted between them. The players to the right of the T-shirt are unsorted.

Note that partial sorting did not take place in the bubble sort. In that algorithm a group of data items was completely sorted at any given time; in the insertion sort, a group of items is only partially sorted.

Inserting the Marked Player in the Appropriate Location

The player where the marker is, whom we'll call the "marked" player, and all the players on her right, are as yet unsorted. This is shown in section A in Figure 5.1.

What we're going to do is insert the marked player in the appropriate place in the (partially) sorted group. However, to do this, we'll need to shift some of the sorted players to the right to make room. To provide a space for this shift, we take the marked player out of line. (In the program this data item is stored in a temporary variable.) This is shown in section B in Figure 5.1.

Now we shift the sorted players to make room. The tallest sorted player moves one space right, into the marked player's spot. Then the next-tallest player moves one space right, into the tallest player's spot, and so on.

When does this shifting process stop? Imagine that you and the marked player are walking down the line to the left. At each position you shift another player to the right, but you also compare the marked player with the player about to be shifted. The shifting process stops when you've shifted the last player who is taller than the marked player. The last shift opens up the space where the marked player, when inserted, will be in (partially) sorted order. This is shown in section C in Figure 5.1.

FIGURE 5.1

The insertion sort on baseball players.

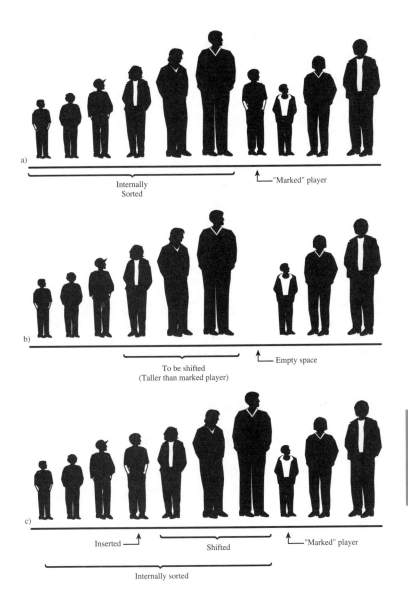

a)

Internally
Sorted

↑— "Marked" player

b)

To be shifted
(Taller than marked player)

↑— Empty space

c)

Inserted —↑

Shifted

↑— "Marked" player

Internally sorted

5

Now the partially sorted group has one more player, and the unsorted group has one fewer. The marker T-shirt is moved one space to the right, so it's again in front of the leftmost, unsorted player. This process is repeated until all the unsorted players have been inserted (hence the name *insertion* sort) into the appropriate place in the partially sorted group.

The insertSort Workshop Applet

Use the insertSort Workshop applet to demonstrate the insertion sort. Unlike the other sorting applets, it's probably more instructive to begin with 100 random bars rather than 10.

To Do: Sort 100 Bars

1. Change to 100 bars with the Size button.

2. Click Run to watch the bars sort themselves before your very eyes.

3. You'll see that the short red `outer` arrow marks the dividing line between the partially sorted bars to the left and the unsorted bars to the right.

4. The blue `inner` arrow keeps starting from `outer` and zipping to the left, looking for the proper place to insert the marked bar.

Figure 5.2 shows how this looks when about a third of the bars are partially sorted.

FIGURE 5.2

The insertSort Workshop applet with 100 bars.

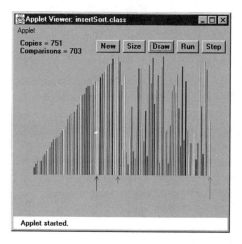

The marked bar is stored in the temporary variable pointed to by the magenta arrow at the right end of the graph, but the contents of this variable are replaced so often it's hard to see what's there (unless you slow down to single-step mode).

Sorting 100 bars gives us a big-picture view of the process. Sorting 10 bars lets us focus on the details.

To Do: Sort 10 Bars

Use Size to switch to 10 bars. (If necessary, use New to make sure the bars are in random order.)

▼ To Do

1. At the beginning, `inner` and `outer` point to the second bar from the left (array index 1), and the first message is `Will copy outer to temp`. This will make room for the shift. (There's no arrow for `inner-1`, but of course it's always one bar to the left of `inner`.)

2. Click the Step button. The bar at `outer` will be copied to `temp`. A copy means that there are now two bars with the same height and color shown on the graph. This is slightly misleading because a real C++ program would probably have two pointers pointing to the same object, not two objects. However, showing two identical bars is meant to convey the idea of copying the pointer.

3. What happens next depends on whether the first two bars are already in order (smaller on the left). If they are, you'll see `Have compared inner-1 and temp, no copy necessary`.

4. If the first two bars are not in order, the message is `Have compared inner-1 and temp, will copy inner-1 to inner`. This is the shift that's necessary to make room for the value in `temp` to be reinserted. There's only one such shift on this first pass; more shifts will be necessary on subsequent passes. The situation is shown in Figure 5.3.

FIGURE 5.3

The insertSort Workshop applet with 10 bars.

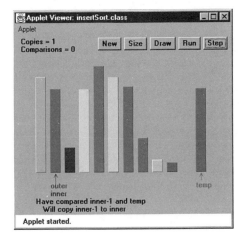

5. On the next click, you'll see the copy take place from `inner-1` to `inner`. Also, the `inner` arrow moves one space left. The new message is `Now inner is 0, so no copy necessary`. The shifting process is complete.

6. No matter which of the first two bars was shorter, the next click will show you `Will copy temp to inner`. This will happen, but if the first two bars were initially in order, you won't be able to tell a copy was performed because `temp` and

▼

▼ `inner` hold the same bar. Copying data over the top of the same data might seem inefficient, but the algorithm runs faster if it doesn't check for this possibility, which happens comparatively infrequently.

7. Now the first two bars are partially sorted (sorted with respect to each other), and the `outer` arrow moves one space right, to the third bar (index 2). The process repeats, with the `Will copy outer to temp` message. On this pass through the sorted data, there might be no shifts, one shift, or two shifts, depending on where the third bar fits among the first two.

8. Continue to single-step the sorting process. Again, it's easier to see what's happening after the process has run long enough to provide some sorted bars on the left. Then you can see how just enough shifts take place to make room for the reinser-
▲ tion of the bar from `temp` into its proper place.

Now that we've seen how the insertion sort works, let's look at how it is implemented in C++.

Implementing the Insertion Sort in C++

Listing 5.1 shows the member function that carries out the insertion sort, extracted from the `insertSort.cpp` program.

INPUT **LISTING 5.1** THE `insertionSort()` MEMBER FUNCTION

```
void insertionSort()
    {
    int in, out;

    for(out=1; out<nElems; out++)      //out is dividing line
        {
        double temp = v[out];          //remove marked item
        in = out;                      //start shifts at out
        while(in>0 && v[in-1] >= temp) //until one is smaller,
            {
            v[in] = v[in-1];           //shift item to right
            --in;                      //go left one position
            }
        v[in] = temp;                  //insert marked item
        } //end for
    } //end insertionSort()
```

ANALYSIS In the outer `for` loop, `out` starts at 1 and moves right; it marks the leftmost unsorted data. In the inner `while` loop, `in` starts at `out` and moves left, until either `temp` is smaller than the array element there, or it can't go left any further. Each pass through the `while` loop shifts another sorted element one space right.

It might be hard to see the relationbetween the steps in the Workshop applet and the code, so Figure 5.4 presents a flow diagram of the `insertionSort()` member function, with the corresponding messages from the insertSort Workshop applet. Listing 5.2 shows the complete `insertSort.cpp` program.

FIGURE 5.4

The flow diagram for `insertSort()`.

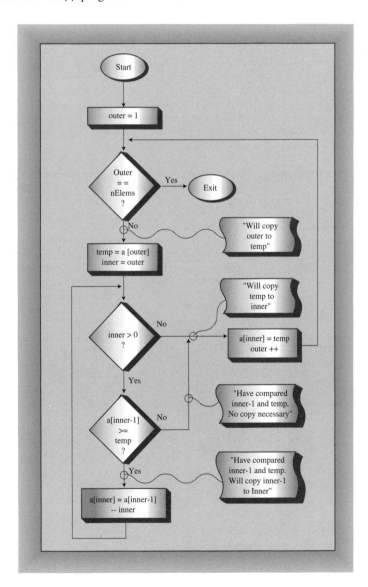

INPUT   **LISTING 5.2**   THE `insertSort.cpp` PROGRAM

```cpp
//insertSort.cpp
//demonstrates insertion sort
#include <iostream>
#include <vector>
using namespace std;
//--------------------------------------------------------------
class ArrayIns
   {
   private:
      vector<double> v;             //vector v
      int nElems;                   //number of data items
//--------------------------------------------------------------
   public:
   ArrayIns(int max) : nElems(0)    //constructor
      {
      v.resize(max);                //size the vector
      }
//--------------------------------------------------------------
   void insert(double value)        //put element into array
      {
      v[nElems] = value;            //insert it
      nElems++;                     //increment size
      }
//--------------------------------------------------------------
   void display()                   //displays array contents
      {
      for(int j=0; j<nElems; j++)   //for each element,
         cout << v[j] << " ";       //display it
      cout << endl;
      }
//--------------------------------------------------------------
   void insertionSort()
      {
      int in, out;

      for(out=1; out<nElems; out++)    //out is dividing line
         {
         double temp = v[out];         //remove marked item
         in = out;                     //start shifts at out
         while(in>0 && v[in-1] >= temp) //until one is smaller,
            {
            v[in] = v[in-1];           //shift item to right
            --in;                      //go left one position
            }
         v[in] = temp;                 //insert marked item
         } //end for
      } //end insertionSort()
//--------------------------------------------------------------
```

```
    };  //end class ArrayIns
///////////////////////////////////////////////////////////////
int main()
    {
    int maxSize = 100;              //array size
    ArrayIns arr(maxSize);          //create array

    arr.insert(77);                 //insert 10 items
    arr.insert(99);
    arr.insert(44);
    arr.insert(55);
    arr.insert(22);
    arr.insert(88);
    arr.insert(11);
    arr.insert(00);
    arr.insert(66);
    arr.insert(33);

    arr.display();                  //display items
    arr.insertionSort();            //insertion-sort them
    arr.display();                  //display them again
    return 0;
    }  //end main()
```

OUTPUT Here's the output from the insertSort.cpp program; it's the same as that from the bubbleSort.cpp program in Hour 4.

```
77 99 44 55 22 88 11 0 66 33
0 11 22 33 44 55 66 77 88 99
```

Invariants in the Insertion Sort

At the end of each pass, following the insertion of the item from temp, the data items with smaller indices than outer are partially sorted.

Efficiency of the Insertion Sort

How many comparisons and copies does this algorithm require? On the first pass, it compares a maximum of one item. On the second pass, it's a maximum of two items, and so on, up to a maximum of N–1 comparisons on the last pass. This is

```
1 + 2 + 3 + ... + N-1 = N*(N-1)/2
```

However, because on each pass an average of only half of the maximum number of items are actually compared before the insertion point is found, we can divide by 2, which gives the following equation:

```
N*(N-1)/4
```

5

Notice that the insertion sort algorithm involves copying rather than swapping. A swap requires three copies (A to temp, B to A, and temp to B). The number of copies is approximately the same as the number of comparisons. However, a copy isn't as time-consuming as a swap, so for random data the insertion sort algorithm runs more than twice as fast as the bubble sort.

In any case, like the bubble sort, the insertion sort runs in $O(N^2)$ time for random data.

For data that is already sorted or almost sorted, the insertion sort does much better. When data is in order, the condition in the `while` loop is never true, so it becomes a simple statement in the outer loop, which executes N–1 times. In this case the algorithm runs in $O(N)$ time. If the data is almost sorted, insertion sort runs in almost $O(N)$ time, which makes it a simple and efficient way to order a file that is only slightly out of order.

However, for data arranged in inverse sorted order, every possible comparison and shift is carried out, so the insertion sort runs no faster than the bubble sort. You can check this using the reverse-sorted data option (toggled with New) in the insertSort Workshop applet.

Let's change our focus from the sorting algorithm to what is being sorted.

Sorting Objects

For simplicity we've applied the sorting algorithms we've looked at thus far to a primitive data type: `double`. However, sorting routines will more likely be applied to objects than to primitive types. Accordingly, we show a C++ program, `objectSort.cpp`, that sorts an array of `Person` objects (last seen in the `classDataArray.cpp` program in Hour 3, "Ordered Arrays").

Implementing C++ Code to Sort Objects

The algorithm used is the insertion sort from the last section. The `Person` objects are sorted by `lastName`; this is the key data member, represented by a variable of the C++ class `string`. The `objectSort.cpp` program is shown in Listing 5.3.

INPUT   **LISTING 5.3**   THE `objectSort.cpp` PROGRAM

```
//objectSort.cpp
//demonstrates sorting objects (uses insertion sort)
#include <iostream>
#include <string>
```

```cpp
#include <vector>
using namespace std;
//////////////////////////////////////////////////////////////
class Person
    {
    private:
        string lastName;
        string firstName;
        int age;
    public:
//------------------------------------------------------------
    Person(string last, string first, int a) :    //constructor
            lastName(last), firstName(first), age(a)
        {  }
//------------------------------------------------------------
    void displayPerson()
        {
        cout << "   Last name: " << lastName;
        cout << ", First name: " << firstName;
        cout << ", Age: " << age << endl;
        }
//------------------------------------------------------------
    string getLast()                    //get last name
        { return lastName; }
    }; //end class Person
//////////////////////////////////////////////////////////////
class ArrayInOb
    {
    private:
        vector<Person*> v;              //vect of ptrs to Persons
        int nElems;                     //number of data items
    public:
//------------------------------------------------------------
    ArrayInOb(int max) : nElems(0)      //constructor
        {
        v.resize(max);                  //size the vector
        }
//------------------------------------------------------------
                                        //put person into array
    void insert(string last, string first, int age)
        {
        v[nElems] = new Person(last, first, age);
        nElems++;                       //increment size
        }
//------------------------------------------------------------
    void display()                      //displays array contents
        {
        for(int j=0; j<nElems; j++)     //for each element,
            v[j]->displayPerson();      //display it
```

continues

LISTING 5.3   CONTINUED

```
        }
//-------------------------------------------------------------
    void insertionSort()
        {
        int in, out;

        for(out=1; out<nElems; out++)
            {
            Person* temp = v[out];        //out is dividing line
            in = out;                     //start shifting at out
                                          //until smaller one found,
            while( in>0 && v[in-1]->getLast() > temp->getLast() )
                {
                v[in] = v[in-1];          //shift item to the right
                --in;                     //go left one position
                }
            v[in] = temp;                 //insert marked item
            }   //end for
        }   //end insertionSort()
//-------------------------------------------------------------
    };   //end class ArrayInOb
/////////////////////////////////////////////////////////////////
int main()
        {
        int maxSize = 100;               //array size
        ArrayInOb arr(maxSize);          //create array

        arr.insert("Evans", "Patty", 24);
        arr.insert("Smith", "Doc", 59);
        arr.insert("Smith", "Lorraine", 37);
        arr.insert("Smith", "Paul", 37);
        arr.insert("Yee", "Tom", 43);
        arr.insert("Hashimoto", "Sato", 21);
        arr.insert("Stimson", "Henry", 29);
        arr.insert("Velasquez", "Jose", 72);
        arr.insert ("Vang", "Minh", 22);
        arr.insert("Creswell", "Lucinda", 18);

        cout << "Before sorting:" << endl;
        arr.display();                   //display items

        arr.insertionSort();             //insertion-sort them

        cout << "After sorting:" << endl;
        arr.display();                   //display them again
        return 0;
        }   //end main()
```

OUTPUT   Here's the output of this program:

```
Before sorting:
    Last name: Evans, First name: Patty, Age: 24
    Last name: Smith, First name: Doc, Age: 59
    Last name: Smith, First name: Lorraine, Age: 37
    Last name: Smith, First name: Paul, Age: 37
    Last name: Yee, First name: Tom, Age: 43
    Last name: Hashimoto, First name: Sato, Age: 21
    Last name: Stimson, First name: Henry, Age: 29
    Last name: Velasquez, First name: Jose, Age: 72
    Last name: Vang, First name: Minh, Age: 22
    Last name: Creswell, First name: Lucinda, Age: 18

After sorting:
    Last name: Creswell, First name: Lucinda, Age: 18
    Last name: Evans, First name: Patty, Age: 24
    Last name: Hashimoto, First name: Sato, Age: 21
    Last name: Smith, First name: Doc, Age: 59
    Last name: Smith, First name: Lorraine, Age: 37
    Last name: Smith, First name: Paul, Age: 37
    Last name: Stimson, First name: Henry, Age: 29
    Last name: Vang, First name: Minh, Age: 22
    Last name: Velasquez, First name: Jose, Age: 72
    Last name: Yee, First name: Tom, Age: 43
```

Another Feature of Sorting Algorithms: Stability

5

Sometimes it matters what happens to data items that happen to have equal keys. For example, you might have employee data arranged alphabetically by last names. (That is, the last names were used as key values in the sort.) Now you want to sort the data by zip code, but you want all the items with the same zip code to continue to be sorted by last names. You want the algorithm to sort only what needs to be sorted, and to leave everything else in its original order. Some sorting algorithms retain this secondary ordering; they're said to be *stable*.

The insertion sort, like the bubble sort in the last hour, is stable. For example, notice the output of the `objectSort.cpp` program. There are three persons with the last name of Smith. Initially the order is Doc Smith, Lorraine Smith, and Paul Smith. After the sort, this ordering is preserved, despite the fact that the various Smith objects have been moved to new locations.

Comparing the Simple Sorts

There's probably no point in using the bubble sort, unless you don't have your algorithm book handy. The bubble sort is so simple you can write it from memory. Even so, it's practical only if the amount of data is small. (For a discussion of what "small" means, see Hour 24, "When to Use What.")

The insertion sort is the most versatile of the basic sorts, and is the best bet in most situations, assuming the amount of data is small or the data is almost sorted. For larger amounts of data, quicksort is generally considered the fastest approach; we'll examine it in Hour 13, "Quicksort."

We've compared the sorting algorithms in terms of speed. Another consideration for any algorithm is how much memory space it needs. Both the bubble sort and the insertion sort carry out their operations *in place*, meaning that beside the initial array, very little extra memory is required. Both sorts require an extra variable to store an item temporarily while it's being swapped or moved.

> You can recompile the sample programs, such as bubbleSort.cpp, to sort larger amounts of data. By timing them for larger sorts, you can get an idea of the differences between them, and how long it takes to sort different amounts of data on your particular system.

Summary

In this hour, you've learned the following:

- Although all the simple sorts execute in $O(N^2)$ time, some can be substantially faster than others.
- The insertion sort is the most commonly used of the $O(N^2)$ sorts.
- A sort is stable if the order of elements with the same key is retained.
- None of the basic sorts require more than a single temporary variable in addition to the original array.

Q&A

Q If both the bubble sort and the insertion sort run in O(N²) time, why not use the bubble sort, which is simpler to program?

A Besides being somewhat faster for random data, the insertion sort is much faster for data that is only slightly out of order.

Q Is there special code in the insertion sort to keep it from "unordering" items with the same key? In other words, why is it stable?

A There's no special code. Stability is just a fringe benefit of the insertion sort. The algorithm doesn't need to make any special effort.

Workshop

The Workshop helps you solidify what you learned in this hour. See Appendix A, "Quiz Answers," for quiz answers.

Quiz

1. What does *partially sorted* mean?

2. During the insertion sort, where is the marked item placed?

3. What is one reason the insertion sort is more efficient than the sorted group?

4. True or false: When using the insertion sort on N items, memory space for N*2 items is required.

5. True or false: The insertion sort runs in O(N²) time, the same as the bubble sort.

6. Define the term *stable* as applied to sorting.

7. When would you use a bubble sort as opposed to an insertion sort?

Exercise

Take the numbered cards from one suit of a deck of cards. Assume the ace is 1. Shuffle these 10 cards and lay them out in a line. Now sort them using the insertion sort algorithm. You can use a penny to designate the marked card.

PART II
Abstract Data Types

Hour

HOUR 6

Stacks

So far we've been looking at one kind of data structure: the array (often implemented as a vector). In this chapter we'll examine a different kind of structure: a stack. You'll learn

- How stacks differ philosophically from arrays
- How a stack operates
- How to create stacks in C++
- Some applications for stacks

A Different Way to Think About Data Structure

Stacks, which we'll discuss in this hour, and queues, which we'll talk about in Hour 7, "Queues and Priority Queues," are similar in many ways. However, there are significant differences between stacks and queues on the one hand and on the other hand the data structure (arrays) we've seen in previous hours. We'll discuss three of these differences before we examine the details of stacks. The differences are the common uses for the data structures, the way the structures are accessed, and their degree of abstraction.

Uses for Stacks and Queues: Programmer's Tools

The array—the data storage structure we've been examining thus far—as well as many other structures we'll encounter later in this book (linked lists, trees, and so on), are appropriate for the kind of data you might find in a database application. They're typically used for personnel records, inventories, financial data, and so on—data that corresponds to real-world objects or activities. These structures facilitate access to data: They make it easy to insert, delete, and search for particular items.

The structures and algorithms we'll examine in this hour and the next, on the other hand, are more often used as programmer's tools. They're primarily conceptual aids rather than full-fledged data storage devices. Their lifetime is typically shorter than that of the database-type structures. They are created and used to carry out a particular task during the operation of a function within a program; when the task is completed, they're discarded.

Stacks and Queues: Restricted Access to Data

In an array, any item can be accessed, either immediately—if its index number is known—or by searching through a sequence of cells until it's found. In stacks and queues, however, access is restricted: Only one item can be read or removed at a given time.

The interface of these structures is designed to enforce this restricted access. Access to other items is (in theory) not allowed.

Stacks and Queues: More Abstract

Stacks and queues are more abstract entities than arrays and many other data storage structures. They're defined primarily by their interface—the permissible operations that can be carried out on them. The underlying mechanism used to implement them is typically not visible to their users.

For example, the underlying mechanism for a stack can be an array, as we will show in this chapter, or it can be a linked list. We'll return to the topic of one data structure being implemented by another when we discuss Abstract Data Types (ADTs) in Hour 9, "Abstract Data Types."

To better understand these ideas, let's look at how stacks work.

Understanding Stacks

A stack allows access to only one data item: the last item inserted. If you remove this item, you can access the next-to-last item inserted, and so on. This is a useful capability in many programming situations. In this section, we'll see how a stack can be used to check whether parentheses, braces, and brackets are balanced in a computer program source file. Stacks also play a vital role in parsing (analyzing) arithmetic expressions such as 3*(4+5).

A stack is also a handy aid when you're programming algorithms for certain complex data structures. In Hour 16, "Traversing Binary Trees," for example, we'll see a stack is used in the code that traverses the nodes of a tree.

Most microprocessors (like the one in your computer) use a stack-based architecture. When a member function is called, its return address and arguments are pushed onto a stack, and when the function returns they're popped off. The stack operations are built into the microprocessor.

Some older pocket calculators used a stack-based paradigm. Instead of entering arithmetic expressions using parentheses, you pushed intermediate results onto a stack.

Two Real-World Stack Analogies

To understand the idea of a stack, let's look at some analogies. The first one is provided by the U.S. Postal Service. Many people, when they get their mail, toss it onto a stack on the hall table, or into an "in" basket at work. Then, when they have a spare moment, they process the accumulated mail from the top down. First they open the letter on the top of the stack and take appropriate action—paying the bill, throwing it away, or whatever. When the first letter has been disposed of, they examine the next letter down, which is now the top of the stack, and deal with that. Eventually they work their way down to the letter on the bottom of the stack (which is now the top). Figure 6.1 shows a stack of mail.

This "do the top one first" approach works all right as long as you can easily process all the mail in a reasonable time. If you can't, there's the danger that letters on the bottom of the stack won't be examined for months, and the bills they contain will become overdue.

Of course, many people don't rigorously follow this top-to-bottom approach. They may, for example, take the mail off the bottom of the stack, so as to process the oldest letter first. Or they might shuffle through the mail before they begin processing it and put higher-priority letters on top. In these cases, their mail system is no longer a stack in the computer-science sense of the word. If they take letters off the bottom, it's a queue; and if they prioritize it, it's a priority queue. We'll look at these possibilities in the next hour.

6

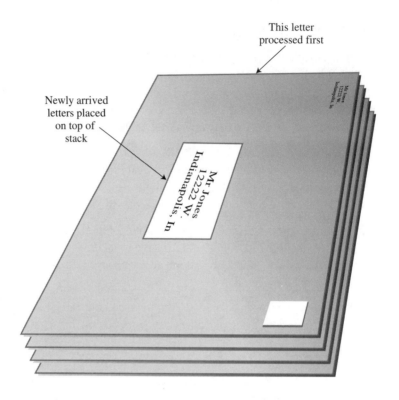

FIGURE 6.1

A stack of letters.

Another stack analogy is the tasks you perform during a typical workday. You're busy on a long-term project (A), but you're interrupted by a coworker asking you for temporary help with another project (B). While you're working on B, someone from Accounting stops by for a meeting about travel expenses (C), and during this meeting you get an emergency call from someone in Sales and spend a few minutes troubleshooting a bulky product (D). When you're finished with call D, you resume meeting C; when you're finished with C, you resume project B, and when you're finished with B you can (finally!) get back to project A. Lower-priority projects are "stacked up" waiting for you to return to them.

NEW TERM Placing a data item on the top of the stack is called *pushing* it. Removing it from the top of the stack is called *popping* it. These are the primary stack operations. A stack is said to be a Last-In-First-Out (LIFO) storage mechanism because the last item inserted is the first one to be removed.

The Stack Workshop Applet

Let's use the Stack Workshop applet to get an idea what stacks do. When you start this applet, you'll see four buttons: New, Push, Pop, and Peek, as shown in Figure 6.2. We'll cover these next.

FIGURE 6.2

The Stack Workshop applet.

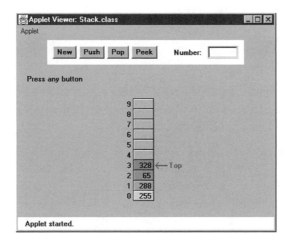

The Stack Workshop applet is based on an array, so you'll see an array of data items. Although it's based on an array, a stack restricts access, so you can't access any data item as you would an array.

New

The stack in the Workshop applet starts with four data items already inserted. If you want to start with an empty stack, the New button creates a new stack with no items. The next three buttons carry out the significant stack operations.

Push

To insert a data item on the stack, use the button labeled Push. After the first press of this button, you'll be prompted to enter the key value of the item to be pushed. After typing it into the text field, a few more presses will insert the item on the top of the stack.

A red arrow always points to the top of the stack; that is, the last item inserted. Notice how during the insertion process, one step (button press) increments (moves up) the Top arrow, and the next step actually inserts the data item into the cell. If you reversed the

6

order, you would overwrite the existing item at Top. When writing the code to implement a stack, it's important to keep in mind the order in which these two steps are executed.

If the stack is full and you try to push another item, you'll get the `Can't insert: stack is full` message. (Theoretically, an ADT stack doesn't become full, but the array implementing it does.)

Pop

To remove a data item from the top of the stack, use the Pop button. The value popped appears in the Number text field; this corresponds to a `pop()` routine returning a value.

Again, notice the two steps involved: First, the item is removed from the cell pointed to by Top, and then Top is decremented to point to the highest occupied cell. This is the reverse of the sequence used in the push operation.

The pop operation shows an item actually being removed from the array, and the cell color becoming gray to show the item has been removed. This is a bit misleading in terms of operations on computer memory, in that deleted items actually remain in the array until written over by new data. However, they cannot be accessed after the Top marker drops below their position, so conceptually they are gone, as the applet shows.

When you've popped the last item off the stack, the Top arrow points to –1, below the lowest cell. This indicates that the stack is empty. If the stack is empty and you try to pop an item, you'll get the `Can't pop: stack is empty` message.

Peek

Push and pop are the two primary stack operations. However, it's sometimes useful to be able to read the value from the top of the stack without removing it. The peek operation does this. By pushing the Peek button a few times, you'll see the value of the item at Top copied to the Number text field, but the item is not removed from the stack, which remains unchanged.

Notice that you can only peek at the top item. By design, all the other items are invisible to the stack user.

Stack Size

Stacks are typically small, temporary data structures, which is why we've shown a stack of only 10 cells. Of course, stacks in real programs might need a bit more room than this, but it's surprising how small a stack needs to be. A very long arithmetic expression, for example, can be parsed with a stack of only a dozen or so cells.

Now that we've seen what stacks do, let's see how they're implemented in C++.

Implementing a Stack in C++

Let's examine a program, Stack.cpp, that implements a stack using a class called StackX. Listing 6.1 contains this class and a short main() routine to exercise it.

INPUT **LISTING 6.1** THE Stack.cpp PROGRAM

```
//Stack.cpp
//demonstrates stacks
#include <iostream>
#include <vector>
using namespace std;
////////////////////////////////////////////////////////////////
class StackX
   {
   private:
      int maxSize;                    //size of stack vector
      vector<double> stackVect;       //stack vector
      int top;                        //top of stack
   public:
//--------------------------------------------------------------
   StackX(int s) : maxSize(s), top(-1)  //constructor
      {
      stackVect.reserve(maxSize);     //size the vector
      }
//--------------------------------------------------------------
   void push(double j)               //put item on top
      {
      stackVect[++top] = j;          //increment top,
      }                              //insert item
//--------------------------------------------------------------
   double pop()                      //take item from top
      {
      return stackVect[top--];       //access item,
      }                              //decrement top
//--------------------------------------------------------------
   double peek()                     //peek at top of stack
      {
      return stackVect[top];
      }
//--------------------------------------------------------------
   bool isEmpty()                    //true if stack is empty
      {
      return (top == -1);
      }
//--------------------------------------------------------------
   bool isFull()                     //true if stack is full
```

continues

6

LISTING 6.1   CONTINUED

```
        {
        return (top == maxSize-1);
        }
//---------------------------------------------------------------
   };  //end class StackX
///////////////////////////////////////////////////////////////
int main()
        {
        StackX theStack(10);              //make new stack, size 10
        theStack.push(20);                //push items onto stack
        theStack.push(40);
        theStack.push(60);
        theStack.push(80);

        while( !theStack.isEmpty() )      //until it's empty,
            {                             //delete item from stack
            double value = theStack.pop();
            cout << value << " ";         //display it
            } //end while
        cout << endl;
        return 0;
        } //end main()
```

OUTPUT   The main() function creates a stack that can hold 10 items, pushes 4 items onto the stack, and then displays all the items by popping them off the stack until it's empty. Here's the output:

```
80 60 40 20
```

Notice how the order of the data is reversed. Because the last item pushed is the first one popped, the 80 appears first in the output.

This version of the StackX class holds data elements of type double. As noted in the last hour, you can change this to any other type, including object types.

StackX Class Member Functions

As in previous programs, the data storage mechanism within the class is a vector. Here it's called stackVect.

The constructor creates a new stack of a size specified in its argument. The data members of the stack are a variable to hold its maximum size (the size of the vector), the vector itself, and a variable, top, which stores the index of the item on the top of the stack.

The push() member function increments top so it points to the space just above the previous top, and stores a data item there. Notice that top is incremented before the item is inserted.

The pop() member function returns the value at top and then decrements top. This effectively removes the item from the stack; it's inaccessible, although the value remains in the vector (until another item is pushed into the cell).

The peek() member function simply returns the value at top, without changing the stack.

The isEmpty() and isFull() member functions return true if the stack is empty or full, respectively. The top variable is at -1 if the stack is empty and maxSize-1 if the stack is full.

Figure 6.3 shows how push() and pop() work.

FIGURE 6.3

Operation of the StackX *class member functions.*

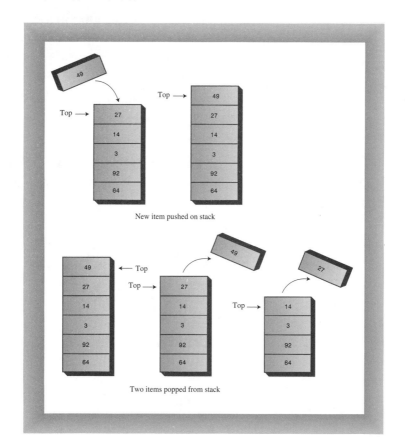

New item pushed on stack

Two items popped from stack

6

Error Handling

There are different philosophies about how to handle stack errors. What happens if you try to push an item onto a stack that's already full? Or pop an item from a stack that's empty?

In `Stack.cpp` we've left the responsibility for handling such errors up to the class user. The user should always check to be sure the stack is not full before pushing a new item:

```
if( !theStack.isFull() )
   theStack.push(item);
else
   cout << "Can't insert, stack is full";
```

In the interest of simplicity, we've left this code out of the `main()` routine (and anyway, in this simple program, we know the stack isn't full because it has just been initialized). We do include the check for an empty stack when `main()` calls `pop()`.

Many stack classes check for these errors internally, in the `push()` and `pop()` member functions. This is the preferred approach. In C++, a good solution for a stack class that discovers such errors is to throw an exception, which can then be caught and processed by the class user.

Now that we've seen how to program a stack in general, let's look at some programs that solve real problems by using a stack.

Stack Example 1: Reversing a Word

For our first example of using a stack, we'll examine a very simple task: reversing a word. When you run the program, it asks you to type in a word. When you press Enter, it displays the word with the letters in reverse order.

A stack is used to reverse the letters. First the characters are extracted one by one from the input string and pushed onto the stack. Then they're popped off the stack and displayed. Because of its last-in-first-out characteristic, the stack reverses the order of the characters. Listing 6.2 shows the code for the `reverse.cpp` program.

INPUT   **LISTING 6.2** THE `reverse.cpp` PROGRAM

```
//reverse.cpp
//stack used to reverse a word
#include <iostream>
#include <vector>
#include <string>
using namespace std;
```

```
///////////////////////////////////////////////////////////////
class StackX
   {
   private:
      int maxSize;
      vector<char> stackVect;        //vector holds stack
      int top;
   public:
//--------------------------------------------------------------
   StackX(int max) : maxSize(max), top(-1)        //constructor
      {
      stackVect.resize(maxSize);   //size the vector
      }
//--------------------------------------------------------------
   void push(char j)                //put item on top of stack
      { stackVect[++top] = j;   }
//--------------------------------------------------------------
   char pop()                       //take item from top of stack
      {  return stackVect[top--];   }
//--------------------------------------------------------------
   char peek()                      //peek at top of stack
      {  return stackVect[top];   }
//--------------------------------------------------------------
   bool isEmpty()                   //true if stack is empty
      { return (top == -1); }
//--------------------------------------------------------------
   };  //end class StackX
///////////////////////////////////////////////////////////////
class Reverser
   {
   private:
      string input;                //input string
      string output;               //output string
   public:
//--------------------------------------------------------------
   Reverser(string in) : input(in) //constructor
      {  }
//--------------------------------------------------------------
   string doRev()                   //reverse the word
      {
      int stackSize = input.length(); //get max stack size
      StackX theStack(stackSize);  //make stack

      for(int j=0; j<input.length(); j++)
         {
         char ch = input[j];       //get a char from input
         theStack.push(ch);        //push it
         }
      output = "";
      while( !theStack.isEmpty() )
```

6

continues

LISTING 6.2   CONTINUED

```
            {
            char ch = theStack.pop(); //pop a char,
            output = output + ch;      //append to output
            }
        return output;
        }  //end doRev()
//----------------------------------------------------------------
    };  //end class Reverser
////////////////////////////////////////////////////////////////////
int main()
    {
    string input, output;

    while(true)
        {
        cout << "Enter a word: ";
        cin >> input;              //read a word from kbd
        if( input.length() < 2 )   //quit if one character
           break;
                                   //make a Reverser
        Reverser theReverser(input);
        output = theReverser.doRev(); //use it
        cout << "Reversed: " << output << endl;
        }  //end while
    return 0;
    }  //end main()
```

ANALYSIS We've created a class Reverser to handle the reversing of the input string. Its key component is the member function doRev(), which carries out the reversal, using a stack. The stack is created within doRev(), which sizes it according to the length of the input string.

In main() we get a string from the user, create a Reverser object with this string as an argument to the constructor, call this object's doRev() member function, and display the return value, which is the reversed string. Here's some sample interaction with the program:

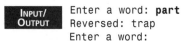

```
Enter a word: part
Reversed: trap
Enter a word:
```

Stack Example 2: Delimiter Matching

One common use for stacks is to parse certain kinds of text strings. Typically the strings are lines of code in a computer language, and the programs parsing them are compilers.

To give the flavor of what's involved, we'll show a program that checks the delimiters in a line of text typed by the user. This text doesn't need to be a line of real C++ code (although it could be), but it should use delimiters the same way C++ does. The delimiters are the braces { and }, brackets [and], and parentheses (and). Each opening or left delimiter should be matched by a closing or right delimiter; that is, every '{' should be followed by a matching '}', and so on. Also, opening delimiters that occur later in the string should be closed before those occurring earlier. Here are some examples:

```
c[d]        // correct
a{b[c]d}e    // correct
a{b(c]d}e    // not correct; ] doesn't match (
a[b{c}d]e}   // not correct; nothing matches final }
a{b(c)       // not correct; Nothing matches opening {
```

Opening Delimiters on the Stack

The program works by reading characters from the string one at a time and placing opening delimiters, when it finds them, on a stack. When the program reads a closing delimiter from the input, it pops the opening delimiter from the top of the stack and attempts to match it with the closing delimiter. If the delimiters are not the same type (there's an opening brace but a closing parenthesis, for example), an error has occurred. Also, if there is no opening delimiter on the stack to match a closing one, or if a delimiter remains on the stack when the parse has ended, an error has occurred.

Let's see what happens on the stack for a typical correct string:

```
a{b(c[d]e)f}
```

Table 6.1 shows how the stack looks as each character is read from this string. The entries in the second column show the stack contents, reading from the bottom of the stack on the left to the top on the right.

As it's read, each opening delimiter is placed on the stack. Each closing delimiter read from the input is matched with the opening delimiter popped from the top of the stack. If they form a pair, all is well. Nondelimiter characters are not inserted on the stack; they're ignored.

6

TABLE 6.1 STACK CONTENTS IN DELIMITER MATCHING

Character Read	Stack Contents
a	
{	{
b	{

continues

TABLE 6.1 CONTINUED

Character Read	Stack Contents
(	{(
c	{(
[	{([
d	{([
]	{(
e	{(
)	{
f	{
}	

This approach works because pairs of delimiters that are opened last should be closed first. This matches the last-in-first-out property of the stack.

C++ Code for `brackets.cpp`

The code for the parsing program, `brackets.cpp`, is shown in Listing 6.3. We've placed `check()`, the member function that does the parsing, in a class called `BracketChecker`.

INPUT   **LISTING 6.3**   THE `brackets.cpp` PROGRAM

```
//brackets.cpp
//stacks used to check matching brackets
#include <iostream>
#include <string>
#include <vector>
using namespace std;
////////////////////////////////////////////////////////////////
class StackX
    {
    private:
        int maxSize;                    //size of vector
        vector<char> stackVect;         //vector for stack
        int top;                        //top of stack
    public:
//---------------------------------------------------------------
    StackX(int s) : maxSize(s), top(-1)  //constructor
        { stackVect.resize(maxSize); }
//---------------------------------------------------------------
    void push(char j)                //put item on top of stack
        { stackVect[++top] = j; }
//---------------------------------------------------------------
```

```
      char pop()                        //take item from top of stack
         { return stackVect[top--]; }
//------------------------------------------------------------
      char peek()                       //peek at top of stack
         { return stackVect[top]; }
//------------------------------------------------------------
      bool isEmpty()                    //true if stack is empty
         { return (top == -1); }
//------------------------------------------------------------
      };  //end class StackX
////////////////////////////////////////////////////////////
class BracketChecker
   {
   private:
      string input;                          //inputstring
   public:
//------------------------------------------------------------
   BracketChecker(string in) : input(in)    //constructor
      {  }
//------------------------------------------------------------
   void check()
      {
      int stackSize = input.length();      //get max stack size
      StackX theStack(stackSize);          //make stack
      bool isError = false;                //error flag

      for(int j=0; j<input.length(); j++)  //get chars in turn
         {
         char ch = input[j];               //get char
         switch(ch)
            {
            case '{':                      //opening symbols
            case '[':
            case '(':
               theStack.push(ch);          //push them
               break;

            case '}':                      //closing symbols
            case ']':
            case ')':
               if( !theStack.isEmpty() )   //if stack not empty,
                  {
                  char chx = theStack.pop();  //pop and check
                  if( (ch=='}' && chx!='{') ||
                      (ch==']' && chx!='[') ||
                      (ch==')' && chx!='(') )
                     {
                     isError = true;
                     cout << "Mismatched delimeter: "
                          << ch << " at " << j << endl;
```

continues

LISTING 6.3   CONTINUED

```
                        }
                  }
                else                          //prematurely empty
                  {
                  isError = true;
                  cout << "Misplaced delimiter: "
                        << ch << " at " << j << endl;
                  }
               break;
            default:     //no action on other characters
               break;
            } //end switch
         } //end for
      //at this point, all characters have been processed
      if( !theStack.isEmpty() )
         cout << "Missing right delimiter" << endl;
      else if( !isError )
         cout << "OK" << endl;
      } //end check()
//-------------------------------------------------------------
   }; //end class BracketChecker
////////////////////////////////////////////////////////////////
int main()
   {
   string input;
   while(true)
      {
      cout << "Enter string containing delimiters "
          << "(no whitespace): ";
      cin >> input;           //read a string from kbd
      if( input.length() == 1 )   //quit if 'q', etc.
         break;
                              //make a BracketChecker
      BracketChecker theChecker(input);
      theChecker.check();     //check brackets
      } //end while
   return 0;
   } //end main()
```

ANALYSIS   The check() routine uses the StackX class from the last program. Notice how easy it is to reuse this class. All the code you need is in one place. This is one of the payoffs for object-oriented programming.

The main() routine repeatedly reads a line of text from the user, creates a BracketChecker object with this text string as an argument, and then calls the check()

member function for this `BracketChecker` object. If it finds any errors, the `check()` member function displays them; otherwise, the syntax of the delimiters is correct.

If it can, the `check()` function reports the character number where it discovered the error (starting at 0 on the left), and the incorrect character it found there. For example, for the input string

```
a{b(c]d}e
```

the output from `check()` will be

```
Mismatched delimeter: ] at 5
```

Using the Stack as a Conceptual Aid

Notice how convenient the stack is in the `brackets.cpp` program. You could have set up an array to do what the stack does, but you would have had to worry about keeping track of an index to the most recently added character, as well as other bookkeeping tasks. The stack is conceptually easier to use. By providing limited access to its contents, using the `push()` and `pop()` member functions, the stack has made your program easier to understand and less error-prone. (Carpenters will also tell you it's safer to use the right tool for the job.)

Efficiency of Stacks

Items can be both pushed and popped from a stack in constant O(1) time. That is, the time is not dependent on how many items are in the stack, and is therefore very quick. No comparisons or moves are necessary. Of course access is, by design, restricted to a single item.

Summary

In this hour, you've learned the following:

- A stack allows access to the last item inserted, at the top of the stack.
- The important stack operations are pushing (inserting) an item onto the top of the stack and popping (removing) the item from the top.
- A stack is often helpful in parsing a string of characters, among other applications.
- A stack can be implemented with an array or with another mechanism, such as a linked list.

6

Q&A

Q What do stacks have to do with sorting, which you talked about in the last hour?

A Well, not too much. A stack is a data structure, whereas sorting is an algorithm. The only reason they're close together in this book is that they're about the same degree of difficulty.

Q Wouldn't it be more efficient for `main()` just to use an array or vector of its own, and keep track of the indices itself?

A It might be slightly more efficient, but the point of using a separate stack class is to make programs easier to write and less error-prone.

Workshop

The Workshop helps you solidify what you learned in this hour. See Appendix A for quiz answers.

Quiz

1. True or false: A stack works on the first-in-first-out (FIFO) principle.
2. Name two ways stacks and queues differ from arrays.
3. True or false: A good analogy for a stack is the line of people waiting at the bank teller's window.
4. Define *push* and *pop*.
5. True or false: If there's only one item in a stack, the bottom of the stack is the same as the top.
6. In the C++ code that pushes an item onto a stack, should you insert the item first or increment the top first?

Exercise

Think of at least one real-world situation (other than those discussed in this hour) that uses the stack principle. What corresponds to the push and pop operations in this situation?

HOUR 7

Queues and Priority Queues

A queue is similar to a stack, except that you put items into one end of a queue and remove them from the other. A priority queue is a specialized queue in which the items are stored in order. In this hour you'll learn

- How a queue works
- How to create a queue in C++
- How a priority queue works
- How to create a priority queue in C++

Queues

NEW TERM The word *queue* is British for *line* (the kind you wait in). In Britain, to "queue up" means to get in line. In computer science a queue is a data structure that is similar to a stack, except that in a queue the first item inserted is the first to be removed (FIFO). In a stack, as we've seen, the last item inserted is the first to be removed (LIFO).

A queue works like the line at the movies: the first person to join the rear of the line is the first person to reach the front of the line and buy a ticket. The last person to line up is the last person to buy a ticket (or—if the show is sold out—to fail to buy a ticket). Figure 7.1 shows how this looks.

FIGURE 7.1

A queue of people.

People join the queue at the rear

People leave the queue at the front

Queues are used as a programmer's tool as stacks are. They're also used to model real-world situations such as people waiting in line at a bank, airplanes waiting to take off, or data packets waiting to be transmitted over the Internet.

There are various queues quietly doing their job in your computer's (or the network's) operating system. There's a printer queue where print jobs wait for the printer to be available. A queue also stores keystroke data as you type at the keyboard. This way, if you're using a word processor but the computer is briefly doing something else when you hit a key, the keystroke won't be lost; it waits in the queue until the word processor has time to read it. Using a queue guarantees the keystrokes stay in order until they can be processed.

The Queue Workshop Applet

Start up the Queue Workshop applet. You'll see a queue with four items preinstalled, as shown in Figure 7.2.

This applet demonstrates a queue based on an array. This is a common approach, although linked lists are also commonly used to implement queues. (We'll explore this issue in Hour 9, "Abstract Data Types.")

The two basic queue operations are *inserting* an item, which is placed at the rear of the queue, and *removing* an item, which is taken from the front of the queue. This is similar to a person joining the rear of a line of moviegoers, and, having arrived at the front of the line and purchased a ticket, removing himself from the front of the line.

FIGURE 7.2

The Queue Workshop applet.

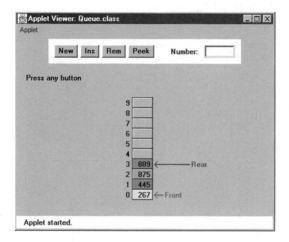

The terms for insertion and removal in a stack are fairly standard; everyone says *push* and *pop*. Standardization hasn't progressed this far with queues. *Insert* is also called *put* or *add* or *enque*, whereas *remove* might be called *delete* or *get* or *de-que*. The rear of the queue, where items are inserted, is also called the *back* or *tail* or *end*. The front, where items are removed, might also be called the *head*. We'll use the terms insert, remove, front, and rear.

Inserting a New Item

By repeatedly pressing the Ins button in the Queue Workshop applet, you can insert a new item. After the first press, you're prompted to enter a key value for a new item into the Number text field; this should be a number from 0 to 999. Subsequent presses will insert an item with this key at the rear of the queue, and increment the Rear arrow so it points to the new item.

Removing an Item

Similarly, you can remove the item at the front of the queue using the Rem button. The item is removed, the item's value is stored in the Number field (corresponding to the remove() member function returning a value), and the Front arrow is incremented. In the applet, the cell that held the deleted item is grayed to show it's gone. In a normal implementation, it would remain in memory but would not be accessible because Front had moved past it. The insert and remove operations are shown in Figure 7.3.

7

FIGURE 7.3

Operation of the Queue
class member func-
tions.

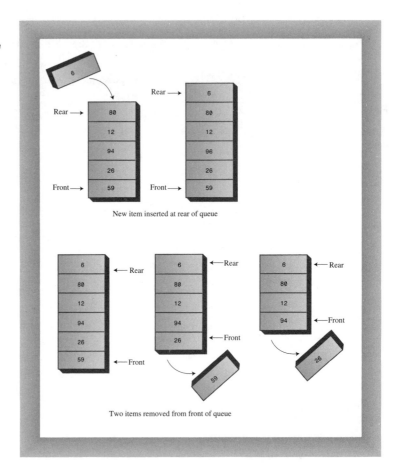

New item inserted at rear of queue

Two items removed from front of queue

Unlike the situation in a stack, the items in a queue don't always extend all the way down to index 0 in the array. After some items are removed, Front will point at a cell with a higher index, as shown in Figure 7.4.

Notice that in this figure Front lies below Rear in the array; that is, Front has a lower index. As we'll see in a moment, this isn't always true.

Peeking at an Item

We show one other queue operation, peek. This finds the value of the item at the front of the queue without removing the item. (Like insert and remove, when applied to a queue, peek is also called by a variety of other names.) If you press the Peek button, you'll see the value at Front transferred to the Number box. The queue is unchanged. This `peek()` member function returns the value at the front of the queue. Some queue implementations have a `rearPeek()` and a `frontPeek()` member function, but usually you want to know what you're about to remove, not what you just inserted.

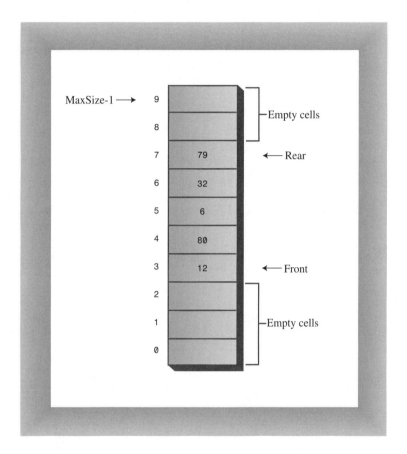

FIGURE 7.4

A queue with some items removed.

Creating a New Queue with New

If you want to start with an empty queue, you can use the New button to create one.

The Empty and Full Errors

If you try to remove an item when there are no more items in the queue, you'll get the `Can't remove, queue is empty` error message. If you try to insert an item when all the cells are already occupied, you'll get the `Can't insert, queue is full` message.

7

A Circular Queue

When you insert a new item in the queue in the Workshop applet, the Front arrow moves upward, toward higher numbers in the array. When you remove an item, Rear also moves upward. Try these operations with the Workshop applet to convince yourself it's true.

> You might find the way a queue works counter-intuitive because the people in a line at the movies all move forward, toward the front, when a person leaves the line. We could move all the items in a queue whenever we deleted one, but that wouldn't be very efficient. Instead we keep all the items in the same place and move the front and rear of the queue.

The trouble with moving the front and rear forward is that pretty soon the rear of the queue is at the end of the array (the highest index). Even if there are empty cells at the beginning of the array, because you've removed them with Rem, you still can't insert a new item because Rear can't go any further. Or can it? This situation is shown in Figure 7.5.

FIGURE 7.5

Rear arrow at the end of the array.

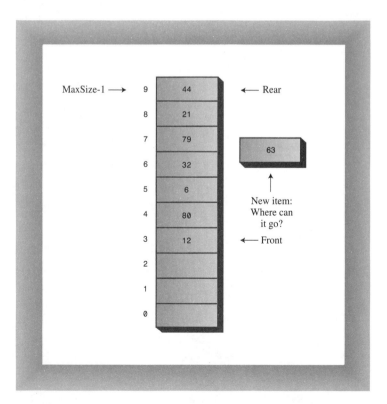

Wrapping Around

NEW TERM To avoid the problem of not being able to insert more items into the queue even when it's not full, the Front and Rear arrows *wrap around* to the beginning of the array. The result is a *circular queue* (sometimes called a *ring buffer*).

To Do: Investigate Wraparound with the Workshop Applet

1. Insert enough items to bring the Rear arrow to the top of the array (index 9).

2. Remove some items from the front of the array.

3. Insert another item.

4. You'll see the Rear arrow wrap around from index 9 to index 0; the new item will be inserted there. This is shown in Figure 7.6.

FIGURE 7.6

Rear arrow wraps around.

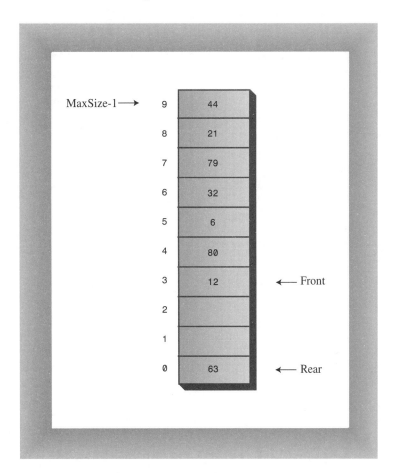

NEW TERM Insert a few more items. The Rear arrow moves upward as you would expect. Notice that after Rear has wrapped around, it's now below Front, the reverse of the original arrangement. You can call this a *broken sequence*: the items in the queue are in two different sequences in the array.

NEW TERM Delete enough items so that the Front arrow also wraps around. Now you're back to the original arrangement, with Front below Rear. The items are in a single *contiguous sequence*.

Now that we've seen how queues work, let's look at some C++ code that implements a queue.

C++ Code for a Queue

The queue.cpp program features a Queue class with insert(), remove(), peek(), isFull(), isEmpty(), and size() member functions.

The main() program creates a queue of five cells, inserts four items, removes three items, and inserts four more. The sixth insertion invokes the wraparound feature. All the items are then removed and displayed. The output looks like this:

```
40 50 60 70 80
```

Listing 7.1 shows the Queue.cpp program.

INPUT   **LISTING 7.1**   THE Queue.cpp PROGRAM

```cpp
//Queue.cpp
//demonstrates queue
#include <iostream>
#include <vector>
using namespace std;
////////////////////////////////////////////////////////////////
class Queue
   {
   private:
      int maxSize;
      vector<int> queVect;
      int front;
      int rear;
      int nItems;
   public:
//--------------------------------------------------------------
                                       //constructor
   Queue(int s) : maxSize(s), front(0), rear(-1), nItems(0)
      { queVect.resize(maxSize); }
//--------------------------------------------------------------
```

```
    void insert(int j)          //put item at rear of queue
       {
       if(rear == maxSize-1)      //deal with wraparound
          rear = -1;
       queVect[++rear] = j;       //increment rear and insert
       nItems++;                  //one more item
       }
//-------------------------------------------------------------
    int remove()                //take item from front of queue
       {
       int temp = queVect[front++];  //get value and incr front
       if(front == maxSize)       //deal with wraparound
          front = 0;
       nItems--;                  //one less item
       return temp;
       }
//-------------------------------------------------------------
    int peekFront()             //peek at front of queue
       { return queVect[front]; }
//-------------------------------------------------------------
    bool isEmpty()              //true if queue is empty
       { return (nItems==0); }
//-------------------------------------------------------------
    bool isFull()               //true if queue is full
       { return (nItems==maxSize); }
//-------------------------------------------------------------
    int size()                  //number of items in queue
       { return nItems; }
//-------------------------------------------------------------
    };  //end class Queue
////////////////////////////////////////////////////////////////
int main()
    {
    Queue theQueue(5);              //queue holds 5 items

    theQueue.insert(10);            //insert 4 items
    theQueue.insert(20);
    theQueue.insert(30);
    theQueue.insert(40);

    theQueue.remove();              //remove 3 items
    theQueue.remove();              //    (10, 20, 30)
    theQueue.remove();

    theQueue.insert(50);            //insert 4 more items
    theQueue.insert(60);            //    (wraps around)
    theQueue.insert(70);
    theQueue.insert(80);
```

continues

7

Listing 7.1　CONTINUED

```
         while( !theQueue.isEmpty() )    //remove and display
            {                            //   all items
            int n = theQueue.remove();   //(40, 50, 60, 70, 80)
            cout << n << " ";
            }
         cout << endl;
         return 0;
         }  //end main()
```

We've chosen an approach in which Queue class data members include not only front and rear, but also the number of items currently in the queue: nItems. Some queue implementations don't use this data member; we'll show this alternative later.

The insert() Member Function

The insert() member function assumes that the queue is not full. We don't show it in main(), but normally you should call insert() only after calling isFull() and getting a return value of false. (It's usually preferable to place the check for fullness in the insert() routine, and cause an exception to be thrown if an attempt was made to insert into a full queue.)

Normally, insertion involves incrementing rear and inserting at the cell rear now points to. However, if rear is at the top of the array (actually a vector), at maxSize-1, then it must wrap around to the bottom of the array before the insertion takes place. This is done by setting rear to –1, so when the increment occurs rear will become 0, the bottom of the array. Finally nItems is incremented.

The remove() Member Function

The remove() member function assumes that the queue is not empty. You should call isEmpty() to ensure this is true before calling remove(), or build this error-checking into remove().

Removal always starts by obtaining the value at front and then incrementing front. However, if this puts front beyond the end of the array, it must then be wrapped around to 0. The return value is stored temporarily while this possibility is checked. Finally, nItems is decremented.

The peek() Member Function

The peek() member function is straightforward: it returns the value at front. Some implementations allow peeking at the rear of the array as well; such routines are called something like peekFront() and peekRear() or just front() and rear().

The `isEmpty()`, `isFull()`, and `size()` Member Functions

The `isEmpty()`, `isFull()`, and `size()` member functions provide the information implied by their names. They all rely on the `nItems` data member, respectively checking whether it's 0, whether it's `maxSize`, or returning its value.

Implementing the Queue Class Without an Item Count

The inclusion of the data member `nItems` in the `Queue` class imposes a slight overhead on the `insert()` and `remove()` member functions in that they must respectively increment and decrement this variable. This might not seem like an excessive penalty, but if you're dealing with huge numbers of insertions and deletions, it might influence performance.

Accordingly, some implementations of queues do without an item count and rely on the `front` and `rear` data members to figure out whether the queue is empty or full and how many items are in it. When this is done, the `isEmpty()`, `isFull()`, and `size()` routines become surprisingly complicated because the sequence of items may be either broken or contiguous, as we've seen.

Also, a strange problem arises. The `front` and `rear` pointers assume certain positions when the queue is full, but they can assume these exact same positions when the queue is empty. The queue can then appear to be full and empty at the same time.

This problem can be solved by making the array (vector) one cell larger than the maximum number of items that will be placed in it. Listing 7.2 shows a `Queue` class that implements this no-count approach. This class uses the no-count implementation.

INPUT   **LISTING 7.2**   THE `Queue` CLASS WITHOUT `nItems`

```
class Queue
   {
   private:
      int maxSize;
      vector<int>(queVect);
      int front;
      int rear;
   public:
//-------------------------------------------------------------
                              //constructor
   Queue(int s) : maxSize(s+1), front(0), rear(-1)
      {
      queVect.resize(maxSize);
      }
//-------------------------------------------------------------
```

continues

7

LISTING 7.2   CONTINUED

```cpp
    void insert(int j)              //put item at rear of queue
       {
       if(rear == maxSize-1)
          rear = -1;
       queVect[++rear] = j;
       }
//------------------------------------------------------------
    int remove()                    //take item from front of queue
       {
       int temp = queVect[front++];
       if(front == maxSize)
          front = 0;
       return temp;
       }
//------------------------------------------------------------
    int peek()                      //peek at front of queue
       {
       return queVect[front];
       }
//------------------------------------------------------------
    bool isEmpty()                  //true if queue is empty
       {
       return ( rear+1==front ¦¦ (front+maxSize-1==rear) );
       }
//------------------------------------------------------------
    bool isFull()                   //true if queue is full
       {
       return ( rear+2==front ¦¦ (front+maxSize-2==rear) );
       }
//------------------------------------------------------------
    int size()                      //(assumes queue not empty)
       {
       if(rear >= front)            //contiguous sequence
          return rear-front+1;
       else                         //broken sequence
          return (maxSize-front) + (rear+1);
       }
//------------------------------------------------------------
    };   //end class Queue
```

Notice the complexity of isFull(), isEmpty(), and size() member functions. This no-count approach is seldom needed in practice, so we'll refrain from discussing it in detail.

Efficiency of Queues

As with a stack, items can be inserted and removed from a queue in O(1) time. Because of the wraparound feature, some insertions and deletions might actually take substantially longer than others, but this doesn't change the Big O time.

> **NEW TERM** A *deque* is a double-ended queue. You can insert items at either end, and delete them from either end. The member functions might be called `insertLeft()` and `insertRight()`, and `removeLeft()` and `removeRight()`.
>
> If you restrict yourself to `insertLeft()` and `removeLeft()` (or their equivalents on the right), the deque acts like a stack. If you restrict yourself to `insertLeft()` and `removeRight()`, (or the opposite pair), it acts like a queue.
>
> A deque provides a more versatile data structure than either a stack or a queue, and is sometimes used in container class libraries to serve both purposes. However, it's not used as often as stacks and queues, so we won't explore it further here.

Let's move from queues to this hour's second major topic, a related data structure called a priority queue.

Priority Queues

A priority queue is a more specialized data structure than a stack or a queue. However, it's a useful tool in a surprising number of situations. Like an ordinary queue, a priority queue has a front and a rear, and items are inserted in the rear and removed from the front. However, in a priority queue, items are ordered by key value, so that the item with the lowest key (or in some implementations the highest key) is always at the front. Items are inserted in the proper position to maintain the order.

Here's how the mail sorting analogy applies to a priority queue. Every time the postman hands you a letter, you insert it into your pile of pending letters according to its priority. If it must be answered immediately (the phone company is about to disconnect your modem line), it goes on top, but if it can wait for a leisurely answer (a letter from your Aunt Mabel), it goes on the bottom.

When you have time to answer your mail, you start by taking the letter off the top (the front of the queue), thus ensuring that the most important letters are answered first. This is shown in Figure 7.7.

7

FIGURE 7.7

Letters in a priority queue.

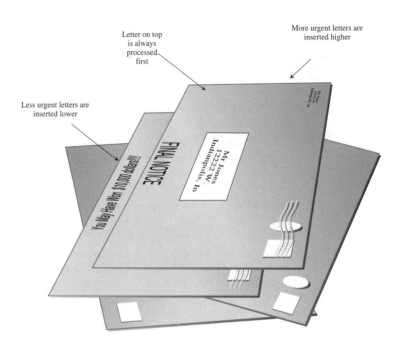

Letter on top is always processed first

More urgent letters are inserted higher

Less urgent letters are inserted lower

Like stacks and queues, priority queues are often used as programmer's tools. They are used in various ways in certain computer systems. In a preemptive multitasking operating system, for example, programs may be placed in a priority queue so the highest-priority program is the next one to receive a time-slice that allows it to execute.

In many situations you want access to the item with the lowest key value (which might represent the cheapest or shortest way to do something). Thus the item with the smallest key has the highest priority. Somewhat arbitrarily, we'll assume that's the case in this discussion, although there are other situations in which the highest key has the highest priority.

Besides providing quick access to the item with the smallest key, you also want a priority queue to provide fairly quick insertion. For this reason, priority queues are, as we noted earlier, often implemented with a data structure called a heap. However, we'll show a priority queue implemented by a simple array. This implementation suffers from slow insertion, but it's simpler and is appropriate when the number of items isn't high or insertion speed isn't critical.

The PriorityQ Workshop Applet

 The PriorityQ Workshop applet implements a priority queue with an array, in which the items are kept in sorted order. It's an *ascending-priority* queue, in which the item with the smallest key has the highest priority and is the one accessed with remove(). (If the highest-key item were accessed, it would be a *descending-priority* queue.)

The minimum-key item is always at the top (highest index) in the array, and the largest item is always at index 0. Figure 7.8 shows the arrangement when the applet is started. Initially there are five items in the queue.

FIGURE 7.8

The PriorityQ Workshop applet.

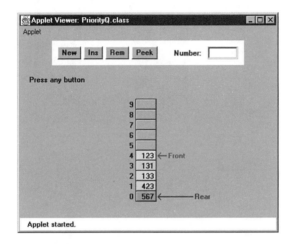

Inserting a New Item

Try inserting an item. You'll be prompted to type the new item's key value into the Number data member. Choose a number that will be inserted somewhere in the middle of the values already in the queue. For example, in Figure 7.8 you might choose 300. Then, as you repeatedly press Ins, you'll see that the items with smaller keys are shifted up to make room. A black arrow shows which item is being shifted. After the appropriate position is found, the new item is inserted into the newly created space.

Notice that there's no wraparound in this implementation of the priority queue. Insertion is slow of necessity because the proper in-order position must be found, but deletion is fast. A wraparound implementation wouldn't improve the situation. Note too that the Rear arrow never moves; it always points to index 0 at the bottom of the array.

Deleting an Item

The item to be removed is always at the top of the array (in both ascending and descending queues), so removal is quick and easy; the item is removed and the Front arrow

moves down to point to the new top of the array. No comparisons or shifting are
necessary.

Figure 7.9

Operation of the
`PriorityQ` *class mem-*
ber functions.

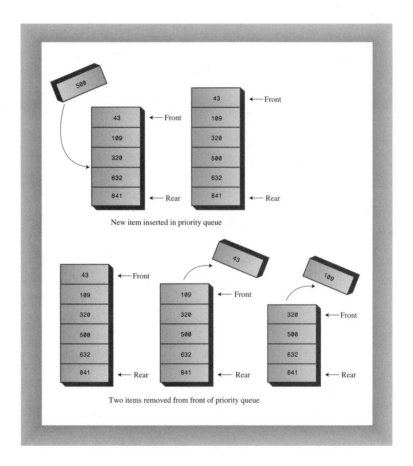

In the PriorityQ Workshop applet, we show Front and Rear arrows to provide a comparison with an ordinary queue, but they're not really necessary. The algorithms know that
the front of the queue is always at the top of the array at `nItems-1`, and they insert items
in order, not at the rear. Figure 7.9 shows the operation of the `PriorityQ` class member
functions.

Peek and New

You can peek at the minimum item (find its value without removing it) with the Peek
button, and you can create a new, empty, priority queue with the New button.

The implementation shown in the PriorityQ Workshop applet isn't very efficient for insertion, which involves moving an average of half the items.

Another approach, which also uses an array, makes no attempt to keep the items in sorted order. New items are simply inserted at the top of the array. This makes insertion very quick, but unfortunately it makes deletion slow because the smallest item must be searched for. This requires examining all the items and shifting half of them, on the average, down to fill in the hole. Generally, the quick-deletion approach shown in the Workshop applet is preferred.

C++ Code for a Priority Queue

The C++ code for a simple array-based priority queue is shown in Listing 7.3.

INPUT   **LISTING 7.3**   THE priorityQ.cpp PROGRAM

```cpp
//priorityQ.cpp
//demonstrates priority queue
#include <iostream>
#include <vector>
using namespace std;
//////////////////////////////////////////////////////////////
class PriorityQ
    {
    //vector in sorted order, from max at 0 to min at size-1
    private:
        int maxSize;
        vector<double> queVect;
        int nItems;
    public:
//--------------------------------------------------------------
    PriorityQ(int s) : maxSize(s), nItems(0)   //constructor
        { queVect.resize(maxSize); }
//--------------------------------------------------------------
    void insert(double item)   //insert item
        {
        int j;

        if(nItems==0)                          //if no items,
            queVect[nItems++] = item;          //insert at 0
        else                                   //if items,
            {
            for(j=nItems-1; j>=0; j--)         //start at end,
                {
```

continues

7

LISTING 7.3 CONTINUED

```cpp
             if( item > queVect[j] )        //if new item larger,
                 queVect[j+1] = queVect[j]; //shift upward
             else                           //if smaller,
                 break;                      //done shifting
             } //end for
         queVect[j+1] = item;                //insert it
         nItems++;
         } //end else (nItems > 0)
     } //end insert()
//------------------------------------------------------------
   double remove()                          //remove minimum item
      { return queVect[--nItems]; }
//------------------------------------------------------------
   double peekMin()                         //peek at minimum item
      { return queVect[nItems-1]; }
//------------------------------------------------------------
   bool isEmpty()                           //true if queue is empty
      { return (nItems==0); }
//------------------------------------------------------------
   bool isFull()                            //true if queue is full
      { return (nItems == maxSize); }
//------------------------------------------------------------
   };  //end class PriorityQ
////////////////////////////////////////////////////////////////
int main()
    {
    PriorityQ thePQ(5);                 //priority queue, size 5

    thePQ.insert(30);                   //unsorted insertions
    thePQ.insert(50);
    thePQ.insert(10);
    thePQ.insert(40);
    thePQ.insert(20);

    while( !thePQ.isEmpty() )
       {                                //sorted removals
       double item = thePQ.remove();
       cout << item << " ";             //10, 20, 30, 40, 50
       } //end while
    cout << endl;
    return 0;
    } //end main()
```

OUTPUT In main() we insert five items in random order, and then remove and display them. The smallest item is always removed first, so the output is

```
10, 20, 30, 40, 50
```

ANALYSIS The insert() member function checks whether there are any items; if not, it inserts one at index 0. Otherwise, the function starts at the top of the array and shifts existing items upward until it finds the place where the new item should go. Then it inserts the new item and increments nItems. Note that if there's any chance the priority queue is full you should check for this possibility with isFull() before using insert().

The front and rear data members aren't necessary as they were in the Queue class because, as we noted, front is always at nItems-1 and rear is always at 0.

The remove() member function is simplicity itself: it decrements nItems and returns the item from the top of the array. The peekMin() member function is similar, except it doesn't decrement nItems. The isEmpty() and isFull() member functions check whether nItems is 0 or maxSize, respectively.

Efficiency of Priority Queues

In the priority-queue implementation we show here, insertion runs in O(N) time, whereas deletion takes O(1) time because of the need to shift items to fill the hole left by the deleted item.

Summary

In this hour, you've learned the following:

- Queues and priority queues, like stacks, are data structure usually used to simplify certain programming operations.
- In these data structures, only one data item can be immediately accessed.
- A queue allows access to the first item that was inserted.
- The important queue operations are inserting an item at the rear of the queue and removing the item from the front of the queue.
- A queue can be implemented as a circular queue, which is based on an array in which the indices wrap around from the end of the array to the beginning.
- A priority queue allows access to the smallest (or sometimes the largest) item.
- The important priority queue operations are inserting an item in sorted order and removing the item with the smallest key.

7

Q&A

Q **The code for the circular queue, with the wraparound feature, seems pretty complicated. Do I really need to know how to write this code?**

A That depends. If you're using an existing queue class, like the one in the C++ STL, you don't need to know anything about how it works. But if you're writing your own container classes, you'll need to understand the details.

Q **How often will I really need to use queues and priority queues in my code?**

A After you know about the concepts, it's surprising how often you'll find them useful. It depends on the kind of programming you do, of course. In some projects they'll never be necessary. But if you're working in systems programming, compiler design or simulations, they're used frequently. They're also used in more advanced data structures, such as graphs (which are beyond the scope of this book).

Workshop

The Workshop helps you solidify what you learned in this hour. See Appendix A for quiz answers.

Quiz

1. Give a one-sentence description of how a queue works.

2. In the C++ code for a queue, when you insert an item, which do you do first: insert the item, increment `Rear`, or check whether `Rear` is at the end of the array?

3. Why is wraparound necessary for (at least some implementations of) queues but not for stacks?

4. What does it mean when we say the `remove()` member function for a queue "assumes" the queue is not empty?

5. What's the difference between a queue and a priority queue?

6. Why is wraparound necessary in priority queues?

7. True or false: Assuming array implementations, insertion and deletion in queues and priority queues operate in O(1) time.

Exercise

We all use queues and priority queues conceptually in our daily lives to decide what activities to execute next. Think of some examples where you apply these concepts in your own life. For example, if three different people at work ask you to do different things, which do you do first? Is the arrangement you chose a queue or a priority queue?

HOUR 8

Linked Lists

Linked lists are versatile data structures that feature fast insertion and deletion. In this hour we'll learn

- The advantages and disadvantages of linked lists
- How linked lists works
- How to create a linked list in C++

In Hours 2, "Arrays" and 3, "Ordered Arrays," we saw that arrays had certain disadvantages as data storage structures. In an unordered array, searching is slow, whereas in an ordered array, insertion is slow. In both kinds of arrays deletion is slow. Also, the size of an array can't be changed after it's created (although it can be changed in a vector).

The linked list solves some of these problems. Linked lists are probably the second most commonly used general-purpose storage structures after arrays.

The linked list is a versatile mechanism suitable for use in many kinds of general-purpose data-storage applications. It can also replace an array as the basis for other storage structures such as stacks and queues. In fact, you can use a linked list in many cases where you use an array. By doing so you can greatly improve insertion and deletion performance.

Linked lists aren't the solution to all data storage problems, but they are surprisingly versatile and conceptually simpler than some other popular structures such as trees.

We'll devote three hours to linked lists. In this hour we'll look at simple linked lists. In Hour 9, "Abstract Data Types," we'll see how using linked lists to implement stacks and queues demonstrates the idea of Abstract Data Types (ADTs). In Hour 10, "Specialized Lists," we'll examine sorted lists and doubly linked lists.

Understanding Links

NEW TERM In a linked list, each data item is embedded in a link. A *link* is an object of a class called something like Link. Because there are many similar links in a list, it makes sense to use a separate class for them, distinct from the linked list itself. Each link object contains a pointer (which we'll call pNext) to the next link in the list. A data member in the list itself contains a pointer to the first link. This is shown in Figure 8.1.

FIGURE 8.1

Links in a list.

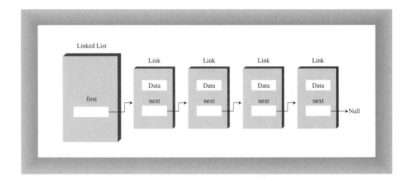

Here's part of the definition of a class Link. It contains some data and a pointer to the next link:

```
class Link
    {
    public:
    int iData;      //data
    double dData;   //data
    Link* pNext;    //pointer to next link
    };
```

NEW TERM This kind of class definition is sometimes called *self-referential* because it contains a data member—pNext in this case—which is a pointer to the same type as itself.

8

We show only two data items in the link: an `int` and a `double`. In a typical application there would be many more. A personnel record, for example, might have name, address, Social Security number, title, salary, and many other fields. Often a pointer to an object that contains this data is used instead of the data items themselves:

```
class Link
   {
   public:
   inventoryItem* pItem;    //pointer to object holding data
   Link* pNext;             //pointer to next link
   };
```

Structure Defined by Relationship, Not Position

Let's examine one of the major ways in which linked lists differ from arrays. In an array each item occupies a particular position. This position can be directly accessed using an index number. It's like a row of houses: you can find a particular house using its address.

In a list the only way to find a particular element is to follow along the chain of links. It's more like human relations. Maybe you ask Harry where Bob is. Harry doesn't know, but he thinks Jane might know, so you go and ask Jane. Jane saw Bob leave the office with Sally, so you call Sally's cell phone. She dropped Bob off at Peter's office, so...but you get the idea. You can't access a data item directly; you must use relationships between the items to locate it. You start with the first item, go to the second, and then the third, and so on, until you find what you're looking for. Let's see how a Workshop applet demonstrates lists.

The LinkList Workshop Applet

The LinkList Workshop applet provides three list operations. You can insert a new data item, search for a data item with a specified key, and delete a data item with a specified key. These operations are the same ones we explored in the Array Workshop applet in Hour 2; they're suitable for a general-purpose database application. However, the way these operations are implemented is quite different.

Figure 8.2 shows how the LinkList Workshop applet looks when it's started up. Initially there are 13 links on the list.

Inserting a New Link

If you think 13 is an unlucky number, you can insert a new link. Click on the Ins button, and you'll be prompted to enter a key value between 0 and 999. Subsequent presses will generate a link with this data in it, as shown in Figure 8.3.

FIGURE 8.2

The LinkList Workshop applet.

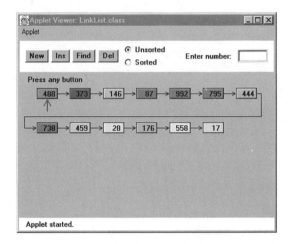

FIGURE 8.3

A new link being inserted.

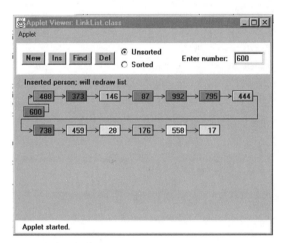

In this version of a linked list, new links are always inserted at the beginning of the list. This is the simplest approach, although it's also possible to insert links anywhere in the list, as we'll see later in this hour in the section "Finding and Removing Specific Links."

A final press on Ins will redraw the list so the newly inserted link lines up with the other links. This redrawing doesn't represent anything happening in the list itself, it just makes the display look neater.

Using the Find Button

Here's how to use the Find button to find a link with a key value you specify.

To Do: Find a Link

1. The Find button allows you to find a link with a specified key value.

2. When prompted, type in the value of an existing link, preferably one somewhere in the middle of the list.

3. As you continue to press the button, you'll see the red arrow move along the list, looking for the link. A message informs you when the link is found.

4. If you type a nonexistent key value, the arrow will search all the way to the end of the list before reporting that the item can't be found.

Using the Del Button

Using the Del button, you can also delete a link with a specified key value.

To Do: Delete a Link

1. Type in the value of an existing link, and repeatedly press Del.

2. Again the arrow will move along the list, looking for the link.

3. When it finds the link, it simply removes it and connects the arrow from the previous link straight across to the following link. This is how links are removed: the pointer to the preceding link is changed to point to the following link.

4. A final key press redraws the picture, but again this just provides evenly spaced links for aesthetic reasons; the length of the arrows doesn't correspond to anything in the program.

Creating Unsorted and Sorted Lists

The LinkList Workshop applet can create both unsorted and sorted lists. Unsorted is the default. We'll show how to use the applet for sorted lists when we discuss them in Hour 10.

Now that we've seen how linked lists look, let's examine how they're implemented in C++.

Implementing a Simple Linked List

Our first sample program, linkList.cpp, demonstrates a simple linked list. The only operations allowed in this version of a list are

- Inserting an item at the beginning of the list
- Removing the item at the beginning of the list
- Iterating through the list to display its contents

These operations are fairly easy to carry out, so we'll start with them. (As we'll see in Hour 9, "Abstract Data Types," these operations are also all you need to use a linked list as the basis for a stack.)

Before we get to the complete linkList.cpp program, we'll look at some important parts of the Link and LinkList classes.

The Link Class

You've already seen the data part of the Link class. Listing 8.1 shows the complete class definition:

INPUT   LISTING 8.1   THE Link CLASS

```
class Link
   {
   public:
      int iData;                  //data item
      double dData;               //data item
      Link* pNext;                //ptr to next link in list
//-----------------------------------------------------------
   Link(int id, double dd) :      //constructor
                        iData(id), dData(dd), pNext(NULL)
      {  }
//-----------------------------------------------------------
   void displayLink()             //display ourself {22, 2.99}
      {
      cout << "{" << iData << ", " << dData << "} ";
      }
//-----------------------------------------------------------
   }; //end class Link
```

ANALYSIS   In addition to the data, there's a constructor and a member function, displayLink(), that displays the link's data in the format {22, 2.99}. Object purists would probably object to naming this member function displayLink(), arguing that it should be simply display(). This would be in the spirit of polymorphism, but it makes the listing somewhat harder to understand when you see a statement like the following and you've forgotten whether pCurrent points to a Link object, a LinkList object, or something else:

```
pCurrent->display();
```

The constructor initializes the data. There's no need to initialize the pNext data member because it's automatically set to NULL when it's created. (Although it could be set to NULL explicitly, for clarity.) The NULL value means it doesn't refer to anything, which is the situation until the link is connected to other links.

> We've made the storage type of the Link fields (iData and so on) public. If they were private we would need to provide public methods to access them, which would require extra code, thus making the listing longer and harder to read. Ideally, for security we would probably want to restrict Link-object access to public methods of the LinkList class.

The LinkList Class

The LinkList class contains only one data item: a pointer to the first link on the list (see Listing 8.2). This pointer is called pFirst. It's the only permanent information the list maintains about the location of any of the links. It finds the other links by following the chain of pointers from pFirst, using each link's pNext data member.

INPUT   **LISTING 8.2**   THE LinkList CLASS

```
class LinkList
   {
   private:
     Link* pFirst;                //ptr to first link on list
   public:
//-------------------------------------------------------------
   LinkList()  : pFirst(NULL)     //constructor
      {  }                        //(no links on list yet)
//-------------------------------------------------------------
   bool isEmpty()                 //true if list is empty
      { return pFirst==NULL; }
//-------------------------------------------------------------
   ...                            //other methods go here
};  //end class LinkList
```

ANALYSIS   The constructor for LinkList sets pFirst to NULL. When pFirst has the value NULL, we know there are no items on the list. If there were any items, pFirst would contain a pointer to the first one. As we'll see, the isEmpty() member function uses this fact to determine if the list is empty.

The insertFirst() Member Function

The insertFirst() member function of LinkList inserts a new link at the beginning of the list. This is the easiest place to insert a link because pFirst already points to the first

link. To insert the new link, we need only set the pNext data member in the newly created link to point to the old first link, and then change pFirst so it points to the newly
created link. This is shown in Figure 8.4.

FIGURE 8.4

Inserting a new link.

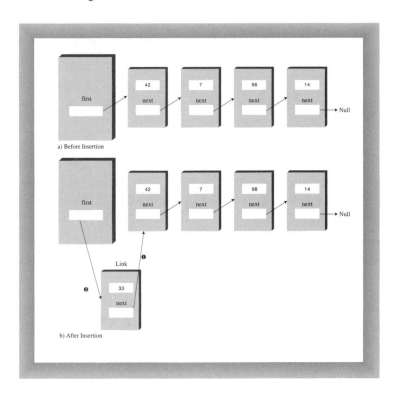

In insertFirst() we begin by creating the new link using the data passed as arguments.
Then we change the link pointers as we just noted.

```
//insert at start of list
   void insertFirst(int id, double dd)
       {                          //make new link
       Link* pNewLink = new Link(id, dd);
       pNewLink->pNext = pFirst;   //newLink-->old first
       pFirst = pNewLink;          //first-->newLink
       }
```

ANALYSIS   The arrows --> in the comments in the last two statements mean that a link (or
                the pFirst data member) connects to the next (downstream) link. (In doubly
linked lists we'll see upstream connections as well, symbolized by <-- arrows.) Compare
these two statements with Figure 8.4. Make sure you understand how the statements

cause the links to be changed, as shown in the figure. This kind of pointer-manipulation is the heart of linked list algorithms.

Notice that we've created a new link with new. This implies we'll need to delete the link from memory if at some point we remove it from the list.

The removeFirst() Member Function

In the LinkList Workshop applet we used the term "delete" to describe removing a link from a list. When we talk about a C++ implementation of a linked list we must be careful with our terminology. In C++, delete is an operator used to remove an object from memory. In listings we'll use the term "remove" to refer to a link being taken out of a list.

The removeFirst() member function is the reverse of insertFirst(). It disconnects the first link by rerouting pFirst to point to the second link. This second link is found by looking at the pNext data member in the first link.

```
void removeFirst()             //delete first link
    {                          //(assumes list not empty)
    Link* pTemp = pFirst;      //save first
    pFirst = pFirst->pNext;    //unlink it: first-->old next
    delete pTemp;              //delete old first
    }
```

ANALYSIS The second statement is all you need to remove the first link from the list. Figure 8.5 shows how pFirst is rerouted to delete the object. We also need to delete the removed link from memory, so we save a pointer to it in pTemp, and then delete it in the last statement. This prevents a "memory leak" caused by an accumulation of links deleted from the list but still taking up space in memory. (We'll examine memory leaks again in the next program.)

Notice that the removeFirst() member function assumes the list is not empty. Before calling it, your program should verify this with the isEmpty() member function.

The displayList() Member Function

To display the list, you start at pFirst and follow the chain of pointers from link to link. A variable pCurrent points to each link in turn. It starts off pointing to pFirst, which holds a pointer to the first link. The following statement changes pCurrent to point to the next link because that's what's in the pNext data member in each link:

```
pCurrent = pCurrent->pNext;
```

FIGURE 8.5

Deleting a link.

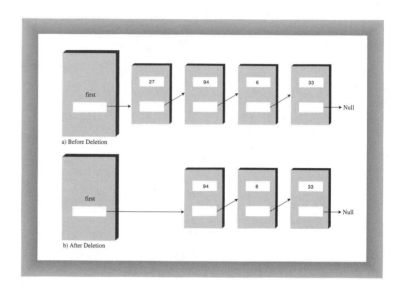

Here's the entire `displayList()` member function:

```
void displayList()
     {
     cout << "List (first-->last): ";
     Link* pCurrent = pFirst;    //start at beginning of list
     while(pCurrent != NULL)     //until end of list,
        {
        pCurrent->displayLink(); //print data
        pCurrent = pCurrent->pNext;  //move to next link
        }
     cout << endl;
     }
```

ANALYSIS The end of the list is indicated by the `pNext` data member in the last link pointing to `NULL` rather than another link. How did this data member get to be `NULL`? It started that way when the link was constructed and was never given any other value because it was always at the end of the list. The `while` loop uses this condition to terminate itself when it reaches the end of the list. Figure 8.6 shows how `pCurrent` steps along the list.

At each link, the `displayList()` member function calls the `displayLink()` member function to display the data in the link.

FIGURE 8.6

Stepping along the list.

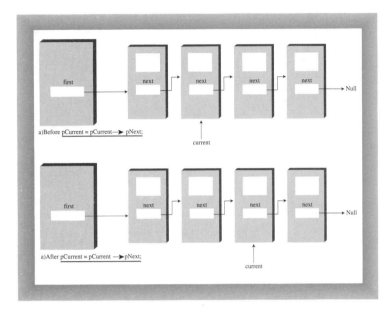

The `linkList.cpp` Program

Listing 8.3 shows the complete `linkList.cpp` program. You've already seen all the components except the `main()` routine.

INPUT   **LISTING 8.3**   THE `linkList1.cpp` PROGRAM

```
//linkList.cpp
//demonstrates linked list
#include <iostream>
using namespace std;
/////////////////////////////////////////////////////////////////
class Link
   {
   public:
      int iData;                 //data item
      double dData;              //data item
      Link* pNext;               //ptr to next link in list
//-------------------------------------------------------------
   Link(int id, double dd) :     //constructor
                   iData(id), dData(dd), pNext(NULL)
      {  }
//-------------------------------------------------------------
   void displayLink()            //display ourself {22, 2.99}
```

continues

LISTING 8.3   CONTINUED

```
      {
      cout << "{" << iData << ", " << dData << "} ";
      }
//--------------------------------------------------------------
   }; //end class Link
/////////////////////////////////////////////////////////////////
class LinkList
   {
   private:
      Link* pFirst;                 //ptr to first link on list
   public:
//--------------------------------------------------------------
   LinkList()  : pFirst(NULL)     //constructor
      { }                          //(no links on list yet)
//--------------------------------------------------------------
   bool isEmpty()                 //true if list is empty
      { return pFirst==NULL; }
//--------------------------------------------------------------
                                  //insert at start of list
   void insertFirst(int id, double dd)
      {                           //make new link
      Link* pNewLink = new Link(id, dd);
      pNewLink->pNext = pFirst;   //newLink-->old first
      pFirst = pNewLink;          //first-->newLink
      }
//--------------------------------------------------------------
   Link* getFirst()               //return first link
      { return pFirst; }
//--------------------------------------------------------------
   void removeFirst()             //delete first link
      {                           //(assumes list not empty)
      Link* pTemp = pFirst;       //save first
      pFirst = pFirst->pNext;     //unlink it: first-->old next
      delete pTemp;               //delete old first
      }
//--------------------------------------------------------------
   void displayList()
      {
      cout << "List (first-->last): ";
      Link* pCurrent = pFirst;    //start at beginning of list
      while(pCurrent != NULL)     //until end of list,
         {
         pCurrent->displayLink(); //print data
         pCurrent = pCurrent->pNext;  //move to next link
         }
      cout << endl;
      }
//--------------------------------------------------------------
```

8

```
   };   //end class LinkList
//////////////////////////////////////////////////////////////
int main()
   {
   LinkList theList;                        //make new list

   theList.insertFirst(22, 2.99);           //insert four items
   theList.insertFirst(44, 4.99);
   theList.insertFirst(66, 6.99);
   theList.insertFirst(88, 8.99);

   theList.displayList();                   //display list

   while( !theList.isEmpty() )              //until it's empty,
      {
      Link* pTemp = theList.getFirst();   //get first link
                                          //display its key
      cout << "Removing link with key " << pTemp->iData << endl;
      theList.removeFirst();               //remove it
      }
   theList.displayList();                   //display empty list
   return 0;
   }   //end main()
```

ANALYSIS   In main() we create a new list, insert four new links into it with insertFirst(), and display it. Then, in the while loop, we repeatedly display the first item with getFirst() and remove it with removeFirst() until the list is empty. The empty list is then displayed.

OUTPUT   Here's the output from linkList.cpp:

```
List (first-->last): {88, 8.99} {66, 6.99} {44, 4.99} {22, 2.99}
Removing link with key 88
Removing link with key 66
Removing link with key 44
Removing link with key 22
List (first-->last):
```

We've examined a barebones linked list program. Now let's look at a program with some additional features.

Finding and Removing Specified Links

Our next sample program adds methods to search a linked list for a data item with a specified key value, and to remove an item with a specified key value. These, along with insertion at the start of the list, are the same operations carried out by the LinkList Workshop applet. The complete linkList2.cpp program is shown in Listing 8.4.

INPUT   **LISTING 8.4**   THE `linkList2.cpp` PROGRAM

```cpp
//linkList2.cpp
//demonstrates linked list
#include <iostream>
using namespace std;
//////////////////////////////////////////////////////////////////
class Link
   {
   public:
      int iData;                  //data item (key)
      double dData;               //data item
      Link* pNext;                //next link in list
//----------------------------------------------------------------
   Link(int id, double dd) :      //constructor
               iData(id), dData(dd), pNext(NULL)
      {  }
//----------------------------------------------------------------
   void displayLink()             //display ourself: {22, 2.99}
      {
      cout << "{" << iData << ", " << dData << "} ";
      }
   };  //end class Link
//////////////////////////////////////////////////////////////////
class LinkList
   {
   private:
      Link* pFirst;               //ptr to first link on list
   public:
//----------------------------------------------------------------
   LinkList()  : pFirst(NULL)     //constructor
      {  }                        //(no links on list yet)
//----------------------------------------------------------------
   ~LinkList()                    //destructor (deletes links)
      {
      Link* pCurrent = pFirst;    //start at beginning of list
      while(pCurrent != NULL)     //until end of list,
         {
         Link* pOldCur = pCurrent;   //save current link
         pCurrent = pCurrent->pNext; //move to next link
         delete pOldCur;             //delete old current
         }
      }
//----------------------------------------------------------------
   void insertFirst(int id, double dd)
      {                                //make new link
      Link* pNewLink = new Link(id, dd);
      pNewLink->pNext = pFirst;   //it points to old first link
      pFirst = pNewLink;          //now first points to this
      }
```

```
//------------------------------------------------------------
   Link* find(int key)              //find link with given key
      {                             //(assumes non-empty list)
      Link* pCurrent = pFirst;           //start at 'first'
      while(pCurrent->iData != key)      //while no match,
         {
         if(pCurrent->pNext == NULL)     //if end of list,
            return NULL;                 //didn't find it
         else                            //not end of list,
            pCurrent = pCurrent->pNext;  //go to next link
         }
      return pCurrent;                    //found it
      }
//------------------------------------------------------------
   bool remove(int key)             //remove link with given key
      {                             //(assumes non-empty list)
      Link* pCurrent = pFirst;      //search for link
      Link* pPrevious = pFirst;
      while(pCurrent->iData != key)
         {
         if(pCurrent->pNext == NULL)
            return false;           //didn't find it
         else
            {
            pPrevious = pCurrent; //go to next link
            pCurrent = pCurrent->pNext;
            }
         }                           //found it
      if(pCurrent == pFirst)       //if first link,
         pFirst = pFirst->pNext;   //change first
      else                                    //otherwise,
         pPrevious->pNext = pCurrent->pNext; //bypass it
      delete pCurrent;             //delete link
      return true;                 //successful removal
      }
//------------------------------------------------------------
   void displayList()               //display the list
      {
      cout << "List (first-->last): ";
      Link* pCurrent = pFirst;     //start at beginning of list
      while(pCurrent != NULL)      //until end of list,
         {
         pCurrent->displayLink();     //print data
         pCurrent = pCurrent->pNext; //move to next link
         }
      cout << endl;
      }
//------------------------------------------------------------
   }; //end class LinkList
```

continues

LISTING 8.4   CONTINUED

```
///////////////////////////////////////////////////////////////////
int main()
   {
   LinkList theList;                        //make list

   theList.insertFirst(22, 2.99);           //insert 4 items
   theList.insertFirst(44, 4.99);
   theList.insertFirst(66, 6.99);
   theList.insertFirst(88, 8.99);

   theList.displayList();                   //display list

   int findKey = 44;                        //find item
   Link* pFind = theList.find(findKey);
   if( pFind != NULL)
      cout << "Found link with key " << pFind->iData << endl;
   else
      cout << "Can't find link" << endl;

   int remKey = 66;                         //remove item
   bool remOK = theList.remove(remKey);
   if( remOK )
      cout << "Removed link with key " << remKey << endl;
   else
      cout << "Can't remove link" << endl;

   theList.displayList();                   //display list
   return 0;
   }  //end main()
```

ANALYSIS   The main() routine makes a list, inserts four items, and displays the resulting list. It then searches for the item with key 44, removes the item with key 66, and displays the list again.

OUTPUT   Here's the output:

```
List (first-->last): {88, 8.99} {66, 6.99} {44, 4.99} {22, 2.99}
Found link with key 44
Deleted link with key 66
List (first-->last): {88, 8.99} {44, 4.99} {22, 2.99}
```

The find() Member Function

The find() member function works much like the displayList() member function seen in the linkList.cpp program. The pointer pCurrent initially points to pFirst, and then steps its way along the links by setting itself repeatedly to pCurrent->pNext. At each link, find() checks whether that link's key is the one it's looking for. If it is, it returns with a pointer to that link. If it reaches the end of the list without finding the desired link, it returns NULL.

The remove() Member Function

The remove() member function is similar to find() in the way it searches for the link to be removed. However, it needs to maintain a pointer not only to the current link (pCurrent), but to the link preceding the current link (pPrevious). This is because if it removes the current link, it must connect the preceding link to the following link, as shown in Figure 8.7. The only way to remember the location of the preceding link is to maintain a pointer to it.

FIGURE 8.7

Removing a specified link.

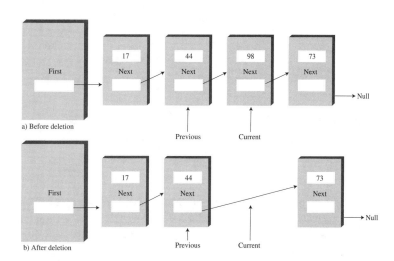

a) Before deletion

b) After deletion

At each cycle through the while loop, just before pCurrent is set to pCurrent->pNext, pPrevious is set to pCurrent. This keeps it pointing at the link preceding pCurrent.

To remove the current link after it's found, the pNext data member of the previous link is set to the next link. A special case arises if the current link is the first link because the first link is pointed to by the LinkList's pFirst data member and not by another link. In this case the link is removed by changing pFirst to point to pFirst->pNext, as we saw in the linkList2.cpp program with the removeFirst() member function. Here's the code that covers these two possibilities:

```
if(pCurrent == pFirst)                 //if first link,
   pFirst = pFirst->pNext;             //   change first
else                                    //otherwise,
   pPrevious->pNext = pCurrent->pNext; //   bypass it
```

Avoiding Memory Leaks

To create a linked list, the LinkList program creates a LinkList object. During the operation of the linked list, the insertFirst() member function of this object creates Link objects using the C++ new operator. When the LinkList object is destroyed (in this program because it goes out of scope when main() terminates), the Link objects that have been created will remain in memory unless we take steps to delete them.

Accordingly, in the destructor for the LinkList class, we install code to step through the list and apply the delete operator to each link. For the same reason, the remove() member function must delete a link after it has been removed from the list.

We've seen methods to insert and remove items at the start of a list, and to find a specified item and remove a specified item. You can imagine other useful list methods. For example, an insertAfter() member function could find a link with a specified key value and insert a new link following it.

The Efficiency of Linked Lists

Insertion and deletion at the beginning of a linked list are very fast. They involve changing only one or two pointers, which takes O(1) time.

Finding or deleting a specified item requires searching through, on the average, half the items in the list. This requires O(N) comparisons. An array is also O(N) for these operations, but the linked list is nevertheless faster because nothing needs to be moved when an item is inserted or removed. The increased efficiency can be significant, especially if a copy takes much longer than a comparison.

Of course, another important advantage of linked lists over arrays is that the linked list uses exactly as much memory as it needs, and can expand to fill all available memory. The size of an array is fixed when it's created; this usually leads to inefficiency because the array is too large, or to running out of room because the array is too small. Vectors, which are expandable arrays, might solve this problem to some extent, but they usually expand in fixed-sized increments (such as doubling the size of the array whenever it's about to overflow). This use of memory is still not as efficient as a linked list.

8

Summary

In this hour, you've learned the following:

- A linked list consists of one linkedList object and a number of link objects.
- The linkedList object contains a pointer, often called pFirst, to the first link in the list.
- Each link object contains data and a pointer, often called pNext, to the next link in the list.
- A pNext value of NULL signals that a link is the last one on the list.
- Inserting an item at the beginning of a linked list involves setting the new link's pNext data member to point to the old first link, and changing pFirst to point to the new link.
- Deleting a link at the beginning of a list involves setting pFirst to point to pFirst->pNext.
- When a link is removed from a list it must also be deleted from memory to avoid a memory leak.
- To traverse a linked list, you start at pFirst; then go from link to link, using each link's pNext data member to find the next link.
- A link with a specified key value can be found by traversing the list. After it is found, an item can be displayed, removed, or operated on in other ways.
- A new link can be inserted before or after a link with a specified key value, following a traversal to find this link.

Q&A

Q How do I know when to use a linked list instead of an array?

A You should consider a linked list when there will be lots of insertions of new data items or deletions of existing items.

Q When shouldn't I use a linked list?

A Don't use a linked list if you need frequent access to data items with a specified key, or to arbitrary items in the list (such as the access provided by array indices).

Workshop

The Workshop helps you solidify what you learned in this hour. See Appendix A for quiz answers.

Quiz

1. What one piece of data must be included in a link class?

2. What one piece of data must be included in a linked list class?

3. Deleting a link from a linked list involves only one change in the list's structure. What is it?

4. How do you get from the current link to the next link?

5. What task must be carried out by both the `find(int key)` and `remove(int key)` member functions?

6. How many objects of the linked list class are normally used to implement a linked list?

7. What task should be carried out by the destructor of a linked list class in a C++ program?

Exercise

There's a somewhat imperfect analogy between a linked list and a railroad train, where individual cars represent links. Imagine how you would carry out various linked list operations, such as those implemented by the member functions `insertFirst()`, `removeFirst()`, and `remove(int key)` from the `LinkList` class in this hour. Also implement an `insertAfter()` function. You'll need some sidings and switches. You can use a model train set if you have one. Otherwise, try drawing tracks on a piece of paper and using business cards for train cars.

HOUR 9

Abstract Data Types

In this hour we'll shift gears and discuss a topic that's more general than linked lists or arrays: Abstract Data Types (ADTs). What is an ADT? Roughly speaking, it's a way of looking at a data structure: focusing on what it does, and ignoring how it does it.

In an ADT the concept of a certain kind of data structure is separated from the underlying implementation. Stacks and queues can be considered examples of abstract data types. We've already seen stacks and queues implemented by arrays (actually vectors).

To clarify the separation of a data structure and its implementation, we'll show how stacks and queues can be implemented as linked lists rather than arrays. This will demonstrate the "abstract" nature of stacks and queues. After we've explored these specific examples, we'll discuss the concept of abstract data types. In this hour you'll learn

- How to implement a stack using a linked list
- How to create a double-ended linked list
- How to implement a queue using a double-ended linked list

- How implementing one data structure with another demonstrates the concept of ADTs
- How the concept of ADTs aids in program design

> This hour is unusual. In previous hours we talked about specific data structures such as arrays and linked lists. We demonstrated these data structures by showing how they could be implemented and used. In this hour we'll be talking about something less concrete: the concepts of abstraction and abstract data types. Here we'll demonstrate abstraction by showing the relationships between data structures.

A Stack Implemented By a Linked List

Let's see how a stack can be implemented by a linked list rather than an array. As we'll see later, this (and the following example) will demonstrate the idea of abstraction.

Implementing push() and pop()

When we created a stack in Hour 6, "Stacks," we used a C++ vector (which is basically an array) to hold the stack's data. The stack's push() and pop() operations were carried out by vector operations such as

```
stackVect[++top] = data;
```

and

```
data = stackVect[top--];
```

which insert data into, and take it out of, a vector.

We can also use a linked list to hold a stack's data. In this case the push() and pop() operations would be carried out by operations like

```
theList.insertFirst(data)
```

and

```
data = theList.deleteFirst()
```

The user of the stack class calls push() and pop() to insert and delete items, without knowing, or needing to know, whether the stack is implemented as an array or as a linked list.

Implementing a Stack Based on a Linked List

Listing 9.1 shows how a stack class called LinkStack can be implemented using the
LinkList class instead of an array. (Object purists would argue that the name LinkStack
should be simply Stack because users of this class shouldn't need to know that it's
implemented as a list.)

INPUT   **LISTING 9.1**   THE linkStack() PROGRAM

```
//linkStack.cpp
//demonstrates a stack implemented as a list
#include <iostream>
using namespace std;
////////////////////////////////////////////////////////////////
class Link
   {
   public:
      double dData;              //data item
      Link* pNext;               //next link in list
//-------------------------------------------------------------
   Link(double dd) : dData(dd), pNext(NULL)
      {  }                       //constructor
//-------------------------------------------------------------
   void displayLink()    //display ourself
      { cout << dData << " "; }
//-------------------------------------------------------------
   }; //end class Link
////////////////////////////////////////////////////////////////
class LinkList
   {
   private:
      Link* pFirst;              //ptr to first item on list
   public:
//-------------------------------------------------------------
   LinkList() : pFirst(NULL)     //constructor
      {  }
//-------------------------------------------------------------
   ~LinkList()                   //destructor (deletes links)
      {
      Link* pCurrent = pFirst;   //start at beginning of list
      while(pCurrent != NULL)    //until end of list,
         {
         Link* pOldCur = pCurrent;   //save current link
         pCurrent = pCurrent->pNext; //move to next link
         delete pOldCur;             //delete old current
         }
      }
//-------------------------------------------------------------
```

continues

LISTING 9.1 CONTINUED

```
    bool isEmpty()                  //true if list is empty
       { return (pFirst==NULL); }
//---------------------------------------------------------------
    void insertFirst(double dd)     //insert at start of list
       {                            //make new link
       Link* pNewLink = new Link(dd);
       pNewLink->pNext = pFirst;    //newLink --> old first
       pFirst = pNewLink;           //first --> newLink
       }
//---------------------------------------------------------------
    double deleteFirst()            //delete first item
       {                            //(assumes list not empty)
       Link* pTemp = pFirst;        //save old first link
       pFirst = pFirst->pNext;      //remove it: first-->old next
       double key = pTemp->dData;   //remember data
       delete pTemp;                //delete old first link
       return key;                  //return deleted link's data
       }
//---------------------------------------------------------------
    void displayList()              //display all links
       {
       Link* pCurrent = pFirst;     //start at beginning of list
       while(pCurrent != NULL)      //until end of list,
          {
          pCurrent->displayLink();  //print data
          pCurrent = pCurrent->pNext;  //move to next link
          }
       cout << endl;
       }
//---------------------------------------------------------------
    };  //end class LinkList
/////////////////////////////////////////////////////////////////
class LinkStack
    {
    private:
       LinkList* pList;             //pointer to linked list
    public:
//---------------------------------------------------------------
    LinkStack()                     //constructor
       { pList = new LinkList; }     //make a linked list
//---------------------------------------------------------------
    ~LinkStack()                    //destructor
       { delete pList; }            //delete the linked list
//---------------------------------------------------------------
    void push(double j)             //put item on top of stack
       { pList->insertFirst(j); }
//---------------------------------------------------------------
    double pop()                    //take item from top of stack
```

```
        { return pList->deleteFirst(); }
//-------------------------------------------------------------
    bool isEmpty()                    //true if stack is empty
        { return ( pList->isEmpty() ); }
//-------------------------------------------------------------
    void displayStack()
        {
        cout << "Stack (top-->bottom): ";
        pList->displayList();
        }
//-------------------------------------------------------------
    };  //end class LinkStack
///////////////////////////////////////////////////////////////
int main()
    {
    LinkStack theStack;             //make stack

    theStack.push(20);              //push items
    theStack.push(40);

    theStack.displayStack();        //display stack (40, 20)

    theStack.push(60);              //push items
    theStack.push(80);

    theStack.displayStack();        //display (80, 60, 40, 20,)

    theStack.pop();                 //pop items (80, 60)
    theStack.pop();

    theStack.displayStack();        //display stack (40, 20)
    return 0;
    }   //end main()
```

ANALYSIS The main() routine creates a stack object, pushes two items on it, displays the stack, pushes two more items, and displays it again. Finally it pops two items and displays the stack again.

OUTPUT Here's the output:

```
Stack (top-->bottom): 40 20
Stack (top-->bottom): 80 60 40 20
X-80
X-60
Stack (top-->bottom): 40 20
X-40
X-20
```

Focusing on Class Relationships

Notice the overall organization of this program. The main() routine relates only to the LinkStack class. The LinkStack class relates only to the LinkList class. There's no communication between main() and the LinkList class.

More specifically, when a statement in main() calls the push() operation in the LinkStack class, this member function in turn calls insertFirst() in the LinkList class to actually insert data. Similarly, pop() calls deleteFirst() to delete an item, and displayStack() calls displayList() to display the stack. To the class user, writing code in main(), there's no difference between using the list-based LinkStack class and using the array-based stack class from the Stack.cpp program in Hour 6.

Implementing a stack with a linked list rather than an array shows how we can disconnect what the user of a class sees (the interface) from the underlying implementation. We'll look at another example in the next two sections.

Double-Ended Lists

In the next section, "Implementing a Queue Using a Linked List," we'll show a queue implemented with a linked list. However, it's hard to implement a queue using the simple linked list we saw in the last hour. A specialized kind of linked list, called a double-ended list, is much more satisfactory. Accordingly, we'll explore the double-ended list first.

Accessing Both Ends of a List

A double-ended list is similar to an ordinary linked list, but it has one additional feature: a reference to the last link as well as to the first. Figure 9.1 shows what this looks like.

FIGURE 9.1

A double-ended list.

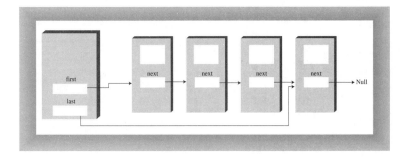

The reference to the last link permits you to insert a new link directly at the end of the list just as easily as at the beginning. Of course you can insert a new link at the end of an ordinary single-ended list by iterating through the entire list until you reach the end, but this is very inefficient.

Access to the end of the list as well as the beginning makes the double-ended list suitable for certain situations that a single-ended list can't handle efficiently, such as implementing a queue.

Implementing a Double-Ended List

Listing 9.2 contains the firstLastList.cpp program, which demonstrates a double-ended list. (Incidentally, don't confuse the double-ended list with the doubly linked list, which we'll explore later in Hour 10, "Specialized Lists.")

INPUT   **LISTING 9.2**   THE firstLastList.cpp PROGRAM

```cpp
//firstLastList.cpp
//demonstrates list with first and last references
#include <iostream>
using namespace std;
/////////////////////////////////////////////////////////////
class Link
    {
    public:
        double dData;                   //data item
        Link* pNext;                    //ptr to next link in list
//------------------------------------------------------------
    Link(double d) : dData(d), pNext(NULL)  //constructor
        {  }
//------------------------------------------------------------
    void displayLink()                  //display this link
        { cout << dData << " "; }
//------------------------------------------------------------
    }; //end class Link
/////////////////////////////////////////////////////////////
class FirstLastList
    {
    private:
        Link* pFirst;                   //ptr to first link
        Link* pLast;                    //ptr to last link
    public:
//------------------------------------------------------------
    FirstLastList() : pFirst(NULL), pLast(NULL)   //constructor
```

continues

LISTING 9.2   CONTINUED

```
        { }
//-------------------------------------------------------------
    ~FirstLastList()                //destructor
        {                           //  (deletes all links)
        Link* pCurrent = pFirst;    //start at beginning
        while(pCurrent != NULL)     //until end of list,
            {
            Link* pTemp = pCurrent;     //remember current
            pCurrent = pCurrent->pNext; //move to next link
            delete pTemp;               //delete old current
            }
        }
//-------------------------------------------------------------
    bool isEmpty()                  //true if no links
        { return pFirst==NULL; }
//-------------------------------------------------------------
    void insertFirst(double dd)     //insert at front of list
        {
        Link* pNewLink = new Link(dd); //make new link

        if( isEmpty() )             //if empty list,
            pLast = pNewLink;       //newLink <-- last
        pNewLink->pNext = pFirst;   //newLink --> old first
        pFirst = pNewLink;          //first --> newLink
        }
//-------------------------------------------------------------
    void insertLast(double dd)      //insert at end of list
        {
        Link* pNewLink = new Link(dd); //make new link
        if( isEmpty() )             //if empty list,
            pFirst = pNewLink;      //first --> newLink
        else
            pLast->pNext = pNewLink;   //old last --> newLink
        pLast = pNewLink;           //newLink <-- last
        }
//-------------------------------------------------------------
    void removeFirst()              //remove first link
        {                           //(assumes non-empty list)
        Link* pTemp = pFirst;       //remember first link
        if(pFirst->pNext == NULL)   //if only one item
            pLast = NULL;           //NULL <-- last
        pFirst = pFirst->pNext;     //first --> old next
        delete pTemp;               //delete the link
        }
//-------------------------------------------------------------
    void displayList()
        {
        cout << "List (first-->last): ";
        Link* pCurrent = pFirst;    //start at beginning
```

```
        while(pCurrent != NULL)         //until end of list,
            {
            pCurrent->displayLink();     //print data
            pCurrent = pCurrent->pNext; //move to next link
            }
        cout << endl;
        }
//-------------------------------------------------------------
    }; //end class FirstLastList
//////////////////////////////////////////////////////////////
int main()
    {
    FirstLastList theList;             //make a new list

    theList.insertFirst(22);           //insert at front
    theList.insertFirst(44);
    theList.insertFirst(66);

    theList.insertLast(11);            //insert at rear
    theList.insertLast(33);
    theList.insertLast(55);

    theList.displayList();             //display the list

    cout << "Deleting first two items" << endl;
    theList.removeFirst();             //remove first two items
    theList.removeFirst();

    theList.displayList();             //display again
    return 0;
        } //end main()
```

ANALYSIS For simplicity, in this program we've reduced the number of data items in each link from two to one. This makes it easier to display the link contents. (Remember that in a serious program there would be many more data items, or perhaps a pointer to another object containing many data items.)

This program inserts three items at the front of the list, inserts three more at the end, and displays the resulting list. It then deletes the first two items and displays the list again.

OUTPUT Here's the output from Listing 9.2:

```
List (first-->last): 66 44 22 11 33 55
Deleting first two items
List (first-->last): 22 11 33 55
```

Notice how repeated insertions at the front of the list reverse the order of the items, whereas repeated insertions at the end preserve the order.

Pointers to Both Ends of the List

The double-ended list class is called the FirstLastList. As discussed, it has two data items, first and last, which point to the first item and the last item in the list. If there is only one item in the list, both first and last point to it, and if there are no items, they are both NULL.

The class has a new member function, insertLast(), that inserts a new item at the end of the list. This involves modifying pLast->pNext to point to the new link, and then changing pLast to point to the new link, as shown in Figure 9.2.

FIGURE 9.2

Insertion at the end of a list.

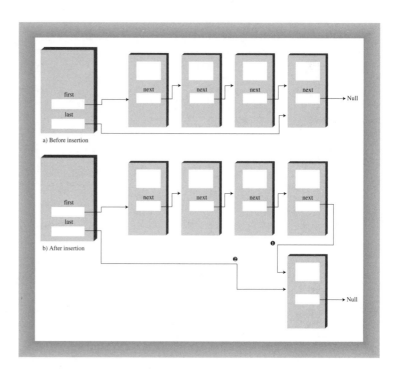

Insertion and Deletion Routines

The insertion and deletion routines are similar to those in a single-ended list. However, both insertion routines must watch out for the special case when the list is empty prior to the insertion. That is, if isEmpty() is true, insertFirst() must set pLast to the new link, and insertLast() must set pFirst to the new link.

If you are inserting at the beginning with insertFirst(), pFirst is set to point to the new link, although when inserting at the end with insertLast(), pLast is set to point to the new link. Deleting from the start of the list is also a special case if it's the only item on the list: pLast must be set to point to NULL in this case.

Unfortunately, making a list double-ended doesn't help you to delete the last link because there is still no reference to the next-to-last link, whose pNext field would need to be changed to NULL if the last link were deleted. To conveniently delete the last link, you would need a doubly linked list, which we'll look at in Hour 10. (Of course, you could also traverse the entire list to find the last link, but that's not very efficient.)

Now that we understand double-ended lists, let's see how to use one to implement a queue.

Implementing a Queue Using a Linked List

Listing 9.3 shows a queue implemented as a double-ended linked list. You can compare this with the Queue.cpp program in Hour 7, "Queues and Priority Queues."

INPUT   **LISTING 9.3**   THE linkQueue() PROGRAM

```
//linkQueue.cpp
//demonstrates queue implemented as double-ended list
#include <iostream>
using namespace std;
///////////////////////////////////////////////////////////
class Link
   {
   public:
      double dData;                 //data item
      Link* pNext;                  //ptr to next link in list
//-------------------------------------------------------------
   Link(double d) :dData(d), pNext(NULL)  //constructor
      {  }
//-------------------------------------------------------------
   void displayLink()              //display this link
      { cout << dData << " "; }
//-------------------------------------------------------------
   };  //end class Link
///////////////////////////////////////////////////////////
class FirstLastList
   {
   private:
      Link* pFirst;                 //ptr to first link
      Link* pLast;                  //ptr to last link
   public:
//-------------------------------------------------------------
```

continues

LISTING 9.3   CONTINUED

```cpp
    FirstLastList() : pFirst(NULL), pLast(NULL)  //constructor
       {  }
//----------------------------------------------------------
    ~FirstLastList()                    //destructor
       {                                //  (deletes all links)
       Link* pCurrent = pFirst;         //start at beginning
       while(pCurrent != NULL)          //until end of list,
          {
          Link* pTemp = pCurrent;       //remember current
          pCurrent = pCurrent->pNext;   //move to next link
          delete pTemp;                 //delete old current
          }
       }
//----------------------------------------------------------
    bool isEmpty()                      //true if no links
       { return pFirst==NULL; }
//----------------------------------------------------------
    void insertLast(double dd)          //insert at end of list
       {
       Link* pNewLink = new Link(dd);   //make new link
       if( isEmpty() )                  //if empty list,
          pFirst = pNewLink;            //first --> newLink
       else
          pLast->pNext = pNewLink;      //old last --> newLink
       pLast = pNewLink;                //newLink <-- last
       }
//----------------------------------------------------------
    double removeFirst()                //delete first link
       {                                //(assumes non-empty list)
       Link* pTemp = pFirst;            //remember first link
       double temp = pFirst->dData;
       if(pFirst->pNext == NULL)        //if only one item
          pLast = NULL;                 //null <-- last
       pFirst = pFirst->pNext;          //first --> old next
       delete pTemp;                    //delete the link
       return temp;
       }
//----------------------------------------------------------
    void displayList()
       {
       Link* pCurrent = pFirst;         //start at beginning
       while(pCurrent != NULL)          //until end of list,
          {
          pCurrent->displayLink();      //print data
          pCurrent = pCurrent->pNext;   //move to next link
          }
       cout << endl;
```

```
        }
//---------------------------------------------------------------
   };  //end class FirstLastList
/////////////////////////////////////////////////////////////class
LinkQueue
   {
   private:
      FirstLastList theList;
   public:
//---------------------------------------------------------------
   bool isEmpty()            //true if queue is empty
      { return theList.isEmpty(); }
//---------------------------------------------------------------
   void insert(double j)      //insert, rear of queue
      { theList.insertLast(j); }
//---------------------------------------------------------------
   double remove()            //remove, front of queue
      { return theList.removeFirst();  }
//---------------------------------------------------------------
   void displayQueue()
      {
      cout << "Queue (front-->rear): ";
      theList.displayList();
      }
//---------------------------------------------------------------
   };  //end class LinkQueue
/////////////////////////////////////////////////////////////
int main()
      {
      LinkQueue theQueue;        //make a queue

      theQueue.insert(20);       //insert items
      theQueue.insert(40);

      theQueue.displayQueue();   //display queue (20, 40)

      theQueue.insert(60);       //insert items
      theQueue.insert(80);

      theQueue.displayQueue();   //display queue (20, 40, 60, 80)

      cout << "Removing two items" << endl;
      theQueue.remove();         //remove items (20, 40)
      theQueue.remove();

      theQueue.displayQueue();   //display queue (60, 80)
      return 0;
      }   //end main()
```

ANALYSIS The program creates a queue, inserts two items, inserts two more items, and removes two items; following each of these operations the queue is displayed. Here's the output:

OUTPUT
```
Queue (front-->rear): 20 40
Queue (front-->rear): 20 40 60 80
Removing two items
X-20
X-40
Queue (front-->rear): 60 80
X-60
X-80
```

Here the member functions insert() and remove() in the LinkQueue class are implemented by the insertLast() and deleteFirst() member functions of the FirstLastList class. We've substituted a linked list for the array used to implement the queue in the Queue program of Hour 7.

Data Types and Abstraction

The LinkStack and LinkQueue programs emphasize that stacks and queues are conceptual entities, separate from their implementations. Stacks and queues can be implemented equally well by arrays or by linked lists. What's important about a stack is the push() and pop() operations and how they're used, not the underlying mechanism used to implement these operations. Similarly, what's important about a queue is the insert() and remove() functions seen by the class user.

The LinkStack and LinkQueue programs demonstrate the concept of abstract data types. Now that we've seen examples of the concept, let's explore the concept itself.

Where does the term *Abstract Data Type* come from? Let's look at the "data type" part of it first, and then return to "abstract."

What We Mean by *Data Types*

The phrase "data type" covers a lot of ground. It was first applied to built-in types such as int and double. This is probably what you first think of when you hear the term.

When you talk about a primitive type, you're actually referring to two things: a data item with certain characteristics, and permissible operations on that data. For example, type int variables in C++ can have whole-number values in a certain range (for example, between $-2,147,483,648$ and $+2,147,483,647$ in some implementations), and the operators +, -, *, /, and so on can be applied to them. The data type's permissible operations are an inseparable part of its identity; understanding the type means understanding what operations can be performed on it.

With the advent of C++, it became possible to create your own data types using classes. Some of these data types represent numerical quantities that are used in ways similar to primitive types. You can, for example, define a class for time (with data members for hours, minutes, and seconds), a class for fractions (with numerator and denominator data members), and a class for extra-long numbers (with characters in a string representing the digits). All these can be added and subtracted like `int` and `double`.

The phrase "data type" seems to fit naturally with such quantity-oriented classes. However, it is also applied to classes that don't have this quantitative aspect. In fact, *any* class represents a data type, in the sense that a class comprises data (data members) and permissible operations on that data (member functions).

By extension, when a data storage structure like a stack or queue is represented by a class, it too can be referred to as a data type. A stack is different in many ways from an `int`, but they are both defined as a certain arrangement of data and a set of operations on that data.

What We Mean by *Abstraction*

NEW TERM   The word *abstract* means "considered apart from detailed specifications or implementation." An *abstraction* is the essence or set of important characteristics of some entity. The office of president, for example, is an abstraction, considered apart from the individual who happens to occupy that office. The powers and responsibilities of the office remain the same, while individual office-holders come and go.

Abstract Data Types and OOP

In object-oriented programming, then, an abstract data type is a class considered without regard to its implementation. It's a description of the data in the class (data members), a list of operations (member functions) that can be carried out on that data, and instructions on how to use those operations. Specifically excluded are the details of how the member functions carry out their tasks. As a class user, you're told what member functions to call, how to call them, and the results you can expect, but not how they work.

Abstract Data Types and Data Structures

The meaning of *abstract data type* is further extended when it's applied to data structures like stacks and queues. As with any class, it means the data and the operations that can be performed on it, but in this context even the fundamentals of how the data is stored become invisible to the user. Users not only don't know how the member functions work, they also don't know what structure is used to store the data.

For the stack, the user knows that `push()` and `pop()` (and perhaps a few other member functions) exist and how they work. The user doesn't (at least not usually) need to know how push() and pop() work, or whether data is stored in an array, a linked list, or some other data structure like a tree.

The Interface

NEW TERM An ADT specification is often called an *interface*. It's what the class user sees; usually its public member functions. In a stack class, push(), pop(), and similar member functions form the interface.

ADT Lists

NEW TERM Now that we know what an abstract data type is, we can mention another one: the list. A *list* (sometimes called a linear list) is a group of items arranged in a linear order. That is, they're lined up in a certain way, like beads on a string or houses on a street. Lists support certain fundamental operations. You can insert an item, delete an item, and usually read an item from a specified location (the third item, for example).

Don't confuse the ADT list with the linked list we've been discussing in this hour. A list is defined by its interface: the specific member functions used to interact with it. This interface can be implemented by various structures, including arrays and linked lists. The list is an abstraction of such data structures.

Using ADTs as a Design Tool

The ADT concept is a useful aid in the software design process. If you need to store data, start by considering the operations that need to be performed on that data. Do you need access to the last item inserted? The first one? An item with a specified key? An item in a certain position? Answering such questions leads to the definition of an ADT. Only after the ADT is completely defined should you worry about the details of how to represent the data and how to code the member functions that access the data.

By decoupling the specification of the ADT from the implementation details, you can simplify the design process. You also make it easier to change the implementation at some future time. If the users relate only to the ADT interface, you should be able to change the implementation without "breaking" the user's code.

Of course, after the ADT has been designed, the underlying data structure must be carefully chosen to make the specified operations as efficient as possible. If you need random access to element N, for example, the linked-list representation isn't so good because random access isn't an efficient operation for a linked list. You'd be better off with an array.

Abstract is a Relative Term

Remember that the ADT concept is only a conceptual tool. Data storage structures are not divided cleanly into some that are ADTs and some that are used to implement ADTs. A linked list, for example, doesn't need to be wrapped in a list interface to be useful; it can act as an ADT on its own, or it can be used to implement another data type such as a queue. A linked list can be implemented using an array, and an array-type structure can be implemented using a linked list. What's an ADT and what's a more basic structure must be determined in a given context.

9

Summary

In this hour, you've learned the following:

- An Abstract Data Type (ADT) is a class considered without reference to its implementation.

- Stacks and queues are examples of ADTs. They can be implemented using either arrays or linked lists.

- An ADT simplifies program design by allowing you focus on the essentials of a data storage structure, without worrying (at least initially) about its implementation.

- A double-ended list allows easy insertion at the end of the list.

- A double-ended list maintains a pointer to the last link in the list, often called `last`, as well as to the first.

Q&A

Q I'm a little unclear on the point of all this ADT stuff.

A In large programming projects it's helpful to start designing a program by focusing on the interface a class will present to its users, without worrying until later how it will be implemented. You don't need to know too much about ADTs and the philosophy behind them to understand this book, which is more concerned with the nuts and bolts of how data structures work. But the idea of ADTs is important in software engineering.

Q How do I decide whether to implement a stack or queue as a vector or a linked list?

A In many cases it doesn't matter how you implement a stack or queue. Both vectors and linked lists provide fast O(1) performance for insertion and deletion. A priority queue is a different matter because you need to rearrange the elements to keep them in sorted order when you insert a new one. Here a linked list might be a better choice because you don't need to move half the elements (on average) to insert a new one.

Workshop

The Workshop helps you solidify what you learned in this hour. See Appendix A for quiz answers.

Quiz

1. When you implement a stack using a linked list rather than an array, what is the chief difference noticed by a user of the stack class?

2. True or false: An abstract C++ class is one whose interface is not yet clearly defined.

3. What does *implementation* mean?

4. What is an ADT?

5. Is a stack an example of an ADT?

6. Would it make sense to implement an array using a stack?

7. Is a linked list an example of an ADT?

Exercise

Write a C++ program that uses a linked list to implement a priority queue. You can modify the priorityQ.cpp program from Hour 7. This linked list could be the LinkList class from the linkStack.cpp program in this hour.

HOUR 10

Specialized Lists

In this hour we'll look at two specialized linked lists: sorted lists and doubly linked lists. Sorted lists are used as implementations of ADTs such as priority queues. They're also used for sorting. Doubly linked lists are a more versatile (although more complex) variation on ordinary lists. (Don't confuse them with double-ended lists, which we discussed in Hour 9, "Abstract Data Types.") In this hour you'll learn

- How a sorted list works
- How to create a sorted list
- How a sorted list can be used to sort data
- How a doubly linked list works
- How to create a doubly linked list

Sorted Lists

NEW TERM In the linked lists we've seen thus far, there was no requirement that data be stored in order. However, for certain applications it's useful to maintain the data in sorted order within the list. A list with this characteristic is called a *sorted list*.

In a sorted list, the items are arranged in sorted order by key value. Deletion is often limited to the smallest (or the largest) item in the list, which is at the start of the list,
although sometimes find() and remove() member functions, which search through the
list for specified links, are used as well.

In general you can use a sorted list in most situations where you use a sorted array. The
advantages of a sorted list over a sorted array are speed of insertion (because elements
don't need to be moved) and the fact that a list can expand to fill available memory,
whereas an array is limited to a fixed size. (A vector eliminates the second problem.)
However, a sorted list is somewhat more difficult to implement than a sorted array.

Later in this hour we'll look at one application for sorted lists: sorting data. A sorted list
can also be used to implement a priority queue.

The LinkList Workshop Applet

The LinkList Workshop applet introduced in Hour 8, "Linked Lists," demonstrates sorted
as well as unsorted lists. Let's see how to insert data in a sorted list.

To Do: Insert Data into the Sorted List

1. Use the New button to create a new list with about 20 links, and when prompted,
   click on the Sorted button. The result is a list with data in sorted order, as shown in
   Figure 10.1.

FIGURE 10.1

*The LinkList Workshop
applet with a sorted
list.*

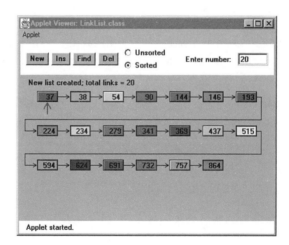

2. Use the Ins button to insert a new item. Type in a value that will fall somewhere in
   the middle of the list.

▼   3. Watch as the algorithm traverses the links, looking for the appropriate insertion
       place.
    4. When it finds it, it inserts the new link, as shown in Figure 10.2.

FIGURE 10.2

A newly inserted link.

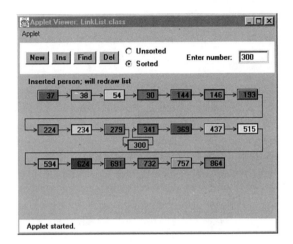

10

▲

With the next press of Ins, the list will be redrawn to regularize its appearance. You can
also find a specified link using the Find button, and delete a specified link using the Del
button.

Implementing an Insertion Function in C++

The insertion function is more complicated for sorted lists than for unsorted lists. To
insert an item into a sorted list, the algorithm must first search through the list until it
finds the appropriate place to put the item. This place is just before the first item that's
larger, as shown in Figure 10.2.

After the algorithm finds where to put the item, it can be inserted in the usual way by
changing pNext in the new link to point to the next link, and changing pNext in the previous link to point to the new link. However, there are some special cases to consider:
The link might need to be inserted at the beginning of the list, or it might need to go at
the end. Let's look at the code:

```
void insert(double key)              //insert, in order
     {
     Link* pNewLink = new Link(key); //make new link
     Link* pPrevious = NULL;         //start at first
     Link* pCurrent = pFirst;
                                     //until end of list,
     while(pCurrent != NULL && key > pCurrent->dData)
```

```
    {                               //or key > current,
    pPrevious = pCurrent;
    pCurrent = pCurrent->pNext;  //go to next item
    }
if(pPrevious==NULL)                 //at beginning of list
    pFirst = pNewLink;              //first --> newLink
else                                //not at beginning
    pPrevious->pNext = pNewLink;    //old prev --> newLink
pNewLink->pNext = pCurrent;         //newLink --> old current
}  //end insert()
```

ANALYSIS We need to maintain a pPrevious pointer as we move along, so we can modify
the previous link's pNext data member to point to the new link. After creating the
new link, we prepare to search for the insertion point by setting pCurrent to pFirst in
the usual way. We also set pPrevious to NULL; this is important because later we'll use
this null value to determine if we're still at the beginning of the list.

The while loop is similar to those we've used before to search for the insertion point, but
there's an added condition. The loop terminates when the key of the link currently being
examined (pCurrent->dData) is no longer smaller than the key of the link being inserted
(key). This is the most usual case, where a key is inserted somewhere in the middle of
the list.

However, the while loop also terminates if pCurrent is NULL. This happens at the end of
the list (the pNext data member of the pLast element is NULL), or if the list is empty to
begin with (pFirst is NULL). Thus when the while loop terminates, we might be at the
beginning, the middle, or the end of the list, or the list might be empty. If we're at the
beginning or the list is empty, pPrevious will be NULL, so we set pFirst to the new link.
Otherwise, we're in the middle of the list, or at the end, and we set pPrevious->pNext to
the new link. In any case we set the new link's pNext data member to pCurrent. If we're
at the end of the list, pCurrent is NULL, so the new link's pNext data member is appropriately set to this value.

Implementing a Sorted List

The sortedList.cpp example shown in Listing 10.1 presents a SortedList class with
insert(), remove(), and displayList() member functions. Only the insert() routine
is different from its counterpart in unsorted lists.

INPUT   **LISTING 10.1**   THE sortedList.cpp PROGRAM

```
//sortedList.cpp
//demonstrates sorted list
#include <iostream>
```

```
using namespace std;
////////////////////////////////////////////////////////////
class Link
   {
   public:
      double dData;                     //data item
      Link* pNext;                      //next link in list
//-----------------------------------------------------------
   Link(double dd) : dData(dd), pNext(NULL)  //constructor
      {  }
//-----------------------------------------------------------
   void displayLink()                   //display this link
      { cout << dData << " "; }
   };  //end class Link
////////////////////////////////////////////////////////////
class SortedList
   {
   private:
      Link* pFirst;                     //ptr to first link
   public:
//-----------------------------------------------------------
   SortedList() : pFirst(NULL)          //constructor
      {  }
//-----------------------------------------------------------
   ~SortedList()                        //destructor
      {                                 //   (deletes links)
      Link* pCurrent = pFirst;          //start at first
      while(pCurrent != NULL)           //until end of list,
         {
         Link* pOldCur = pCurrent;      //save current link
         pCurrent = pCurrent->pNext;    //move to next link
         delete pOldCur;                //delete old current
         }
      }
//-----------------------------------------------------------
   bool isEmpty()                       //true if no links
      { return (pFirst==NULL); }
//-----------------------------------------------------------
   void insert(double key)              //insert, in order
      {
      Link* pNewLink = new Link(key);   //make new link
      Link* pPrevious = NULL;           //start at first
      Link* pCurrent = pFirst;
                                        //until end of list,
      while(pCurrent != NULL && key > pCurrent->dData)
         {                              //or key > current,
         pPrevious = pCurrent;
         pCurrent = pCurrent->pNext;    //go to next item
         }
      if(pPrevious==NULL)               //at beginning of list
```

continues

LISTING 10.1   CONTINUED

```
            pFirst = pNewLink;            //first --> newLink
         else                             //not at beginning
            pPrevious->pNext = pNewLink;  //old prev --> newLink
         pNewLink->pNext = pCurrent;      //newLink --> old current
         }  //end insert()
//-------------------------------------------------------------
   void remove()                          //remove first link
      {                                    //(assumes non-empty list)
      Link* pTemp = pFirst;                //save first
      pFirst = pFirst->pNext;              //new first --> next
      delete pTemp;                        //delete old first link
      }
//-------------------------------------------------------------
   void displayList()
      {
      cout << "List (first-->last): ";
      Link* pCurrent = pFirst;             //start at beginning of list
      while(pCurrent != NULL)              //until end of list,
         {
         pCurrent->displayLink();          //print data
         pCurrent = pCurrent->pNext;       //move to next link
         }
      cout << endl;
      }
   };  //end class SortedList
////////////////////////////////////////////////////////////////
int main()
   {
   SortedList theSortedList;     //create new list
   theSortedList.insert(20);     //insert 2 items
   theSortedList.insert(40);

   theSortedList.displayList();  //display list (20, 40)

   theSortedList.insert(10);     //insert 3 more items
   theSortedList.insert(30);
   theSortedList.insert(50);

   theSortedList.displayList();  //display list
                                 //   (10, 20, 30, 40, 50)
   theSortedList.remove();       //remove smallest item

   theSortedList.displayList();  //display list (20, 30, 40, 50)
   return 0;
   }  //end main()
```

ANALYSIS In main() we insert two items with key values 20 and 40. Then we insert three more items, with values 10, 30, and 50. These are inserted at the beginning of the list, in the middle, and at the end; showing that the insert() routine correctly handles these special cases. Finally we remove one item to show removal is always from the front of the list. After each change the list is displayed.

OUTPUT Here's the output from sortedList.cpp:

```
List (first-->last): 20 40
List (first-->last): 10 20 30 40 50
List (first-->last): 20 30 40 50
```

Efficiency of Sorted Linked Lists

Insertion and deletion of arbitrary items in the sorted linked list require O(N) comparisons (N/2 on the average) because the appropriate location must be found by stepping through the list. However, the minimum value can be found, or deleted, in O(1) time because it's at the beginning of the list. If an application frequently accesses the minimum item, and fast insertion isn't critical, a sorted linked list is an effective choice.

Next we'll look at an application for sorted lists.

List Insertion Sort

A sorted list can be used as a fairly efficient sorting mechanism. For example, assume you have an array of unsorted data items. If you take the items from the array and insert them one by one into the sorted list, they'll be placed in sorted order automatically. If you then remove them from the list and put them back in the array, the array will be sorted.

It turns out this is substantially more efficient than the more usual insertion sort within an array, described in Hour 5, "The Insertion Sort." This is because fewer copies are necessary. It's still an $O(N^2)$ process because inserting each item into the sorted list involves comparing a new item with an average of half the items already in the list, and there are N items to insert, resulting in about $N^2/4$ comparisons. However, each item is copied only twice: once from the array to the list, and once from the list to the array. N×2 copies compares favorably with the insertion sort within an array, where there are about N^2 copies.

Listing 10.2 shows the listInsertionSort.cpp program, which starts with an array of unsorted items of type link, inserts them into a sorted list (using a constructor), and then removes them and places them back into the array.

LISTING 10.2   THE `listInsertionSort.cpp` PROGRAM

```cpp
//listInsertionSort.cpp
//demonstrates sorted list used for sorting
#include <iostream>
#include <cstdlib>                  //for random numbers
#include <ctime>                    //for random seed
using namespace std;
//////////////////////////////////////////////////////////////
class Link
    {
    public:
        double dData;               //data item
        Link* pNext;                //next link in list
//--------------------------------------------------------------
    Link(double dd) : dData(dd), pNext(NULL)    //constructor
        {  }
//--------------------------------------------------------------
    };  //end class Link
//////////////////////////////////////////////////////////////
class SortedList
    {
    private:
        Link* pFirst;               //ptr to first item on list
    public:
//--------------------------------------------------------------
        SortedList() : pFirst(NULL)  //constructor (no args)
            {  }                     //initialize list
//--------------------------------------------------------------
                                     //constructor
    SortedList(Link** linkArr, int length) : pFirst(NULL)
        {                            //(initialized with array)
        for(int j=0; j<length; j++)  //copy array
            insert( linkArr[j] );    //to list
        }
//--------------------------------------------------------------
    void insert(Link* pArg)          //insert (in order)
        {
        Link* pPrevious = NULL;       //start at first
        Link* pCurrent = pFirst;
                                      //until end of list,
        while(pCurrent != NULL && pArg->dData > pCurrent->dData)
            {                         //or key > current,
            pPrevious = pCurrent;
            pCurrent = pCurrent->pNext; //go to next item
            }
        if(pPrevious==NULL)           //at beginning of list
            pFirst = pArg;            //first --> k
```

```
      else                          //not at beginning
         pPrevious->pNext = pArg;   //old prev --> k
      pArg->pNext = pCurrent;       //k --> old currnt
      } //end insert()
//--------------------------------------------------------------
   Link* remove()                   //return & delete first link
      {                             //(assumes non-empty list)
      Link* pTemp = pFirst;         //save first
      pFirst = pFirst->pNext;       //delete first
      return pTemp;                 //return value
      }
//--------------------------------------------------------------
   }; //end class SortedList
//////////////////////////////////////////////////////////////
int main()
   {
   int j;
   time_t aTime;                    //seed random numbers
   srand(static_cast<unsigned>(time(&aTime)) );
   const int size = 10;             //array size

   Link* linkArray[size];           //array of ptrs to links

   for(j=0; j<size; j++)            //fill with ptrs to links
      {
      int n = rand() % 99;          //random number (0 to 99)
      Link* pNewLink = new Link(n); //make link
      linkArray[j] = pNewLink;      //put ptr to link in array
      }

   cout << "Unsorted array: ";      //display array contents
   for(j=0; j<size; j++)
      cout << linkArray[j]->dData << " ";
   cout << endl;
                                    //create new list
   SortedList theSortedList(linkArray, size); //initialized
                                    //with array
   for(j=0; j<size; j++)            //links from list to array
      linkArray[j] = theSortedList.remove();

   cout << "Sorted Array: ";        //display array contents
   for(j=0; j<size; j++)
      cout << linkArray[j]->dData << " ";
   cout << endl;

   for(j=0; j<size; j++)            //delete individual links
      delete linkArray[j];
   return 0;
   } //end main()
```

10

OUTPUT This program displays the values in the array before the sorting operation, and again afterward. Here's some sample output:

```
Unsorted array: 59 69 41 56 84 15 86 81 37 35
Sorted array:   15 35 37 41 56 59 69 81 84 86
```

The output will be different each time because the initial values are generated randomly.

ANALYSIS A new constructor for `SortedList` takes an array of `Link` objects as an argument, and inserts the entire contents of this array into the newly created list. This helps make things easier for the client (the `main()` routine) because the array is copied automatically when the list is created.

We've also made a change to the `insert()` routine in this program. It now accepts a `Link` object as an argument, rather than a `double`. We do this so we can store `Link` objects in the array and insert them directly into the list. In the `sortedList.cpp` program, it was more convenient to have the `insert()` routine create each `Link` object, using the `double` value passed as an argument.

The downside of the list insertion sort, compared with an array-based insertion sort, is that it takes somewhat more than twice as much memory: The array and linked list must be in memory at the same time. However, if you have a sorted linked list class handy, the list insertion sort is a convenient way to sort arrays that aren't too large.

We've examined one specialized kind of linked list, the sorted list. Now let's look at another, the doubly linked list.

Doubly Linked Lists

In a doubly linked list, each link contains a pointer to the previous link as well as to the next link. (Don't confuse this with a double-ended list, where the links are the same as a normal singly linked list but the list maintains a pointer to the end of the list.) Why do we need this added pointer in each link?

The Problem with Singly Linked Lists

A potential problem with ordinary singly linked lists is that it's difficult to traverse backward along the list. Consider the following statement:

```
pCurrent = pCurrent->pNext;
```

This statement causes the program to step to the next link, but in a singly linked list there's no corresponding way to step to the previous link. Depending on the application, this could pose problems.

For example, imagine a text editor in which a linked list is used to store the text. Each text line on the screen is stored as a string object embedded in a link. When the editor's user moves the cursor downward on the screen, the program steps to the next link to manipulate or display the new line. But what happens if the user moves the cursor upward? In an ordinary linked list, you'd need to return pCurrent (or its equivalent) to the start of the list and then step all the way down again to the new current link. This isn't very efficient. You want to make a single step upward.

Implementing a Doubly Linked List

The doubly linked list provides the capability to traverse backward as well as forward through the list. The secret is that each link has two pointers to other links instead of one. The first pointer is to the next link, as in ordinary lists. The second is to the previous link. This is shown in Figure 10.3.

10

FIGURE 10.3

A doubly linked list.

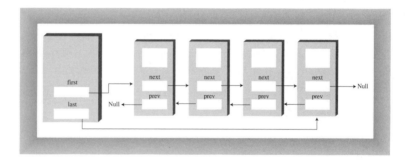

The beginning of the specification for the Link class in a doubly linked list looks like this:

```
class Link
   {
   public:
   double dData;       //data item
   Link* pNext;        //next link in list
   Link* pPrevious;    //previous link in list
   };
```

Now we have a pointer, pPrevious, to the previous link as well as to the next link.

The downside of doubly linked lists is that every time you insert or delete a link you must deal with four links instead of two: two attachments to the previous link and two attachments to the following one. Also, of course, each link is a little bigger because of the extra pointer.

A doubly linked list doesn't necessarily need to be a double-ended list (including a pointer to the last element on the list as well as the first) but doing so is useful, so we'll include it in our example.

We'll show the complete listing for the doublyLinked.cpp program soon, but first let's examine some of the member functions in its doublyLinkedList class.

Displaying the List

Two display member functions demonstrate traversal of a doubly linked list. The displayForward() member function is the same as the displayList() member function we've seen in ordinary linked lists. The displayBackward() member function is similar, but starts at the last element in the list and proceeds toward the start of the list, going to each element's pPrevious data member. This code fragment shows how this works:

```
Link* pCurrent = pLast;            //start at end
while(pCurrent != NULL)            //until start of list,
   pCurrent = pCurrent->pPrevious; //move to previous link
```

Incidentally, some people take the view that because you can go either way equally easily on a doubly linked list, there is no preferred order and therefore terms like previous and next are inappropriate. If you prefer, you can substitute order-neutral terms such as left and right.

Inserting New Links

We've included several insertion routines in the DoublyLinkedList class. The insertFirst() member function inserts at the beginning of the list, insertLast() inserts at the end, and insertAfter() inserts following an element with a specified key.

Unless the list is empty, the insertFirst() routine changes the pPrevious data member in the old pFirst link to point to the new link, and changes the pNext data member in the new link to point to the old pFirst link. Finally it sets pFirst to point to the new link. This is shown in Figure 10.4.

If the list is empty, the pLast data member must be changed instead of the pFirst->pPrevious data member. Here's the code:

```
void insertFirst(double dd)        //insert at front of list
   {
   Link* pNewLink = new Link(dd);  //make new link

   if( isEmpty() )                 //if empty list,
      pLast = pNewLink;            //newLink <-- last
   else
      pFirst->pPrevious = pNewLink; //newLink <-- old first
```

```
    pNewLink->pNext = pFirst;      //newLink --> old first
    pFirst = pNewLink;             //first --> newLink
    }
```

FIGURE 10.4

*Insertion at the
beginning.*

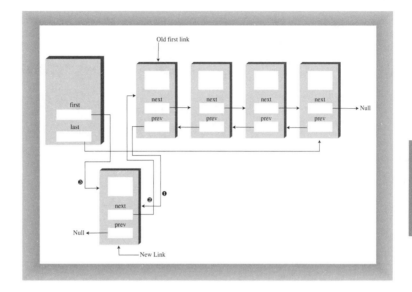

The insertLast() member function is the same process applied to the end of the list;
it's a mirror image of insertFirst().

The insertAfter() member function inserts a new link following the link with a specified key value. It's a bit more complicated because four connections must be made. First
the link with the specified key value must be found. This is handled the same way as the
find() routine in the linkedList2 program in Hour 8, "Linked Lists." Then, assuming
we're not at the end of the list, two connections must be made between the new link and
the next link, and two more between pCurrent and the new link. This is shown in Figure 10.5.

If the new link will be inserted at the end of the list, its pNext data member must point to
NULL, and pLast must point to the new link. Here's the insertAfter() code that deals
with the links:

```
if(pCurrent==pLast)            //if last link,
    {
    pNewLink->pNext = NULL;    //newLink --> null
    pLast = pNewLink;          //newLink <-- last
    }
else                           //not last link,
```

```
{                                      //newLink --> old next
pNewLink->pNext = pCurrent->pNext;
                                       //newLink <-- old next
pCurrent->pNext->pPrevious = pNewLink;
}
pNewLink->pPrevious = pCurrent;  //old current <-- newLink
pCurrent->pNext = pNewLink;      //old current --> newLink
```

FIGURE 10.5

Insertion at an arbi-trary location.

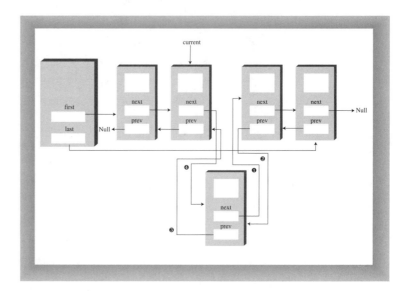

Perhaps you're unfamiliar with the use of two -> operators in the same expression. It's a natural extension of a single -> operator. The following expression means the pPrevious data member of the link referred to by the pNext data member in the link pCurrent:

```
pCurrent->pNext->pPrevious
```

Deleting Links

There are three deletion routines: removeFirst(), removeLast(), and removeKey(). The first two are fairly straightforward. In removeKey(), the key being deleted is pCurrent. Assuming the link to be deleted is neither the first nor the last one in the list, the pNext data member of pCurrent->pPrevious (the link before the one being deleted) is set to point to pCurrent->pNext (the link following the one being deleted), and the pPrevious data member of pCurrent->pNext is set to point to pCurrent->pPrevious. This disconnects the current link from the list. Figure 10.6 shows how this disconnection looks, and the following two statements carry it out:

```
pCurrent->pPrevious->pNext = pCurrent->pNext;
pCurrent->pNext->pPrevious = pCurrent.pPrevious;
```

FIGURE 10.6

Deleting an arbitrary link.

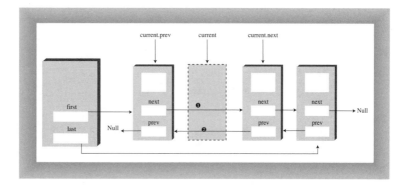

The situations in which the link to be deleted is either the first or last in the list are special cases, because pFirst or pLast must be set to point to the next or the previous link. Here's the code from removeKey() for dealing with link connections:

```
if(pCurrent==pFirst)              //found it; first item?
   pFirst = pCurrent->pNext;      //first --> old next
else                             //not first
                                 //old previous --> old next
   pCurrent->pPrevious->pNext = pCurrent->pNext;

if(pCurrent==pLast)               //last item?
   pLast = pCurrent->pPrevious;   //old previous <-- last
else                             //not last
                                 //old previous <-- old next
   pCurrent->pNext->pPrevious = pCurrent->pPrevious;
```

C++ Code for a Doubly Linked List

Listing 10.3 shows the complete doublyLinked.cpp program, which includes all the routines just discussed.

INPUT   **LISTING 10.3**   THE doublyLinked.cpp PROGRAM

```
//doublyLinked.cpp
//demonstrates doubly-linked list
#include <iostream>
using namespace std;
///////////////////////////////////////////////////////////////
class Link
   {
   public:
      double dData;                   //data item
      Link* pNext;                    //next link in list
```

continues

LISTING 10.3   CONTINUED

```cpp
      Link* pPrevious;               //previous link in list
   public:
//------------------------------------------------------------
   Link(double dd) :                 //constructor
            dData(dd), pNext(NULL), pPrevious(NULL)
      {  }
//------------------------------------------------------------
   void displayLink()                //display this link
      { cout << dData << " "; }
//------------------------------------------------------------
   }; //end class Link
////////////////////////////////////////////////////////////////
class DoublyLinkedList
   {
   private:
      Link* pFirst;                  //pointer to first item
      Link* pLast;                   //pointer to last item
   public:
//------------------------------------------------------------
   DoublyLinkedList() :              //constructor
            pFirst(NULL), pLast(NULL)
      {  }
//------------------------------------------------------------
   ~DoublyLinkedList()               //destructor (deletes links)
      {
      Link* pCurrent = pFirst;       //start at beginning of list
      while(pCurrent != NULL)        //until end of list,
         {
         Link* pOldCur = pCurrent;   //save current link
         pCurrent = pCurrent->pNext; //move to next link
         delete pOldCur;             //delete old current
         }
      }
//------------------------------------------------------------
   bool isEmpty()                    //true if no links
      { return pFirst==NULL; }
//------------------------------------------------------------
   void insertFirst(double dd)       //insert at front of list
      {
      Link* pNewLink = new Link(dd); //make new link

      if( isEmpty() )                //if empty list,
         pLast = pNewLink;           //newLink <-- last
      else
         pFirst->pPrevious = pNewLink; //newLink <-- old first
      pNewLink->pNext = pFirst;      //newLink --> old first
      pFirst = pNewLink;             //first --> newLink
      }
```

```
//--------------------------------------------------------------
   void insertLast(double dd)          //insert at end of list
      {
      Link* pNewLink = new Link(dd);   //make new link
      if( isEmpty() )                  //if empty list,
         pFirst = pNewLink;            //first --> newLink
      else
         {
         pLast->pNext = pNewLink;      //old last --> newLink
         pNewLink->pPrevious = pLast;  //old last <-- newLink
         }
      pLast = pNewLink;                //newLink <-- last
      }
//--------------------------------------------------------------
   void removeFirst()                  //remove first link
      {                                //(assumes non-empty list)
      Link* pTemp = pFirst;
      if(pFirst->pNext == NULL)        //if only one item
         pLast = NULL;                 //null <-- last
      else
         pFirst->pNext->pPrevious = NULL;  //null <-- old next
      pFirst = pFirst->pNext;          //first --> old next
      delete pTemp;                    //delete old first
      }
//--------------------------------------------------------------
   void removeLast()                   //remove last link
      {                                //(assumes non-empty list)
      Link* pTemp = pLast;
      if(pFirst->pNext == NULL)        //if only one item
         pFirst = NULL;                //first --> null
      else
         pLast->pPrevious->pNext = NULL;  //old previous --> null
      pLast = pLast->pPrevious;        //old previous <-- last
      delete pTemp;                    //delete old last
      }
//--------------------------------------------------------------
                                       //insert dd just after key
   bool insertAfter(double key, double dd)
      {                                //(assumes non-empty list)
      Link* pCurrent = pFirst;         //start at beginning
      while(pCurrent->dData != key)    //until match is found,
         {
         pCurrent = pCurrent->pNext;   //move to next link
         if(pCurrent == NULL)
            return false;              //didn't find it
         }
      Link* pNewLink = new Link(dd);   //make new link

      if(pCurrent==pLast)              //if last link,
         {
```

continues

LISTING 10.3 CONTINUED

```
            pNewLink->pNext = NULL;      //newLink --> null
            pLast = pNewLink;            //newLink <-- last
            }
        else                             //not last link,
            {                            //newLink --> old next
            pNewLink->pNext = pCurrent->pNext;
                                         //newLink <-- old next
            pCurrent->pNext->pPrevious = pNewLink;
            }
        pNewLink->pPrevious = pCurrent; //old current <-- newLink
        pCurrent->pNext = pNewLink;     //old current --> newLink
        return true;                     //found it, did insertion
        }
//-----------------------------------------------------------------
    bool removeKey(double key)           //remove item w/ given key
        {                                //(assumes non-empty list)
        Link* pCurrent = pFirst;         //start at beginning
        while(pCurrent->dData != key)    //until match is found,
            {
            pCurrent = pCurrent->pNext; //move to next link
            if(pCurrent == NULL)
                return false;            //didn't find it
            }
        if(pCurrent==pFirst)             //found it; first item?
            pFirst = pCurrent->pNext;    //first --> old next
        else                             //not first
                                         //old previous --> old next
            pCurrent->pPrevious->pNext = pCurrent->pNext;

        if(pCurrent==pLast)              //last item?
            pLast = pCurrent->pPrevious;  //old previous <-- last
        else                             //not last
                                         //old previous <-- old next
            pCurrent->pNext->pPrevious = pCurrent->pPrevious;
        delete pCurrent;                 //delete item
        return true;                     //successful deletion
        }
//-----------------------------------------------------------------
    void displayForward()
        {
        cout << "List (first-->last): ";
        Link* pCurrent = pFirst;         //start at beginning
        while(pCurrent != NULL)          //until end of list,
            {
            pCurrent->displayLink();     //display data
            pCurrent = pCurrent->pNext; //move to next link
            }
        cout << endl;
```

```
        }
//------------------------------------------------------------
    void displayBackward()
        {
        cout << "List (last-->first): ";
        Link* pCurrent = pLast;          //start at end
        while(pCurrent != NULL)          //until start of list,
            {
            pCurrent->displayLink();     //display data
            pCurrent = pCurrent->pPrevious; //go to previous link
            }
        cout << endl;
        }
//------------------------------------------------------------
    };  //end class DoublyLinkedList
////////////////////////////////////////////////////////////////
int main()
        {
        DoublyLinkedList theList;        //make a new list

        theList.insertFirst(22);         //insert at front
        theList.insertFirst(44);
        theList.insertFirst(66);

        theList.insertLast(11);          //insert at rear
        theList.insertLast(33);
        theList.insertLast(55);

        theList.displayForward();        //display list forward
        theList.displayBackward();       //display list backward

        cout << "Deleting first, last, and 11" << endl;
        theList.removeFirst();           //remove first item
        theList.removeLast();            //remove last item
        theList.removeKey(11);           //remove item with key 11

        theList.displayForward();        //display list forward

        cout << "Inserting 77 after 22, and 88 after 33" << endl;
        theList.insertAfter(22, 77);  //insert 77 after 22
        theList.insertAfter(33, 88);  //insert 88 after 33

        theList.displayForward();        //display list forward
        return 0;
        }   //end main()
```

ANALYSIS In main() we insert some items at the beginning of the list and at the end, display the items going both forward and backward, delete the first and last items and the item with key 11, display the list again (forward only), insert two items using the `insertAfter()` member function, and display the list again. Here's the output:

OUTPUT

```
List (first-->last): 66 44 22 11 33 55
List (last-->first): 55 33 11 22 44 66
Deleting first, last, and 11
List (first-->last): 44 22 33
Inserting 77 after 22, and 88 after 33
List (first-->last): 44 22 77 33 88
```

The deletion member functions and the `insertAfter()` member function assume that the list isn't empty. Although for simplicity we don't show it in `main()`, `isEmpty()` should be used to verify that there's something in the list before attempting such insertions and deletions.

A doubly linked list can be used as the basis for a deque, mentioned in Hour 7, "Queues and Priority Queues." In a deque you can insert and delete at either end, and the doubly linked list provides this capability.

Summary

In this hour, you learned the following:

- In a sorted linked list, the links are arranged in order of ascending (or sometimes descending) key value.

- Insertion in a sorted list takes O(N) time because the correct insertion point must be found. Deletion of the smallest link takes O(1) time.

- A sorted list is the basis for the list insertion sort.

- The list insertion sort is faster than the ordinary insertion sort, but requires twice as much memory space.

- In a doubly linked list, each link contains a pointer to the previous link as well as the next link.

- A doubly linked list permits backward traversal as well as deletion from the end of the list.

Q&A

Q **When would I use a sorted list?**

A When you want quick access to the item with the smallest (or largest) key. This is what a priority queue does. The advantage of a sorted-list implementation over a sorted-array implementation is that you don't need to move any items to insert a new one; just rearrange some pointers. That makes it more efficient, although harder to program.

Q **When would I use the list insertion sort?**

A In specialized situations. If you've already created a sorted linked list, you've done most of the sort already. To finish the sort, just copy the list into an array. This takes O(N) time, so it's very fast.

Q **Are doubly linked lists important?**

A The list in many class libraries is a doubly linked list. This is true of the `list` class in the C++ STL. The doubly linked list is far more versatile than a singly linked list, and only slightly less efficient.

10

Workshop

The Workshop helps you solidify what you learned in this hour. See Appendix A for quiz answers.

Quiz

1. What is the advantage of a sorted list over an unsorted list?
2. What is the advantage of a sorted list over a sorted array?
3. True or false: It takes O(N) time to insert an item in a sorted list.
4. How does the insertion sort work?
5. Besides its use in the insertion sort, what's another application for the sorted list?
6. What is the advantage of a doubly linked list over a singly linked list?
7. What is the main disadvantage of a doubly linked list?

Exercise

Write a C++ program that uses a sorted list to implement a priority queue. You can start with the `priorityQ.cpp` program from Hour 7, "Queues and Priority Queues," and add the `sortedList` class from the `sortedList.cpp` program in this hour. (For extra credit, write a program that uses a doubly linked list to implement a deque.)

PART III

Recursion and Quicksort

Hour

Hour 11

Recursion

Recursion is a programming technique in which a function (or member function) calls itself. This might sound like a strange thing to do, or even a catastrophic mistake. Recursion is, however, one of the most interesting, and surprisingly effective, techniques in programming. Like pulling yourself up by your bootstraps (you do have bootstraps, don't you?), recursion seems incredible when you first encounter it. However, it not only works, it also provides a unique conceptual framework for solving many problems. In this hour we will

- Introduce recursion
- Show an example using triangular numbers
- Show an example using anagrams
- Show an example using a binary search
- Discuss the relationship between stacks and recursion

Demonstrating Recursion with Triangular Numbers

As an example of recursion, let's examine two approaches to an ancient problem. It's said that the Pythagoreans, a band of mathematicians in ancient Greece who worked under Pythagoras (of Pythagorean theorem fame), felt a mystical connection with the series of numbers 1, 3, 6, 10, 15, 21, … (where the … means the series continues indefinitely). Can you find the next member of this series?

The nth term in the series is obtained by adding n to the previous term. Thus the second term is found by adding 2 to the first term (which is 1), giving 3. The third term is 3 added to the second term (which is 3) giving 6, and so on. The numbers in this series are called *triangular numbers* because they can be visualized as a triangular arrangement of objects, shown as little squares in Figure 11.1.

FIGURE 11.1

The triangular numbers.

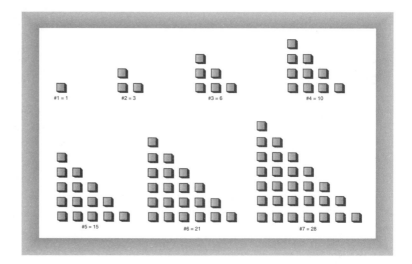

Finding the *n*th Term Using a Loop

Suppose you wanted to find the value of some arbitrary nth term in the series; say the fourth term (whose value is 10). How would you calculate it? Looking at Figure 11.2, you might decide that the value of any term could be obtained by adding up all the vertical columns of squares.

In the fourth term, the first column has four little squares, the second column has three, and so on. Adding 4+3+2+1 gives 10.

FIGURE 11.2

Triangular number as columns.

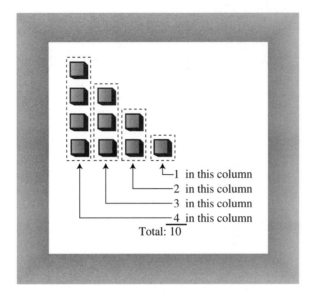

-1 in this column
-2 in this column
-3 in this column
-4 in this column
Total: 10

The following `triangle()` function uses this column-based technique to find a triangular number. It sums all the columns, from a height of n to a height of 1.

```
int triangle(int n)
   {
   int total = 0;

   while(n > 0)              // until n is 1
      {
      total = total + n;   // add n (column height) to total
      --n;                  // decrement column height
      }
   return total;
   }
```

The function cycles around the loop n times, adding n to `total` the first time, n-1 the second time, and so on down to 1, quitting the loop when n becomes 0.

Finding the *n*th Term Using Recursion

The loop approach might seem straightforward, but there's another way to look at this problem. The value of the *n*th term can be thought of as the sum of only two things, instead of a whole series. These are

1. The first (tallest) column, which has the value n.

2. The sum of all the remaining columns.

This is shown in Figure 11.3.

11

FIGURE **11.3**

Triangular number as column plus triangle.

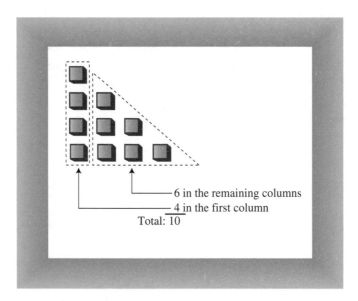

6 in the remaining columns
4 in the first column
Total: 10

Finding the Remaining Columns

If we knew about a function that found the sum of all the remaining columns, we could write our `triangle()` member function, which returns the value of the *n*th triangular number, like this:

```
int triangle(int n)
   {
   return( n + sumRemainingColumns(n) );   // (incomplete version)
   }
```

But what have we gained here? It looks like it's just as hard to write the `sumRemainingColumns()` function as to write the `triangle()` function in the first place.

However, notice in Figure 11.3 that the sum of all the remaining columns for term *n* is the same as the sum of all the columns for term *n*–1. Thus, if we knew about a function that summed all the columns for term n, we could call it with an argument of n-1 to find the sum of all the *remaining* columns for term n:

```
int triangle(int n)
   {
   return( n + sumAllColumns(n-1) );   // (incomplete version)
   }
```

But when you think about it, the `sumAllColumns()` function is doing exactly the same thing the `triangle()` function is. That is, summing all the columns for some number *n* passed as an argument. So why not use the `triangle()` function itself, instead of some other function? That would look like this:

```
int triangle(int n)
   {
   return( n + triangle(n-1) );   // (incomplete version)
   }
```

It might seem amazing that a function can call itself, but why shouldn't it be able to? A function call is (among other things) a transfer of control to the start of the function. This transfer of control can take place from within the function as well as from outside.

Passing the Buck

All this might seem like passing the buck. Someone tells me to find the ninth triangular number. I know this is 9 plus the eighth triangular number, so I call Harry and ask him to find the eighth triangular number. When I hear back from him, I'll add 9 to whatever he tells me, and that will be the answer.

Harry knows the eighth triangular number is 8 plus the seventh triangular number, so he calls Sally and asks her to find the seventh triangular number. This process continues with each person passing the buck to another one.

Where does this buck-passing end? Someone at some point must be able to figure out an answer that doesn't involve asking another person to help him. If this didn't happen, there would be an infinite chain of people asking other people questions—a sort of arithmetic Ponzi scheme that would never end. In the case of `triangle()`, this would mean the function calling itself over and over in an infinite series that would hang the program.

The Buck Stops Here

To prevent an infinite regress, the person who is asked to find the first triangular number of the series, when *n* is 1, must know, without asking anyone else, that the answer is 1. There are no smaller numbers to ask anyone about, there's nothing left to add to anything else, so the buck stops there. We can express this by adding a condition to the `trian-gle()` function:

```
int triangle(int n)
   {
   if(n==1)
      return 1;
   else
      return( n + triangle(n-1) );
   }
```

NEW TERM   The condition that leads to a recursive function returning without making another recursive call is referred to as the *base case*. It's critical that every recursive function has a base case to prevent infinite recursion and the consequent demise of the program.

The `triangle.cpp` Program

Does recursion actually work? If you run the `triangle.cpp` program, you'll see that it does. This program uses recursion to calculate triangular numbers. Enter a value for the term number, n, and the program will display the value of the corresponding triangular number. Listing 11.1 shows the `triangle.cpp` program.

INPUT   **LISTING 11.1** THE `triangle.cpp` PROGRAM

```cpp
// triangle.cpp
// evaluates triangular numbers
#include <iostream>
using namespace std;
//-----------------------------------------------------------
int main()
   {
   int theNumber;
   int triangle(int);

   cout << "Enter a number: ";
   cin >> theNumber;
   int theAnswer = triangle(theNumber);
   cout << "Triangle=" << theAnswer << endl;
   return 0;
   }  // end main()
//-----------------------------------------------------------
int triangle(int n)
   {
   if(n==1)
      return 1;
   else
      return  ( n + triangle(n-1) );
   }
```

ANALYSIS   The `main()` routine prompts the user for a value for n, calls `triangle()`, and displays the return value. The `triangle()` function calls itself repeatedly to do all the work.

    Here's some sample output:

```
Enter a number: 1000
Triangle = 500500
```

If you're skeptical of the results returned from `triangle()`, you can check them by using the following formula:

nth triangular number = $(n^2+n)/2$

What the `triangle()` Function Is Really Doing

Let's modify the `triangle()` function to provide an insight into what's happening when it executes. We'll insert some output statements to keep track of the arguments and return values:

```
int triangle(int n)
   {
   cout << "Entering: n=" << n << endl;
   if(n==1)
      {
      cout << "Returning 1" << endl;
      return 1;
      }
   else
      {
      int temp = n + triangle(n-1);
      cout << "Returning " << temp << endl;
      return temp;
      }
   }
```

INPUT/ OUTPUT

Here's the interaction when this function is substituted for the earlier `triangle()` function and the user enters 5:

```
Enter a number: 5

Entering: n=5
Entering: n=4
Entering: n=3
Entering: n=2
Entering: n=1
Returning 1
Returning 3
Returning 6
Returning 10
Returning 15

Triangle = 15
```

ANALYSIS

Each time the `triangle()` function calls itself, its argument, which starts at 5, is reduced by 1. The function plunges down into itself again and again until its

11

argument is reduced to 1. Then it returns. This triggers an entire series of returns. The function rises back up, phoenix-like, out of the discarded versions of itself. Each time it returns, it adds the value of n it was called with to the return value from the function it called.

The return values replay the series of triangular numbers, until the answer is returned to main(). Figure 11.4 shows how each invocation of the triangle() function can be imagined as being "inside" the previous one.

FIGURE **11.4**

The recursive
triangle() *member*
function.

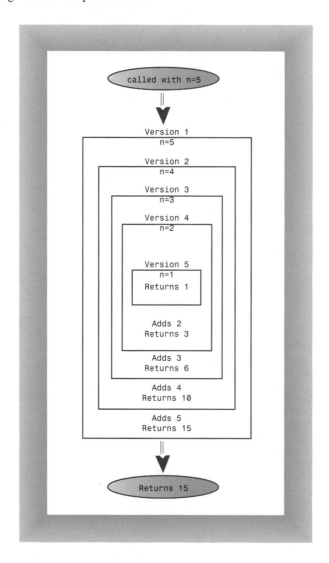

Notice that, just before the innermost version returns a 1, there are actually five different incarnations of triangle() in existence at the same time. The outer one was passed the argument 5; the inner one was passed the argument 1.

> We might note that factorials can also be calculated recursively. The factorial of an integer is the product of the integer multiplied by all the integers smaller than itself. Thus the factorial of 5 is 5*4*3*2*1, which is 120. The algorithm is much the same as for triangular numbers, except that the function returns n*factorial(n-1) instead of n+triangle(n-1).

We've seen an example of recursion at work in calculating triangular numbers. Now let's step back and take a broader view of recursion.

Characteristics of Recursive Functions

Although it's short, the triangle() function possesses the key features common to all recursive routines:

- It calls itself.
- When it calls itself, it does so to solve a smaller problem.
- There's some version of the problem that is simple enough that the routine can solve it, and return, without calling itself.

In each successive call of a recursive function to itself, the argument becomes smaller (or perhaps a range described by multiple arguments becomes smaller), reflecting the fact that the problem has become "smaller" or easier. When the argument or range reaches a certain minimum size, a condition is triggered (the base case) and the function returns without calling itself.

Is Recursion Efficient?

Calling a function involves certain overhead. Control must be transferred from the location of the call to the beginning of the function. In addition, the arguments to the function, and the address to which the function should return, must be pushed onto an internal stack so that the function can access the argument values and know where to return.

In the case of the triangle() function, it's probable that, as a result of this overhead, the while loop approach executes more quickly than the recursive approach. The penalty

11

might not be significant, but if there are a large number of function calls as a result of a recursive function, it might be desirable to eliminate the recursion. We'll talk about this more at the end of this hour in the section "Recursion and Stacks."

Another inefficiency is that memory is used to store all the intermediate arguments and return values on the system's internal stack. This might cause problems if there is a large amount of data, leading to stack overflow.

Recursion is usually used because it simplifies a problem conceptually, not because it's inherently more efficient.

Mathematical Induction

Recursion is the programming equivalent of mathematical induction. Mathematical induction is a way of defining something in terms of itself. (The term is also used to describe a related approach to proving theorems.) Using induction, we could define the triangular numbers mathematically by saying

$tri(n) = 1$ (if $n = 1$)

$tri(n) = n + tri(n–1)$ (if $n > 1$)

Defining something in terms of itself might seem circular, but in fact it's perfectly valid (provided there's a base case).

Next, to clarify recursion further, let's look at another program example where recursion is helpful. This one is less mathematical than the triangular numbers example.

Demonstrating Recursion with Anagrams

Here's a situation where recursion provides a neat solution to a problem. Suppose you want to list all the anagrams of a specified word, that is, all possible letter-combinations (whether they make a real English word or not) that can be made from the letters of the original word. We'll call this *anagramming* a word. Anagramming cat, for example, would produce

- cat
- cta
- atc
- act
- tca
- tac

Try anagramming some words yourself. You'll find that the number of possibilities is the factorial of the number of letters. For 3 letters there are 6 possible words, for 4 letters there are 24 words, for 5 letters, 120 words, and so on. (This assumes that all letters are distinct; if there are multiple instances of the same letter, there will be fewer possible words.)

Conceptualizing the Anagram Process

How would you write a program to anagram a word? Here's one approach. Assume the word has *n* letters.

1. Anagram the rightmost *n*–1 letters.

2. Rotate all *n* letters.

3. Repeat these steps *n* times.

NEW TERM To *rotate* the word means to shift all the letters one position left, except for the leftmost letter, which "rotates" back to the right, as shown in Figure 11.5.

FIGURE 11.5

Rotating a word.

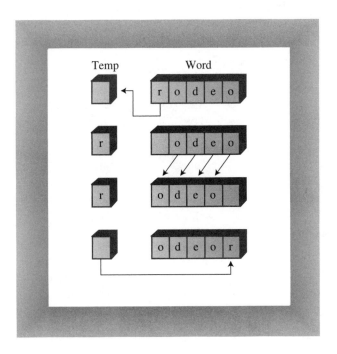

Rotating the word *n* times gives each letter a chance to begin the word. While the selected letter occupies this first position, all the other letters are then anagrammed (arranged in every possible position). For cat, which has only three letters, rotating the remaining two letters simply switches them. The sequence is shown in Table 11.1.

TABLE 11.1   ANAGRAMMING THE WORD *CAT*

Word	Display Word?	First Letter	Remaining Letters	Action
cat	Yes	c	at	Rotate at
cta	Yes	c	ta	Rotate ta
cat	No	c	at	Rotate cat
atc	Yes	a	tc	Rotate tc
act	Yes	a	ct	Rotate ct
atc	No	a	tc	Rotate atc
tca	Yes	t	ca	Rotate ca
tac	Yes	t	ac	Rotate ac
tca	No	t	ca	Rotate tca
cat	No	c	at	Done

Notice that we must rotate back to the starting point with two letters before performing a 3-letter rotation. This leads to sequences like cat, cta, cat. The redundant combinations aren't displayed.

How do we anagram the rightmost *n*–1 letters? By calling ourselves. The recursive ana-gram function takes the size of the word to be anagrammed as its only parameter. This word is understood to be the rightmost *n* letters of the complete word. Each time ana-gram calls itself, it does so with a word one letter smaller than before, as shown in Figure 11.6.

The base case occurs when the size of the word to be anagrammed is only one letter. There's no way to rearrange one letter, so the function returns immediately. Otherwise, it anagrams all but the first letter of the word it was given and then rotates the entire word. These two actions are performed *n* times, where *n* is the size of the word.

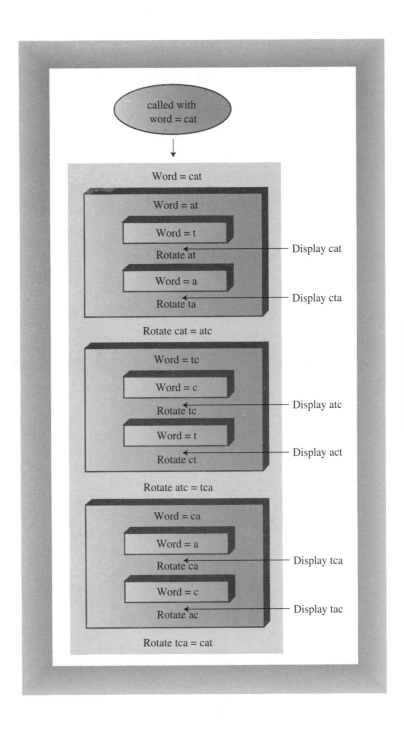

FIGURE 11.6

The recursive `anagram()` *member function.*

Implementing Anagramming in C++

Here's the recursive routine `anagram()`, which carries out the operations we've been discussing:

```
void word::anagram(int newSize)
    {
    if(newSize == 1)                    //if too small,
        return;                         //go no further

    for(int j=0; j<newSize; j++)        //for each position,
        {
        anagram(newSize-1);             //anagram remaining
        if(newSize==2)                  //if innermost,
            displayWord();              //   display it
        rotate(newSize);                //rotate word
        }
    }
```

Each time the `anagram()` function calls itself, the size of the word is one letter smaller, and the starting position is one cell further to the right, as shown in Figure 11.7.

FIGURE 11.7

Smaller and smaller words.

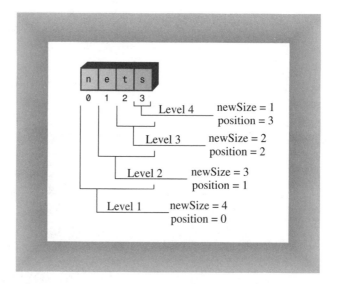

Listing 11.2 shows the complete `anagram.cpp` program. We use a class to represent the word to be anagrammed. Member functions of the class allow the word to be displayed, anagrammed, and rotated. The `main()` routine gets a word from the user, creates a word object with this word as an argument to the constructor, and calls the `anagram()` member function to anagram the word.

```
//anagram.cpp
//creates anagrams
#include <iostream>
#include <string>
using namespace std;
//////////////////////////////////////////////////////////////
class word
   {
   private:
      int size;                         //length of input word
      int count;                        //numbers in display
      string workStr;                   //workspace
      void rotate(int);                 //rotate part of workStr
      void displayWord();               //display workStr
   public:
      word(string);                     //constructor
      void anagram(int);                //anagram ourselves
   };
//-----------------------------------------------------------
                                        //constructor
word::word(string inpStr) : workStr(inpStr), count(0)
   {                                    //initialize workStr
   size = inpStr.length();              //number of characters
   }
//-----------------------------------------------------------
void word::anagram(int newSize)
   {
   if(newSize == 1)                     //if too small,
      return;                           //go no further

   for(int j=0; j<newSize; j++)         //for each position,
      {
      anagram(newSize-1);               //anagram remaining
      if(newSize==2)                    //if innermost,
         displayWord();                 //   display it
      rotate(newSize);                  //rotate word
      }
   }
//-----------------------------------------------------------
//rotate left all chars from position to end
void word::rotate(int newSize)
   {
   int j;
   int position = size - newSize;
   char temp = workStr[position];       //save first letter
   for(j=position+1; j<size; j++)       //shift others left
      workStr[j-1] = workStr[j];
```

continues

LISTING 11.2   CONTINUED

```
    workStr[j-1] = temp;                 //put first on right
    }
//-------------------------------------------------------------
void word::displayWord()
    {
    if(count < 99)                       //spaces before one-
       cout << " ";                      //or two-digit numbers
    if(count < 9)
       cout << " ";
    cout << ++count << " ";              //number
    cout << workStr << "    ";
    if(count%6 == 0)
       cout << endl;
    }
///////////////////////////////////////////////////////////////
int main()
    {
    string input;
    int length;

    cout << "Enter a word: ";            //get word
    cin >> input;
    length = input.length();             //get its length

    word theWord(input);                 //make a word object
    theWord.anagram(length);             //anagram it
    return 0;
    }   //end main()
```

ANALYSIS   The `rotate()` member function rotates the word one position left as described earlier. The `displayWord()` member function displays the entire word and also displays a count to make it easy to see how many words have been displayed.

Here's some sample interaction with the program:

```
Enter a word: cats
     1 cats      2 cast      3 ctsa      4 ctas      5 csat      6 csta
     7 atsc      8 atcs      9 asct     10 astc     11 acts     12 acst
    13 tsca     14 tsac     15 tcas     16 tcsa     17 tasc     18 tacs
    19 scat     20 scta     21 satc     22 sact     23 stca     24 stac
```

(Is it only coincidence that scat is an anagram of cats?) You can use the program to anagram 5-letter or even 6-letter words. However, because the factorial of 6 is 720, this might generate more words than you want to know about.

Let's move on now to an example where recursion helps out with a programming task.

Demonstrating Recursion in a Binary Search

Remember the binary search we discussed in Hour 3, "Ordered Arrays"? We wanted to find a given cell in an ordered array using the fewest number of comparisons. The solution was to divide the array in half, see which half the desired cell lay in, divide that half in half again, and so on. Here's what the original find() member function looked like:

```
int find(double searchKey)
    {
    int lowerBound = 0;
    int upperBound = nElems-1;
    int curIn;

    while(true)
        {
        curIn = (lowerBound + upperBound ) / 2;
        if(v[curIn]==searchKey)
            return curIn;              //found it
        else if(lowerBound > upperBound)
            return nElems;             //can't find it
        else                           //divide range
            {
            if(v[curIn] < searchKey)
                lowerBound = curIn + 1; //it's in upper half
            else
                upperBound = curIn - 1; //it's in lower half
            }  //end else divide range
        }  //end while
    }  //end find()
```

You might want to reread the section "Conducting a Binary Search with the find() Member Function" in Hour 3, which describes how this function works. Also, run the Ordered Workshop applet from that hour if you want to see a binary search in action.

Using Recursion to Replace the Loop

We can transform this loop-based function into a recursive function quite easily. In the loop-based approach, we change lowerBound or upperBound to specify a new range, and then cycle through the loop again. Each time through the loop we divide the range (roughly) in half.

In the recursive approach, instead of changing lowerBound or upperBound, we call the find function again with the new value of lowerBound or upperBound as arguments. The loop disappears, and its place is taken by the recursive calls. We call this new find function recFind(). Here's how it looks:

```
int recFind(double searchKey, int lowerBound, int upperBound)
    {
```

```
int curIn;

curIn = (lowerBound + upperBound ) / 2;
if(v[curIn]==searchKey)
   return curIn;                    //found it
else if(lowerBound > upperBound)
   return nElems;                   //can't find it
else                               //divide range
   {
   if(v[curIn] < searchKey)      //it's in upper half
      return recFind(searchKey, curIn+1, upperBound);
   else                           //it's in lower half
      return recFind(searchKey, lowerBound, curIn-1);
   } //end else divide range
} //end recFind()
```

The class user, represented by main(), might not know how many items are in the array when it calls find(), and in any case shouldn't be burdened with having to know what values of upperBound and lowerBound to set initially. Therefore we supply an intermediate public function, find(), which main() calls with only one argument: the value of the search key. The find() member function supplies the proper initial values of lowerBound and upperBound (0 and nElems-1) and then calls the private, recursive function recFind(). The find() member function looks like this:

```
public int find(double searchKey)
   {
   return recFind(searchKey, 0, nElems-1);
   }
```

Listing 11.3 shows the complete binarySearch.cpp program, which incorporates the recursive recFind() and find() routines.

INPUT   **LISTING 11.3**   THE binarySearch.cpp PROGRAM

```
//binarySearch.cpp
//demonstrates recursive binary search
#include <iostream>
#include <vector>
using namespace std;
/////////////////////////////////////////////////////////////////
class ordArray
   {
   private:
      vector<double> v;                //vector v
      int nElems;                      //number of data items
   public:
      //------------------------------------------------------------
      ordArray(int max)                //constructor
```

```
   {
   v.resize(max);                    //size the array
   nElems = 0;
   }
//------------------------------------------------------------
int getSize()                        //return # of elements
   { return nElems; }
//------------------------------------------------------------
int find(double searchKey)           //initial find()
   {
   return recFind(searchKey, 0, nElems-1);
   }
//------------------------------------------------------------
                                     //recursive find()
int recFind(double searchKey, int lowerBound, int upperBound)
   {
   int curIn;

   curIn = (lowerBound + upperBound ) / 2;
   if(v[curIn]==searchKey)
      return curIn;                  //found it
   else if(lowerBound > upperBound)
      return nElems;                 //can't find it
   else                             //divide range
      {
      if(v[curIn] < searchKey)      //it's in upper half
         return recFind(searchKey, curIn+1, upperBound);
      else                          //it's in lower half
         return recFind(searchKey, lowerBound, curIn-1);
      } //end else divide range
   } //end recFind()
//------------------------------------------------------------
void insert(double value)  //put element into array
   {
   int j;
   for(j=0; j<nElems; j++)           //find where it goes
      if(v[j] > value)               //(linear search)
         break;
   for(int k=nElems; k>j; k--)       //move bigger ones up
      v[k] = v[k-1];
   v[j] = value;                     //insert it
   nElems++;                         //increment size
   } //end insert()
//------------------------------------------------------------
void display()                       //displays array contents
   {
   for(int j=0; j<nElems; j++)           //for each element,
      cout << v[j] << " ";  //display it
   cout << endl;
```

continues

LISTING 11.3   CONTINUED

```
        }
//------------------------------------------------------------
    };  //end class ordArray
////////////////////////////////////////////////////////////////
int main()
        {
        int maxSize = 100;              //array size
        ordArray arr(maxSize);          //ordered array

        arr.insert(72);                 //insert items
        arr.insert(90);
        arr.insert(45);
        arr.insert(126);
        arr.insert(54);
        arr.insert(99);
        arr.insert(144);
        arr.insert(27);
        arr.insert(135);
        arr.insert(81);
        arr.insert(18);
        arr.insert(108);
        arr.insert(9);
        arr.insert(117);
        arr.insert(63);
        arr.insert(36);

        arr.display();                  //display array

        int searchKey = 27;             //search for item
        if( arr.find(searchKey) != arr.getSize() )
           cout << "Found " << searchKey << endl;
        else
           cout << "Can't find " << searchKey << endl;
        return 0;
        }   //end main()
```

ANALYSIS   In main() we insert 16 items into the array. The insert() member function arranges them in sorted order, and then they're displayed. Finally we use find() to try to find the item with a key value of 27.

OUTPUT   Here's some sample output:

```
9 18 27 36 45 54 63 72 81 90 99 108 117 126 135 144
Found 27
```

In binarySearch.cpp there are 16 items in an array. Figure 11.8 shows how the recFind() member function in this program calls itself over and over, each time with a smaller range than before. When the innermost version of the function finds the desired item, which has the key value 27, it returns with the index value of the item, which is 2 (as can be seen in the display of ordered data). This value is then returned from each version of recFind() in turn; finally find() returns it to the class user.

FIGURE 11.8

The recursive recFind() *member function.*

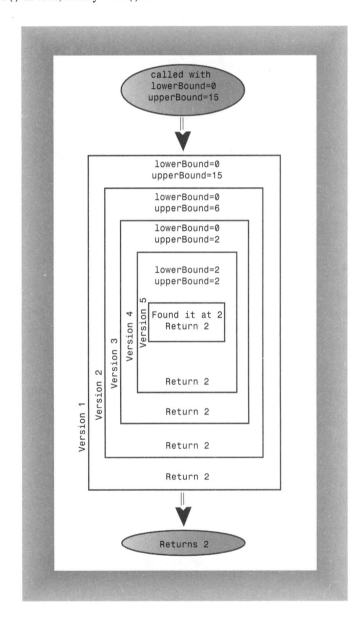

11

The recursive binary search has the same Big O efficiency as the nonrecursive version: O(logN). It is somewhat more elegant, but might be slightly slower.

Understanding Divide-and-Conquer Algorithms

NEW TERM The recursive binary search is an example of the *divide-and-conquer* approach. You divide the big problem into two smaller problems and solve each one separately. The solution to the smaller problems is the same: you divide each one into two even smaller problems and solve them. The process continues until you get to the base case, which can be solved easily, with no further division into halves.

The divide-and-conquer approach is commonly used with recursion, although, as we saw in the binary search in Hour 3, you can also use a nonrecursive approach.

A divide-and-conquer approach usually involves a function that contains two recursive calls to itself, one for each half of the problem. In the binary search, there are two such calls, but only one of them is actually executed. The mergesort, which we'll encounter in Hour 12, "Applied Recursion," actually executes both recursive calls (to sort two halves of an array).

Recursion Versus Stacks

Some algorithms lend themselves to a recursive approach, some don't. As we've seen, the recursive `triangle()` and binary search functions can be implemented more efficiently using a simple loop. However, various divide-and-conquer algorithms, such as mergesort, work very well as a recursive routine.

Often an algorithm is easy to conceptualize as a recursive function, but in practice the recursive approach proves to be inefficient. In such cases, it might be useful to transform the recursive approach into a nonrecursive approach. Such a transformation can often make use of a stack.

There is a close relationship between recursion and stacks. In fact, most compilers implement recursion by using stacks. As we noted, when a function is called, the compiler pushes the function arguments and the return address (where control will go when the function returns) on the stack, and then transfers control to the function. When the function returns, the compiler pops these values off the stack. The arguments disappear, and control returns to the return address.

In theory, any algorithm that uses recursion can be systematically transformed into one that uses a stack. In practice, however, it's usually more practical to rethink the algorithm from the ground up, using a stack-based approach instead of a recursive approach.

Listing 11.4 shows what happens when we do that with the `triangle()` member function.

INPUT **LISTING 11.4** THE stackTriangle.cpp PROGRAM

```cpp
//stackTriangle.cpp
//evaluates triangular numbers, stack replaces recursion
#include <iostream>
#include <vector>
using namespace std;
////////////////////////////////////////////////////////////////
class StackX
    {
    private:
        int maxSize;                //size of stack array
        vector<int>(stackVect) ;    //stack vector
        int top;                    //top of stack
    public:
//------------------------------------------------------------
    StackX(int s) : maxSize(s), top(-1)  //constructor
        { stackVect.resize(maxSize); }
//------------------------------------------------------------
    void push(int p)                //put item on top of stack
        { stackVect[++top] = p; }
//------------------------------------------------------------
    int pop()                       //take item from top of stack
        { return stackVect[top--]; }
//------------------------------------------------------------
    int peek()                      //peek at top of stack
        { return stackVect[top]; }
//------------------------------------------------------------
    bool isEmpty()                  //true if stack is empty
        { return (top == -1); }
//------------------------------------------------------------
    };  //end class StackX
////////////////////////////////////////////////////////////////
int main()
    {
    int theNumber;
    int theAnswer;
    int stackTriangle(int);

    cout << "Enter a number: ";
    cin >> theNumber;
    theAnswer = stackTriangle(theNumber);
    cout << "Triangle=" << theAnswer << endl;
    return 0;
```

continues

LISTING 11.4   CONTINUED

```
    }  //end main()
//--------------------------------------------------------------
int stackTriangle(int number)
    {
    StackX theStack(10000);        //make a big stack
    int answer = 0;                //initialize answer

    while(number > 0)              //until n is 1,
        {
        theStack.push(number);     //push value
        --number;                  //decrement value
        }
    while( !theStack.isEmpty() )   //until stack empty,
        {
        int newN = theStack.pop(); //pop value,
        answer += newN;            //add to answer
        }
    return answer;
    }
```

ANALYSIS   In this program we use a stack class called StackX. In main() there are two
loops. In the first, the numbers from *n* down to 1 are pushed onto the stack. In
the second, they're removed from the stack and summed. The result is the triangular
number for *n*.

Of course, in this program you can see by inspection that you can eliminate the stack
entirely and use a simple loop. However, in more complicated algorithms the stack must
remain.

Often you'll need to experiment to see whether a recursive function, a stack-based
approach, or a simple loop is the most efficient (or practical) way to handle a particular
situation.

Summary

In this hour, you learned the following:

- A recursive function calls itself repeatedly, with a different argument value each
  time.

- Some value of its arguments causes a recursive function to return without calling
  itself. This is called the *base case*.

- When the innermost instance of a recursive function returns, the process "unwinds" by completing pending instances of the function, going from the latest back to the original call.

- A triangular number is the sum of itself and all numbers smaller than itself. (*Number* means *integer* in this context.) For example, the triangular number of 4 is 10, because 4+3+2+1 = 10.

- Triangular numbers can be calculated using a recursive function, a simple loop, or a stack-based approach.

- The anagram of a word (all possible combinations of its *n* letters) can be found recursively by repeatedly rotating all its letters and anagramming the rightmost *n*–1 of them.

- A binary search can be carried out recursively by checking which half of a sorted range the search key is in, and then doing the same thing with that half.

- Any operation that can be carried out with recursion can be carried out with a stack.

- A recursive approach might be inefficient. If so, it can sometimes be replaced with a simple loop or a stack-based approach.

Q&A

Q **Recursion seems weird and complicated. Do I really need to know about it?**

A After you get used to recursion it's a very powerful conceptual tool. Sooner or later you'll encounter a problem that could be solved in a simple way using recursion.

Q **Isn't it easier to think in terms of a loop-based approach to problems?**

A Some situations are hard to visualize in terms of loops, but are easy in terms of recursion.

Workshop

The Workshop helps you solidify what you learned in this hour. See Appendix A for quiz answers.

Quiz

1. Complete the sentence: A recursive function is one that…

2. The value of the eighth triangular number is…

3. True or false: Recursion is used because it is more efficient.

4. What is a base case?

5. Describe briefly how to anagram a word.

6. What's the advantage of the recursive approach to binary searches, as opposed to the loop approach?

7. True or false: A recursive approach can be replaced with a stack-based approach.

8. In a recursive approach to a binary search, what two things does the recursive function call itself to do?

Exercise

Write a C++ program that uses recursion to calculate the factorial of a number. Factorials are mentioned in the note at the end of the section "What the `triangle()` Function is Really Doing" in this hour.

HOUR 12

Applied Recursion

In this hour we'll show recursion at work in two quite different contexts. We'll demonstrate recursion in

- The Towers of Hanoi puzzle
- A sorting process called mergesort

The first of these demonstrates dramatically how a seemingly complicated problem can be solved very simply using recursion. The second shows recursion in a more serious context, and also serves as an introduction to advanced sorting processes, which we'll explore in Hours 13, "Quicksort," and 14, "Improving Quicksort."

The Towers of Hanoi

The Towers of Hanoi is an ancient puzzle consisting of a number of disks placed on three columns, as shown in Figure 12.1.

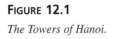

FIGURE **12.1**

The Towers of Hanoi.

The disks all have different diameters and holes in the middle so they will fit over the columns. All the disks start out on column A. The object of the puzzle is to transfer all the disks from column A to column C. Only one disk can be moved at a time, and no disk can be placed on a disk that's smaller than itself.

There's an ancient myth that somewhere in India, in a remote temple, monks labor day and night to transfer 64 golden disks from one of three diamond-studded towers to another. When they are finished, the world will end. Any alarm you might feel, however, will be dispelled when you see how long it takes to solve the puzzle for far fewer than 64 disks.

We'll show first how a Workshop applet solves this puzzle. Then we'll present C++ code that uses recursion to solve it.

The Towers Workshop Applet

Start up the Towers Workshop applet. You can attempt to solve the puzzle yourself by using the mouse to drag the topmost disk to another tower. Figure 12.2 shows how this looks after several moves have been made.

There are three ways to use the Workshop applet.

- You can attempt to solve the puzzle manually, by dragging the disks from tower to tower.

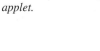

FIGURE 12.2

The Towers Workshop applet.

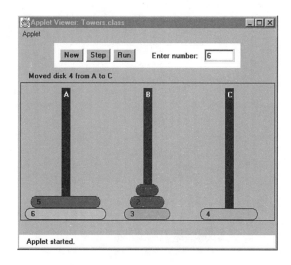

- You can repeatedly press the Step button to watch the algorithm solve the puzzle. At each step in the solution, a message is displayed, telling you what the algorithm is doing.

- You can press the Run button and watch the algorithm solve the puzzle with no intervention on your part; the disks zip back and forth between the posts.

To restart the puzzle, type in the number of disks you want to use, from 1 to 10, and press New twice. (After the first press, you're asked to verify that restarting is what you want to do.) The specified number of disks will be arranged on tower A. After you drag a disk with the mouse, you can't use Step or Run; you must start over with New. However, you can switch to Manual in the middle of stepping or running, and you can switch to Step when you're running, and Run when you're stepping.

Try solving the puzzle manually with a small number of disks, say 3 or 4. Work up to higher numbers. The applet gives you the opportunity to learn intuitively how the problem is solved.

Moving Subtrees

NEW TERM Let's call the initial tree-shaped (or pyramid-shaped) arrangement of disks on tower A a *tree*. As you experiment with the applet, you'll begin to notice that smaller tree-shaped stacks of disks are generated as part of the solution process. Let's call these smaller trees, containing fewer than the total number of disks, *subtrees*. For example, if you're trying to transfer 4 disks, you'll find that one of the intermediate steps involves a subtree of 3 disks on tower B, as shown in Figure 12.3.

12

FIGURE 12.3

A subtree on tower B.

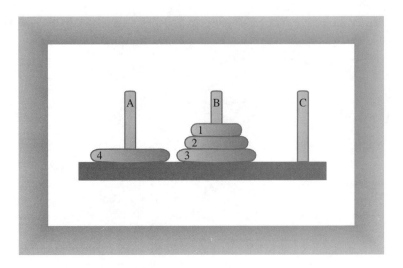

These subtrees form many times in the solution of the puzzle. This is because the creation of a subtree is the only way to transfer a larger disk from one tower to another: all the smaller disks must be placed on an intermediate tower, where they naturally form a subtree.

Here's a rule of thumb that might help when you solve the puzzle manually. If the subtree you're trying to move has an odd number of disks, start by moving the topmost disk directly to the tower where you want the subtree to go. If you're trying to move a subtree with an even number of disks, start by moving the topmost disk to the intermediate tower.

The Recursive Algorithm

The solution to the Towers of Hanoi puzzle can be expressed recursively using the notion of subtrees. Suppose you want to move all the disks from a source tower (call it S) to a destination tower (call it D). You have an intermediate tower available (call it I). Assume there are n disks on tower S. Here's how you would carry out the algorithm.

To Do: The Towers of Hanoi Algorithm

1. Move the subtree consisting of the top $n-1$ disks from S to I.

2. Move the remaining (largest) disk from S to D.

3. Move the subtree from I to D.

When you begin, the source tower is A, the intermediate tower is B, and the destination tower is C. Figure 12.4 shows the three steps for this situation.

FIGURE **12.4**

Recursive solution to Towers of Hanoi puzzle.

First, the subtree consisting of disks 1, 2, and 3 is moved to the intermediate tower B. Then the largest disk, 4, is moved to tower C. Then the subtree is moved from B to C.

Of course, this doesn't solve the problem of how to move the subtree consisting of disks 1, 2, and 3 to tower B because you can't move a subtree all at once; you must move it one disk at a time. Moving the 3-disk subtree is not so easy. However, it's easier than moving 4 disks.

As it turns out, moving 3 disks from A to the destination tower B can be done with the same 3 steps as moving 4 disks. That is, move the subtree consisting of the top 2 disks from tower A to intermediate tower C; then move disk 3 from A to B. Then move the subtree back from C to B.

12

How do you move a subtree of two disks from A to C? Move the subtree consisting of only one disk (1) from A to B. This is the base case: when you're moving only one disk, you just move it; there's nothing else to do. Then move the larger disk (2) from A to C, and replace the subtree (disk 1) on it.

Now that we've seen how to solve the Towers of Hanoi puzzle with the Workshop applet, let's look at some C++ code that does the same thing.

Implementing the Towers of Hanoi in C++

The towers.cpp program solves the Towers of Hanoi puzzle using this recursive approach. It communicates the moves by displaying them; this requires much less code than displaying the towers graphically. It's up to the human reading the list to actually carry out the moves.

The code is simplicity itself. The main() routine makes a single call to the recursive member function doTowers(). This function then calls itself recursively until the puzzle is solved. In this version, shown in Listing 12.1, there are initially only 3 disks, but you can recompile the program with any number.

INPUT   **LISTING 12.1**   THE towers.cpp PROGRAM

```cpp
//towers.cpp
//solves Towers of Hanoi puzzle
#include <iostream>
using namespace std;
void doTowers(int, char, char, char);          //prototype
//--------------------------------------------------------------
int main()
   {
   int nDisks;                                 //number of disks

   cout << "Enter number of disks: ";          //get # of disks
   cin >> nDisks;
   doTowers(nDisks, 'A', 'B', 'C');            //solve it
   return 0;
   }
//--------------------------------------------------------------
void doTowers(int topN, char src, char inter, char dest)
   {
   if(topN==1)                                 //display
      cout << "Disk 1 from " << src << " to " << dest << endl;
   else
      {
      doTowers(topN-1, src, dest, inter);      //src to inter

      cout << "Disk " << topN                  //display
```

```
                    << " from " << src << " to " << dest << endl;
               doTowers(topN-1, inter, src, dest);      //inter to dest
               }
          }
```

OUTPUT Remember that three disks are moved from A to C. Here's the output from the
program:

```
Disk 1 from A to C
Disk 2 from A to B
Disk 1 from C to B
Disk 3 from A to C
Disk 1 from B to A
Disk 2 from B to C
Disk 1 from A to C
```

The arguments to doTowers() are the number of disks to be moved, and the source
(from), intermediate (inter), and destination (to) towers to be used. The number of
disks decreases by one each time the function calls itself. The source, intermediate, and
destination towers also change.

Here is the output with additional notations that show when the member function is
entered and when it returns, and its arguments. The notations also show whether a disk is
moved because it's the base case (a subtree consisting of only one disk) or because it's
the remaining bottom disk after a subtree has been moved.

OUTPUT
```
Enter (3 disks): s=A, i=B, d=C
   Enter (2 disks): s=A, i=C, d=B
      Enter (1 disk): s=A, i=B, d=C
         Base case: move disk 1 from A to C
      Return (1 disk)
      Move bottom disk 2 from A to B
      Enter (1 disk): s=C, i=A, d=B
         Base case: move disk 1 from C to B
      Return (1 disk)
   Return (2 disks)
   Move bottom disk 3 from A to C
   Enter (2 disks): s=B, i=A, d=C
      Enter (1 disk): s=B, i=C, d=A
         Base case: move disk 1 from B to A
      Return (1 disk)
      Move bottom disk 2 from B to C
      Enter (1 disk): s=A, i=B, d=C
         Base case: move disk 1 from A to C
      Return (1 disk)
   Return (2 disks)
Return (3 disks)
```

12

ANALYSIS If you study this output along with the source code for `doTower()`, it should become clear exactly how the method works. It's amazing that such a small amount of code can solve such a seemingly complicated problem.

Next we'll look at a final example of recursion. Besides recursion, this example will introduce you to an advanced sorting method.

Mergesort

In this example we'll use recursion to sort data using the mergesort algorithm. This is a much more efficient sorting technique than those we saw in Hours 4, "The Bubble Sort," and 5, "The Insertion Sort," at least in terms of speed. Although the bubble and insertion sorts take $O(N^2)$ time, the mergesort is $O(N*logN)$. The graph in Figure 3.5 (in Hour 3, "Ordered Arrays") shows how much faster this is. For example, if N (the number of items to be sorted) is 10,000, then N^2 is 100,000,000, whereas N*logN is only 40,000. If sorting this many items required 40 seconds with the mergesort, it would take almost 28 hours for the insertion sort.

The mergesort is also fairly easy to implement. It's conceptually easier than quicksort, which we'll encounter in the next hour.

The downside of the mergesort is that it requires an additional array in memory, equal in size to the one being sorted. If your original array barely fits in memory, the mergesort won't work. However, if you have enough space and don't require the ultimate in speed, it's a good choice.

Merging Two Sorted Arrays

The heart of the mergesort algorithm is the merging of two already-sorted arrays. Merging two sorted arrays A and B creates a third array, C, that contains all the elements of A and B, also arranged in sorted order. We'll examine the merging process first; later we'll see how it's used in sorting.

Imagine two sorted arrays. They don't need to be the same size. Let's say array A has 4 elements and array B has 6 elements. They will be merged into an array C that starts with 10 empty cells. Figure 12.5 shows how this looks.

In the figure, the circled numbers indicate the order in which elements are transferred from A and B to C. Table 12.1 shows the comparisons necessary to determine which element will be copied. The steps in the table correspond to the steps in the figure. Following each comparison, the smaller element is copied to A.

FIGURE **12.5**

Merging two arrays.

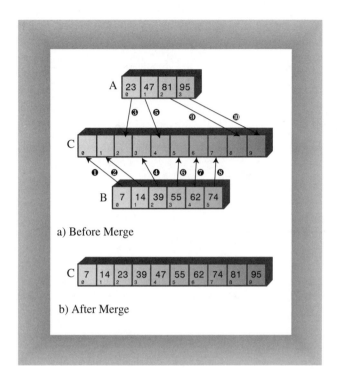

a) Before Merge

b) After Merge

TABLE 12.1   MERGING OPERATIONS

Step	Comparison (If Any)	Copy
1	Compare 23 and 7	Copy 7 from B to C
2	Compare 23 and 14	Copy 14 from B to C
3	Compare 23 and 39	Copy 23 from A to C
4	Compare 39 and 47	Copy 39 from B to C
5	Compare 55 and 47	Copy 47 from A to C
6	Compare 55 and 81	Copy 55 from B to C
7	Compare 62 and 81	Copy 62 from B to C
8	Compare 74 and 81	Copy 74 from B to C
9		Copy 81 from A to C
10		Copy 95 from A to C

12

Notice that because B is empty following step 8, no more comparisons are necessary; all the remaining elements are simply copied from A into C.

Listing 12.2 shows a C++ program that carries out the merge shown in Figure 12.5 and Table 12.1.

INPUT   **LISTING 12.2**   THE `merge.cpp` PROGRAM

```
//merge.cpp
//demonstrates merging two arrays into a third
#include <iostream>
using namespace std;
//--------------------------------------------------------------
void merge( int[], int, int[], int, int[] );
void display(int[], int);                  //prototypes
//--------------------------------------------------------------
int main()
   {
   int arrayA[] = {23, 47, 81, 95};        //source A
   int arrayB[] = {7, 14, 39, 55, 62, 74}; //source B
   int arrayC[10];                         //destination

   merge(arrayA, 4, arrayB, 6, arrayC); //merge A+B-->C
   display(arrayC, 10);                  //display result
   return 0;
   } //end main()
//--------------------------------------------------------------
void merge( int arrayA[], int sizeA,     //merge A and B into C
            int arrayB[], int sizeB,
            int arrayC[] )
   {
   int aDex=0, bDex=0, cDex=0;

   while(aDex < sizeA && bDex < sizeB)  //neither array empty
      if( arrayA[aDex] < arrayB[bDex] )
         arrayC[cDex++] = arrayA[aDex++];
      else
         arrayC[cDex++] = arrayB[bDex++];

   while(aDex < sizeA)                      //arrayB is empty,
      arrayC[cDex++] = arrayA[aDex++];  //but arrayA isn't

   while(bDex < sizeB)                      //arrayA is empty,
      arrayC[cDex++] = arrayB[bDex++];  //but arrayB isn't
   } //end merge()
//--------------------------------------------------------------
void display(int theArray[], int size)  //display array
   {
```

```
for(int j=0; j<size; j++)
   cout << theArray[j] << " ";
cout << endl;
}
```

ANALYSIS In main() the arrays arrayA, arrayB, and arrayC are created; then the merge() member function is called to merge arrayA and arrayB into arrayC, and the resulting contents of arrayC are displayed. Here's the output:

OUTPUT 7 14 23 39 47 55 62 74 81 95

The merge()function has three while loops. The first steps along both arrayA and arrayB, comparing elements and copying the smaller of the two into arrayC.

The second while loop deals with the situation when all the elements have been transferred out of arrayB, but arrayA still has remaining elements. (This is what happens in the example, where 81 and 95 remain in arrayA.) The loop simply copies the remaining elements from arrayA into arrayC.

The third loop handles the similar situation when all the elements have been transferred out of arrayA, but arrayB still has remaining elements; they are copied to arrayC.

Sorting by Merging

The idea in the mergesort is to divide an array in half, sort each half, and then use the merge() member function to merge the two halves into a single sorted array. How do you sort each half? This hour is about recursion, so you probably already know the answer: You divide the half into two quarters, sort each of the quarters, and merge them to make a sorted half.

Similarly each pair of 8ths is merged to make a sorted quarter, each pair of 16ths is merged to make a sorted 8th, and so on. You divide the array again and again until you reach a subarray with only one element. This is the base case; it's assumed an array with one element is already sorted.

We've seen that generally something is reduced in size each time a recursive member function calls itself, and built back up again each time the member function returns. In mergeSort() the range is divided in half each time this member function calls itself, and each time it returns it merges two smaller ranges into a larger one.

As mergeSort() returns from finding two arrays of one element each, it merges them into a sorted array of two elements. Each pair of resulting 2-element arrays is then merged into a 4-element array. This process continues with larger and larger arrays until

12

the entire array is sorted. This is easiest to see when the original array size is a power of 2, as shown in Figure 12.6.

FIGURE 12.6

Merging larger and larger arrays.

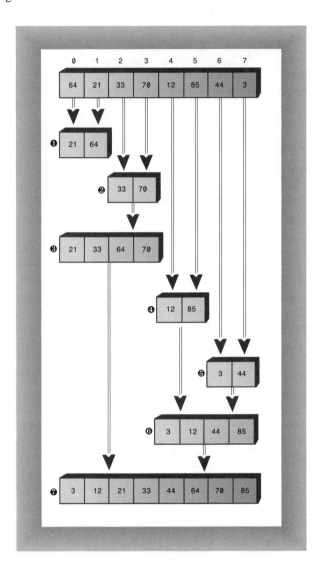

First, in the bottom half of the array, range 0–0 and range 1–1 are merged into range 0–1. Of course, 0–0 and 1–1 aren't really ranges; they're only one element, so they are base cases. Similarly, 2–2 and 3–3 are merged into 2–3. Then ranges 0–1 and 2–3 are merged into 0–3.

In the top half of the array, 4–4 and 5–5 are merged into 4–5, 6–6 and 7–7 are merged into 6–7, and 4–5 and 6–7 are merged into 4–7. Finally the top half, 0–3, and the bottom half, 4–7, are merged into the complete array, 0–7, which is now sorted.

When the array size is not a power of 2, arrays of different sizes must be merged. For example, Figure 12.7 shows the situation when the array size is 12. Here an array of size 2 must be merged with an array of size 1 to form an array of size 3.

FIGURE 12.7

Array size not a power of 2.

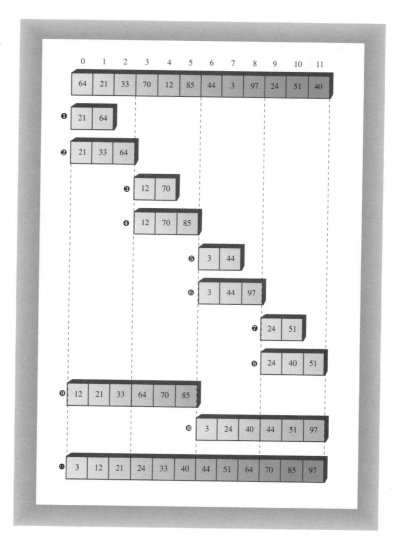

First the 1-element ranges 0–0 and 1–1 are merged into the 2-element range 0–1. Then range 0–1 is merged with the 1-element range 2–2. This creates the 3-element range 0–2. It's merged with the 3-element range 3–5. The process continues until the array is sorted.

Notice that in mergesort we don't merge two separate arrays into a third one, as we demonstrated in the merge.cpp program. Instead, we merge parts of a single array into itself.

You might wonder where all these subarrays are located in memory. In the algorithm, a workspace array of the same size as the original array is created. The subarrays are stored in sections of the workspace array. This means that subarrays in the original array are copied to appropriate places in the workspace array. After each merge, the workspace array is copied back into the original array.

The mergeSort Workshop Applet

All this is easier to appreciate when you see it happening before your very eyes. Start up the mergeSort Workshop applet. Repeatedly pressing the Step button will execute mergeSort step by step. Figure 12.8 shows what it looks like after the first three presses.

FIGURE 12.8

The mergeSort Workshop applet.

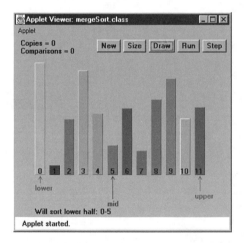

The Lower and Upper arrows show the range currently being considered by the algorithm, and the Mid arrow shows the middle part of the range. The range starts as the entire array and then is halved each time the mergeSort() member function calls itself. When the range is one element, mergeSort() returns immediately; that's the base case. Otherwise, the two subarrays are merged. The applet provides messages, such as Entering mergeSort: 0-5, to tell you what it's doing and the range it's operating on.

Many steps involve the mergeSort() member function calling itself or returning. Comparisons and copies are performed only during the merge process, when you'll see messages like Merged 0-0 and 1-1 into workspace. You can't see the merge happening because the workspace isn't shown. However, you can see the result when the appropriate section of the workspace is copied back into the original (visible) array: The bars in the specified range will appear in sorted order.

First, the first two bars will be sorted, then the first three bars, then the two bars in the range 3–4, then the three bars in the range 3–5, then the six bars in the range 0–5, and so on, corresponding to the sequence shown in Figure 12.7. Eventually all the bars will be sorted.

You can cause the algorithm to run continuously by pressing the Run button. You can stop this process at any time by pressing Step, single-step as many times as you want, and resume running by pressing Run again.

As in the other sorting Workshop applets, pressing New resets the array with a new group of unsorted bars, and toggles between random and inverse arrangements. The Size button toggles between 12 bars and 100 bars.

It's especially instructive to watch the algorithm run with 100 inversely sorted bars. The resulting patterns show clearly how each range is sorted individually and merged with its other half, and how the ranges grow larger and larger.

Implementing Mergesort in C++

In a moment we'll look at the entire mergeSort.cpp program. First, let's focus on the member function that carries out the mergesort. Here is the function:

```
void DArray::recMergeSort(vector<double> workSpace,
                          int lowerBound, int upperBound)
   {
   if(lowerBound == upperBound)        //if range is 1,

      return;                          //no use sorting
   else
      {                                //find midpoint
      int mid = (lowerBound+upperBound) / 2;
                                       //sort low half
      recMergeSort(workSpace, lowerBound, mid);
                                       //sort high half
      recMergeSort(workSpace, mid+1, upperBound);
                                       //merge them
      merge(workSpace, lowerBound, mid+1, upperBound);
      } //end else
   } //end recMergeSort()
```

12

As you can see, beside the base case, there are only four statements in this member function. The first computes the midpoint, the next two are recursive calls to recMergeSort() (one for each half of the array), and the fourth is a call to merge() to merge the two sorted halves. The base case occurs when the range contains only one element (lowerBound==upperBound) and results in an immediate return.

In the mergeSort.cpp program, the mergeSort() member function is the one actually seen by the class user. It creates the array workSpace[], and then calls the recursive routine recMergeSort() to carry out the sort. The creation of the workspace array is handled in mergeSort() because doing it in recMergeSort() would cause the array to be created anew with each recursive call, which is an inefficiency.

The merge() member function in the previous merge.cpp program operated on three separate arrays: two source arrays and a destination array. The merge() routine in the mergeSort.cpp program operates on a single array: the theArray member of the DArray class. The arguments to this merge() function are the starting point of the low-half subarray, the starting point of the high-half subarray, and the upper bound of the high-half subarray. The function calculates thesizes of the subarrays based on this information.

Listing 12.3 shows the complete mergeSort.cpp program. This program uses a variant of the array classes from Hour 2, "Arrays," adding the mergeSort() and recMergeSort() member functions to the DArray class. The main() routine creates an array, inserts 12 items, displays the array, sorts the items with mergeSort(), and displays the array again.

INPUT   **LISTING 12.3**   THE mergeSort.cpp PROGRAM

```cpp
//mergeSort.cpp
//demonstrates recursive merge sort
#include <iostream>
#include <vector>
using namespace std;
////////////////////////////////////////////////////////////////
class DArray
    {
    private:
        vector<double>(theVect);        //vector of doubles
        int nElems;                     //number of data items
        void recMergeSort(vector<double>, int, int);
        void merge(vector<double>, int, int, int);
    public:
//-------------------------------------------------------------
        DArray(int max) : nElems(0)     //constructor
            {
            theVect.resize(max);        //size vector
            }
```

```
//--------------------------------------------------------------
   void insert(double value)        //put element into array
      {
      theVect[nElems] = value;       //insert it
      nElems++;                      //increment size
      }
//--------------------------------------------------------------
   void display()                   //displays array contents
      {
      for(int j=0; j<nElems; j++)    //for each element,
         cout << theVect[j] << " ";  //display it
      cout << endl;
      }
//--------------------------------------------------------------
   void mergeSort()                 //called by main()
      {                             //provides workspace
      vector<double>(workSpace);
      workSpace.resize(nElems);
      recMergeSort(workSpace, 0, nElems-1);
      }
   }; //end class DArray
//--------------------------------------------------------------
void DArray::recMergeSort(vector<double> workSpace,
                          int lowerBound, int upperBound)
   {
   if(lowerBound == upperBound)     //if range is 1,
      return;                       //no use sorting
   else
      {                             //find midpoint
      int mid = (lowerBound+upperBound) / 2;
                                    //sort low half
      recMergeSort(workSpace, lowerBound, mid);
                                    //sort high half
      recMergeSort(workSpace, mid+1, upperBound);
                                    //merge them
      merge(workSpace, lowerBound, mid+1, upperBound);
      }   //end else
   }  //end recMergeSort()
//--------------------------------------------------------------
void DArray::merge(vector<double> workSpace, int lowPtr,
                   int highPtr, int upperBound)
   {
   int j = 0;                       //workspace index
   int lowerBound = lowPtr;
   int mid = highPtr-1;
   int n = upperBound-lowerBound+1; //# of items

   while(lowPtr <= mid && highPtr <= upperBound)
      if( theVect[lowPtr] < theVect[highPtr] )
         workSpace[j++] = theVect[lowPtr++];
```

continues

LISTING 12.3 CONTINUED

```
        else
           workSpace[j++] = theVect[highPtr++];

     while(lowPtr <= mid)
        workSpace[j++] = theVect[lowPtr++];

     while(highPtr <= upperBound)
        workSpace[j++] = theVect[highPtr++];

     for(j=0; j<n; j++)
        theVect[lowerBound+j] = workSpace[j];
     }  //end merge()
//////////////////////////////////////////////////////////////
int main()
   {
   const int maxSize = 100;          //array size
   DArray arr(maxSize);              //create "array"

   arr.insert(64);                   //insert items
   arr.insert(21);
   arr.insert(33);
   arr.insert(70);
   arr.insert(12);
   arr.insert(85);
   arr.insert(44);
   arr.insert(3);
   arr.insert(99);
   arr.insert(0);
   arr.insert(108);
   arr.insert(36);

   arr.display();                    //display items
   arr.mergeSort();                  //merge-sort the array
   arr.display();                    //display items again
   return 0;
   }  //end main()
```

OUTPUT The output from the program is simply the display of the unsorted and sorted arrays:

```
64 21 33 70 12 85 44 3 99 0 108 36
0 3 12 21 33 36 44 64 70 85 99 108
```

If we put additional statements in the recMergeSort() member function, we could generate a running commentary on what the program does during a sort. The following output shows how this might look for the 4-item array {64, 21, 33, 70}. (You can think of this as the lower half of the array in Figure 12.6.)

```
Entering 0-3
   Will sort low half of 0-3
   Entering 0-1
      Will sort low half of 0-1
         Entering 0-0
         Base-Case Return 0-0
      Will sort high half of 0-1
         Entering 1-1
         Base-Case Return 1-1
      Will merge halves into 0-1
   Return 0-1                       theArray=21 64 33 70
   Will sort high half of 0-3
   Entering 2-3
      Will sort low half of 2-3
         Entering 2-2
         Base-Case Return 2-2
      Will sort high half of 2-3
         Entering 3-3
         Base-Case Return 3-3
      Will merge halves into 2-3
   Return 2-3                       theArray=21 64 33 70
   Will merge halves into 0-3
Return 0-3                          theArray=21 33 64 70
```

ANALYSIS This is roughly the same content as would be generated by the mergeSort Workshop applet if it could sort 4 items. Study of this output, and comparison with the code for recMergeSort() and Figure 12.6, will reveal the details of the sorting process.

Efficiency of the Mergesort

As we noted, the mergesort runs in O(N*logN) time. How do we know this? Let's see how we can figure out the number of times a data item must be copied, and the number of times it must be compared with another data item, during the course of the algorithm. We assume that copying and comparing are the most time-consuming operations—that the recursive calls and returns don't add much overhead. We'll look first at copies, then at comparisons.

Number of Copies

Look again at Figure 12.6. Each cell below the top line represents an element copied from the array into the workspace.

Adding up all the cells in Figure 12.6 (the 7 numbered steps) shows there are 24 copies necessary to sort 8 items. $Log_2 8$ is 3, so $8*log_2 8$ equals 24. This shows that for the case of 8 items, the number of copies is proportional to $N*log_2 N$.

NEW TERM Another way to look at this is that to sort eight items requires three *levels*, each of which involves eight copies. A level means all copies into the same size subarray.

12

In the first level, there are four 2-element subarrays; in the second level, there are two 4-element subarrays; and in the third level, there is one 8-element subarray. Each level has eight elements, so again there are 3*8 or 24 copies.

In Figure 12.6, by considering only half the graph, you can see that eight copies are necessary for an array of four items (steps 1, 2 and 3), and two copies are necessary for two items. Similar calculations provide the number of copies necessary for larger arrays. Table 12.2 summarizes this information.

TABLE 12.2 NUMBER OF OPERATIONS WHEN N IS A POWER OF 2

N	log^2N	Number of Copies into Workspace ($N*log^2N$)	Total Copies	Comparisons Max (Min)
2	1	2	4	1 (1)
4	2	8	16	5 (4)
8	3	24	48	17 (12)
16	4	64	128	49 (32)
32	5	160	320	129 (80)
64	6	384	768	321 (192)
128	7	896	1792	769 (448)

Actually, the items are not only copied into the workspace, they're also copied back into the original array. This doubles the number of copies, as shown in the Total Copies column. The final column of Table 12.2 shows comparisons, which we'll return to in a moment.

It's harder to calculate the number of copies and comparisons when N is not a multiple of 2, but these numbers fall between those that are a power of 2. For 12 items, there are 88 total copies, and for 100 items, 1344 total copies.

Number of Comparisons

In the mergesort algorithm, the number of comparisons is always somewhat less than the number of copies. How much less? Assuming the number of items is a power of 2, for each individual merging operation, the maximum number of comparisons is always one less than the number of items being merged, and the minimum is half the number of items being merged. You can see why this is true in Figure 12.9, which shows two possibilities when trying to merge two arrays of four items each.

FIGURE 12.9

Maximum and minimum comparisons.

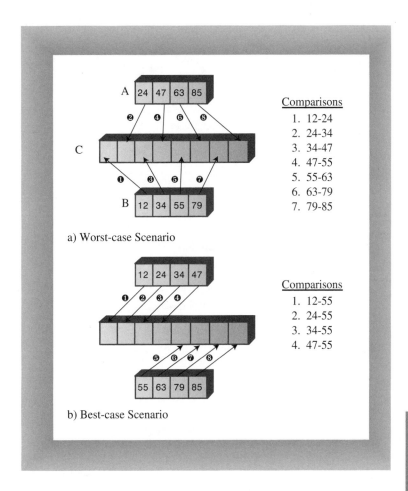

a) Worst-case Scenario

Comparisons
1. 12-24
2. 24-34
3. 34-47
4. 47-55
5. 55-63
6. 63-79
7. 79-85

b) Best-case Scenario

Comparisons
1. 12-55
2. 24-55
3. 34-55
4. 47-55

In the first case, the items interleave, and seven comparisons must be made to merge them. In the second case, all the items in one array are smaller than all the items in the other, so only four comparisons need be made.

There are many merges for each sort, so we must add the comparisons for each one. Referring to Figure 12.6, you can see that seven merge operations are required to sort eight items. The number of items being merged and the resulting number of comparisons are shown in Table 12.3.

TABLE 12.3 COMPARISONS INVOLVED IN SORTING EIGHT ITEMS

Step Number	1	2	3	4	5	6	7	Totals
Number of Items Being Merged (N)	2	2	4	2	2	4	8	24
Maximum Comparisons (N–1)	1	1	3	1	1	3	7	17
Minimum Comparisons (N/2)	1	1	2	1	1	2	4	12

For each merge, the maximum number of comparisons is one fewer than the number of items. Adding these figures for all the merges gives us a total of 17.

The minimum number of comparisons is always half the number of items being merged, and adding these figures for all the merges results in 12 comparisons. Similar arithmetic results in the Comparisons columns for Table 12.2. The actual number of comparisons to sort a specific array depends on how the data is arranged, but it will be somewhere between the maximum and minimum values.

Summary

In this hour, you've learned the following:

- The Towers of Hanoi puzzle consists of three towers and an arbitrary number of rings.
- The Towers of Hanoi puzzle can be solved recursively by moving all but the bottom disk of a subtree to an intermediate tower, moving the bottom disk to the destination tower, and finally moving the remaining subtree to the destination.
- Merging two sorted arrays means to create a third array that contains all the elements from both arrays in sorted order.
- In mergesort, 1-element subarrays of a larger array are merged into 2-element subarrays, 2-element subarrays are merged into 4-element subarrays, and so on until the entire array is sorted.
- Mergesort requires O(N*logN) time.
- Mergesort requires a workspace equal in size to the original array.

- For triangular numbers, anagrams, and the binary search shown in the last hour, the recursive function contains only one call to itself. (There are two shown in the code for the binary search, but only one is used on any given pass through the member function's code.)

- For the Towers of Hanoi and mergesort in this hour, the recursive member function contains two calls to itself.

Q&A

Q Isn't this Towers of Hanoi example sort of frivolous? I mean, I'll probably never program anything like it.

A The point of the Towers of Hanoi example is to show how recursion can sometimes make what looks like a difficult problem into a simple one. There might come a time in your own programming when a similar recursive approach saves you a lot of trouble.

Q Do I really need to understand the analysis of how efficient the mergesort is?

A This sort of discussion is important because it shows how to figure out how efficient an algorithm is. You don't need to remember the details, but you should come away with the idea that such analysis, while it isn't totally easy, isn't rocket science either.

Workshop

The Workshop helps you solidify what you learned in this hour. See Appendix A for quiz answers.

12

Quiz

1. Define the term *subtree* as used in our discussion of the Towers of Hanoi puzzle.
2. Briefly describe the recursive solution to the Towers of Hanoi puzzle.
3. True or false: The mergesort is faster than the insertion sort.
4. What does it mean to merge two arrays?
5. Briefly describe the mergesort.
6. What is the base case for the mergesort?
7. What is the Big O efficiency of the mergesort?

Exercise

Calculate how many moves are required to solve the Towers of Hanoi puzzle for different numbers of disks. Create a table showing these results. Express the relationship between the number of moves and the number of disks as an equation.

Hour 13

Quicksort

In this hour we'll introduce the most widely used approach to sorting: quick-sort. Quicksort is based on the idea of partitions. You'll learn

- What partitioning is
- How to implement it
- How partitioning applies to sorting
- How quicksort works
- How to implement quicksort

We discussed simple sorting in Hours 4, "The Bubble Sort," and 5, "The Insertion Sort." The sorts described there—the bubble and insertion sorts—are easy to implement but are rather slow. In Hour 12, "Applied Recursion," we described the mergesort. It runs much faster than the simple sorts, but requires twice as much space as the original array; this is often a serious drawback.

Quicksort operates much faster than the simple sorts; it runs in O(N*logN) time, which is the fastest time for general-purpose sorts. Also, it does not require a large amount of extra memory space, as mergesort does.

Partitioning

Partitioning is the underlying mechanism of quicksort, but it's also a useful operation on its own, so we'll cover it here in its own section.

NEW TERM   To *partition* data is to divide it into two groups, so that all the items with a key value higher than a specified amount are in one group, and all the items with a lower key value are in another.

It's easy to imagine situations where you would want to partition data. Maybe you want to divide your personnel records into two groups: employees who live within 15 miles of the office and those who live farther away. Or a school administrator might want to divide students into those with grade point averages higher and lower than 3.5, so as to know who deserves to be on the dean's list.

The Partition Workshop Applet

Our Partition Workshop applet demonstrates the partitioning process. Figure 13.1 shows 12 bars before partitioning, and Figure 13.2 shows them again after partitioning.

FIGURE 13.1

Twelve bars before partitioning.

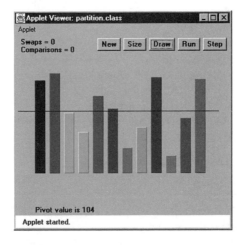

NEW TERM   The horizontal line represents the *pivot value*. This is the value used to determine into which of the two groups an item is placed.

We'll assume that each bar in the applet's graph represents one cell in an array. Items with a key value less than the pivot value go in the left part of the array, and those with a greater (or equal) key go in the right part. (In the section on quicksort, we'll see that the pivot value can be the key value of an actual data item, called the *pivot*. For now, it's just a number.)

FIGURE 13.2

Twelve bars after partitioning.

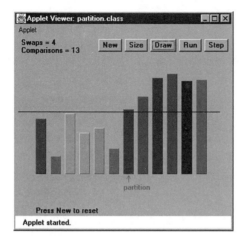

The arrow labeled partition points to the leftmost item in the right (higher) subarray. This value is returned from the partitioning member function, so it can be used by other functions that need to know where the division is.

For a more vivid display of the partitioning process, set the Partition Workshop applet to 100 bars and press the Run button. The leftScan and rightScan markers will zip toward each other, swapping bars as they go. When they meet, the partition is complete.

When you program a partition algorithm, you can choose any value you want for the pivot value, depending on why you're doing the partition (such as choosing a grade point average of 3.5). For variety, the Workshop applet chooses a random number for the pivot value (the horizontal black line) each time New or Size is pressed, but the value is never too far from the average bar height.

After being partitioned, the data is by no means sorted; it has simply been divided into two groups. However, it's more sorted than it was before. As we'll see in the next section, it doesn't take much more trouble to sort it completely.

13

> Notice that partitioning is not stable. That is, each group is not in the same order it was originally. In fact, partitioning tends to reverse the order of some of the data in each group.

Now that you've seen partitioning demonstrated by the Workshop applet, let's look at some C++ code that performs this algorithm.

The `partition.cpp` Program

Listing 13.1 shows the `partition.cpp` program, which includes the `partitionIt()` member function for partitioning an array.

INPUT   **LISTING 13.1**   THE `partition.cpp` PROGRAM

```cpp
//partition.cpp
//demonstrates partitioning an array
#include <iostream>
#include <vector>
#include <cstdlib>                //for random numbers
#include <ctime>                  //for random numbers
using namespace std;
//////////////////////////////////////////////////////////////
class ArrayPar
    {
    private:
        vector<double> theVect;    //vector of doubles
        int nElems;                //number of data items
    public:
//--------------------------------------------------------------
    ArrayPar(int max) : nElems(0)  //constructor
        {
        theVect.resize(max);       //size the vector
        }
//--------------------------------------------------------------
    void insert(double value)      //put element into array
        {
        theVect[nElems] = value;   //insert it
        nElems++;                  //increment size
        }
//--------------------------------------------------------------
    int getSize()                  //return number of items
        { return nElems; }
//--------------------------------------------------------------
    void display()                 //displays array contents
        {
        cout << "A=";
        for(int j=0; j<nElems; j++)      //for each element,
            cout << theVect[j] << " ";   //display it
        cout << endl;
        }
//--------------------------------------------------------------
                                   //partition a range
    int partitionIt(int left, int right, double pivot)
        {
        int leftMark = left - 1;       //right of first elem
        int rightMark = right + 1;     //left of pivot
        while(true)
```

```
          {
          while(leftMark < right &&      //find bigger item
                theVect[++leftMark] < pivot)
              ;  //(nop)

          while(rightMark > left &&      //find smaller item
                theVect[--rightMark] > pivot)
              ;  //(nop)
          if(leftMark >= rightMark)      //if markers cross,
              break;                     //   partition done
          else                           //not crossed, so
              swap(leftMark, rightMark); //  swap elements
          }  //end while(true)
        return leftMark;                 //return partition
        }  //end partitionIt()
//------------------------------------------------------------
    void swap(int dex1, int dex2)  //swap two elements
        {
        double temp;
        temp = theVect[dex1];              //A into temp
        theVect[dex1] = theVect[dex2];     //B into A
        theVect[dex2] = temp;              //temp into B
        }  //end swap(
//------------------------------------------------------------
    };  //end class ArrayPar
////////////////////////////////////////////////////////////
int main()
    {
    time_t aTime;
    int maxSize = 16;                  //array size
    ArrayPar arr(maxSize);             //create the array
    srand( static_cast<unsigned>(time(&aTime)) ); //seed randoms

    for(int j=0; j<maxSize; j++)       //fill array with
        {                              //random numbers
        double n = rand() % 199;
        arr.insert(n);
        }
    arr.display();                     //display unsorted array

    double pivot = 99;                 //pivot value
    cout << "Pivot is " << pivot;
    int size = arr.getSize();
                                       //partition array
    int partDex = arr.partitionIt(0, size-1, pivot);

    cout << ", Partition is at index " << partDex << endl;
    arr.display();                     //display partitioned array
    return 0;
    }  //end main()
```

13

ANALYSIS The main() routine creates an ArrayPar object that holds 16 items of type double with values between 0 and 198. (The array within this object is implemented as an STL vector object.) The pivot value is fixed at 99. The routine inserts 16 random values into ArrayPar, displays them, partitions them by calling the partitionIt() member function, and displays them again. Here's some sample output:

OUTPUT
```
A=149 192 47 152 159 195 61 66 17 167 118 64 27 80 30 105
Pivot is 99, partition is at index 8
A=30 80 47 27 64 17 61 66 195 167 118 159 152 192 149 105
```

You can see that the partition is successful: The first eight numbers in the bottom line are all smaller than the pivot value of 99; the last eight are all larger.

Notice that the partitioning process doesn't necessarily divide the array in half as it does in this example; that depends on the pivot value and key values of the data. There might be more items in one group than in the other.

The Partition Algorithm

The partitioning algorithm works by starting with two markers, one at each end of the array. (The markers are implemented as array index numbers. We could call them pointers, but we don't want them to be confused with C++ pointers.) The marker on the left, leftMark, moves toward the right, and the one of the right, rightMark, moves toward the left. Notice that leftMark and rightMark in the partition.cpp program correspond to leftScan and rightScan in the Partition Workshop applet.

Actually, leftMark is initialized to one position to the left of the first cell, and rightMark to one position to the right of the last cell because they will be incremented and decremented, respectively, before they're used.

Stopping and Swapping

When leftMark encounters a data item smaller than the pivot value, it keeps going because that item is already in the right place. However, when it encounters an item larger than the pivot value, it stops. Similarly, when rightMark encounters an item larger than the pivot, it keeps going, but when it finds a smaller item, it also stops. Two inner while loops, the first for leftMark and the second for rightMark, control this scanning process. A marker stops because its while loop exits. Here's a simplified version of the code that scans for out-of-place items:

```
while( theArray[++leftMark] < pivot )    //find bigger item
   ;  // (nop)
while( theArray[--rightMark] > pivot )   //find smaller item
   ;  // (nop)
swap(leftMark, rightMark);               //swap elements
```

The first `while` loop exits when an item larger than `pivot` is found; the second loop exits when an item smaller than `pivot` is found. When both these loops exit, both `leftMark` and `rightMark` point to items that are in the wrong part of the array, so these items are swapped.

After the swap, the two markers continue on, again stopping at items that are in the wrong part of the array and swapping them. All this activity is nested in an outer `while` loop, as can be seen in the `partitionIt()` member function in Listing 13.1. When the two markers eventually meet, the partitioning process is complete and this outer `while` loop exits.

You can watch the markers in action when you run the Partition Workshop applet with 100 bars. These markers, represented by blue arrows, start at opposite ends of the array and move toward each other, stopping and swapping as they go. The bars between them are unpartitioned; those they've already passed over are partitioned. When they meet, the entire array is partitioned.

Handling Unusual Data

If we were sure that there was a data item at the right end of the array that was smaller than the pivot value, and an item at the left end that was larger, the simplified `while` loops previously shown would work fine. Unfortunately, the algorithm might be called upon to partition data that isn't so well organized.

If all the data is smaller than the pivot value, for example, the `leftMark` variable will go all the way across the array, looking in vain for a larger item, and fall off the right end, creating an `array index out of bounds` error. A similar fate will befall `rightMark` if all the data is larger than the pivot value.

To avoid these problems, extra tests must be placed in the `while` loops to check for the ends of the array: `leftMark<right` in the first loop, and `rightMark>left` in the second. This can be seen in context in Listing 13.1.

In the next major section in this chapter, on quicksort, we'll see that a clever pivot-selection process can eliminate these end-of-array tests. Eliminating code from inner loops is always a good idea if you want to make a program run faster.

Delicate Code

 The code in the `while` loops is rather delicate. For example, you might be tempted to remove the increment operators from the inner `while` loops and use

13

them to replace the nop statements. (*nop* refers to a statement consisting only of a semi-colon, and means *no operation*.) For example, you might try to change this:

```
while(leftMark < right && theArray[++leftMark] < pivot)
    ;   // (nop)
```

to this:

```
while(leftMark < right && theArray[leftMark] < pivot)
    ++leftMark;
```

and similarly for the other inner while loop. This would make it possible for the initial values of the markers to be left and right, which is somewhat clearer than left-1 and right+1.

However, these changes result in the markers being incremented only when the condition is satisfied. The markers must move in any case, so two extra statements within the outer while loop would be required to bump the markers. The nop version is the most efficient solution.

Efficiency of the Partition Algorithm

The partition algorithm runs in O(N) time. It's easy to see this when running the Partition Workshop applet: The two markers start at opposite ends of the array and move toward each other at a more or less constant rate, stopping and swapping as they go. When they meet, the partition is complete. If there were twice as many items to partition, the markers would move at the same rate, but they would have twice as far to go (twice as many items to compare and swap), so the process would take twice as long. Thus the running time is proportional to N.

More specifically, for each partition there will be N+1 or N+2 comparisons. Every item will be encountered and used in a comparison by one or the other of the markers, leading to N comparisons, but the markers overshoot each other before they find out they've "crossed" or gone beyond each other, so there are one or two extra comparisons before the partition is complete. The number of comparisons is independent of how the data is arranged (except for the uncertainty between 1 and 2 extra comparisons at the end of the scan).

The number of swaps, however, does depends on how the data is arranged. If it's inversely ordered, and the pivot value divides the items in half, every pair of values must be swapped, which is N/2 swaps. (Remember in the Partition Workshop applet that the pivot value is selected randomly, so that the number of swaps for inversely sorted bars won't always be exactly N/2.)

For random data, there will be fewer than N/2 swaps in a partition, even if the pivot value is such that half the bars are shorter and half are taller. This is because some bars will already be in the right place (short bars on the left, tall bars on the right). If the pivot value is higher (or lower) than most of the bars, there will be even fewer swaps because only those few bars that are higher (or lower) than the pivot will need to be swapped. On average, for random data, about half the maximum number of swaps take place.

Although there are fewer swaps than comparisons, they are both proportional to N. Thus the partitioning process runs in O(N) time. Running the Workshop applet, you can see that for 12 random bars there are about 3 swaps and 14 comparisons, and for 100 random bars there are about 25 swaps and 102 comparisons.

Now that you've seen how partitioning works, you're ready to understand quicksort, which is based on the partitioning algorithm.

Basic Quicksort

Quicksort is undoubtedly the most popular sorting algorithm, and for good reason: in the majority of situations, it's the fastest, operating in O(N*logN) time. (This is true only for in-memory sorting; for sorting data in disk files, other algorithms, such as mergesort, may be better.) Quicksort was discovered by C.A.R. Hoare in 1962.

To understand quicksort, you should be familiar with the partitioning algorithm described in the last section. Basically the quicksort algorithm operates by partitioning an array into two subarrays, and then calling itself recursively to quicksort each of these subarrays. However, there are some embellishments we can make to this basic scheme. These have to do with the selection of the pivot and the sorting of small partitions. We'll examine these refinements in the next hour.

It's difficult to understand what quicksort is doing before you understand some of the details of how it works, so we'll reverse our usual presentation and show the C++ code for quicksort before presenting the quicksort Workshop applet.

The Quicksort Algorithm

The code for a basic recursive quicksort member function is fairly simple. Here's an example:

```
void recQuickSort(int left, int right)
   {
   if(right-left <= 0)          //if size is 1,
      return;                   //   it's already sorted
   else                         //size is 2 or larger
      {
                                    //partition range
      int partition = partitionIt(left, right);
```

13

```
        recQuickSort(left, partition-1);    //sort left side
        recQuickSort(partition+1, right);   //sort right side
        }
    }
```

As you can see, there are three basic steps (after you check for the base case).

To Do: The Quicksort Algorithm

1. Partition the array or subarray into left (smaller keys) and right (larger keys) groups.

2. Call ourselves to sort the left group.

3. Call ourselves again to sort the right group.

After a partition, all the items in the left subarray are smaller than all those on the right. If we then sort the left subarray, and sort the right subarray, the entire array will be sorted. How do we sort these subarrays? By calling ourselves.

The Arguments to `recQuickSort()`

The arguments to the `recQuickSort()` member function determine the left and right ends of the array (or subarray) it's supposed to sort. The function first checks whether this array consists of only one element. If so, the array is by definition already sorted, and the function returns immediately. This is the base case in the recursion process.

Finding the Boundary

If the array has two or more cells, the algorithm calls the `partitionIt()` member function, described in the last section, to partition it. This member function returns the index number of the *partition*: the left element in the right (larger keys) subarray. The partition marks the boundary between the subarrays. This is shown in Figure 13.3.

After the array is partitioned, `recQuickSort()` calls itself recursively, once for the left part of its array, from `left` to `partition-1`, and once for the right, from `partition+1` to `right`. Note that the data item at the index `partition` is not included in either of the recursive calls. Why not? Doesn't it need to be sorted? The explanation lies in how the pivot value is chosen.

Choosing a Pivot Value

What pivot value should the `partitionIt()` member function use? Here are some relevant ideas:

- The pivot value should be the key value of an actual data item; this item is called the pivot.

- You can pick a data item to be the pivot more or less at random. For simplicity, let's say we always pick the item on the right end of the subarray being partitioned.

- After the partition, if the pivot is inserted at the boundary between the left and right subarrays, it will be in its final sorted position.

FIGURE 13.3

Recursive calls sort subarrays.

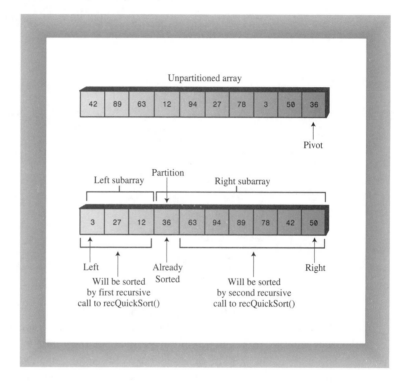

This last point may sound unlikely, but remember that because the pivot's key value is used to partition the array, following the partition the left subarray holds items smaller than the pivot, and the right subarray holds items larger. The pivot starts out on the right, but if it could somehow be placed between these two subarrays, it would be in the right place; that is, in its final sorted position. Figure 13.4 shows how this looks with a pivot whose key value is 36.

This figure is somewhat fanciful because you can't actually take an array apart as we've shown. So how do we move the pivot to its proper place?

13

FIGURE **13.4**

*The pivot and the sub-
arrays.*

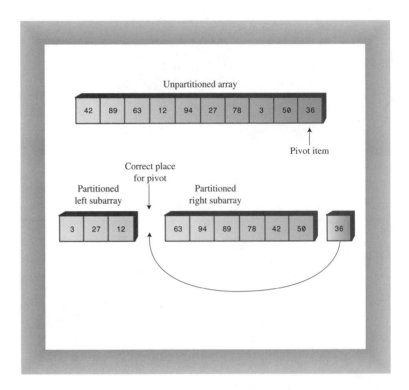

We could shift all the items in the right subarray to the right one cell to make room for the pivot. However, this is inefficient and unnecessary. Remember that all the items in the right subarray, although they are larger than the pivot, are not yet sorted, so they can be moved around, within the right subarray, without affecting anything. Therefore, to simplify inserting the pivot in its proper place, we can simply swap the pivot (36) and the left item in the right subarray, which is 63. This places the pivot in its proper position between the left and right groups. The 63 is switched to the right end, but because it remains in the right (larger) group, the partitioning is undisturbed. This is shown in Figure 13.5.

After it's swapped into the partition's location, the pivot is in its final resting place. All subsequent activity will take place on one side of it or on the other, but the pivot itself won't be moved (or indeed even accessed) again.

FIGURE 13.5

Swapping the pivot.

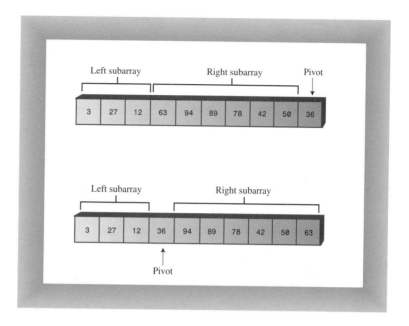

To incorporate the pivot selection process into our recQuickSort() member function, let's make it an overt statement, and send the pivot value to partitionIt() as an argument. Here's how that looks:

```
void recQuickSort(int left, int right)
   {
   if(right-left <= 0)         //if size <= 1,
      return;                  //   already sorted
   else                        //size is 2 or larger
      {
      double pivot = theArray[right];   //rightmost item
                                        //partition range
      int partition = partitionIt(left, right, pivot);
      recQuickSort(left, partition-1);  //sort left side
      recQuickSort(partition+1, right); //sort right side
      }
   }  // end recQuickSort()
```

When we use this scheme of choosing the rightmost item in the array as the pivot, we'll need to modify the partitionIt() member function to exclude this rightmost item from the partitioning process. After all, we already know where it should go after the

13

partitioning process is complete: at the partition, between the two groups. Also, once the partitioning process is completed, we need to swap the pivot from the right end into the partition's location. Listing 13.2 shows the quickSort1.cpp program, which incorporates these features.

INPUT   **LISTING 13.2**   THE quickSort1.cpp PROGRAM

```cpp
//quickSort1.cpp
//demonstrates simple version of quick sort
#include <iostream>
#include<vector>
#include<cstdlib>                         //for random numbers
#include<ctime>                           //for random numbers
using namespace std;
////////////////////////////////////////////////////////////////
class ArrayIns
   {
   private:
      vector<double>(theVect);            //vector of doubles
      int nElems;                         //number of data items
   public:
//------------------------------------------------------------
   ArrayIns(int max) : nElems(0)          //constructor
      {
      theVect.resize(max);                //size the vector
      }
//------------------------------------------------------------
   void insert(double value)              //put element into array
      {
      theVect[nElems] = value;            //insert it
      nElems++;                           //increment size
      }
//------------------------------------------------------------
   void display()                         //displays array contents
      {
      cout << "A=";
      for(int j=0; j<nElems; j++)         //for each element,
         cout << theVect[j] << " ";       //display it
      cout << endl;
      }
//------------------------------------------------------------
   void quickSort()                       //sort array
      {
      recQuickSort(0, nElems-1);          //call recursive sort
      }
//------------------------------------------------------- void
recQuickSort(int left, int right)  //recursive sort
      {
      if(right-left <= 0)                      //if size <= 1,
```

```
        return;                         //   already sorted
      else                              //size is 2 or larger
        {
        double pivot = theVect[right];    //rightmost item
                                          //partition range
        int partition = partitionIt(left, right, pivot);
        recQuickSort(left, partition-1);  //sort left side
        recQuickSort(partition+1, right); //sort right side
        }
      } //end recQuickSort()
//-------------------------------------------------------------
   int partitionIt(int left, int right, double pivot)
      {
      int leftMark = left-1;            //left    (after ++)
      int rightMark = right;            //right-1 (after --)
      while(true)
        {                               //find bigger item
        while( theVect[++leftMark] < pivot )
           ;                            //  (nop)
                                        //find smaller item
        while(rightMark > 0 && theVect[--rightMark] > pivot)
           ;                            //  (nop)

        if(leftMark >= rightMark)       //if pointers cross,
           break;                       //   partition done
        else                            //not crossed, so
           swap(leftMark, rightMark);   //  swap elements
        } //end while(true)
      swap(leftMark, right);            //restore pivot
      return leftMark;                  //return pivot location
      } //end partitionIt()
//-------------------------------------------------------------
   void swap(int dex1, int dex2)        //swap two elements
      {
      double temp = theVect[dex1];      //A into temp
      theVect[dex1] = theVect[dex2];    //B into A
      theVect[dex2] = temp;             //temp into B
      } //end swap(
//-------------------------------------------------------------
   }; //end class ArrayIns
/////////////////////////////////////////////////////////////
int main()
   {
   time_t aTime;
   int maxSize = 16;                    //array size
   ArrayIns arr(maxSize);               //create array
   srand( static_cast<unsigned>(time(&aTime)) );  //seed randoms

   for(int j=0; j<maxSize; j++)         //fill array with
```

continues

LISTING 13.2   CONTINUED

```
    {                                 //random numbers
    double n = rand() % 99;
    arr.insert(n);
    }
arr.display();                        //display items
arr.quickSort();                      //quicksort them
arr.display();                        //display them again
return 0;
} //end main()
```

ANALYSIS The main() routine creates an object of type ArrayIns, inserts 16 random data items of type double in it, displays it, sorts it with the quickSort() member function, and displays the results.

OUTPUT Here's some typical output:

```
A=69 0 70 6 38 38 24 56 44 26 73 77 30 45 97 65
A=0 6 24 26 30 38 38 44 45 56 65 69 70 73 77 97
```

An interesting aspect of the code in the partitionIt() member function is that we've been able to remove the test for the end of the array in the first inner while loop. This test, seen in the earlier partitionIt() member function in the partition.cpp program in Listing 13.1, was

```
leftMark < right
```

It prevented leftMark running off the right end of the array if there was no item there larger than pivot. Why can we eliminate the test? Because we selected the rightmost item as the pivot, so leftMark will always stop there. However, the test is still necessary for rightMark in the second while loop. (In Hour 14, "Improving Quicksort," we'll see how this test can be eliminated as well.)

Choosing the rightmost item as the pivot is thus not an entirely arbitrary choice; it speeds up the code by removing an unnecessary test. Picking the pivot from some other location would not provide this advantage.

The quickSort1 Workshop Applet

At this point you know enough about the quicksort algorithm to understand the nuances of the quickSort1 Workshop applet. We'll use it to examine the big picture first, then the details.

Understanding the Big Picture

To understand the big picture, use the Size button to set the applet to sort 100 random bars, and press the Run button. (Press Draw followed by Run if you find spurious bars in the display.) Following the sorting process, the display will look something like Figure 13.6.

FIGURE 13.6

The quickSort1 Workshop applet with 100 bars.

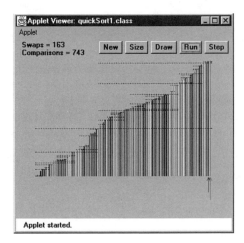

Watch how the algorithm partitions the array into two parts, and then sorts each of these parts by partitioning it into two parts, and so on, creating smaller and smaller subarrays.

When the sorting process is complete, each dotted line provides a visual record of one of the sorted subarrays. The horizontal range of the line shows which bars were part of the subarray, and its vertical position is the pivot value (the height of the pivot). The total length of all these lines on the display is a measure of how much work the algorithm has done to sort the array; we'll return to this topic later.

Each dotted line (except the shortest ones) should have a line below it (probably separated by other, shorter lines) and a line above it that together add up to the same length as the original line (less one bar). These are the two partitions into which each subarray is divided.

Examining the Details

For a more detailed examination of quicksort's operation, switch to the 12-bar display in the quickSort1 Workshop applet and step through the sorting process. You'll see how the pivot value corresponds to the height of the pivot on the right side of the array, how the

13

algorithm partitions the array, swaps the pivot into the space between the two sorted groups, sorts the shorter group (using many recursive calls), and then sorts the larger group.

Figure 13.7 shows all the steps involved in sorting 12 bars. The horizontal brackets under the arrays show which subarray is being partitioned at each step, and the circled numbers show the order in which these partitions are created. A pivot being swapped into place is shown with a dotted arrow. The final position of the pivot is shown as a dotted cell to emphasize that this cell contains a sorted item that will not be changed thereafter. Horizontal brackets under single cells (steps 5, 6, 7, 11, and 12) are base case calls to recQuickSort(); they return immediately.

Sometimes, as in steps 4 and 10, the pivot ends up in its original position on the right side of the array being sorted. In this situation, there is only one subarray remaining to be sorted: that to the left of the pivot. There is no second subarray to its right.

The different steps in Figure 13.7 occur at different levels of recursion, as shown in Table 13.1. The initial call from main() to recQuickSort() is the first level, recQuickSort() calling two new instances of itself is the second level, these two instances calling four more instances is the third level, and so on.

TABLE 13.1   RECURSION LEVELS FOR FIGURE 13.7

Step	Recursion Level
1	1
2, 8	2
3, 7, 9, 12	3
4, 10	4
5, 6, 11	5

The order in which the partitions are created, corresponding to the step numbers, does not correspond with depth. It's not the case that all the first-level partitions are done first, then all the second level ones, and so on. Instead the left group at every level is handled before any of the right groups.

In theory there should be eight steps in the fourth level and 16 in the fifth level, but in this small array we run out of items before these steps are necessary.

FIGURE 13.7

The quicksort process.

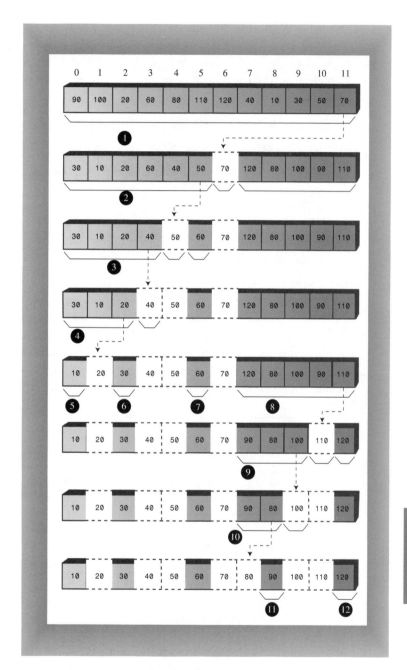

The number of levels in the table shows that with 12 data items, the machine stack needs enough space for 5 sets of arguments and return values; one for each recursion level. This is, as we'll see later, somewhat greater than the logarithm to the base 2 of the number of items: $\log_2 N$. The size of the machine stack is determined by your particular system.

Details to Notice in the Workshop Applet

Here's are some details you might notice as you run the quickSort1 Workshop applet.

You might think that a powerful algorithm like quicksort would not be able to handle subarrays as small as 2 or 3 items. However, this version of the quicksort algorithm is quite capable of sorting such small subarrays; leftScan and rightScan just don't go very far before they meet. For this reason we don't need to use a different sorting scheme for small subarrays. (Although, as we'll see in Hour 14, "Improving Quicksort," handling small subarrays differently might have advantages.)

At the end of each scan, the leftScan variable ends up pointing to the partition—that is, the left element of the right subarray. The pivot is then swapped with the partition to put the pivot in its proper place, as we've seen. As we noted, in steps 3 and 9 of Figure 13.7, leftScan ends up pointing to the pivot itself, so the swap has no effect. This might seem like a wasted swap; you might decide that leftScan should stop one bar sooner. However, it's important that leftScan scan all the way to the pivot, otherwise a swap would unsort the pivot and the partition.

> Be aware that leftScan and rightScan start at left-1 and right. This might look peculiar on the display, especially if left is 0; then leftScan will start at -1. Similarly rightScan initially points to the pivot, which is not included in the partitioning process. These markers start outside the subarray being partitioned because they will be incremented and decremented, respectively, before they're used the first time.

The applet shows ranges as numbers in parentheses; for example, (2–5) means the subarray from index 2 to index 5. The range given in some of the messages might be negative: from a higher number to a lower one: Array partitioned; left (7-6), right (8-8), for example. The (8–8) range means a single cell (8), but what does (7–6) mean? This range isn't real; it simply reflects the values that left and right, the arguments to recQuickSort(), have when this member function is called. Here's the code in question:

```
int partition = partitionIt(left, right, pivot);
recQuickSort(left, partition-1);   //sort left side
recQuickSort(partition+1, right);  //sort right side
```

If `partitionIt()` is called with `left` = 7 and `right` = 8, for example, and happens to return 7 as the partition, the range supplied in the first call to `recQuickSort()` will be (7–6) and the range to the second will be (8–8). This is normal. The base case in `recQuickSort()` is activated by array sizes less than 1 as well as by 1, so it will return immediately for negative ranges. Negative ranges are not shown in Figure 13.7, although they do cause (brief) calls to `recQuickSort()`.

Quicksort has some problems we haven't examined yet. In the next hour we'll see how to solve these problems We'll also discuss the efficiency of quicksort.

Summary

In this hour, you've learned the following:

- To *partition* an array is to divide it into two subarrays, one of which holds items with key values less than a specified value, while the other holds items with keys greater or equal to this value.

- The *pivot value* is the value that determines into which group an item will go during partitioning; items smaller than the pivot value go in the left group, larger items go in the right group.

- Partitioning operates in linear O(N) time, making N plus 1 or 2 comparisons and fewer than N/2 swaps.

- The partitioning algorithm may require extra tests in its inner `while` loops to prevent the indices running off the ends of the array.

- The `quicksort()` function partitions an array and then calls itself twice recursively to sort the two resulting subarrays.

- The pivot value for a partition in quicksort is the key value of a specific item, called the *pivot*.

- In a simple version of quicksort, the pivot can always be the item at the right end of the subarray.

- During the partition the pivot is placed out of the way on the right, and is not involved in the partitioning process.

- Later the pivot is swapped again, into the space between the two partitions. This is its final sorted position.

13

Q&A

Q **There are a lot of nuances in the quicksort code. Do I really need to understand them in detail?**

A Not if you're just going to use a quicksort that someone else has written. Of course, if you're going to write your own quicksort routine, they're important.

Q **Is it really necessary to worry about eliminating a single comparison by choosing the pivot point on the right? This can't speed up the algorithm all that much.**

A Any code in an innermost loop is worth optimizing as much as possible because it will be executed so often.

Q **Can I use the code shown in Listing 13.2 as a general-purpose sorting routine?**

A Before you do that, you should read the material in the next hour. You'll find a better algorithm there.

Workshop

The Workshop helps you solidify what you learned in this hour. See Appendix A for quiz answers.

Quiz

1. What does it mean to partition a number of data items?

2. What is the name given to the value used to separate the two groups into when partitioning?

3. Describe briefly how the C++ code that carries out the partitioning algorithm works.

4. True or false: The partitioning algorithm runs in O(N) time.

5. Briefly describe the operation of the quicksort algorithm.

6. What is the name of the data item whose key is the same as the pivot value?

7. How do we pick the pivot in the quicksort examples in this hour?

Exercise

Shuffle 10 playing cards (ace through 10) and lay them out in a row. Now sort them using the quicksort algorithm. That is, partition them, quicksort the low group, and then quicksort the high group. Pay attention to swapping the pivot card and to the other details described in this hour.

Hour **14**

Improving Quicksort

The quicksort program shown in Hour 13 suffers from a fairly serious efficiency problem if the data supplied to it happens to be inversely sorted. Also, quicksort can be speeded up somewhat by using a different approach to small partitions. In this hour you'll learn

- Why the basic quicksort algorithm runs slowly for inversely sorted data
- How to fix the inverse-data problem using median-of-three partitioning
- How to speed up quicksort by using insertion sort for small partitions

Problems with Inversely Sorted Data

If you use the quickSort1 Workshop applet to sort 100 inversely sorted bars, you'll see that the algorithm runs much more slowly, and that many more dotted horizontal lines are generated, indicating more and larger subarrays are being partitioned. What's happening here?

NEW TERM   The problem is in the selection of the pivot. Ideally, the pivot should be the median of the items being sorted. The *median* or *middle* item is the data item chosen so that exactly half the other items are smaller and half are larger.

That is, half the items should be larger than the pivot, and half smaller. This would result in the array being partitioned into two subarrays of equal size. Two equal subarrays is the optimum situation for the quicksort algorithm. If it has to sort one large and one small array, it's less efficient because the larger subarray has to be subdivided more times.

The worst situation results when a subarray with N elements is divided into one subarray with 1 element and the other with N–1 elements. (This division into 1 cell and N–1 cells can also be seen in steps 3 and 9 in Figure 13.7 in the last hour.) If this 1 and N–1 division happens with every partition, every element requires a separate partition step. This is in fact what takes place with inversely sorted data: In all the subarrays, the pivot is the smallest item, so every partition results in an N–1 elements in one subarray and only the pivot in the other.

To see this unfortunate process in action, step through the quickSort1 Workshop applet with 12 inversely sorted bars. Notice how many more steps are necessary than with random data. In this situation the advantage gained by the partitioning process is lost and the performance of the algorithm degenerates to $O(N^2)$.

Besides being slow, there's another potential problem when quicksort operates in $O(N^2)$ time. When the number of partitions increases, the number of recursive function calls also increases. Every function call takes up room on the machine stack. If there are too many calls, the machine stack can overflow and paralyze the system.

To summarize: In the quickSort1 applet, we select the rightmost element as the pivot. If the data is truly random, this isn't too bad a choice because usually the pivot won't be too close to either end of the array. However, when the data is sorted or inversely sorted, choosing the pivot from one end or the other is a bad idea. Can we improve on our approach to selecting the pivot?

Median-of-Three Partitioning

Many schemes have been devised for picking a better pivot. The method should be simple but have a good chance of avoiding the largest or smallest value. Picking an element at random is simple but—as we've seen—doesn't always result in a good selection. We could examine all the elements and actually calculate which one was the median. This would be the ideal pivot choice, but the process isn't practical because it would take more time than the sort itself.

NEW TERM A compromise solution is to find the median of the first, last, and middle elements of the array, and use this for the pivot. This is called the *median-of-three* approach and is shown in Figure 14.1.

FIGURE 14.1

The median of three.

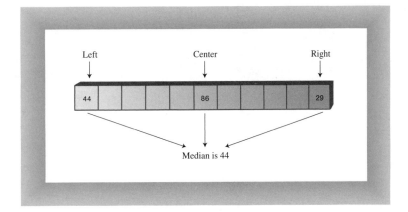

Finding the median of three items is obviously much faster than finding the median of all the items, and yet it successfully avoids picking the largest or smallest item in cases where the data is already sorted or inversely sorted. There are probably some pathological arrangements of data where the median-of-three scheme works poorly, but normally it's a fast and effective technique for finding the pivot.

Besides picking the pivot more effectively, the median-of-three approach has an additional benefit: We can dispense with the `rightMark>left` test in the second inside `while` loop, leading to a small increase in the algorithm's speed. How is this possible?

The test can be eliminated because we can use the median-of-three approach to not only select the pivot, but also to sort the three elements used in the selection process. Figure 14.2 shows how this looks.

NEW TERM After these three elements are sorted, and the median item is selected as the pivot, we are guaranteed that the element at the left end of the subarray is less than (or equal to) the pivot, and the element at the right end is greater than (or equal to) the pivot. This means that the `leftMark` and `rightMark` indices can't step beyond the right or left ends of the array, respectively, even if we remove the `leftMark>right` and `rightMark<left` tests. (The marker will stop, thinking it needs to swap the item, only to find that it has crossed the other marker and the partition is complete.)

14

FIGURE 14.2

Sorting the left, center, and right elements.

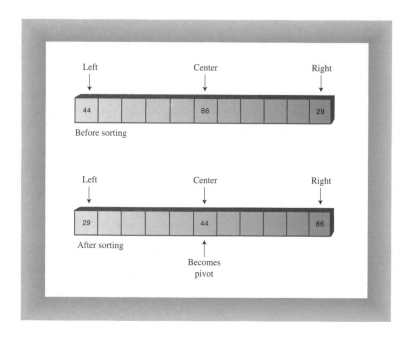

NEW TERM The values at `left` and `right` act as *sentinels* to keep `leftMark` and `rightMark` confined to valid array values. A sentinel in this context is a data item than an algorithm can examine to determine the end of a range.

> Another small benefit to median-of-three partitioning is that after the left, center, and right elements are sorted, the partition process doesn't need to examine these elements again. The partition can begin at `left+1` and `right-1` because `left` and `right` have in effect already been partitioned. We know that `left` is in the correct partition because it's on the left and it's less than the pivot, and `right` is in the correct place because it's on the right and it's greater than the pivot.

Thus, median-of-three partitioning not only avoids $O(N^2)$ performance for already-sorted data, it also allows us to speed up the inner loops of the partitioning algorithm and reduce slightly the number of items that must be partitioned.

Implementing Median-of-Three Partitioning in C++

Listing 14.1 shows the `quickSort2.cpp` program, which incorporates median-of-three partitioning. We use a separate member function, `medianOf3()`, to sort the left, center, and right elements of a subarray. This function returns the value of the pivot, which is then sent to the `partitionIt()` member function.

INPUT   **LISTING 14.1**   THE quickSort2.cpp PROGRAM

```cpp
//quickSort2.cpp
//demonstrates quick sort with median-of-three partitioning
#include <iostream>
#include <vector>
#include <cstdlib>              //for random numbers
#include <ctime>               //for random numbers
using namespace std;
////////////////////////////////////////////////////////////////
class ArrayIns
   {
   private:
      vector<double>(theVect);         //vector of doubles
      int nElems;                      //number of data items
   public:
//---------------------------------------------------------------
   ArrayIns(int max) : nElems(0)      //constructor
      {
      theVect.resize(max);            //size the vector
      }
//---------------------------------------------------------------
   void insert(double value)          //put element into array
      {
      theVect[nElems] = value;        //insert it
      nElems++;                       //increment size
      }
//---------------------------------------------------------------
   void display()                     //displays array contents
      {
      cout << "A=";
      for(int j=0; j<nElems; j++)     //for each element,
         cout << theVect[j] << " ";   //display it
      cout << endl;
      }
//---------------------------------------------------------------
   void quickSort()                   //sort array
      {
      recQuickSort(0, nElems-1);      //call recursive sort
      }
//---------------------------------------------------------------
   void recQuickSort(int left, int right)  //recursive sort
      {
      int size = right-left+1;
      if(size <= 3)                   //manual sort if small
```

14

continues

LISTING **14.1**   CONTINUED

```
               manualSort(left, right);
           else                                  //quicksort if large
               {
               double median = medianOf3(left, right);
               int partition = partitionIt(left, right, median);
               recQuickSort(left, partition-1);
               recQuickSort(partition+1, right);
               }
           }  //end recQuickSort()
//----------------------------------------------------------------
       double medianOf3(int left, int right)
           {
           int center = (left+right)/2;
                                             //order left & center
           if( theVect[left] > theVect[center] )
               swap(left, center);
                                             //order left & right
           if( theVect[left] > theVect[right] )
               swap(left, right);
                                             //order center & right
           if( theVect[center] > theVect[right] )
               swap(center, right);

           swap(center, right-1);            //put pivot on right
           return theVect[right-1];          //return median value
           }  //end medianOf3()
//----------------------------------------------------------------
       void swap(int dex1, int dex2)         //swap two elements
           {
           double temp = theVect[dex1];      //A into temp
           theVect[dex1] = theVect[dex2];    //B into A
           theVect[dex2] = temp;             //temp into B
           }  //end swap(
//----------------------------------------------------------------
                                             //partition a range
       int partitionIt(int left, int right, double pivot)
           {
           int leftMark = left;              //right of first elem
           int rightMark = right - 1;        //left of pivot

           while(true)
               {
               while( theVect[++leftMark] < pivot ) //find bigger
                   ;                                 //   (nop)
               while( theVect[--rightMark] > pivot ) //find smaller
                   ;                                 //   (nop)
               if(leftMark >= rightMark)      //if pointers cross,
```

```
                break;                          //    partition done
            else                                //not crossed, so
                swap(leftMark, rightMark); //swap elements
            }   //end while(true)
        swap(leftMark, right-1);                //restore pivot
        return leftMark;                        //return pivot location
        }   //end partitionIt()
//------------------------------------------------------------
    void manualSort(int left, int right)
        {
        int size = right-left+1;
        if(size <= 1)
            return;                             //no sort necessary
        if(size == 2)
            if( theVect[left] > theVect[right] )
                swap(left, right);
            return;
            }
        else   //size==3, so 3-sort left, center (right-1) & right
            {
            if( theVect[left] > theVect[right-1] )
                swap(left, right-1);                //left, center
            if( theVect[left] > theVect[right] )
                swap(left, right);                  //left, right
            if( theVect[right-1] > theVect[right] )
                swap(right-1, right);               //center, right
            }
        }   //end manualSort()
//------------------------------------------------------------
    };  //end class ArrayIns
////////////////////////////////////////////////////////////////
int main()
    {
    time_t aTime;
    int maxSize = 16;               //array size
    ArrayIns arr(maxSize);          //create the array
    srand( static_cast<unsigned>(time(&aTime)) );  //seed randoms

    for(int j=0; j<maxSize; j++)    //fill array with
        {                           //random numbers
        double n = rand() % 99;
        arr.insert(n);
        }
    arr.display();                  //display items
    arr.quickSort();                //quicksort them
    arr.display();                  //display them again
    return 0;
    }   //end main()
```

14

ANALYSIS This program uses another new member function, manualSort(), to sort subarrays of three or fewer elements. It returns immediately if the subarray is one cell (or less), swaps the cells if necessary if the range is 2, and sorts three cells if the range is 3. The recQuickSort() routine can't be used to sort ranges of 2 or 3 because median partitioning requires at least four cells.

The main() routine and the output of quickSort2.cpp are similar to those of quickSort1.cpp.

The quickSort2 Workshop Applet

The quickSort2 Workshop applet demonstrates the quicksort algorithm using median-of-three partitioning. This applet is similar to the quickSort1 Workshop applet, but starts off sorting the first, center, and left elements of each subarray and selecting the median of these as the pivot value. At least, it does this if the array size is greater than 3. If the subarray is 2 or 3 units, the applet simply sorts it "by hand" without partitioning or recursive calls.

Notice the dramatic improvement in performance when the applet is used to sort 100 inversely ordered bars. No longer is every subarray partitioned into one cell and N–1 cells; instead the subarrays are partitioned roughly in half.

Other than this improvement for ordered data, the quickSort2 Workshop applet produces results similar to quickSort1. It is no faster when sorting random data; its advantages become evident only when sorting ordered data.

Handling Small Partitions

NEW TERM If you use the median-of-three partitioning scheme, it follows that the quicksort algorithm won't work for partitions of three or fewer items. The number 3 in this case is called a *cutoff* point. In the preceding examples we sorted subarrays of 2 or 3 items by hand, using the manualSort() function. Is this the best way?

Using an Insertion Sort for Small Partitions

Another option for dealing with small partitions is to use the insertion sort. When you do this, you aren't restricted to a cutoff of 3. You can set the cutoff to 10, 20, or any other number. It's interesting to experiment with different values of the cutoff to see where the best performance lies. Knuth (see Appendix C, "Further Reading") recommends a cutoff of 9. However, the optimum number depends on your computer, operating system, compiler, and so on.

The quickSort3.cpp program, shown in Listing 14.2, uses an insertion sort to handle subarrays of fewer than 10 cells. The output of this program is similar to those of the other quickSort programs.

OUTPUT   **LISTING 14.2**   THE quickSort3.cpp PROGRAM

```cpp
//quickSort3.cpp
//demonstrates quick sort; uses insertion sort for cleanup
#include <iostream>
#include <vector>
#include <cstdlib>                      //for rand()
#include <ctime>                        //for rand()
using namespace std;
////////////////////////////////////////////////////////////////
class ArrayIns
   {
   private:
      vector<double> theArray;          //array theArray
      int nElems;                       //number of data items
   public:
//--------------------------------------------------------------
   ArrayIns(int max)                    //constructor
      {
      theArray.reserve(max);            //change size of vector
      nElems = 0;                       //no items yet
      }
//--------------------------------------------------------------
   void insert(double value)            //put element into array
      {
      theArray[nElems] = value;         //insert it
      nElems++;                         //increment size
      }
//--------------------------------------------------------------
   void display()                       //displays array contents
      {
      cout << "A=";
      for(int j=0; j<nElems; j++)       //for each element,
         cout << theArray[j] << " ";    //display it
      cout << endl;
      }
//--------------------------------------------------------------
   void quickSort()                     //sort the array
      {
      recQuickSort(0, nElems-1);
//    insertionSort(0, nElems-1);       //(another option)
      }
//--------------------------------------------------------------
```

continues

14

LISTING 14.2   CONTINUED

```
    void recQuickSort(int left, int right)  //recursive quicksort
       {
       int size = right-left+1;
       if(size < 10)                        //insertion sort if small
          insertionSort(left, right);
       else                                 //quicksort if large
          {
          double median = medianOf3(left, right);
          int partition = partitionIt(left, right, median);
          recQuickSort(left, partition-1);
          recQuickSort(partition+1, right);
          }
       } //end recQuickSort()
//-------------------------------------------------------------
    double medianOf3(int left, int right)
       {
       int center = (left+right)/2;
                                            //order left & center
       if( theArray[left] > theArray[center] )
          swap(left, center);
                                            //order left & right
       if( theArray[left] > theArray[right] )
          swap(left, right);
                                            //order center & right
       if( theArray[center] > theArray[right] )
          swap(center, right);

       swap(center, right-1);            //put pivot on right
       return theArray[right-1];         //return median value
       } //end medianOf3()
//-------------------------------------------------------------
    void swap(int dex1, int dex2)        //swap two elements
       {
       double temp = theArray[dex1];     //A into temp
       theArray[dex1] = theArray[dex2];  //B into A
       theArray[dex2] = temp;            //temp into B
       } //end swap(
//-------------------------------------------------------------
    int partitionIt(int left, int right, double pivot)
       {
       int leftMark = left;              //right of first elem
       int rightMark = right - 1;        //left of pivot
       while(true)
          {
          while( theArray[++leftMark] < pivot )  //find bigger
             ;                                    //  (nop)
          while( theArray[--rightMark] > pivot ) //find smaller
```

```
             ;                                    //   (nop)
        if(leftMark >= rightMark)     //if pointers cross,
           break;                     //   partition done
        else                          //not crossed, so
           swap(leftMark, rightMark); //swap elements
        } //end while(true)
     swap(leftMark, right-1);         //restore pivot
     return leftMark;                 //return pivot location
     } //end partitionIt()
//-----------------------------------------------------------
   void insertionSort(int left, int right)  //insertion sort
     {
     int in, out;
                                      //sorted on left of out
     for(out=left+1; out<=right; out++)
        {
        double temp = theArray[out];  //remove marked item
        in = out;                     //start shifts at out
                                      //until one is smaller,
        while(in>left && theArray[in-1] >= temp)
           {
           theArray[in] = theArray[in-1]; //shift item to right
           --in;                      //go left one position
           }
        theArray[in] = temp;          //insert marked item
        } //end for
     } //end insertionSort()
//-----------------------------------------------------------
   };  //end class ArrayIns
////////////////////////////////////////////////////////////
int main()
   {
   int maxSize = 16;                 //array size
   ArrayIns arr(maxSize);            //create array
   time_t aTime;                     //seed random numbers
   srand(static_cast<unsigned>( time(&aTime) ));

   for(int j=0; j<maxSize; j++)      //fill array with
      {                              //random numbers
      double n = rand() % 99;
      arr.insert(n);
      }
   arr.display();                    //display items
   arr.quickSort();                  //quicksort them
   arr.display();                    //display them again
   return 0;
   } //end main()
```

14

ANALYSIS In this example the cutoff is 10. Subarrays smaller than that use the insertion sort. Using the insertion sort for small subarrays turns out to be the fastest approach on our particular installation, but it is not much faster than sorting subarrays of 3 or fewer cells by hand, as in quickSort2.cpp. The numbers of comparisons and copies are reduced substantially in the quicksort phase, but are increased by an almost equal amount in the insertion sort, so the time savings is not dramatic. However, it's probably a worthwhile approach if you are trying to squeeze the last ounce of performance out of quicksort.

Insertion Sort Following Quicksort

Another option is to completely quicksort the array without bothering to sort partitions smaller than the cutoff. This is shown with a commented statement in the quickSort() function. If you activate this statement, you should change recQuickSort() to do nothing for small partitions, rather than calling insertionSort(). When quicksort is finished, the array will be almost sorted. You then apply the insertion sort to the entire array. The insertion sort is supposed to operate efficiently on almost-sorted arrays, and this approach is recommended by some experts, but on our installation it runs very slowly. The insertion sort appears to be happier doing a lot of small sorts than one big one.

Another embellishment recommended by many writers is removing recursion from the quicksort algorithm. This involves rewriting the algorithm to store deferred subarray bounds (left and right) on a stack, and using a loop instead of recursion to oversee the partitioning of smaller and smaller subarrays. The idea in doing this is to speed up the program by removing function calls. However, this idea arose with older compilers and computer architectures, which imposed a large time penalty for each function call. It's not clear that removing recursion is much of an improvement for modern systems, which handle function calls more efficiently.

Efficiency of Quicksort

We've said that quicksort operates in O(N*logN) time. As we saw in the discussion of mergesort in Hour 12, "Applied Recursion," this is generally true of the divide-and-conquer algorithms, in which a recursive function divides a range of items into two groups and then calls itself to handle each group. In this situation the logarithm actually has a base of 2: the running time is proportional to $N*\log_2 N$.

You can get an idea of the validity of this $N*\log_2 N$ running time for quicksort by running one of the quickSort Workshop applets with 100 random bars and examining the resulting dotted horizontal lines.

Each dotted line represents an array or subarray being partitioned: the pointers leftScan and rightScan moving toward each other, comparing data items and swapping when appropriate. We saw in the section on partitioning that a single partition runs in O(N) time. This tells us that the total length of all the lines is proportional to the running time of quicksort. But how long are all the lines? It would be tedious to measure them with a ruler on the screen, but we can visualize them a different way.

There is always one line that runs the entire width of the graph, spanning N bars. This results from the first partition. There will also be two lines (one below and one above the first line) that have an average length of N/2 bars; together they are again N bars long. Then there will be four lines with an average length of N/4 that again total N bars, and then 8 lines, 16, and so on. Figure 14.3 shows how this looks for 1, 2, 4, and 8 lines.

FIGURE 14.3

Lines correspond to partitions.

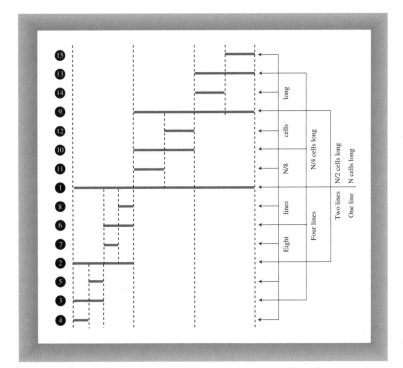

In this figure solid horizontal lines represent the dotted horizontal lines in the quicksort applets, and captions like N/4 cells long indicate average, not actual, line lengths. The circled numbers on the left show the order in which the lines are created.

Each series of lines (the eight N/8 lines, for example) corresponds to a level of recursion. The initial call to recQuickSort() is the first level and makes the first line; the two calls from within the first call—the second level of recursion—make the next two lines; and so on. If we assume we start with 100 cells, the results are shown in Table 14.1.

TABLE 14.1   LINE LENGTHS AND RECURSION

Recursion Level	Step Numbers in Figure 14.3	Average Line Length (Cells)	Number of Lines	Total Length (Cells)
1	1	100	1	100
2	2, 9	50	2	100
3	3, 6, 10, 13	25	4	100
4	4, 5, 7, 8, 11, 12, 14, 15	12	8	96
5	Not shown	6	16	96
6	Not shown	3	32	96
7	Not shown	1	64	64
				Total = 652

Where does this division process stop? If we keep dividing 100 by 2, and count how many times we do this, we get the series 100, 50, 25, 12, 6, 3, 1, which is about 7 levels of recursion. This looks about right on the workshop applets: If you pick some point on the graph and count all the dotted lines directly above and below it, there will be an average of approximately 7. (In Figure 14.3, because not all levels of recursion are shown, only 4 lines intersect any vertical slice of the graph.)

Table 14.1 shows a total of 652 cells. This is only an approximation because of rounding errors, but it's close to 100 times the logarithm to the base 2 of 100, which is 6.65. Thus this informal analysis suggests the validity of the $N*\log_2 N$ running time for quicksort.

More specifically, in the section on partitioning, we found that there should be N+2 comparisons and fewer than N/2 swaps. Multiplying these quantities by $\log_2 N$ for various values of N gives the results shown in Table 14.2.

TABLE 14.2 SWAPS AND COMPARISONS IN QUICKSORT

N	8	12	16	64	100	128
$\log_2 N$	3	3.59	4	6	6.65	7
$N*\log_2 N$	24	43	64	384	665	896
Comparisons: $(N+2)*\log_2 N$	30	50	72	396	678	910
Swaps: Fewer than $N/2*\log_2 N$	12	21	32	192	332	448

The $\log_2 N$ quantity used in Table 14.2 is actually true only in the best-case scenario, where each subarray is partitioned exactly in half. For random data the figure is slightly greater. Nevertheless, the quickSort1 and quickSort2 Workshop applets approximate these results for 12 and 100 bars, as you can see by running them and observing the Swaps and Comparisons fields.

Because they have different cutoff points and handle the resulting small partitions differently, quickSort1 performs fewer swaps but more comparisons than quickSort2. The number of swaps shown in the table is the maximum (which assumes the data is inversely sorted). For random data the actual number of swaps turns out to be one-half to two-thirds of the figures shown.

Summary

In this hour, you've learned the following:

- In the simple version of quicksort, performance is only $O(N^2)$ for already-sorted (or inversely sorted) data.
- In the more advanced version of quicksort, the pivot can be the median of the first, last, and center items in the subarray. This is called *median-of-three* partitioning.
- Median-of-three partitioning effectively eliminates the problem of $O(N^2)$ performance for already-sorted data.
- In median-of-three partitioning, the left, center, and right items are sorted at the same time the median is determined.
- Quicksort operates in $O(N*\log_2 N)$ time (except when the simpler version is applied to already-sorted data).
- Subarrays smaller than a certain size (the *cutoff*) can be sorted by a function other than quicksort.
- The insertion sort is commonly used to sort subarrays smaller than the cutoff.
- The insertion sort can also be applied to the entire array, after it has been sorted down to a cutoff point by quicksort.

14

Q&A

Q If I never try to sort inversely sorted data, isn't it all right to use the simpler technique shown in the `quickSort1.cpp` program in the last hour, instead of the more complicated programs shown in this hour?

A It's all right if you're sure you'll never be faced with inversely sorted data, but why take the chance?

Q Is quicksort really the best approach to sorting?

A Generally it is. It's not the best approach for small amounts of data or almost-sorted data (the insertion sort is better here), or for data stored in external storage like a disk file. There might be other specific situations where it's not optimum, but usually it's a good choice.

Workshop

The Workshop helps you solidify what you learned in this hour. See Appendix A for quiz answers.

Quiz

1. Is there a particular arrangement of data that the naive version of quickSort (where the pivot is always on the right) might have trouble sorting?

2. Why is the naive quicksort so slow for inversely sorted data?

3. What is median-of-three partitioning?

4. Name three ways, besides quicksort, to sort small partitions.

5. Which is the best system?

6. If you use median-of-three partitioning, why can't you use quicksort to sort very small partitions?

7. What is an easy but tedious way to measure the efficiency of the quicksort algorithm, using the Workshop applet?

Exercise

Recompile the quickSort3.cpp program to sort much larger arrays. Make them large enough that you can time the sorting process with a stopwatch. Then experiment with different cutoff points (the subarray size below which the insertion sort is used). Figure out the cutoff that provides the fastest performance on your particular system.

PART IV
Trees

Hour

Hour 15

Binary Trees

In this hour we switch from algorithms—the focus of the last few hours on sorting—to data structures. Binary trees are one of the fundamental data structures used in programming. They provide advantages that the data structures we've seen so far (arrays and lists) cannot. In this hour we'll learn

- Why you would want to use trees
- Some terminology for describing trees
- What binary trees and binary search trees are
- How to go about creating trees
- How to find and insert data in a tree

We'll also present C++ code fragments for these activities. In the next hour we'll find how to visit all the nodes in a tree, and examine a complete C++ program that incorporates the various tree operations.

Why Use Binary Trees?

Why might you want to use a tree? Usually because it combines the advantages of two other structures: an ordered array and a linked list. You can search a tree quickly, as you can an ordered array, and you can also insert and delete items quickly, as you can with a linked list. Let's explore these topics a bit before delving into the details of trees.

Slow Insertion in an Ordered Array

Imagine an array in which all the elements are arranged in order; that is, an ordered array, such as we saw in Hour 3, "Ordered Arrays." As we learned, it's quick to search such an array for a particular value, using a binary search. You check in the center of the array. If the object you're looking for is greater than what you find there, you narrow your search to the top half of the array; if it's less, you narrow your search to the bottom half. Applying this process repeatedly finds the object in O(log N) time. It's also quick to iterate through an ordered array, visiting each object in sorted order.

On the other hand, if you want to insert a new object into an ordered array, you first must find where the object will go, and then move all the objects with greater keys up one space in the array to make room for it. These multiple moves are time-consuming because they require, on average, moving half the items (N/2 moves). Deletion involves the same multimove operation, and is thus equally slow.

If you're going to be doing a lot of insertions and deletions, an ordered array is a bad choice.

Slow Searching in a Linked List

On the other hand, as we saw in Hour 8, "Linked Lists," insertions and deletions are quick to perform on a linked list. They are accomplished simply by changing a few pointers. These operations require O(1) time (the fastest Big O time).

Unfortunately, however, finding a specified element in a linked list is not so easy. You must start at the beginning of the list and visit each element until you find the one you're looking for. Thus you will need to visit an average of N/2 objects, comparing each one's key with the desired value. This is slow, requiring O(N) time. (Notice that times considered fast for a sort are slow for data structure operations.)

You might think you could speed things up by using an ordered linked list, in which the elements were arranged in order, but this doesn't help. You still must start at the beginning and visit the elements in order because there's no way to access a given element without following the chain of pointers to it. (Of course, in an ordered list it's much quicker to visit the nodes in order than it is in a non-ordered list, but that doesn't help to find an arbitrary object.)

Trees to the Rescue

It would be nice if there were a data structure with the quick insertion and deletion of a linked list, and also the quick searching of an ordered array. Trees provide both these characteristics, and are also one of the most interesting data structures.

What Is a Tree?

We'll be mostly interested in a particular kind of tree called a binary tree, but let's start by discussing trees in general before moving on to the specifics of binary trees.

A tree consists of nodes connected by edges. Figure 15.1 shows a tree. In such a picture of a tree (or in our Workshop applet) the nodes are represented as circles, and the edges as lines connecting the circles.

Figure 15.1

A tree.

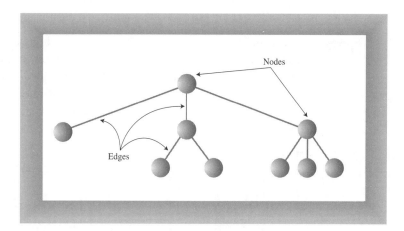

Trees have been studied extensively as abstract mathematical entities, so there's a large amount of theoretical knowledge about them.

> A tree is actually an instance of a more general category called a *graph*.

 New Term   In computer programs, *nodes* often represent data items such as people, car parts, airline reservations, and so on; in other words, the typical items we store in any kind of data structure. In an OOP language like C++ these real-world entities are represented by objects. We've seen such data items stored in arrays and lists; now we'll see them stored in the nodes of trees.

New Term The *lines* (edges) between the nodes represent the way the nodes are related. Roughly speaking, the lines represent convenience: It's easy (and fast) for a program to get from one node to another if there is a line connecting them. In fact, the only way to get from node to node is to follow a path along the lines. Often you are restricted to going in one direction along edges: from the root downward. Edges are likely to be represented in a program by pointers, if the program is written in C++.

Typically there is one node in the top row of a tree, with lines connecting to more nodes on the second row, even more on the third, and so on. Thus trees are small on the top and large on the bottom. This might seem upside-down compared with real trees, but generally a program starts an operation at the small end of the tree, and it's (arguably) more natural to think about going from top to bottom, as in reading text.

New Term There are different kinds of trees. The tree shown in Figure 15.1 has more than two children per node. (We'll see what *children* means in a moment.) However, in this hour we'll be discussing a specialized form of tree called a *binary* tree. Each node in a binary tree has a maximum of two children. More general trees, in which nodes can have more than two children, are called *multiway* trees. We'll see an example in Hour 19, where we discuss 2-3-4 trees.

We've mentioned some aspects of trees in general; now let's look at terms for various parts of trees.

Tree Terminology

Many terms are used to describe particular aspects of trees. You need to know a few of them so our discussion will be comprehensible. Fortunately, most of these terms are related to real-world trees or to family relationships (as in parents and children), so they're not hard to remember. Figure 15.2 shows many of these terms applied to a binary tree.

Path

New Term Think of someone walking from node to node along the edges that connect them. The resulting sequence of nodes is called a *path*.

Root

New Term The node at the top of the tree is called the *root*. There is only one root in a tree. For a collection of nodes and edges to be defined as a tree, there must be one

15

(and only one!) path from the root to any other node. Figure 15.3 shows a non-tree. You can see that it violates this rule.

FIGURE **15.2**

Tree terms.

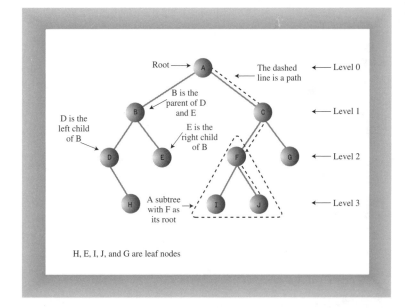

FIGURE **15.3**

A non-tree.

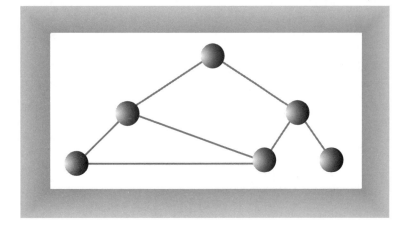

Parent

 Any node (except the root) has exactly one edge running upward to another node. The node above it is called the *parent* of the node.

Child

 Any node can have one or more lines running downward to other nodes. These nodes below a given node are called its *children*.

Leaf

 A node that has no children is called a *leaf node* or simply a *leaf*. There can be only one root in a tree, but there can be many leaves.

Subtree

 Any node can be considered to be the root of a *subtree*, which consists of its children, and its children's children, and so on. If you think in terms of families, a node's subtree contains all its descendants.

Visiting

 A node is *visited* when program control arrives at the node, usually for the purpose of carrying out some operation on the node, such as checking the value of one of its data members, or displaying it. Merely passing over a node on the path from one node to another is not considered to be visiting the node.

Traversing

 To *traverse* a tree means to visit all the nodes in some specified order. For example, you might visit all the nodes in order of ascending key value. There are other ways to traverse a tree, as we'll see in the next hour.

Levels

 The *level* of a particular node refers to how many generations the node is from the root. If we assume the root is Level 0, its children will be Level 1, its grandchildren will be Level 2, and so on.

Keys

 We've seen that one data item in an object is usually designated a *key value*. This value is used to search for the item or perform other operations on it. In tree diagrams, when a circle represents a node holding a data item, the key value of the item is typically shown in the circle. (We'll see many figures later on that show how this looks.)

Binary Trees

 If every node in a tree can have at most two children, the tree is called a *binary tree*. In this hour we'll focus on binary trees because they are the simplest, the most common, and in many situations the most frequently used.

NEW TERM The two children of each node in a binary tree are called the *left child* and the *right child*, corresponding to their positions when you draw a picture of a tree, as shown in Figure 15.2. A node in a binary tree doesn't necessarily have the maximum of two children; it might have only a left child, or only a right child, or it can have no children at all (which means it's a leaf).

NEW TERM The kind of binary tree we'll be dealing with in this discussion is technically called a *binary search tree*. The defining characteristic of a binary search tree is this: A node's left child must have a key less than its parent, and a node's right child must have a key greater than or equal to its parent. Figure 15.4 shows a binary search tree.

15

FIGURE 15.4

A binary search tree.

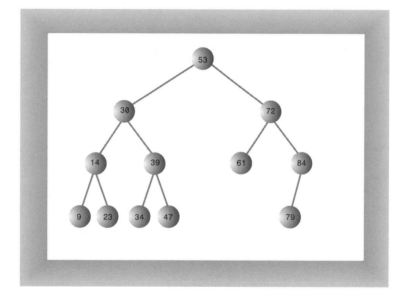

Now that we've learned how to describe the parts of a tree, let's look at a tree structure that you're probably already familiar with.

A Tree Analogy in Your Computer

One commonly encountered tree is the hierarchical file structure in a computer system. The root directory of a given device (designated with the backslash, as in `C:\`, on many systems) is the tree's root. The directories one level below the root directory are its children. There may be many levels of subdirectories. Files are leaves; they have no children of their own.

Clearly a hierarchical file structure is not a binary tree because a directory can have many children. A complete pathname, such as `C:\SALES\EAST\NOVEMBER\SMITH.DAT`, corresponds to the path from the root to the `SMITH.DAT` leaf node. Terms used for file structures, such as root and path, were borrowed from tree theory.

A hierarchical file structure differs in a significant way from the trees we'll be discussing here. In the file structure, subdirectories contain no data; they contain only references to other subdirectories or to files. Only files contain data. In a tree, every node contains data (a personnel record, car part specifications, or whatever). In addition to the data, all nodes (except leaves) contain pointers to other nodes.

Basic Binary Tree Operations

Let's see how to carry out the common binary-tree operations of finding a node with a given key and inserting a new node. For these operations we'll first show how to use the Tree Workshop applet to carry it out; then we'll look at the corresponding C++ code.

The Tree Workshop Applet

Start up the Binary TreeWorkshop applet. You'll see a screen something like that shown in Figure 15.5. However, because the tree in the Workshop applet is randomly generated, it won't look exactly the same as the tree in the figure.

FIGURE 15.5

The Binary Tree Workshop applet.

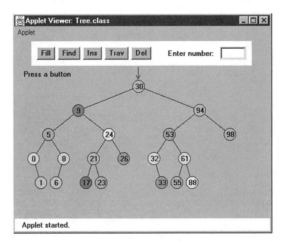

Using the Binary Tree Workshop Applet

The key values shown in the nodes range from 0 to 99. Of course, in a real tree, there would probably be a larger range of key values. For example, if employees' Social Security numbers were used for key values, they would range up to 999,999,999.

Another difference between the Workshop applet and a real tree is that the Workshop applet is limited to a depth of 5; that is, there can be no more than 5 levels from the root

15

to the bottom row. This restriction ensures that all the nodes in the tree will be visible on the screen. In a real tree the number of levels is theoretically unlimited.

Using the Workshop applet, you can create a new tree whenever you want.

To Do: Create a Tree with the Workshop Applet

1. Click the Fill button.
2. A prompt will ask you to enter the number of nodes in the tree. This can vary from 1 to 31, but 15 will give you a representative tree.
3. After typing in the number, click Fill twice more to generate the new tree. You can experiment by creating trees with different numbers of nodes.

Unbalanced Trees

NEW TERM Notice that some of thetrees you generate are *unbalanced*, that is, they have most of their nodes on one side of the root or the other, as shown in Figure 15.6. Individual subtrees may also be unbalanced.

FIGURE 15.6

An unbalanced tree (with an unbalanced subtree).

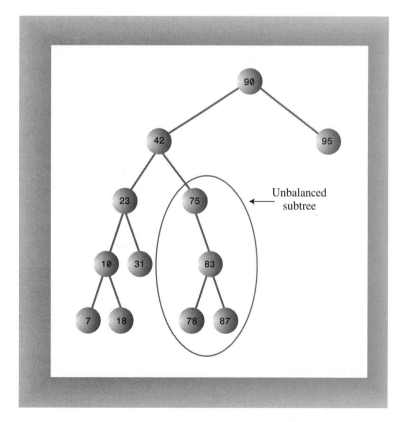

Trees become unbalanced because of the order in which the data items are inserted. If these key values are inserted randomly, the tree will be more or less balanced. However, if an ascending sequence (like 11, 18, 33, 42, 65, and so on) or a descending sequence is generated, all the values will be right children (if ascending) or left children (if descending) and the tree will be unbalanced. The key values in the Workshop applet are generated randomly, but of course some short ascending or descending sequences will be created anyway, which will lead to local imbalances. When you learn how to insert items into the tree in the Workshop applet, you can try building up a tree by inserting such an ordered sequence of items and see what happens.

If you ask for a large number of nodes when you use Fill to create a tree, you might not get as many nodes as you requested. Depending on how unbalanced the tree becomes, some branches might not be able to hold a full number of nodes. This is because the depth of the applet's tree is limited to five; the problem would not arise in a real tree.

If a tree is created by data items whose key values arrive in random order, the problem of unbalanced trees might not be too much of a problem for larger trees because the chances of a long run of numbers in sequence is small. But key values can arrive in strict sequence; for example, when a data-entry person arranges a stack of personnel files into order of ascending employee number before entering the data. When this happens, tree efficiency can be seriously degraded. We'll discuss unbalanced trees and what to do about them in Hour 17, "Red-Black Trees."

Representing the Tree in C++ Code

Let's see how we might implement a binary tree in C++. As with other data structures, there are several approaches to representing a tree in the computer's memory. The most common is to store the nodes at unrelated locations in memory, and connect them using pointers in each node that point to its children. (It's also possible to represent a tree in memory as an array, but we'll ignore that possibility here.)

As we discuss individual operations we'll show code fragments pertaining to that operation. The complete program from which these fragments are extracted can be seen in Listing 16.1 in the next hour.

The Node Class

First, we need a class of node objects. These objects contain the data representing the objects being stored (employees in an employee database, for example) and also pointers to each of the node's two children. Here's how that looks.

```
class Node
   {
   public:
      int iData;                 //data item (key)
```

```
      double dData;              //data item
      Node* pLeftChild;          //this node's left child
      Node* pRightChild;         //this node's right child
//------------------------------------------------------------
                                 //constructor
      Node() : iData(0), dData(0.0), pLeftChild(NULL),
                                  pRightChild(NULL)
         {  }
//------------------------------------------------------------
   void displayNode()        //display ourself: {75, 7.5}
         {
         cout << '{' << iData << ", " << dData << "} ";
         }
   };   //end class Node
```

Some programmers also include a pointer to the node's parent. This simplifies some operations but complicates others, so we don't include it. We do include a member function called displayNode() to display the node's data, but its code isn't relevant here.

There are other approaches to designing class Node. Instead of placing the data items directly into the node, you could use a pointer to an object representing the data item:

```
class Node
   {
   Person* p1;                //pointer to Person object
   Node* pLeftChild;          //pointer to left child
   Node* pRightChild;         //pointer to right child
   };
```

This makes it conceptually clearer that the node and the data item it holds aren't the same thing, but it results in somewhat more complicated code, so we'll stick to the first approach.

The Tree Class

We'll also need a class from which to create the tree itself; the object that holds all the nodes. We'll call this class Tree. It has only one data member: a Node* variable that holds a pointer to the root. It doesn't need data members for the other nodes because they are all accessed from the root.

The Tree class has a number of member functions: for finding and inserting, several for different kinds of traverses, and one to display the tree. Here's a skeleton version:

```
class Tree
   {
   private:
     Node* pRoot;              //first node of tree

   public:
//------------------------------------------------------------
```

```
   Tree() : pRoot(NULL)          //constructor
      { }
//-------------------------------------------------------------
   Node* find(int key)           //find node with given key
      { /*body not shown*/ }
//-------------------------------------------------------------
   void insert(int id, double dd) //insert new node
      { /*body not shown*/ }
//-------------------------------------------------------------
   void traverse(int traverseType)
      { /*body not shown*/ }
//-------------------------------------------------------------
   void displayTree()
      { /*body not shown*/ }
//-------------------------------------------------------------
};   //end class Tree
```

The `main()` Function

Finally, we need a way to perform operations on the tree. Here's how you might write a `main()` routine to create a tree, insert three nodes into it, and then search for one of them:

```
int main()
   {
   Tree theTree;                  //make a tree

   theTree.insert(50, 1.5);       //insert 3 nodes
   theTree.insert(25, 1.7);
   theTree.insert(75, 1.9);

   Node* found = theTree.find(25);  //find node with key 25
   if(found != NULL)
      cout << "Found the node with key 25" << endl;
   else
      cout << "Could not find node with key 25" << endl;
   return 0;
   } // end main()
```

In Listing 16.1 in the next hour the `main()` routine provides a primitive user interface so you can use the keyboard to insert, find, or perform other operations.

Next we'll look at individual tree operations: finding a node and inserting a node. We'll also briefly mention the problem of deleting a node.

Finding a Node

Finding a node with a specific key is the simplest of the major tree operations. Remember that the nodes in a binary search tree correspond to objects containing information. They could be objects representing people, with an employee number as the key and also perhaps name, address, telephone number, salary, and other data members. Or they could represent car parts, with a part number as the key value and data members for quantity on hand, price, and so on. However, the only characteristics of each node that we can see in the Workshop applet are a number and a color. A node is created with these two characteristics, and keeps them throughout its life.

Using the Workshop Applet to Find a Node

Look at the Workshop applet, and pick a node, preferably one near the bottom of the tree (as far from the root as possible). The number shown in this node is its key value. We're going to demonstrate how the Workshop applet finds the node, given the key value.

For purposes of this discussion we'll assume you've decided to find the node representing the item with key value 57, as shown in Figure 15.7. Of course, when you run the Workshop applet you'll get a different tree and will need to pick a different key value.

FIGURE 15.7

Finding node 57.

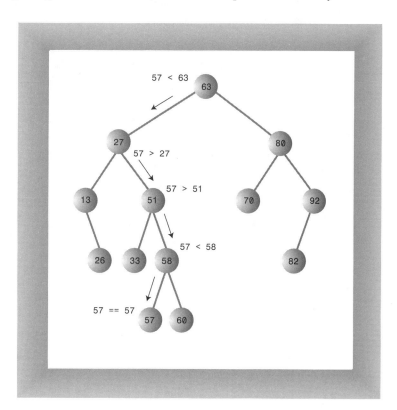

To Do: Find a Node

▼ To Do ▲

1. Click the Find button. The prompt will ask for the value of the node to find.

2. Enter 57 (or whatever the number is on the node you chose). Click Find twice more.

3. Continue to press the Find button. As the Workshop applet looks for the specified node, the prompt will display either `Going to left child` or `Going to right child`, and the red arrow will move down one level to the right or left.

In Figure 15.7 the arrow starts at the root. The program compares the key value 57 with the value at the root, which is 63. The key is less, so the program knows the desired node must be on the left side of the tree; either the root's left child or one of this child's descendants. The left child of the root has the value 27, so the comparison of 57 and 27 will show that the desired node is in the right subtree of 27. The arrow will go to 51, the root of this subtree. Here, 57 is again greater than the 51 node, so we go to the right, to 58, and then to the left, to 57. This time the comparison shows 57 equals the node's key value, so we've found the node we want.

The Workshop applet doesn't do anything with the node after it is found, except to display a message saying it has been found. A serious program would perform some operation on the found node, such as displaying its contents or changing one of its data members.

C++ Code for Finding a Node

Here's the code for the `find()` routine, which is a member function of the `Tree` class.

```
Node* find(int key)              //find node with given key
   {                             //(assumes non-empty tree)
   Node* pCurrent = pRoot;             //start at root
   while(pCurrent->iData != key)       //while no match,
      {
      if(key < pCurrent->iData)        //go left?
         pCurrent = pCurrent->pLeftChild;
      else                             //or go right?
         pCurrent = pCurrent->pRightChild;
      if(pCurrent == NULL)             //if no child,
         return NULL;                  //didn't find it
      }
   return pCurrent;                    //found it
   } //end find()
```

This routine uses the variable `pCurrent` to hold a pointer to the node it is currently examining. The argument `key` is the value to be found. The routine starts at the root. (It has to; this is the only node it can access directly.) That is, it sets `pCurrent` to the root.

Then, in the `while` loop, it compares the value to be found, `key`, with the value of the `iData` member (the key) in the current node. If `key` is less than this data member, `pCurrent` is set to the node's left child. If `key` is greater than (or equal) to the node's `iData` data member, then `pCurrent` is set to the node's right child.

Can't Find the Node

If `pCurrent` becomes equal to `NULL`, we couldn't find the next child node in the sequence; we've reached the end of the line without finding the node we were looking for, so it can't exist. We return `NULL` to indicate this fact.

Found the Node

If the condition of the `while` loop is not satisfied, so that we exit from the bottom of the loop, the `iData` data member of `pCurrent` is equal to `key`; that is, we've found the node we want. We return the node, so that the routine that called `find()` can access any of the node's data.

Efficiency of the Find Operation

As you can see, how long it takes to find a node depends on how many levels down it is situated. In the Workshop applet there can be up to 31 nodes, but no more than 5 levels. Thus you can find any node using a maximum of only 5 comparisons. This is O(log N) time, or more specifically $O(\log_2 N)$ time; the logarithm to the base 2. We'll discuss this further toward the end of the next hour.

Inserting a Node

To insert a node we must first find the place to insert it. This is much the same process as trying to find a node which turns out not to exist, as described in the section on `find`. We follow the path from the root to the appropriate node, which will be the parent of the new node. After this parent is found, the new node is connected as its left or right child, depending on whether the new node's key is less or greater than that of the parent.

Using the Workshop Applet to Insert a Node

Inserting a new node with the Workshop applet is similar to finding an existing node.

To Do: Insert a Node

1. Click the Ins button.
2. You'll be asked to type the key value of the node to be inserted. Let's assume we're going to insert a new node with the value 45. Type this into the text field.

3. Continue to press the Ins button. The red arrow will move down to the insertion
       point and attach the new node.

The first step for the program in inserting a node is to find where it should be inserted.
Figure 15.8a shows how this looks.

FIGURE 15.8

Inserting a node.

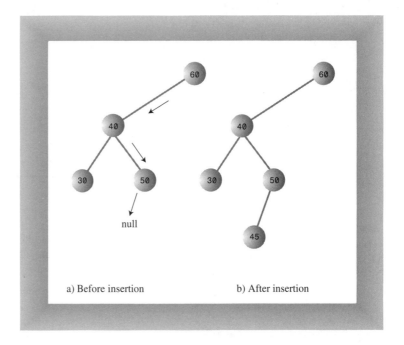

a) Before insertion   b) After insertion

The value 45 is less than 60 but greater than 40, so we arrive at node 50. Now we want
to go left because 45 is less than 50, but 50 has no left child; its pLeftChild data member is NULL. When it sees this NULL, the insertion routine has found the place to attach the
new node. The Workshop applet does this by creating a new node with the value 45 (and
a randomly generated color) and connecting it as the left child of 50, as shown in Figure
15.8b.

C++ Code for Inserting a Node

The insert() function starts by creating the new node, using its arguments to supply the
data.

Next, insert() must determine where to insert the new node. This is done using roughly
the same code as finding a node, described in the section on find(). The difference is
that when you're simply trying to *find* a node and you encounter a NULL (non-existent)

node, you know the node you're looking for doesn't exist, so you return immediately. When you're trying to *insert* a node you insert it (creating it first, if necessary) before returning.

The value to be searched for is the data item passed in the argument id. The while loop uses true as its condition because it doesn't care if it encounters a node with the same value as id; it treats another node with the same key value as if it were simply greater than the key value. (We'll return to the subject of duplicate nodes in the next hour.)

In a real tree (as opposed to the Workshop applet) a place to insert a new node will always be found (unless you run out of memory); when it is, and the new node is attached, the while loop exits with a return statement.

Here's the code for the insert() function:

```
void insert(int id, double dd) //insert new node
   {
   Node* pNewNode = new Node;          //make new node
   pNewNode->iData = id;               //insert data
   pNewNode->dData = dd;
   if(pRoot==NULL)                     //no node in root
      pRoot = pNewNode;
   else                                //root occupied
      {
      Node* pCurrent = pRoot;          //start at root
      Node* pParent;
      while(true)                      //(exits internally)
         {
         pParent = pCurrent;
         if(id < pCurrent->iData)      //go left?
            {
            pCurrent = pCurrent->pLeftChild;
            if(pCurrent == NULL)       //if end of the line,
               {                       //insert on left
               pParent->pLeftChild = pNewNode;
               return;
               }
            }  //end if go left
         else                          //or go right?
            {
            pCurrent = pCurrent->pRightChild;
            if(pCurrent == NULL)       //if end of the line
               {                       //insert on right
               pParent->pRightChild = pNewNode;
               return;
               }
            }  //end else go right
         }  //end while
      }  //end else not root
   }  //end insert()
```

We use a new variable, pParent (a pointer to the parent of pCurrent), to remember the last non-NULL node we encountered (50 in the figure). This is necessary because pCurrent is set to NULL in the process of discovering that its previous value did not have an appropriate child. If we didn't save pParent, we would lose track of where we were.

To insert the new node, change the appropriate child pointer in pParent (the last non-NULL node you encountered) to point to the new node. If you were looking unsuccessfully for pParent's left child, you attach the new node as pParent's left child; if you were looking for its right child, you attach the new node as its right child. In Figure 15.8, 45 is attached as the left child of 50.

Deleting a Node

How do you delete a node? Unfortunately, the deletion process is complex and lengthy, and therefore beyond the scope of this book. There is a Del button in the Tree Workshop applet. You can experiment with this to see how different nodes are deleted in different ways. It's easy to delete a node with no children: just remove it. If a node has one child, it's deleted by attaching its child to its parent. However, if a node has two children, deleting it is quite complicated.

Some programs avoid the complexity of deletion by simply marking a node as "deleted." It's not really deleted, but algorithms can ignore it (except for its connections to other nodes). Consult the books in Appendix C, "Further Reading," for more on deletion.

In the next hour we'll find out how to examine all the nodes in a tree, and present the complete code for tree.cpp.

Summary

In this hour, you've learned the following:

- Trees consist of nodes (circles) connected by edges (lines).
- The root is the topmost node in a tree; it has no parent.
- In a binary tree, a node has at most two children.
- In a binary search tree, all the nodes that are left descendants of node A have key values less than A; all the nodes that are A's right descendants have key values greater than (or equal to) A.
- Trees perform searches, insertions, and deletions in O(log N) time.
- Nodes represent the data-objects being stored in the tree.

- Edges are most commonly represented in a program by pointers to a node's children (and sometimes to its parent).

- An unbalanced tree is one whose root has many more left descendents than right descendants, or vice versa.

- Searching for a node involves comparing the value to be found with the key value of a node, and going to that node's left child if the key search value is less, or to the node's right child if the search value is greater.

- Insertion involves finding the place to insert the new node, and then changing a child data member in its new parent to refer to it.

Q&A

Q Trees seems much more complicated than arrays or linked lists. Are they really useful?

A Trees are probably the single most useful data structure. They have comparatively fast searching, insertion, and deletion, which is not the case with simpler structures. For storing large amounts of data, a tree is usually the first thing you should consider.

Q Don't you sometimes need to rearrange the nodes in a tree when you insert a new node?

A Never. The new node is always attached to a leaf node, or as the missing child of a node with one child. However, when deleting a node rearrangement may be necessary.

Q Can we use the tree we've seen in this hour as a general-purpose data storage structure?

A Only in some circumstances. As we'll discuss in Hour 17, simple trees work poorly when the order of data insertion creates an unbalanced tree.

Workshop

The Workshop helps you solidify what you learned in this hour. See Appendix A for quiz answers.

Quiz

1. The tree class stores the location of only one node. Which node is it?

2. What is the name for a node with no children?

3. True or false: In a binary tree, each node can have a maximum of two children.

4. What does it mean to traverse a tree?

5. What defines a binary search tree (as opposed to a binary tree)?

6. In a tree with N nodes, how many nodes must be examined to find a given node?

7. What are the advantages of using a binary search tree to store data?

Exercise

Cut a few dozen disks from paper or cardboard. Number the disks with a marker and shuffle them. Now pick out disks in random order and make a binary tree out of them, using the insertion procedure discussed in this hour to place each disk in the tree.

HOUR 16

Traversing Binary Trees

In this hour we'll continue our discussion of binary search trees. You'll learn

- What it means to traverse a tree
- Three different kinds of traversals
- How to write C++ code to traverse a tree
- About the efficiency of binary trees

We'll also present the complete C++ listing that ties together the various binary-tree member functions we've seen so far.

Traversing the Tree

Traversing a tree means visiting each node in a specified order. This process is not as commonly used as finding, inserting, and deleting nodes. One reason for this is that traversal is not particularly fast. But traversing a tree has some surprisingly useful applications and is theoretically interesting.

There are three simple ways to traverse a tree. They're called *preorder*, *inorder*, and *postorder*. The order most commonly used for binary search trees is inorder, so let's look at that first, and then return briefly to the other two.

Inorder Traversal

NEW TERM   An *inorder traversal* of a binary search tree will cause all the nodes to be visited in ascending order, based on their key values. If you want to create a sorted list of the data in a binary tree, this is one way to do it.

The simplest way to carry out a traversal is the use of recursion (discussed in Hour 11, "Recursion"). Here's how it works. A recursive function to traverse the tree is called with a node as an argument. Initially, this node is the root. The function must perform only three tasks.

1. Call itself to traverse the node's left subtree.
2. Visit the node.
3. Call itself to traverse the node's right subtree.

Remember that visiting a node means doing something to it: displaying it, writing it to a file, or whatever.

Traversals work with any binary tree, not just with binary search trees. The traversal mechanism doesn't pay any attention to the key values of the nodes; it only concerns itself with whether a node has children.

C++ Code for Traversing

The actual code for inorder traversal is so simple we show it before seeing how traversal looks in the Workshop applet. The routine, inOrder(), performs the three steps already described. The visit to the node consists of displaying the contents of the node. Like any recursive function, there must be a base case: the condition that causes the routine to return immediately, without calling itself. In inOrder() this happens when the node passed as an argument is NULL. Here's the code for the inOrder() member function:

```
void inOrder(Node* pLocalRoot)
    {
    if(pLocalRoot != NULL)
       {
       inOrder(pLocalRoot->pLeftChild);        //left child
       cout << pLocalRoot->iData << " ";        //display node
       inOrder(pLocalRoot->pRightChild);        //right child
       }
    }
```

This member function is initially called with the root as an argument:

```
inOrder(root);
```

After that, the function is on its own, calling itself recursively until there are no more nodes to visit.

Traversing a 3-Node Tree

Let's look at a simple example to get an idea of how this recursive traversal routine works. Imagine traversing a tree with only three nodes: a root (A), with a left child (B), and a right child (C), as shown in Figure 16.1.

16

FIGURE 16.1

inOrder() *member function applied to a 3-node tree.*

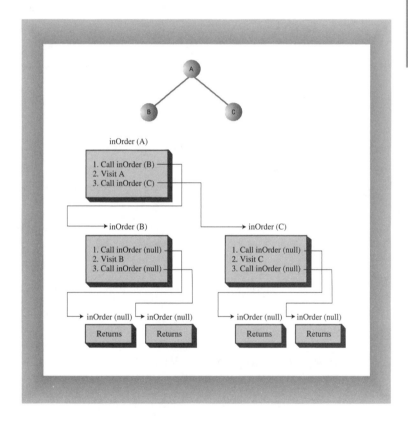

To Do: Follow the Steps of an InOrder Traversal

▼ To Do

1. Start by calling inOrder() with the root A as an argument. This incarnation of inOrder() we'll call inOrder(A).

▼   2. inOrder(A) first calls inOrder() with its left child, B, as an argument. This second incarnation of inOrder() we'll call inOrder(B).

3. inOrder(B) now calls itself with its left child as an argument. However, it has no left child, so this argument is NULL. This creates an invocation of inorder() we could call inOrder(NULL).

4. There are now three instances of inOrder() in existence: inOrder(A), inOrder(B), and inOrder(NULL). However, inOrder(NULL) returns immediately when it finds its argument is NULL. (We all have days like that.)

5. Now inOrder(B) goes on to visit B; we'll assume this means to display it.

6. Then inOrder(B) calls inOrder() again, with its right child as an argument. Again this argument is NULL, so the second inorder(NULL) returns immediately.

7. Now inOrder(B) has carried out tasks 1, 2, and 3, so it returns (and thereby ceases to exist).

8. Now we're back to inOrder(A), just returning from traversing A's left child.

9. We visit A, and then call inOrder() again with C as an argument, creating inOrder(C). Like inOrder(B), inOrder(C) has no children, so task 1 returns with no action, task 2 visits C, and task 3 returns with no action.

10. inOrder(B) now returns to inOrder(A).

▲   11. However, inOrder(A) is now done, so it returns and the entire traversal is complete.

The order in which the nodes were visited is A, B, C; they have been visited *inorder*. In a binary search tree this would be the order of ascending keys.

More complex trees are handled similarly. The inOrder() function calls itself for each node, until it has worked its way through the entire tree.

Traversing with the Workshop Applet

To see what a traversal looks like with the Workshop applet, repeatedly press the Trav button. (There's no need to type in any numbers.)

Table 16.1 shows what happens when you use the Tree Workshop applet to traverse inorder the tree shown in Figure 16.2. This is a slightly more complex than the 3-node tree seen previously. The red arrow starts at the root. Table 16.1 shows the sequence of node keys and the corresponding messages. The key sequence is displayed at the bottom of the Workshop applet screen.

FIGURE 16.2

Traversing a tree inorder.

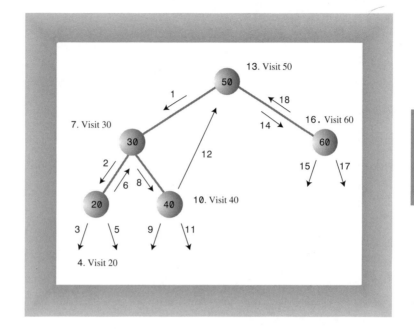

TABLE 16.1 WORKSHOP APPLET TRAVERSAL

Step Number	Red Arrow on Node	Message	List of Nodes Visited
1	50 (root)	Will check left child	
2	30	Will check left child	
3	20	Will check left child	
4	20	Will visit this node	
5	20	Will check right child	20
6	20	Will go to root of previous subtree	20
7	30	Will visit this node	20
8	30	Will check for right child	20 30
9	40	Will check left child	20 30
10	40	Will visit this node	20 30
11	40	Will check right child	20 30 40
12	40	Will go to root of previous subtree	20 30 40
13	50	Will visit this node	20 30 40

continues

16

TABLE 16.1   CONTINUED

Step Number	Red Arrow on Node	Message	List of Nodes Visited
14	50	Will check right child	20 30 40 50
15	60	Will check left child	20 30 40 50
16	60	Will visit this node	20 30 40 50
17	60	Will check for right child	20 30 40 50 60
18	60	Will go to root of previous subtree	20 30 40 50 60
19	50	Done traversal	20 30 40 50 60

It might not be obvious, but for each node, the routine traverses the node's left subtree, visits the node, and traverses the right subtree. For example, for node 30 this happens in steps 2, 7, and 8.

All this isn't as complicated as it looks. The best way to get a feel for what's happening is to traverse a variety of different trees with the Tree Workshop applet.

Preorder and Postorder Traversals

NEW TERM   You can traverse the tree in two ways besides inorder; they're called *preorder* and *postorder*. It's fairly clear why you might want to traverse a tree inorder, but the motivation for preorder and postorder traversals is more obscure. However, these traversals are indeed useful if you're writing programs that parse or analyze algebraic expressions. Let's see why that should be true.

A binary tree (not a binary search tree) can be used to represent an algebraic expression that involves the binary arithmetic operators +, -, /, and *. The root node holds an operator, and the other nodes represent either a variable name (like A, B, or C), or another operator. Each subtree is an algebraic expression.

For example, the binary tree shown in Figure 16.3 represents the algebraic expression

A*(B+C)

NEW TERM   This is called *infix* notation; it's the notation normally used in algebra. Traversing the tree inorder will generate the correct inorder sequence A*B+C, but you'll need to insert the parentheses yourself.

FIGURE 16.3

A tree representing an algebraic expression.

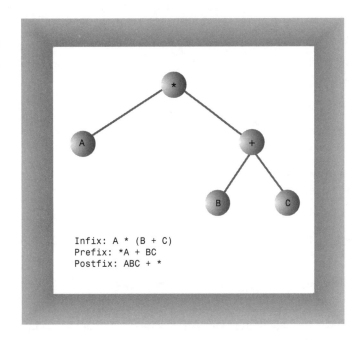

```
Infix: A * (B + C)
Prefix: *A + BC
Postfix: ABC + *
```

16

What's all this got to do with preorder and postorder traversals? Let's see what's involved. For these other traversals the same three tasks are used as for inorder, but in a different sequence. Here's the sequence for a `preorder()` member function:

1. Visit the node.

2. Call itself to traverse the node's left subtree.

3. Call itself to traverse the node's right subtree.

Traversing the tree shown in Figure 16.3 using preorder would generate the expression

`*A+BC`

NEW TERM   This is called *prefix* notation. It's another equally valid way to represent an algebraic expression. One of the nice things about it is that parentheses are never required; the expression is unambiguous without them. Starting on the left, each operator is applied to the next two things in the expression. For the first operator, `*`, these two things are A and +BC. In turn, the expression +BC means "apply + to the next two things in the expression"—which are B and C—so this last expression is B+C in inorder notation. Inserting that into the original expression *A+BC (preorder) gives us A*(B+C) in inorder.

By simply using different traversals, we've transformed one kind of algebraic notation into another.

The postorder traversal member function contains the three tasks arranged in yet another way:

1. Call itself to traverse the node's left subtree.
2. Call itself to traverse the node's right subtree.
3. Visit the node.

For the tree in Figure 16.3, visiting the nodes with a postorder traversal would generate the expression

ABC+*

| NEW TERM | This is called *postfix* notation. Starting on the right, each operator is applied to the two things on its left. First we apply the * to A and BC+.

Following the rule again for BC+, we apply the + to B and C. This gives us (B+C) in infix. Inserting this in the original expression ABC+* (postfix) gives us A*(B+C) infix.

Besides writing different kinds of algebraic expressions, you might find other clever uses for the different kinds of traversals. As we'll see at the end of this hour, we use postorder traversal to delete all the nodes when the tree is destroyed.

The code in Listing 16.1 later in this hour contains member functions for preorder and postorder traversals, as well as for inorder.

Now let's move on from traversals and briefly examine another aspect of binary search trees.

Finding Maximum and Minimum Values

I should note how easy it is to find the maximum and minimum values in a binary search tree. In fact, it's so easy we don't include it as an option in the Workshop applet, nor show code for it in Listing 16.1. Still, it's important to understand how it works.

For the minimum value, go to the left child of the root; then go to the left child of that child, and so on, until you come to a node that has no left child. This node is the minimum, as shown in Figure 16.4.

FIGURE 16.4

The minimum value of a tree.

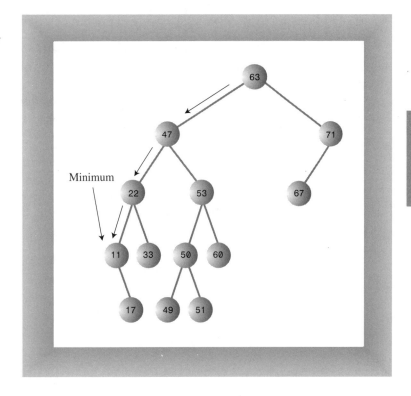

Here's some code that returns the node with the minimum key value:

```
Node* minimum()      // returns node with minimum key value
   {
   Node* pCurrent, pLast;
   pCurrent = pRoot;                    //start at root
   while(pCurrent != NULL)              //until the bottom,
      {
      pLast = pCurrent;                 //remember node
      pCurrent = pCurrent->pLeftChild;  //go to left child
      }
   return pLast;
   }
```

For the maximum value in the tree, follow the same procedure but go from right child to right child until you find a node with no right child. This node is the maximum. The code is the same except that the last statement in the loop is

```
pCurrent = pCurrent->pRightChild;  // go to right child
```

The Efficiency of Binary Trees

As you've seen, most operations with trees involve descending the tree from level to level to find a particular node. How long does it take to do this? In a full tree, about half the nodes are on the bottom level. (Actually there's one more node on the bottom row than in the rest of the tree.) Thus about half of all searches or insertions or deletions require finding a node on the lowest level. (An additional quarter of these operations require finding the node on the next-to-lowest level, and so on.)

During a search we need to visit one node on each level. So we can get a good idea how long it takes to carry out these operations by knowing how many levels there are. Assuming a full tree, Table 16.2 shows how many levels are necessary to hold a given number of nodes.

TABLE 16.2   NUMBER OF LEVELS FOR SPECIFIED NUMBER OF NODES

Number of Nodes	Number of Levels
1	1
3	2
7	3
15	4
31	5
...	...
1,023	10
...	...
32,767	15
...	...
1,048,575	20
...	...
33,554,432	25
...	...
1,073,741,824	30

This situation is very much like the ordered array discussed in Hour 3, "Ordered Arrays." In that case, the number of comparisons for a binary search was approximately equal to the base-2 logarithm of the number of cells in the array. Here, if we call the number of nodes in the first column N, and the number of levels in the second column L, we can say that N is 1 less than 2 raised to the power L, or

```
N = 2ᴸ - 1
```

Adding 1 to both sides of the equation, we have

```
N+1 = 2ᴸ
```

This is equivalent to

```
L = log₂(N+1)
```

Thus the time needed to carry out the common tree operations is proportional to the base-2 log of N. In Big O notation we say such operations take O(log N) time.

If the tree isn't full, analysis is difficult. We can say that for a tree with a given number of levels, average search times will be shorter for the non-full tree than the full tree because fewer searches will proceed to lower levels.

Compare the tree to the other data-storage structures we've discussed so far. In an unordered array or a linked list containing 1,000,000 items, it would take you on the average 500,000 comparisons to find the one you wanted. But in a tree of 1,000,000 items, it takes 20 (or fewer) comparisons.

In an ordered array you can find an item equally quickly, but inserting an item requires, on the average, moving 500,000 items. Inserting an item in a tree with 1,000,000 items requires 20 or fewer comparisons, plus a small amount of time to connect the item.

Similarly, deleting an item from a 1,000,000-item array requires moving an average of 500,000 items. We haven't investigated deletion, but it can be shown that deletion time is also proportional to the log of the number of nodes. Thus a tree provides high efficiency for all the common data-storage operations.

Traversing is not as fast as the other operations. However, traversals are probably not very commonly carried out in a typical large database. They're more appropriate when a tree is used as an aid to parsing algebraic or similar expressions, which are probably not too long anyway.

Now we'll look at another issue that we've examined earlier in relation to other data structures: duplicate keys.

Duplicate Keys

In the code shown for insert(), and in the Workshop applet, a node with a duplicate key will be inserted as the right child of its twin.

The problem is that the find() routine will find only the first of two (or more) duplicate nodes. The find() routine could be modified to check an additional data item, to distinguish data items even when the keys were the same, but this would be (at least somewhat) time-consuming.

One option is to simply forbid duplicate keys. When duplicate keys are excluded by the nature of the data (employee ID numbers, for example) there's no problem. Otherwise, you need to modify the insert() routine to check for equality during the insertion process, and abort the insertion if a duplicate is found.

The Fill routine in the Workshop applet excludes duplicates when generating the random keys.

In the next section we'll show the complete program that includes all the member functions and code fragments we've looked at so far in Hour 15, "Binary Trees," and in this hour.

Implementing a Binary Search Tree in C++

Besides implementing a binary search tree, the tree.cpp program also features a primitive user interface. This allows the user to chose an operation (finding, inserting, traversing and displaying the tree) by entering characters. The display routine uses character output to generate a picture of the tree. Figure 16.5 shows how this looks.

FIGURE 16.5

Output of the tree.cpp *program.*

In the figure, the user has typed s to display the tree, typed i and 48 to insert a node with that value, and then s again to display the tree with the additional node. The 48 appears in the lower display.

The available commands are the characters s, i, f, t, and q, for show, insert, find, traverse, and quit. The i and f options ask for the key value of the node to be operated on. The t option gives you a choice of traversals: 1 for preorder, 2 for inorder, and 3 for postorder. The key values are then displayed in that order.

The display created by the program shows the nodes as key values arranged in something of a tree shape; however, you'll need to imagine the edges connecting the nodes. Two dashes (--) represent a node that doesn't exist at a particular position in the tree. The program initially creates some nodes so the user will have something to see before any insertions are made. You can modify this initialization code to start with any nodes you want, or with no nodes (which is good nodes).

16

You can experiment with this program as you can with the Workshop applet, but unlike the Workshop applet, it doesn't show you the steps involved in carrying out an operation; it does everything at once. Listing 16.1 shows the complete tree.cpp program.

INPUT   **LISTING 16.1**   THE tree.cpp PROGRAM

```
//tree.cpp
//demonstrates binary tree
#include <iostream>
#include <stack>
using namespace std;
/////////////////////////////////////////////////////////////////
class Node
   {
   public:
      int iData;               //data item (key)
      double dData;            //data item
      Node* pLeftChild;        //this node's left child
      Node* pRightChild;       //this node's right child
//--------------------------------------------------------------
                               //constructor
      Node() : iData(0), dData(0.0), pLeftChild(NULL),
                               pRightChild(NULL)
         {  }
//--------------------------------------------------------------
      ~Node()                  //destructor
         { cout << "X-" << iData << " "; }
//--------------------------------------------------------------
      void displayNode()       //display ourself: {75, 7.5}
         {
         cout << '{' << iData << ", " << dData << "} ";
         }
   };  //end class Node
/////////////////////////////////////////////////////////////////
```

continues

LISTING 16.1   CONTINUED

```cpp
class Tree
    {
    private:
      Node* pRoot;                   //first node of tree

    public:
//--------------------------------------------------------------
    Tree() : pRoot(NULL)           //constructor
        {  }
//--------------------------------------------------------------
    Node* find(int key)            //find node with given key
        {                          //(assumes non-empty tree)
       Node* pCurrent = pRoot;           //start at root
       while(pCurrent->iData != key)     //while no match,
          {
          if(key < pCurrent->iData)        //go left?
             pCurrent = pCurrent->pLeftChild;
          else                             //or go right?
             pCurrent = pCurrent->pRightChild;
          if(pCurrent == NULL)             //if no child,
             return NULL;                  //didn't find it
          }
       return pCurrent;                  //found it
        }  //end find()
//--------------------------------------------------------------
    void insert(int id, double dd) //insert new node
        {
       Node* pNewNode = new Node;         //make new node
       pNewNode->iData = id;              //insert data
       pNewNode->dData = dd;
       if(pRoot==NULL)                    //no node in root
          pRoot = pNewNode;
       else                               //root occupied
          {
          Node* pCurrent = pRoot;         //start at root
          Node* pParent;
          while(true)                     //(exits internally)
             {
             pParent = pCurrent;
             if(id < pCurrent->iData)       //go left?
                {
                pCurrent = pCurrent->pLeftChild;
                if(pCurrent == NULL)        //if end of the line,
                   {                        //insert on left
                   pParent->pLeftChild = pNewNode;
                   return;
                   }
                }  //end if go left
```

```
          else                        //or go right?
            {
            pCurrent = pCurrent->pRightChild;
            if(pCurrent == NULL)       //if end of the line
               {                       //insert on right
               pParent->pRightChild = pNewNode;
               return;
               }
            }  //end else go right
         }  //end while
      }  //end else not root
   }  //end insert()
//------------------------------------------------------------
   void traverse(int traverseType)
      {
      switch(traverseType)
         {
         case 1: cout << "\nPreorder traversal: ";
                 preOrder(pRoot);
                 break;
         case 2: cout << "\nInorder traversal:  ";
                 inOrder(pRoot);
                 break;
         case 3: cout << "\nPostorder traversal: ";
                 postOrder(pRoot);
                 break;
         }
      cout << endl;
      }
//------------------------------------------------------------
   void preOrder(Node* pLocalRoot)
      {
      if(pLocalRoot != NULL)
         {
         cout << pLocalRoot->iData << " ";    //display node
         preOrder(pLocalRoot->pLeftChild);    //left child
         preOrder(pLocalRoot->pRightChild);   //right child
         }
      }
//------------------------------------------------------------
   void inOrder(Node* pLocalRoot)
      {
      if(pLocalRoot != NULL)
         {
         inOrder(pLocalRoot->pLeftChild);     //left child
         cout << pLocalRoot->iData << " ";    //display node
         inOrder(pLocalRoot->pRightChild);    //right child
         }
      }
```

16

continues

LISTING 16.1   CONTINUED

```
//--------------------------------------------------------------
   void postOrder(Node* pLocalRoot)
      {
      if(pLocalRoot != NULL)
         {
         postOrder(pLocalRoot->pLeftChild);   //left child
         postOrder(pLocalRoot->pRightChild);  //right child
         cout << pLocalRoot->iData << " ";    //display node
         }
      }
//--------------------------------------------------------------
   void displayTree()
      {
      stack<Node*> globalStack;
      globalStack.push(pRoot);
      int nBlanks = 32;
      bool isRowEmpty = false;

      cout <<
      "....................................................";
      cout << endl;
      while(isRowEmpty==false)
         {
         stack<Node*> localStack;
         isRowEmpty = true;

         for(int j=0; j<nBlanks; j++)
            cout << ' ';

         while(globalStack.empty()==false)
            {
            Node* temp = globalStack.top();
            globalStack.pop();
            if(temp != NULL)
               {
               cout << temp->iData;
               localStack.push(temp->pLeftChild);
               localStack.push(temp->pRightChild);

               if(temp->pLeftChild != NULL ||
                                 temp->pRightChild != NULL)
                  isRowEmpty = false;
               }
            else
               {
               cout << "--";
               localStack.push(NULL);
```

```
                    localStack.push(NULL);
                    }
                for(int j=0; j<nBlanks*2-2; j++)
                    cout << ' ';
                }  //end while globalStack not empty
            cout << endl;
            nBlanks /= 2;
            while(localStack.empty()==false)
                {
                globalStack.push( localStack.top() );
                localStack.pop();
                }
            }  //end while isRowEmpty is false
        cout <<
        "....................................................";
        cout << endl;
        }  //end displayTree()
//-------------------------------------------------------------
    void destroy()                          //deletes all nodes
        { destroyRec(pRoot); }              //start at root
//-------------------------------------------------------------
    void destroyRec(Node* pLocalRoot)       //delete nodes in
        {                                   //   this subtree
        if(pLocalRoot != NULL)
            {                                   //uses postOrder
            destroyRec(pLocalRoot->pLeftChild);  //left subtree
            destroyRec(pLocalRoot->pRightChild); //right subtree
            delete pLocalRoot;              //delete this node
            }
        }
//-------------------------------------------------------------
    };  //end class Tree
/////////////////////////////////////////////////////////////
int main()
    {
    int value;
    char choice;
    Node* found;
    Tree theTree;                           //create tree

    theTree.insert(50, 5.0);                //insert nodes
    theTree.insert(25, 2.5);
    theTree.insert(75, 7.5);
    theTree.insert(12, 1.2);
    theTree.insert(37, 3.7);
    theTree.insert(43, 4.3);
    theTree.insert(30, 3.0);
    theTree.insert(33, 3.3);
    theTree.insert(87, 8.7);
```

continues

LISTING 16.1   CONTINUED

```
theTree.insert(93, 9.3);
theTree.insert(97, 9.7);

while(choice != 'q')                        //interact with user
    {                                       //until user types 'q'
    cout << "Enter first letter of ";
    cout << "show, insert, find, traverse or quit: ";
    cin >> choice;
    switch(choice)
       {
       case 's':                            //show the tree
          theTree.displayTree();
          break;
       case 'i':                            //insert a node
          cout << "Enter value to insert: ";
          cin >> value;
          theTree.insert(value, value + 0.9);
          break;
       case 'f':                            //find a node
          cout << "Enter value to find: ";
          cin >> value;
          found = theTree.find(value);
          if(found != NULL)
             {
             cout << "Found: ";
             found->displayNode();
             cout << endl;
             }
          else
             cout << "Could not find " << value << endl;
          break;
       case 't':                            //traverse the tree
          cout << "Enter traverse type (1=preorder, "
               << "2=inorder, 3=postorder): ";
          cin >> value;
          theTree.traverse(value);
          break;
       case 'q':                            //quit the program
          theTree.destroy();
          cout << endl;
          break;
       default:
          cout << "Invalid entry\n";
       } //end switch
    } //end while
return 0;
} //end main()
```

To avoid memory leaks, all the nodes in the tree should be deleted when the tree is destroyed. We've included code to delete the nodes when the user quits the program. Pressing q causes the program to call the destroy() member function of Tree before terminating. This routine uses postorder traversal to visit every node and delete it. (The nodes are probably sorry they answered the door.) Postorder is necessary because a node can't be deleted until both its subtrees are deleted, so visiting it must take place last.

16

Summary

In this hour, you've learned the following:

- Traversing a tree means visiting all its nodes in some order.

- The simple traversals are preorder, inorder, and postorder.

- An inorder traversal visits nodes in order of ascending keys.

- Preorder and postorder traversals are useful for parsing algebraic expressions, among other things.

- Nodes with duplicate key values might cause trouble because only the first one can be found in a search.

- All the common operations on a binary search tree can be carried out in O(log N) time.

Q&A

Q Will I really need to traverse a tree in a typical programming situation?

A It's most common to traverse a tree inorder. This allows you to extract data from a tree in a useful way, so it can be displayed or copied to another data structure. The other traversals are less often used.

Q Do I need to understand the C++ code to understand how to use a tree?

A As with other data structures and algorithms in this book, the answer is, "Not usually."

Workshop

The Workshop helps you solidify what you learned in this hour. See Appendix A for quiz answers.

Quiz

1. What three tasks should a recursive function execute to perform an inorder traversal?

2. What is the base case in such traversals?

3. Here's an expression in postfix notation: AB+C-. Express this in infix notation.

4. Describe how to find the node with the maximum key value in a binary search tree.

5. The number of steps involved searching and insertion in a binary tree is proportional to what aspect of the tree?

6. The efficiency of binary search trees in Big O notation is _____.

7. In C++, what two data members must the Node class contain?

Exercise

Use the Binary Tree Workshop applet (or the `tree.cpp` sample program) to transform the following infix expression into both prefix and postfix forms:

(A+B) * (C-D)

Hour **17**

Red-Black Trees

A red-black tree is a binary search tree with some special features. Ordinary binary search trees, which we explored in Hours 15, "Binary Trees" and 16, "Traversing Binary Trees," have an unfortunate defect: If data is inserted in a non-random sequence, the tree might become unbalanced, seriously degrading its performance. A red-black tree can fix this by ensuring that the tree remains balanced at all times. In this hour we'll learn

- How unbalanced trees degrade performance
- The characteristics of red-black trees
- The color rules
- How to use the RBTree Workshop applet
- How to rotate a subtree

In the next hour we'll see how to use these techniques to insert a new node into a tree while keeping the tree balanced.

Ordinary binary search trees offer important advantages as data storage devices: You can quickly search for an item with a given key, and you can also quickly insert or delete an item. Other data storage structures, such as arrays, sorted arrays, and linked lists, perform one or the other of these activities slowly. Thus binary search trees might appear to be the ideal data storage structure.

Ordinary binary search trees work well if the data is inserted into the tree in random order. However, they become much slower if data is inserted in already-sorted order (17, 21, 28, 36,…) or inversely sorted order (36, 28, 21, 17,…). When the values to be inserted are already ordered, a binary tree becomes unbalanced. With an unbalanced tree, the ability to quickly find (or insert or delete) a given element is lost.

Red-black trees, which we'll explore in this hour and the next one, are the most common way to keep trees balanced. There are other approaches. We'll mention some at the end of the next hour, and examine one, the 2-3-4 tree, in Hours 19, "2-3-4 Trees," and 20, "Implementing 2-3-4 Trees." However, the red-black tree is in most cases the most efficient balanced tree, at least when data is stored in memory as opposed to external files.

Our Approach to the Discussion

We'll explain insertion into red-black trees a little differently than we have explained insertion into other data structures. Red-black trees are not trivial to understand. Because of this and also because of a multiplicity of symmetrical cases (for left or right children, and inside or outside grandchildren), the actual code is more lengthy and complex than one might expect. It's therefore hard to learn about the algorithm by examining code.

For this reason, we're going to concentrate on conceptual understanding rather than coding details. In this we will be aided by the RBTree Workshop applet. We'll describe how you can work in partnership with the applet to insert new nodes into a tree. Including a human into the insertion routine certainly slows it down, but it also makes it easier for the human to understand how the process works.

We'll discuss some characteristics of red-black trees first, then examine how the RBTree Workshop applet works, and then use the applet to carry out some experiments that will introduce some common red-black tree operations.

Balanced and Unbalanced Trees

Before we begin our investigation of red-black trees, let's review how trees become unbalanced. Fire up the Tree Workshop applet from Hour 15 (not this hour's RBTree applet). Use the Fill button to create a tree with only one node. Then insert a series of nodes whose keys are in either ascending or descending order. The result will be something like that in Figure 17.1.

FIGURE **17.1**

*Items inserted in
ascending order.*

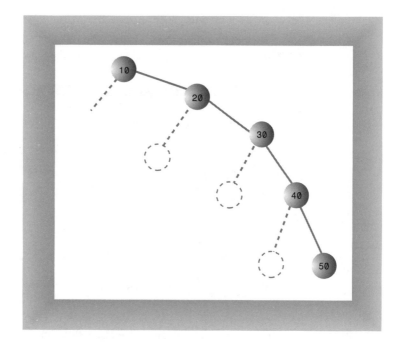

The nodes arrange themselves in a line with no branches. Because each node is larger
than the previously inserted one, every node is a right child, so all the nodes are on one
side of the root. The tree is maximally unbalanced. If you inserted items in descending
order, every node would be the left child of its parent; the tree would be unbalanced on
the other side.

Performance Degenerates to O(N)

When there are no branches, the tree becomes, in effect, a linked list. The arrangement of
data is one-dimensional instead of two-dimensional. As with a linked list, you must now
search through (on the average) half the items to find the one you're looking for. In this
situation the speed of searching is reduced to O(N), instead of O(log N) as it is for a balanced tree. Searching through 10,000 items in such an unbalanced tree would require an
average of 5,000 comparisons, whereas for a balanced tree with random insertions it
requires only 14. For presorted data you might just as well use a linked list in the first
place.

Data that's only partly sorted will generate trees that are only partly unbalanced. If you use the Tree Workshop applet from Hour 15 to attempt to generate trees with 31 nodes, you'll see that some of them are more unbalanced than others, as shown in Figure 17.2.

FIGURE 17.2

A partially unbalanced tree.

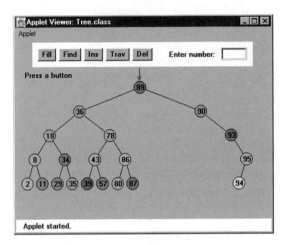

Although not as bad as a maximally unbalanced tree, this situation is not optimal for searching times.

In the Tree Workshop applet, trees can become partially unbalanced, even with randomly generated data, because the amount of data is so small that even a short run of ordered numbers will have a big effect on the tree. Also a very small or very large key value can cause an unbalanced tree by not allowing the insertion of many nodes on one side or the other. A root of 3, for example, allows only two more nodes to be inserted to its left.

With a realistic amount of random data it's not likely a tree would become seriously unbalanced. However, there might be runs of sorted data that will partially unbalance a tree. Searching partially unbalanced trees will take time somewhere between O(N) and O(log N), depending on how badly the tree is unbalanced.

Balanced Trees to the Rescue

To guarantee the quick O(log N) search times a tree is capable of, we need to ensure that our tree is always balanced (or at least almost balanced). This means that each node in a tree must have roughly the same number of descendents on its left side as it has on its right.

In a red-black tree, balance is achieved during insertion (and also deletion, but we'll ignore that here). As an item is being inserted, the insertion routine checks that certain characteristics of the tree are not violated. If they are, it takes corrective action, restructuring the tree as necessary. By maintaining these characteristics, the tree is kept balanced.

Red-Black Tree Characteristics

What are these mysterious tree characteristics? There are two, one simple and one more complicated:

- The nodes are colored.
- During insertion and deletion, rules are followed that preserve various arrangements of these colors.

Colored Nodes

In a red-black tree, every node is either black or red. These are arbitrary colors; blue and yellow would do just as well. In fact, the whole concept of saying that nodes have "colors" is somewhat arbitrary. Some other analogy could have been used instead: We could say that every node is either heavy or light, or yin or yang. However, colors are convenient labels. A data member, which can be Boolean, (isRed, for example), is added to the node class to embody this color information.

In the RBTree Workshop applet, the red-black characteristic of a node is shown by its border color. The center color, as it was in the Tree applet in Hour 15, is simply a randomly generated data member of the node.

When we speak of a node's color in this hour we'll almost always be referring to its red-black border color. In the figures (except the screen shot of Figure 17.3) we'll show black nodes as dark and red nodes as white with a double border.

Red-Black Rules

When inserting (or deleting) a new node, certain rules, which we call the *red-black rules*, must be followed. If they're followed, the tree will be balanced. Let's look briefly at these rules:

1. Every node is either red or black.
2. The root is always black.
3. If a node is red, its children must be black (although the converse isn't necessarily true).
4. Every path from the root to a leaf, or to a null child, must contain the same number of black nodes.

NEW TERM   The *null child* referred to in Rule 4 is a place where a child could be attached to a nonleaf node. In other words, it's the potential left child of a node with a right child, or the potential right child of a node with a left child. This will make more sense as we go along.

NEW TERM   The number of black nodes on a path from root to leaf is called the *black height*. Another way to state Rule 4 is that the black height must be the same for all paths from the root to a leaf.

The red-black rules probably seem completely mysterious. It's not obvious how they will lead to a balanced tree, but they do; some very clever people invented them. Copy them onto a sticky note, and keep it on your computer. You'll need to refer to them often in the course of this hour.

You can see how the rules work by using the RBTree Workshop applet. We'll do some experiments with this applet in a moment.

Duplicate Keys

What happens if there's more than one data item with the same key? This presents a slight problem in red-black trees. It's important that nodes with the same key are distributed on both sides of other nodes with the same key. That is, if keys arrive in the order 50, 50, 50, you want the second 50 to go to the right of the first one, and the third 50 to go to the left of the first one. Otherwise, the tree becomes unbalanced.

This could be handled by some kind of randomizing process in the insertion algorithm. However, the search process then becomes more complicated if all items with the same key must be found.

It's simpler to outlaw items with the same key. In this discussion we'll assume duplicates aren't allowed.

The Actions

What actions can you take if one of the red-black rules is broken? There are two, and only two, possibilities:

- You can change the colors of nodes.
- You can perform rotations.

Changing the color of a node means changing its red-black border color (not the center color). A rotation is a rearrangement of the nodes that hopefully leaves the tree more balanced.

At this point such concepts probably seem very abstract, so let's become familiar with the RBTree Workshop applet, which can help to clarify things.

Using the RBTree Workshop Applet

Figure 17.3 shows what the RBTree Workshop applet looks like after some nodes have been inserted. (It might be hard to tell the difference between red and black node borders in the figure, but they should be clear on a color monitor.)

FIGURE 17.3

The RBTree Workshop applet.

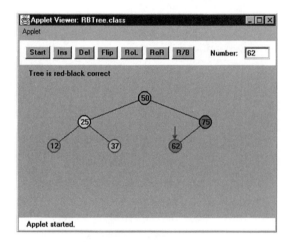

There are quite a few buttons in the RBTree applet. We'll briefly review what they do, although at this point some of the descriptions might be a bit puzzling. Soon we'll do some experimenting with these buttons.

Clicking on a Node

The red arrow points to the currently selected node. It's this node whose color is changed or which is the top node in a rotation. You select a node by single-clicking it with the mouse. This moves the red arrow to the node.

The Start Button

When you first start the Workshop applet, and also when you press the Start button, you'll see that a tree is created that contains only one node. Because an understanding of red-black trees focuses on using the red-black rules during the insertion process, it's more convenient to begin with the root and construct the tree by inserting additional nodes. To simplify future operations, the initial root node is always given a value of 50. (You select your own numbers for subsequent insertions.)

The Ins Button

The Ins button causes a new node to be created, with the value that was typed into the Number box, and then inserted into the tree. (At least this is what happens if no color flips are necessary. See the section on the Flip button for more on this possibility.)

Notice that the Ins button does a complete insertion operation with one push; multiple pushes are not required as they were with the Tree Workshop applet in Hour 15. The focus in the RBTree applet is not on the process of finding the place to insert the node, which is similar to that in ordinary binary search trees, but on keeping the tree balanced; so the applet doesn't show the individual steps in the insertion. This can be unnerving until you get used to it.

The Del Button

Pushing the Del button causes the node with the key value typed into the Number box to be deleted. As with the Ins button, this takes place immediately after the first push; multiple pushes are not required.

The Del button and the Ins button use the basic insertion algorithms; the same as those in the Tree Workshop applet. This is how the work is divided between the applet and the user: The applet does the insertion, but it's (mostly) up to the user to make the appropriate changes to the tree to ensure the red-black rules are followed and the tree thereby becomes balanced.

The Flip Button

If there is a black parent with two red children, and you place the red arrow on the parent by clicking on the node with the mouse, when you press the Flip button the parent will become red and the children will become black. That is, the colors are flipped between the parent and children. You'll learn later why this is a desirable thing to do.

If you try to flip the root, it will remain black, so as not to violate Rule 2, but its children will change from red to black.

The RoL Button

This button carries out a left rotation. To rotate a group of nodes, first single-click the mouse to position the arrow at the topmost node of the group to be rotated. (For a left rotation, the top node must have a right child.) Then click the button. We'll examine rotations in detail later.

The RoR Button

This button performs a right rotation. Position the arrow on the top node to be rotated, making sure it has a left child; then click the button.

The R/B Button

The R/B button changes a red node to black, or a black node to red. Single-click the mouse to position the red arrow on the node, and then push the button. (This button changes the color of a single node; don't confuse it with the Flip button, which changes three nodes at once.)

Text Messages

NEW TERM Messages in the text box below the buttons tell you whether the tree is red-black correct. The tree is *red-black correct* if it adheres to rules 1 to 4, listed previously. If it's not correct, you'll see messages advising which rule is being violated. In some cases the red arrow will point to where the violation occurred.

Where's the Find Button?

In red-black trees, a search routine operates exactly as it did in the ordinary binary search trees described in Hour 15. It starts at the root, and, at each node it encounters (the current node), it decides whether to go to the left or right child by comparing the key of the current node with the search key.

We don't include a Find button in the RBTree applet because you already understand this process and our attention will be on manipulating the red-black aspects of the tree.

Experimenting

Now that you're familiar with the RBTree buttons, let's do some simple experiments to get a feel for what the applet does. The idea here is to learn to manipulate the applet's controls. Later you'll use these skills to balance the tree.

Experiment 1: Simple Insertions

Let's try inserting some nodes into the red-black tree and seeing what happens to the red-black rules.

To Do: Insert New Nodes

▼ To Do

1. Press Start to clear any extra nodes. You'll be left with the root node, which always has the value 50.

2. Insert a new node with a value smaller than the root, say 25, by typing the number into the Number box and pressing the Ins button. This doesn't cause any rule violations, so the message continues to say Tree is red-black correct.

3. Insert a second node that's larger than the root, say 75. The tree is still red-black correct. It's also balanced; there are the same number of nodes on the right of the only nonleaf node (the root) as there are on its left. The result is shown in Figure 17.4.

FIGURE 17.4

A balanced tree.

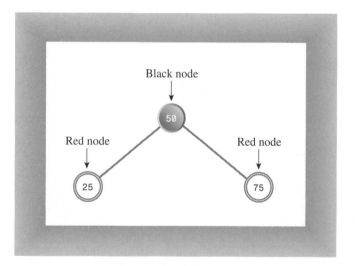

▲

Notice that newly inserted nodes are always colored red (except for the root). This is not an accident. It's less likely that inserting a red node will violate the red-black rules than inserting a black one.

This is because if the new red node is attached to a black one, no rule is broken. It doesn't create a situation where there are two red nodes together (Rule 3), and it doesn't change the black height in any of the paths (Rule 4). Of course, if you attach a new red node to a red node, Rule 3 will be violated. However, with any luck this will only happen half the time. Whereas, if it were possible to add a new black node, it would always change the black height for its path, violating Rule 4.

Also, it's easier to fix violations of Rule 3 (parent and child are both red) than Rule 4 (black heights differ), as we'll see later.

Experiment 2: Rotations

Let's try some rotations.

To Do: Rotate the Tree to the Right

To Do ▼

1. Start with the three nodes as shown in Figure 17.4.

2. Position the red arrow on the root (50) by clicking it with the mouse. This node will be the top node in the rotation.

3. Now perform a right rotation by pressing the RoR button. The nodes all shift to new positions, as shown in Figure 17.5.

FIGURE 17.5

Following a right rotation.

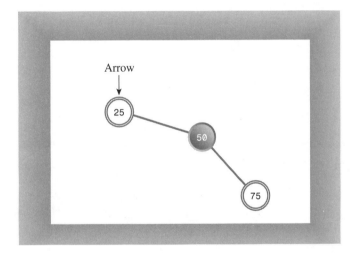

In this right rotation, the parent or top node moves into the place of its right child, the left child moves up and takes the place of the parent, and the right child moves down to become the grandchild of the new top node.

Notice that the tree is now unbalanced; there are more nodes to the right of the root than to the left. Also, the message indicates that the red-black rules are violated, specifically Rule 2 (the root is always black). Don't worry about this yet. Instead, rotate the other way.

To Do: Rotate the Tree to the Left

To Do

1. Position the red arrow on 25, which is now the root (the arrow should already point to 25 after the previous rotation).

2. Click the RoL button to rotate left. The nodes will return to the position of Figure 17.4.

Experiment 3: Color Flips

A color flip changes the colors of a parent and its two children. Let's see how this works.

To Do: Perform a Color Flip

▼ To Do

1. Start with the position of Figure 17.4, with nodes 25 and 75 inserted in addition to 50 in the root position. Note that the parent (the root) is black and both its children are red.

2. Now try to insert another node. No matter what value you use, you'll see the message Can't Insert: Needs color flip. As we mentioned, a color flip is necessary whenever, during the insertion process, a black node with two red children is encountered.

3. The red arrow should already be positioned on the black parent (the root node), so click the Flip button.

4. The root's two children change from red to black. Ordinarily the parent would change from black to red, but this is a special case because it's the root: it remains black to avoid violating Rule 2. Now all three nodes are black. The tree is still red-black correct.

5. Now click the Ins button again to insert the new node. Figure 17.6 shows the result if the newly inserted node has the key value 12.

FIGURE 17.6

Colors flipped, new node inserted.

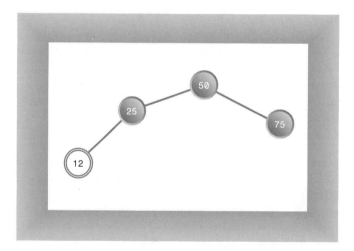

▲

The tree is still red-black correct. The root is black, there's no situation where a parent and child are both red, and all the paths have the same number of black nodes (2). Adding the new red node didn't change the red-black correctness.

Experiment 4: An Unbalanced Tree

Now let's see what happens when you try to do something that leads to an unbalanced tree. In Figure 17.6 one path has one more node than the other. This isn't very unbalanced, and no red-black rules are violated, so neither we nor the red-black algorithms need to worry about it. However, suppose that one path differs from another by two or more levels (where level is the same as the number of nodes along the path). In this case the red-black rules will always be violated, and we'll need to rebalance the tree.

To Do: Create an Unbalanced Tree

1. Insert a 6 into the tree of Figure 17.6.

2. You'll see the message Error: parent and child are both red. Rule 3 has been violated, as shown in Figure 17.7.

FIGURE 17.7

Parent and child are both red.

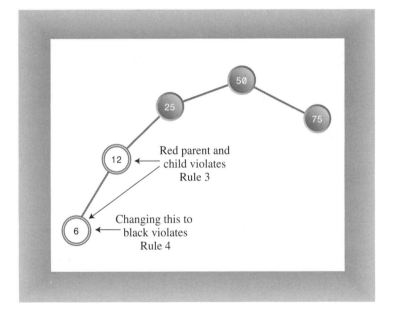

How can we fix things so Rule 3 isn't violated? An obvious approach is to change one of the offending nodes to black. Let's try changing the child node, 6.

To Do: Try to Balance the Tree

1. Position the red arrow on node 6.

2. Press the R/B button. The node becomes black.

The good news is we fixed the problem of both parent and child being red. The bad news is that now the message says Error: Black heights differ. The path from the root to node 6 has three black nodes in it, while the path from the root to node 75 has only two. Thus Rule 4 is violated. It seems we can't win. This problem can be fixed with a rotation and some color changes. How to do this will be the topic of Hour 18, "Red-Black Tree Insertions."

Experimenting on Your Own

Experiment with the RBTree Workshop applet on your own. Insert more nodes and see what happens. See if you can use rotations and color changes to achieve a balanced tree. Does keeping the tree red-black correct seem to guarantee an (almost) balanced tree?

Try inserting ascending keys (50, 60, 70, 80, 90) and then restart with the Start button and try descending keys (50, 40, 30, 20, 10). Ignore the messages; we'll see what they mean later. These are the situations that get the ordinary binary search tree into trouble. Can you still balance the tree?

The Red-Black Rules and Balanced Trees

Try to create a tree which is unbalanced by two or more levels but is red-black correct. As it turns out, this is impossible. That's why the red-black rules keep the tree balanced. If one path is more than one node longer than another, it must either have more black nodes, violating Rule 4, or it must have two adjacent red nodes, violating Rule 3. Convince yourself that this is true by experimenting with the applet.

Null Children

Rule 4 specifies all paths that go from the root to any leaf or to any null children must have the same number of black nodes. Remember that a null child is a child that a non-leaf node might have, but doesn't. Thus in Figure 17.8 the path from 50 to 25 to the right child of 25 (its null child) has only one black node, which is not the same as the paths to 6 and 75, which have 2. This arrangement violates Rule 4, although both paths to leaf nodes have the same number of black nodes.

Remember that the term *black height* is the number of black nodes from a given node to the root. In Figure 17.8 the black height of the root (50) is 1, from the root to 25 is still 1, from the root to 12 is 2, and so on.

We've experimented with various red-black operations: simple insertions, some easy rotations, and color flips. Now let's see how to use these operations to balance a tree.

FIGURE 17.8

Path to a null child.

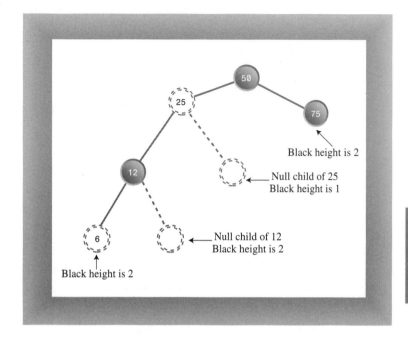

Black height is 2

Null child of 25
Black height is 1

Null child of 12
Black height is 2

Black height is 2

Rotations

To balance a tree, it's necessary to physically rearrange the nodes. If all the nodes are on the left of the root, for example, you need to move some of them over to the right side. This is done using *rotations*. In this section we'll learn what rotations are and how to execute them.

NEW TERM *Rotations* are ways to rearrange nodes. They were designed to do the following two things:

- Raise some nodes and lower others to help balance the tree.
- Ensure that the characteristics of a binary search tree are not violated.

Recall that in a binary search tree the left children of any node have key values less than the node, whereas its right children have key values greater or equal to the node. If the rotation didn't maintain a valid binary search tree it wouldn't be of much use because the search algorithm, as we saw in Hour 15, relies on the search-tree arrangement.

Note that color rules and node color changes are only used to help decide when to perform a rotation; fiddling with the colors doesn't accomplish anything by itself; it's the rotation that's the heavy hitter. Color rules are like rules of thumb for building a house (such as "exterior doors open inward"), whereas rotations are like the hammering and sawing needed to actually build it.

Simple Rotations

In Experiment 2 we tried rotations to the left and right. These rotations were easy to visualize because they involved only three nodes. Let's clarify some aspects of this process.

What's Rotating?

The term *rotation* can be a little misleading. The nodes themselves aren't rotated, it's the relationship between them that changes. One node is chosen as the "top" of the rotation. If we're doing a right rotation, this "top" node will move down and to the right, into the position of its right child. Its left child will move up to take its place.

Remember that the top node isn't the "center" of the rotation. If we talk about a car tire, the top node doesn't correspond to the hubcap, it's more like the topmost part of the tire tread.

The rotation we described in Experiment 2 was performed with the root as the top node, but of course any node can be the top node in a rotation, provided it has the appropriate child.

Mind the Children

You must be sure that if you're doing a right rotation, the top node has a left child. Otherwise there's nothing to rotate into the top spot. Similarly, if you're doing a left rotation, the top node must have a right child.

The Weird Crossover Node

Rotations can be more complicated than the three-node example we've discussed so far. Let's see an example.

To Do: Rotate More Than Three Nodes

▼ To Do

1. Click Start, which puts 50 at the root.

2. Insert nodes with following values, in this order: 25, 75, 12, 37.

3. When you try to insert the 12, you'll see the `Can't insert: needs color flip` message.

4. Just click the Flip button. The parent and children change color. Then click Ins again to complete the insertion of the 12.

▼   5. Finally, insert the 37. The resulting arrangement is shown in Figure 17.9a.

FIGURE 17.9

*Rotation with
crossover node.*

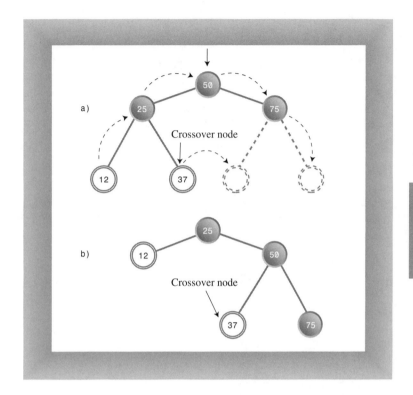

17

6. Now we'll try the rotation. Place the arrow on the root (don't forget this!) and press the RoR button. All the nodes move. The 12 follows the 25 up, and the 50 follows the 75 down.

But what's this? The 37 has detached itself from the 25, whose right child it was, and become instead the left child of 50. Some nodes go up, some nodes go down, but the 37 moves *across*. The result is shown in Figure 17.9b. The rotation has caused a violation of Rule 4; we'll see how to fix this later.

NEW TERM In the original position of Figure 17.9a, the 37 is called an *inside grandchild* of the top node, 50. (The 12 is an *outside grandchild*.) The inside grandchild, if it's the child of the node that's going up (which is the left child of the top node in a right rotation) is always disconnected from its parent and reconnected to its former grandparent. It's like becoming your own uncle (although it's best not to dwell too long on this analogy).

Subtrees on the Move

We've shown individual nodes changing position during a rotation, but entire subtrees can move as well. To see this, try the following.

To Do: Make a Subtree Cross Over

1. Click Start to put 50 at the root

2. Insert the following sequence of nodes in order: 25, 75, 12, 37, 62, 87, 6, 18, 31, 43.

3. Click Flip whenever you can't complete an insertion because of the Can't insert: needs color flip message. The resulting arrangement is shown in Figure 17.10a.

FIGURE 17.10

Subtree motion during rotation.

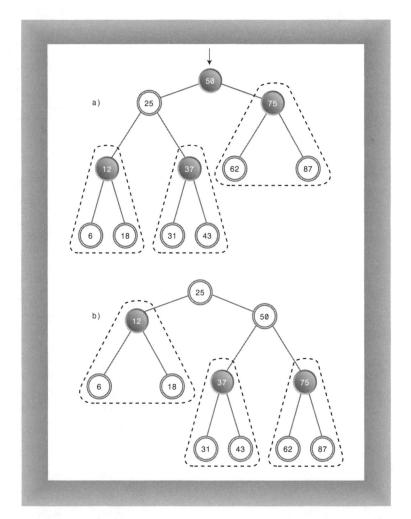

▼   4. Position the arrow on the root, 50.

▲   5. Now press RoR.

Wow! (Or is it WoW?) A lot of nodes have changed position. The result is shown in Figure 17.10b. Here's what happens:

- The top node (50) goes to its right child.
- The top node's left child (25) goes to the top.
- The entire subtree of which 12 is the root moves up.
- The entire subtree of which 37 is the root moves across to become the left child of 50.
- The entire subtree of which 75 is the root moves down.

You'll see the `Error: root must be black` message but you can ignore it for the time being. You can flip back and forth by alternately pressing RoR and RoL with the arrow on the top node. Do this and watch what happens to the subtrees, especially the one with 37 as its root.

The figures show the subtrees encircled by dotted triangles. Note that the relations of the nodes within each subtree are unaffected by the rotation. The entire subtree moves as a unit. The subtrees can be larger (have more descendants) than the three nodes we show in this example. No matter how many nodes there are in a subtree, they will all move together during a rotation.

Human Beings Versus Computers

This is pretty much all you need to know about what a rotation does. To cause a rotation, you position the arrow on the top node, then press RoR or RoL. Of course, in a real red-black tree insertion algorithm, rotations happen under program control, without human intervention.

However, notice that in your capacity as a human being, you could probably balance any tree just by looking at it and performing appropriate rotations. Whenever a node has a lot of left descendants and not too many right ones, you rotate it right, and vice versa.

Unfortunately, computers aren't very good at "just looking" at a pattern. They work better if they can follow a few simple rules. That's what the red-black scheme provides, in the form the color coding and the four color rules.

In the next hour we'll see how color rules and rotations are used to maintain a balanced tree during the insertion process.

Summary

In this hour, you've learned the following:

- It's important to keep a binary search tree balanced to ensure that the time necessary to find a given node is kept as short as possible, that is, O(log N).
- Inserting data that has already been sorted can create a maximally unbalanced tree, which results in search times of O(N).
- In the red-black balancing scheme, each node is given a new characteristic: a color that can be either red or black.
- A set of rules, called red-black rules, specifies permissible ways that nodes of different colors can be arranged.
- These rules are applied while inserting (or deleting) a node.
- A color flip changes a black node with two red children to a red node with two black children.
- In a rotation, one node is designated the top node.
- A right rotation moves the top node into the position of its right child, and the top node's left child into its position.
- A left rotation moves the top node into the position of its left child, and the top node's right child into its position.

Q&A

Q Why can't I forget about red-black trees, and just use an ordinary binary tree? I could simply tell anyone entering data not to enter it in order.

A Sometimes you can get away with this approach. However, in most situations Murphy's Law will dictate that someone will enter data sequentially.

Q Why don't you let the Workshop applet do all the work during an insertion, as in the Tree applet?

A So much happens in a red-black insertion that it would be hard to learn anything by watching the applet. By involving the reader, we make it easier to see what's happening.

Q The red-black rules seem so arbitrary, I can't believe they can work to balance a tree.

A It can be hard to believe. But wait until you read Hours 19 and 20, on 2-3-4 trees. They cast light on the red-black rules by looking at them from a completely different perspective.

Workshop

The Workshop helps you solidify what you learned in this hour. See Appendix A for quiz answers.

Quiz

1. Why is a balanced tree desirable?

2. How is the tree kept balanced?

3. How do the red-black algorithms know what rotations to perform?

4. What is black height?

5. Name the red-black rules.

6. What actions can the red-black algorithms perform to keep a tree balanced?

7. In what ways can the colors of nodes be changed?

8. True or false: During a rotation, an entire subtree can be unattached from its parent and reattached to another node.

17

Exercise

Use the RBTree Workshop applet to create a tree with seven nodes. During the insertion of new nodes, try to make the tree as unbalanced as possible. Ignore the red-black rule violations. After the tree is created, try to balance it using rotations. A tree is considered balanced if no path from root to leaf differs by more than one level. Try the exercise with different arrangements of nodes and with more nodes.

Hour **18**

Red-Black Tree Insertions

In the last hour we introduced some of the concepts used in red-black trees, notably rotations and the color rules. In this hour we'll use these concepts to insert new nodes into the tree, while at the same time keeping it balanced. You'll learn

- That insertion involves searching down the tree, performing rotations and color flips on the way.
- How to perform color flips on the way down the tree.
- How to perform rotations on the way down the tree.
- How to insert the node once the insertion point is found.

As we noted in the last hour, because of its complexity we won't show any C++ code for red-black trees. Instead we'll explore the process using the RBTree Workshop applet.

Although most of this hour will be concerned with the insertion process, at the end of the hour we'll also touch briefly on several other topics such as deletion and red-black tree efficiency.

Inserting a New Node

We'll discuss the insertion process in two stages: first a brief preview, and then a more extensive discussion. Don't worry if the preview leaves unanswered questions.

NEW TERM Our approach to insertion is called *top-down* insertion. This means that some structural changes might be made to the tree as the search routine descends the tree looking for the place to insert the node.

NEW TERM Another approach is *bottom-up* insertion. This involves finding the place to insert the node and then working back up through the tree making structural changes. Bottom-up insertion is less efficient because two passes must be made through the tree, so we don't cover it here.

Preview of Our Approach

In the discussion that follows we'll use X, P, and G to designate a pattern of related nodes. X is a node that has caused a rule violation. (Sometimes X refers to a newly inserted node, and sometimes to the child node when a parent and child have a red-red conflict.)

- X is a particular node.
- P is the parent of X.
- G is the grandparent of X (the parent of P).

On the way down the tree to find the insertion point, you perform a color flip whenever you find a black node with two red children (a violation of Rule 2). Sometimes the flip causes a red-red conflict (a violation of Rule 3) between a parent and child. Call the red child X and the red parent P. The conflict can be fixed with a single rotation or a double rotation, depending on whether X is an outside or inside grandchild of G. Following color flips and rotations, you continue down to the insertion point and insert the new node.

After you've inserted the new node X, if P is black you simply attach the new red node. If P is red, there are two possibilities: X can be an outside or inside grandchild of G. You perform two color changes (we'll see what they are in a moment). If X is an outside grandchild, you perform one rotation, and if it's an inside grandchild you perform two. This restores the tree to a balanced state.

Now we'll recapitulate this preview in more detail. We'll divide the discussion into three parts, arranged in order of complexity:

1. Color flips on the way down

2. Rotations once the node is inserted

3. Rotations on the way down

If we were discussing these three parts in strict chronological order, we would examine part 3 before part 2. However, it's easier to talk about rotations at the bottom of the tree than in the middle, and operations 1 and 2 are encountered more frequently than operation 3, so we'll discuss 2 before 3.

Color Flips on the Way Down

The insertion routine in a red-black tree starts off doing essentially the same thing it does in an ordinary binary search tree: It follows a path from the root to the place where the node should be inserted, going left or right at each node depending on the relative size of the node's key and the search key.

However, in a red-black tree, getting to the insertion point is complicated by color flips and rotations. We introduced color flips in Experiment 3 in the last hour; now we'll look at them in more detail.

Imagine the insertion routine proceeding down the tree, going left or right at each node, searching for the place to insert a new node. To make sure the color rules aren't broken, the routine needs to perform color flips when necessary. Here's the rule: Every time the insertion routine encounters a black node that has two red children, it must change the children to black and the parent to red (unless the parent is the root, which always remains black).

How does a color flip affect the red-black rules? For convenience, let's call the node at the top of the triangle, the one that's red before the flip, P for parent. We'll call P's left and right children X1 and X2. This is shown in Figure 18.1a.

Color Flips Leave Black Heights Unchanged

Figure 18.1b shows the nodes after the color flip. The flip leaves unchanged the number of black nodes on the path from the root on down through P to the leaf or null nodes. All such paths go through P, and then through either X1 or X2. Before the flip, only P is black, so the triangle (consisting of P, X1, and X2) adds one black node to each of these paths.

18

FIGURE 18.1

Color flip.

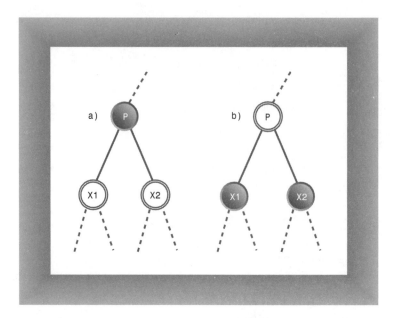

After the flip, P is no longer black, but both L and R are, so again the triangle contributes one black node to every path that passes through it. So a color flip can't cause Rule 4 to be violated.

Color flips are helpful because they make red leaf nodes into black leaf nodes. This makes it easier to attach new red nodes without violating Rule 3.

Color Flips Can Create Red-Red Conflict

Although Rule 4 is not violated by a color flip, Rule 3 (a node and its parent can't both be red) might be. If the parent of P is black, there's no problem when P is changed from black to red. However, if the parent of P is red, then, after the color change, we'll have two reds in a row.

This needs to be fixed before we continue down the path to insert the new node. We can correct the situation with rotations, as we'll soon see.

> When Rule 3 (a node and its parent can't both be red) is violated, rotations are used to correct the problem.

Flipping the Root

What about the root? Remember that a color flip of the root and its two children leaves the root, as well as its children, black. This avoids violating Rule 2. Does this affect the other red-black rules? Clearly there are no red-to-red conflicts because we've made more nodes black and none red. Thus Rule 3 isn't violated. Also, because the root and one or the other of its two children are in every path, the black height of every path is increased the same amount; that is, by 1. Thus Rule 4 isn't violated either.

Finally, Just Insert the Node

After you've worked your way down to the appropriate place in the tree, performing color flips (and rotations, which we'll look at later) if necessary on the way down, you can then insert the new node as described in Hours 15 and 16 for an ordinary binary search tree. However, that's not the end of the story.

Rotations After the Node Is Inserted

The insertion of the new node might cause the red-black rules to be violated. (Try some insertions with the RBTree Workshop applet to verify this.) Therefore, following the insertion, we must check for rule violations and take appropriate steps.

Remember that as described earlier, the newly inserted node, which we'll call X, is always red. X can be located in various positions relative to P and G, as shown in 18.2.

Remember that a node X is an outside grandchild if it's on the same side of its parent P that P is of its parent G. That is, X is an outside grandchild if either it's a left child of P and P is a left child of G, or it's a right child of P and P is a right child of G. Conversely, X is an inside grandchild if it's on the opposite side of its parent P that P is of its parent G.

If X is an outside grandchild, it may be either the left or right child of P, depending on whether P is the left or right child of G. Two similar possibilities exist if X is an inside grandchild. It's these four situations that are shown in Figure 18.2. This multiplicity of what we might call "handed" (left or right) variations is one reason the red-black insertion routine is challenging to program.

The action we take to restore the red-black rules is determined by the colors and configuration of the newly inserted node X and its relatives. Perhaps surprisingly, there are only three major ways that nodes can be arranged (not counting the handed variations already mentioned). Each possibility must be dealt with in a different way to preserve red-black correctness and thereby lead to a balanced tree. We'll list the three possibilities briefly in the following list, and then discuss each one in detail in its own section. Figure 18.3 shows what the possibilities look like. Remember that X is always red.

FIGURE **18.2**

*Handed variations of
node being inserted.*

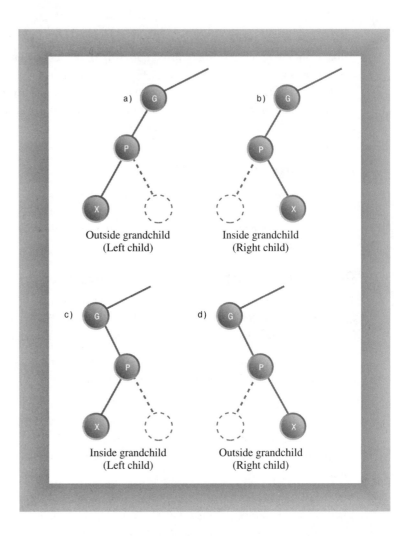

1. P is black.

2. P is red and X is an outside grandchild of G.

3. P is red and X is an inside grandchild of G.

It might seem that this list doesn't cover all the possibilities. We'll return to this question after we've explored these three.

FIGURE 18.3

Three post-insertion possibilities.

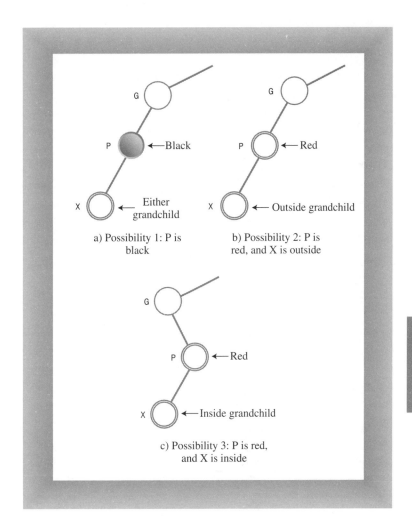

a) Possibility 1: P is black

b) Possibility 2: P is red, and X is outside

c) Possibility 3: P is red, and X is inside

18

Possibility 1: P Is Black

If P is black, we get a free ride. The node we've just inserted is always red. If its parent is black, there's no red-to-red conflict (Rule 3), and no addition to the number of black nodes (Rule 4). Thus no color rules are violated. We don't need to do anything else. The insertion is complete.

Possibility 2: P Is Red, X Is Outside

If P is red and X is an outside grandchild, we need a single rotation and some color changes. Let's set this up with the RBTree Workshop applet so we can see what we're talking about. Start with the usual 50 at the root, and insert 25, 75, and 12. You'll need to do a color flip before you insert the 12.

Now insert 6, which is X, the new node. Figure 18.4a shows how this looks. The message on the Workshop applet says Error: parent and child both red, so we know we need to take some action. In this situation, we can take three steps to restore red-black correctness and thereby balance the tree.

FIGURE 18.4

P is red, X is an outside grandchild.

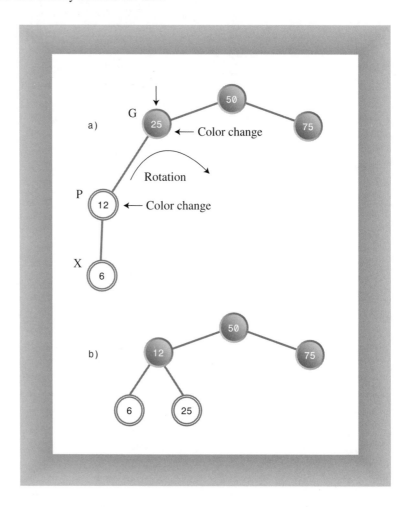

To Do: Balance with a Single Rotation

1. Switch the color of X's grandparent G (25 in this example).
2. Switch the color of X's parent P (12).

▲

3. Rotate with X's grandparent G (25) at the top, in the direction that raises X (6). This is a right rotation in the example.

As you've learned, to switch colors, put the arrow on the node and press the R/B button. To rotate right, put the arrow on the top node and press RoR. When you've completed the three steps, the Workshop applet will inform you that the Tree is red/black correct. It's also more balanced than it was, as shown in Figure 18.4b.

In this example, X was an outside grandchild and a left child. There's a symmetrical situation when the X is an outside grandchild but a right child. Try this by creating the tree 50, 25, 75, 87, 93 (with color flips when necessary). Fix it by changing the colors of 75 and 87, and rotating left with 75 at the top. Again the tree is balanced.

Possibility 3: P Is Red and X Is Inside

If P is red and X is an inside grandchild, we need two rotations and some color changes. To see this one in action, use the Workshop applet to create the tree 50, 25, 75, 12, 18. (Again you'll need a color flip before you insert the 12.) The result is shown in Figure 18.5a.

Note that the 18 node is an inside grandchild. It and its parent are both red, so again you see the error message Error: parent and child both red.

Fixing this arrangement is slightly more complicated. If we try to rotate right with the grandparent node G (25) at the top, as we did in Possibility 2, the inside grandchild X (18) moves across rather than up, so the tree is no more balanced than before. (Try this, and then rotate back, with 12 at the top, to restore it.) A different solution is needed.

The trick when X is an inside grandchild is to perform *two* rotations rather than one. The first changes X from an inside grandchild to an outside grandchild, as shown in Figure 18.5b. Now the situation is similar to Possibility 1, and we can apply the same rotation, with the grandparent at the top, as we did before. The result is shown in Figure 18.5c.

We must also recolor the nodes. We do this before doing any rotations. (This order doesn't really matter, but if we wait until after the rotations to recolor the nodes, it's hard to know what to call the nodes.)

To Do: Balance with a Double Rotation

1. Switch the color of X's grandparent (25 in this example).

2. Switch the color of X (*not* its parent; X is 18 here).

3. Rotate with X's parent P at the top (*not* the grandparent; the parent is 12), in the direction that raises X (a left rotation in this example).

4. Rotate again with X's grandparent (25) at the top, in the direction that raises X (a right rotation).

18

FIGURE 18.5

P is red and X is an inside grandchild.

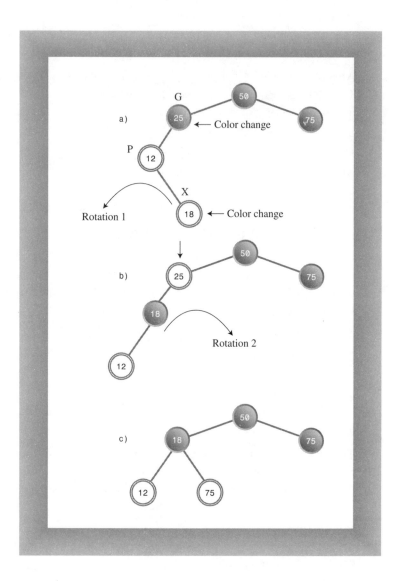

This restores the tree to red-black correctness, and also balances it (as much as possible). As with Possibility 2, there is an analogous case where P is the right child of G rather than the left.

> When X is an outside grandchild, a single rotation (with color changes) restores red-black correctness. When X is an inside grandchild, a double rotation is necessary.

Are There Other Post-Insertion Possibilities?

Do the three post-insertion possibilities just discussed really cover all situations?

Suppose, for example, that X has a sibling S; the other child of P. This might complicate the rotations necessary to insert X. But if P is black, there's no problem inserting X (that's Possibility 1). If P is red, both its children must be black (to avoid violating Rule 3). It can't have a single child S that's black because the black heights would be different for S and the null child. However, we know X is red, so we conclude that it's impossible for X to have a sibling unless P is red.

Another possibility is that G, the grandparent of P, has a child U, the sibling of P and the uncle of X. Again, this would complicate any necessary rotations. However, if P is black, there's no need for rotations when inserting X, as we've seen. So let's assume P is red. Then U must also be red, otherwise the black height going from G to P would be different from that going from G to U. But a black parent with two red children is flipped on the way down, so this situation can't exist either.

Thus the three possibilities discussed above are the only ones that can exist (except that, in Possibilities 2 and 3, X can be a right or left child and G can be a right or left child).

What the Color Flips Accomplished

Suppose that performing a rotation and appropriate color changes caused other violations of the red-black rules to appear further up the tree. One can imagine situations in which you would need to work your way all the way back up the tree, performing rotations and color switches, to remove rule violations.

Fortunately, this situation can't arise. Using color flips on the way down has eliminated the situations in which a rotation could introduce any rule violations further up the tree. It ensures that one or two rotations will restore red-black correctness in the entire tree. Actually proving this is beyond the scope of this book, but such a proof is possible.

It's the color flips on the way down that make insertion in red-black trees more efficient than in other kinds of balanced trees, such as AVL trees. They ensure that you only need to pass through the tree once, on the way down.

Rotations on the Way Down

Now we'll discuss the last of the three operations involved in inserting a node: making rotations on the way down to the insertion point. As we noted, although we're discussing this last, it actually takes place before the node is inserted. We've waited until now to discuss it only because it is easier to explain rotations for a just-installed node than for nodes in the middle of the tree.

During the discussion of color flips during the insertion process, we noted that it's possible for a color flip to cause a violation of Rule 3 (a parent and child can't both be red). We also noted that a rotation can fix this violation.

There are two possibilities, corresponding to Possibility 2 and Possibility 3 during the insertion phase described above. The offending node can be an outside grandchild or it can be an inside grandchild. (In the situation corresponding to Possibility 1, no action is required.)

Outside Grandchild

NEW TERM First we'll examine an example in which the offending node is an outside grandchild. By *offending node* we mean the child in the parent-child pair that caused the red-red conflict.

To Do: Encounter a Rule Violation

1. Start a new tree with the 50 node.

2. Insert the following nodes: 25, 75, 12, 37, 6, and 18. You'll need to do color flips when inserting 12 and 6.

3. Now try to insert a node with the value 3. You'll be told you must do a flip of 12 and its children 6 and 18.

4. Push the Flip button. The flip is carried out, but now the message says Error: parent and child are both red, referring to 25 and its child 12. The resulting tree is shown in Figure 18.6a.

The procedure used to fix this is similar to the post-insertion operation with an outside grandchild, described earlier. We must perform two color switches and one rotation. So we can discuss this in the same terms we did when inserting a node, we'll call the node at the top of the triangle that was flipped (which is 12 in this case) X. This looks a little odd because we're used to thinking of X as the node being inserted, and here it's not even a leaf node. However, these on-the-way-down rotations can take place anywhere within the tree.

FIGURE 18.6

Outside grandchild on the way down.

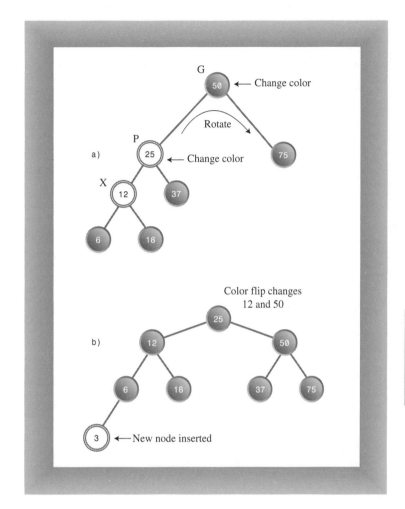

The parent of X is P (25 in this case), and the grandparent of X—the parent of P—is G (50 in this case). We follow the same set of rules we did under Possibility 2, discussed above.

To Do: Fix the Rule Violation

1. Switch the color of X's grandparent G (50 in this example). Ignore the message that the root must be black.

2. Switch the color of X's parent P (25).

3. Rotate with X's grandparent (50) at the top, in the direction that raises X (here a right rotation).

Suddenly, the tree is balanced! It has also become pleasantly symmetrical. It appears to be a bit of a miracle, but it's only a result of following the color rules.

Now the node with value 3 can be inserted in the usual way. Because the node it connects to, 6, is black, there's no complexity about the insertion. One color flip (at 50) is necessary. Figure 18.6b shows the tree after 3 is inserted.

Inside Grandchild

If X is an inside grandchild when a red-red conflict occurs on the way down, two rotations are required to set it right. This situation is similar to the inside grandchild in the post-insertion phase, which we called Possibility 3.

To Do: Encounter a Rule Violation

1. Click Start in the RBTree Workshop applet to begin with 50.

2. Insert 25, 75, 12, 37, 31, and 43. You'll need color flips before 12 and 31.

3. Now try to insert a new node with the value 28.

4. You'll be told it needs a color flip (at 37). But when you perform the flip, 37 and 25 are both red, and you get the Error: parent and child are both red message.

5. Don't press Ins again.

In this situation G is 50, P is 25, and X is 37, as shown in Figure 18.7a.

To cure the red-red conflict, you must do the same two color changes and two rotations as in Possibility 3.

To Do: Fix the Rule Violation

1. Change the color of G (it's 50; ignore the message that the root must be black).

2. Change the color of X (37).

3. Rotate with P (25) as the top, in the direction that raises X (left in this example). The result is shown in Figure 18.7b.

4. Rotate with G as the top, in the direction that raises X (right in this example).

Now you can insert the 28. A color flip changes 25 and 50 to black as you insert it. The result is shown in Figure 18.7c.

This concludes the description of how a tree is kept red-black correct, and therefore balanced, during the insertion process.

FIGURE **18.7**

Inside grandchild on the way down.

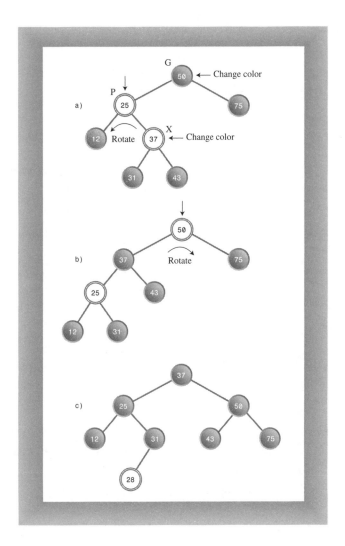

Deletion

As you might recall, coding for deletion in an ordinary binary search tree is considerably harder than for insertion. The same is true in red-black trees, but in addition, the deletion process is, as you might expect, complicated by the need to restore red-black correctness after the node is removed.

In fact, the deletion process is so complicated that many programmers sidestep it in various ways. One approach, as with ordinary binary trees, is to mark a node as deleted without actually deleting it. A search routine that finds the node then knows not to tell anyone about it. This works in many situations, especially if deletions are not a common occurrence. In any case, we're going to forgo a discussion of the deletion process. You can refer to the bibliography if you want to pursue it.

Efficiency of Red-Black Trees

Like ordinary binary search trees, a red-black tree allows for searching, insertion, and deletion in $O(\log_2 N)$ time. Search times should be almost the same in the red-black tree as in the ordinary tree because the red-black characteristics of the tree aren't used during searches. The only penalty is that the storage required for each node is increased slightly to accommodate the red-black color (a Boolean variable).

More specifically, according to Sedgewick (see Appendix C, "Further Reading"), in practice a search in a red-black tree takes about $\log_2 N$ comparisons, and it can be shown that it cannot require more than $2*\log_2 N$ comparisons.

The times for insertion and deletion are increased by a constant factor because of having to perform color flips and rotations on the way down and at the insertion point. On the average, an insertion requires about one rotation. Therefore insertion still takes $O(\log_2 N)$ time, but is slower than insertion in the ordinary binary tree.

Because in most applications there will be more searches than insertions and deletions, there is probably not much overall time penalty for using a red-black tree instead of an ordinary tree. Of course, the advantage is that in a red-black tree sorted data doesn't lead to slow $O(N)$ performance.

Implementing the Insertion Process

Most people will probably use a prewritten library routine to implement a red-black tree. However, if you're writing an insertion routine for red-black trees, all you need to do (irony intended) is to write code to carry out the operations described above. As we noted, showing and describing such code are beyond the scope of this book. However, here's what you'll need to think about.

You'll need to add a red-black data member (which can be type `bool`) to the `Node` class.

You can adapt the insertion routine from the `tree.cpp` program in Hour 16. On the way down to the insertion point, check whether the current node is black and its two children are both red. If so, change the color of all three (unless the parent is the root, which must be kept black).

After a color flip, check that there are no violations of Rule 3. If so, perform the appropriate rotations: one for an outside grandchild, two for an inside grandchild.

When you reach a leaf node, insert the new node as in `tree.cpp`, making sure the node is red. Check again for red-red conflicts, and perform any necessary rotations.

Perhaps surprisingly, your software need not keep track of the black height of different parts of the tree (although you might want to check this during debugging). You only need to check for violations of Rule 3, a red parent with a red child, which can be done locally (unlike checks of black heights, Rule 4, which would require more complex bookkeeping).

If you perform the color flips, color changes, and rotations described earlier, the black heights of the nodes should take care of themselves and the tree should remain balanced. The RBTree Workshop applet reports black-height errors only because the user is not forced to carry out the insertion algorithm correctly.

Other Balanced Trees

There are several other ways to balance a binary tree besides the red-black approach discussed in this hour. We'll briefly mention two possibilities.

AVL Trees

NEW TERM The *AVL tree* is the earliest kind of balanced tree. It's named after its inventors: Adelson-Velskii and Landis. In AVL trees each node stores an additional piece of data: the difference between the heights of its left and right subtrees. This difference may not be larger than 1. That is, the height of a node's left subtree may be no more than one level different from the height of its right subtree.

Following insertion, the root of the lowest subtree into which the new node was inserted is checked. If the height of its children differs by more than 1, a single or double rotation is performed to equalize their heights. The algorithm then moves up and checks the node above, equalizing heights if necessary. This continues all the way back up to the root.

Search times in an AVL tree are O(log N) because the tree is guaranteed to be balanced. However, because two passes through the tree are necessary to insert (or delete) a node, one down to find the insertion point and one up to rebalance the tree, AVL trees are not as efficient as red-black trees and are not used as often.

Multiway Trees

NEW TERM The other important kind of balanced tree is the *multiway tree*, in which each node can have more than two children. We'll look at one version of multiway trees, the 2-3-4 tree, in Hours 19, "2-3-4 Trees," and 20, "Implementing 2-3-4 Trees."

18

One problem with multiway trees is that each node must be larger than for a binary tree because it needs to incorporate a pointer to every one of its children.

Summary

In this hour, you've learned the following:

- Color flips, and sometimes rotations, are applied while searching down the tree to find where a new node should be inserted. These flips simplify returning the tree to red-black correctness following an insertion.
- After a new node is inserted, red-red conflicts are checked again. If a violation is found, appropriate rotations are carried out to make the tree red-black correct.
- These adjustments result in the tree being balanced, or at least almost balanced.
- Adding red-black balancing to a binary tree has only a small negative effect on average performance, and avoids worst-case performance when the data is already sorted.

Q&A

Q Do I really need to understand how red-black trees work?

A Every detail is critical! No, that's not really true. If you're just using a prewritten class, understanding the general idea is probably all you need. Of course, if you're going to write your own red-black tree class, that's another story.

Q Why don't you show any C++ code for red-black trees?

A As we noted earlier, it's so lengthy and complicated it doesn't really help you understand the concepts. Also, you'll probably end up using a prewritten red-black tree class anyway. If you do want to write your own code, we've told you enough to get you started, and we wish you the best of luck.

Workshop

The Workshop helps you solidify what you learned in this hour. See Appendix A for quiz answers.

Quiz

1. During what operations are color changes and rotations applied?

2. What is the principle way a red-black tree is balanced?

3. What is the purpose of the color rules?

4. What is a color flip?

5. What is a rotation?

6. What's an inside grandchild?

7. Briefly describe the insertion process in red-black trees.

8. What do you do when Rule 3, (a parent and its child can't both be red) is violated?

9. How do you know whether to perform a single rotation or a double rotation?

Exercise

Write down 13 random numbers, between 1 and 99, on a piece of paper. Then, using the RBTree Workshop applet, insert nodes with these 13 values into a new tree. As each node is inserted, follow the color rules to keep the tree balanced, performing rotations as necessary. Refer to the lists in the "Outside Grandchild" and "Inside Grandchild" sections if you're not sure how to handle rotations. Try this several times with different sets of numbers.

18

HOUR 19

2-3-4 Trees

NEW TERM   In a binary tree, each node has one data item and can have up to two children. If we allow more data items and children per node, the result is a multiway tree. *2-3-4 trees*, which we'll discuss in this hour and the next one, are multiway trees that can have up to four children and three data items per node.

2-3-4 trees are balanced trees like red-black trees. They're slightly less efficient than red-black trees, but easier to program. In this hour you'll learn:

- How a 2-3-4 tree is organized
- How searching and insertion are carried out
- How node splits keep a 2-3-4 tree balanced

In the next hour we'll look at some C++ code for a 2-3-4 tree, and investigate the surprising relationship between 2-3-4 trees and red-black trees.

Introduction to 2-3-4 Trees

Figure 19.1 shows a small 2-3-4 tree. Each lozenge-shaped node can hold one, two, or three data items.

FIGURE **19.1**

A 2-3-4 tree.

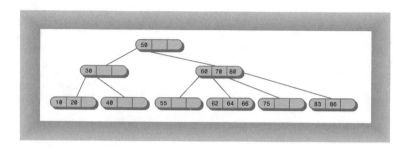

Here the top three nodes have children, and the six nodes on the bottom row are all leaf nodes, which by definition have no children. In a 2-3-4 tree all the leaf nodes are always on the same level.

What's in a Name?

The 2, 3, and 4 in the name 2-3-4 tree refer to how many links to child nodes can potentially exist in a given node. For nonleaf nodes, the following three arrangements are possible:

- A node with one data item always has two children
- A node with two data items always has three children
- A node with three data items always has four children

In short, a nonleaf node must always have one more child than it has data items. Or, to put it symbolically, if the number of child links is L and the number of data items is D, then

```
L = D + 1
```

This is a critical relationship that determines the structure of 2-3-4 trees. A leaf node, by contrast, has no children, but it can nevertheless contain one, two, or three data items. Empty nodes are not allowed.

NEW TERM Because a *2-3-4 tree* can have nodes with up to four children, it's called *a multi-way tree of order 4*.

You might wonder why a 2-3-4 tree isn't called a 1-2-3-4 tree. Can't a node have only one child, as nodes in binary trees can? A binary tree (described in Hours 15 through 18), can be thought of as a multiway tree of order 2 because each node can have up to two children. However, there's a difference (besides the maximum number of children) between binary trees and 2-3-4 trees. In a binary tree, a node can have *up to* two child links. A single link, to its left or to its right child, is also perfectly permissible. The other link has a null value.

In a 2-3-4 tree, on the other hand, nodes with a single link are not permitted. A node with one data item must always have two links, unless it's a leaf, in which case it has no links.

 A node must always have at least two children, unless it's a leaf.

NEW TERM Figure 19.2 shows the possibilities. A node with two links is called a *2-node*, a node with three links is a *3-node*, and a node with 4 links is a *4-node*, but there is no such thing as a 1-node.

FIGURE 19.2

Nodes in a 2-3-4 tree.

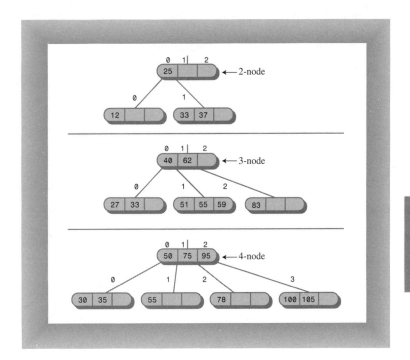

19

2-3-4 Tree Organization

For convenience we number the data items in a link from 0 to 2, and the child links from 0 to 3, as shown in Figure 19.2. The data items in a node are arranged in ascending key order; by convention from left to right (lower to higher numbers).

An important aspect of any tree's structure is the relationship of its links to the key values of its data items. In a binary tree, all children with keys less than the node's key are in a subtree rooted in the node's left child, and all children with keys larger than or equal to the node's key are rooted in the node's right child. In a 2-3-4 tree the principle is the same, but there's more to it, as summarized in the following list:

- All children in the subtree rooted at child 0 have key values less than key 0.
- All children in the subtree rooted at child 1 have key values greater than key 0 but less than key 1.
- All children in the subtree rooted at child 2 have key values greater than key 1 but less than key 2.
- All children in the subtree rooted at child 3 have key values greater than key 2.

These relationships between keys and children are shown in Figure 19.3. Duplicate values are not usually permitted in 2-3-4 trees, so we don't need to worry about comparing equal keys.

FIGURE 19.3

Keys and children.

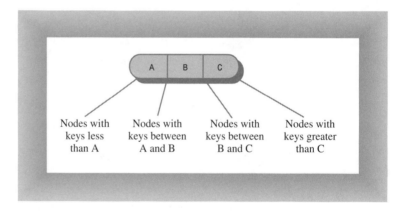

Refer to the tree in Figure 19.1. As in all 2-3-4 trees, the leaves are all on the same level (the bottom row). Upper-level nodes are often not full; that is, they might contain only one or two data items instead of three.

Also, notice that the tree is balanced. It retains its balance even if you insert a sequence of data in ascending (or descending) order. The 2-3-4 tree's self-balancing capability results from the way new data items are inserted, as we'll see in a moment.

Searching for a Data Item

Finding a data item with a particular key is similar to the search routine in a binary tree. You start at the root, and, unless the search key is found there, select the link that leads to the subtree with the appropriate range of values.

For example, here's how to search for the data item with key 64 in the tree in Figure 19.1.

To Do: Search a 2-3-4 Tree

1. Start at the root.

2. You search the root, but don't find the item.

3. Because 64 is larger than 50, you go to child 1, which we will represent as 60/70/80. (Remember that child 1 is on the right of data item 50 because the numbering of children and links starts at 0 on the left of the first item.)

4. You don't find the data item in this node either, so you must go to the next child.

5. In 60/70/80, because 64 is greater than 60 but less than 70, you go again to child 1, which is 62/64/66.

6. This time you find the specified item as child 1.

Inserting a New Data Item

New data items are always inserted in leaves, which are on the bottom row of the tree. If items were inserted in nodes with children, the number of children would need to be changed to maintain the structure of the tree, which stipulates that there should be one more child than data items in a node.

Insertion into a 2-3-4 tree is sometimes quite easy and sometimes rather complicated. In any case the process begins by searching for the appropriate leaf node.

If no full nodes are encountered during the search, insertion is easy. When the appropriate leaf node is reached, the new data item is simply inserted into it. Figure 19.4 shows a data item with key 18 being inserted into a 2-3-4 tree.

Insertion may involve moving one or two other items in a node so the keys will be in the correct order after the new item is inserted. In this example the 23 had to be shifted right to make room for the 18.

FIGURE **19.4**

Insertion with no splits.

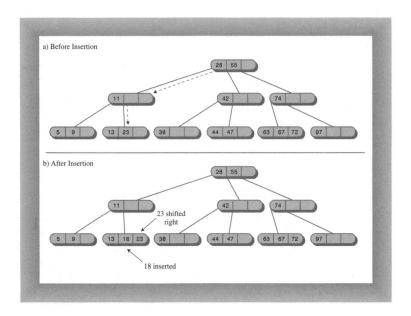

Node Splits

NEW TERM Insertion becomes more complicated if a full node is encountered on the path down to the insertion point. When this happens, the node must be *split*. It's this splitting process that keeps the tree balanced. The kind of 2-3-4 tree we're discussing here is often called a *top-down* 2-3-4 tree because nodes are split on the way down to the insertion point.

Let's name the data items in the node that's about to be split A, B, and C. Here's what happens in a split. (We assume the node being split is not the root; we'll examine splitting the root later.)

- A new, empty node is created. It's a sibling of the node being split, and is placed to its right.
- Data item C is moved into the new node.
- Data item B is moved into the parent of the node being split.
- Data item A remains where it is.
- The rightmost two children are disconnected from the node being split and connected to the new node.

An example of a node split is shown in Figure 19.5. Another way of describing a node split is to say that a 4-node has been transformed into two 2-nodes.

FIGURE 19.5

Splitting a node.

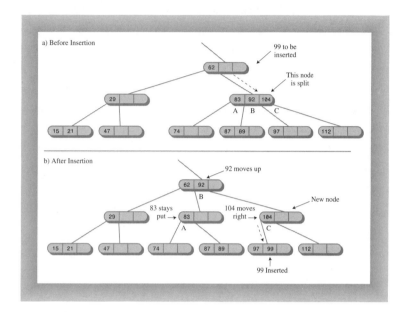

Notice that the effect of the node split is to move data up and to the right. It's this rearrangement that keeps the tree balanced.

Here the insertion required only one node split, but more than one full node might be encountered on the path to the insertion point. When this is the case there will be multiple splits.

Splitting the Root

When a full root is encountered at the beginning of the search for the insertion point, the resulting split is slightly more complicated:

- A new node is created that becomes the new root and the parent of the node being split.
- A second new node is created that becomes a sibling of the node being split.

19

- Data item C is moved into the new sibling.
- Data item B is moved into the new root.
- Data item A remains where it is.
- The two rightmost children of the node being split are disconnected from it and connected to the new right-side node.

Figure 19.6 shows the root being split. This process creates a new root that's at a higher level than the old one. Thus the overall height of the tree is increased by one. Another way to describe splitting the root is to say that a 4-node is split into three 2-nodes.

FIGURE 19.6

Splitting the root.

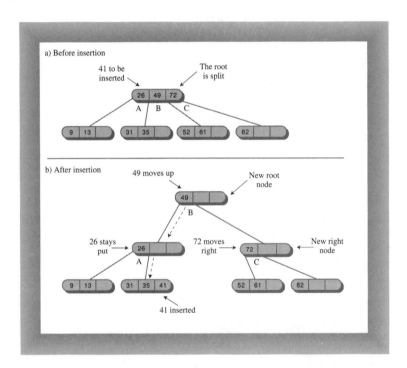

Following a node split, the search for the insertion point continues down the tree. In Figure 19.6, the data item with a key of 41 is inserted into the appropriate leaf.

Splitting Nodes on the Way Down

Notice that because all full nodes are split on the way down, a split can't cause an effect that ripples back up through the tree. The parent of any node that's being split is guaranteed not to be full, and can therefore accept data item B without itself needing to be split.

Of course, if this parent already had two children when its child was split, it will become full. However, that just means that it will be split when the next insertion encounters it.

Figure 19.7 shows a series of insertions into an empty tree. There are four node splits, two of the root and two of leaves.

FIGURE 19.7

Insertions into a 2-3-4 tree.

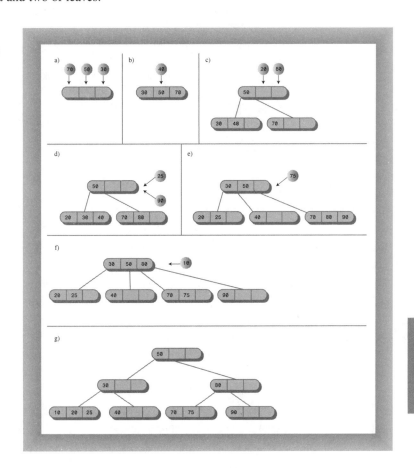

Now that you understand the general idea behind 2-3-4 trees, let's see how they look with a Workshop applet.

The Tree234 Workshop Applet

Operating the Tree234 Workshop applet provides a quick way to see how 2-3-4 trees work. When you start the applet you'll see a screen similar to Figure 19.8. The following sections explain what the various buttons do.

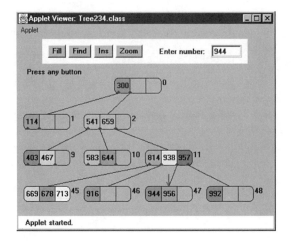

FIGURE **19.8**

*The Tree234 Workshop
applet.*

The Fill Button

When it's first started, the Tree234 Workshop applet inserts 10 data items into the tree.
You can use the Fill button to create a new tree with a different number of data items,
from 0 to 45. Click Fill and type the number into the field when prompted. Another click
will create the new tree.

The tree might not look very full with 45 nodes, but more nodes require more levels,
which won't fit in the display.

The Find Button

You can watch the applet locate a data item with a given key by repeatedly clicking the
Find button.

To Do: Find a Data Item

1. When prompted, type in the appropriate key.

2. Then, as you click the button, watch the red arrow move from node to node as it
   searches for the item.

3. Messages will say something like Went to child number 1. (As we've seen, children are numbered from 0 to 3 from left to right, whereas data items are numbered
   from 0 to 2.)

4. When the arrow reaches the node containing the item (if it exists), you'll see the
   message Found item, number 1 in this node (or whatever item number is
   appropriate).

After a little practice you should be able to predict the path the search will take.

A search involves examining one node on each level. The applet supports a maximum of four levels, so any item can be found by examining only four nodes. Within each nonleaf node, the algorithm examines each data item, starting on the left, to see which child it should go to next. In a leaf node it examines each data item to see whether it contains the specified key. If it can't find such an item in the leaf node, the search fails.

> In the Tree234 Workshop applet it's important to complete each operation before attempting a new one. Continue to click the button until the message says Press any button. This is the signal that an operation is complete.

The Ins Button

The Ins button causes a new data item, with a key specified in the text box, to be inserted in the tree. The algorithm first searches for the appropriate node. If the algorithm encounters a full node along the way, it splits the node before continuing.

Experiment with the insertion process. Watch what happens when there are no full nodes on the path to the insertion point. This is a straightforward process. Then try inserting at the end of a path that includes a full node, either at the root, at the leaf, or somewhere in between. Watch how new nodes are formed and the contents of the node being split are distributed among three different nodes.

The Zoom Button

One of the problems with 2-3-4 trees is that there are a great many nodes and data items just a few levels down. The Tree234 Workshop applet supports only four levels, but there are potentially 64 nodes on the bottom level, each of which can hold up to three data items.

It would be impossible to display so many items at once on one row, so the applet shows only some of them: the children of a selected node. (To see the children of another node, you click on it; we'll discuss that in a moment.) To see a zoomed-out view of the entire tree, click the Zoom button. Figure 19.9 shows what you'll see.

In this view nodes are shown as small rectangles; data items are not shown. Nodes that exist and are visible in the zoomed-in view (which you can restore by clicking Zoom again) are shown in green. Nodes that exist but aren't currently visible in the zoomed-out view are shown in magenta, and nodes that don't exist are shown in gray. These colors are hard to distinguish on the figure; you'll need to view the applet on your color monitor to make sense of the display.

FIGURE **19.9**

The zoomed-out view.

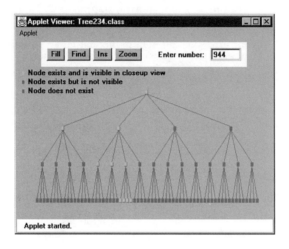

 Using the Zoom button to toggle back and forth between the zoomed-out and zoomed-in views allows you to see both the big picture and the details, and hopefully put the two together in your mind.

Viewing Different Nodes

In the zoomed-in view you can always see all the nodes in the top two rows: there's only one node, the root, in the top row, and only four nodes in the second row. Below the second row things get more complicated because there are too many nodes to fit on the screen: 16 on the third row, and 64 on the fourth. However, you can see any node you want by clicking on its parent, or sometimes its grandparent and then its parent.

A blue triangle at the bottom of a node shows where a child is connected to a node. If a node's children are currently visible, the lines to the children can be seen running from the blue triangles to them. If the children aren't currently visible, there are no lines, but the blue triangles indicate that the node nevertheless has children. If you click on the parent node, its children, and the lines to them, will appear. By clicking the appropriate nodes you can navigate all over the tree.

For convenience, all the nodes are numbered, starting with 0 at the root and continuing up to 85 for the node on the far right of the bottom row. The numbers are displayed to the upper right of each node, as shown in Figure 19.8. Nodes are numbered whether they exist or not, so the numbers on existing nodes probably won't be contiguous.

Figure 19.10 shows a small tree with four nodes in the third row. The user has clicked on node 1, so its two children, numbered 5 and 6, are visible.

FIGURE **19.10**

Selecting the leftmost children.

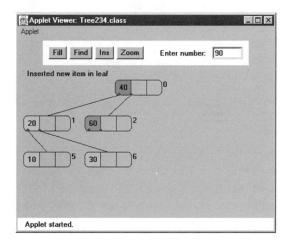

If the user clicks on node 2, its children 9 and 10 will appear, as shown in Figure 19.11.

FIGURE **19.11**

Selecting the rightmost children.

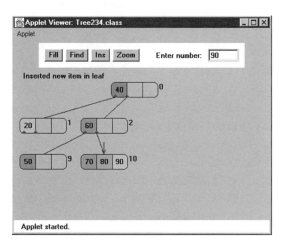

19

These figures show how to switch among different nodes in the third row by clicking nodes in the second row. To switch nodes in the fourth row you'll need to click first on a grandparent in the second row, and then on a parent in the third row.

During searches and insertions with the Find and Ins buttons, the view will change automatically to show the node currently being pointed to by the red arrow.

Experimenting on Your Own

The Tree234 Workshop applet offers a quick way to learn about 2-3-4 trees. Try inserting items into the tree. Watch for node splits. Stop before one is about to happen, and figure out where the three data items from the split node are going to go. Then press Ins again to see if you're right.

As the tree gets larger you'll need to move around it to see all the nodes. Click on a node to see its children (and their children, and so on). If you lose track of where you are, use the Zoom key to see the big picture.

How many data items can you insert in the tree? There's a limit because only four levels are allowed. Four levels can potentially contain $1 + 4 + 16 + 64$ nodes, for a total of 85 nodes (all visible on the zoomed-out display). Assuming a full 3 items per node gives 255 data items. However, the nodes can't all be full at the same time. Long before they fill up, another root split, leading to five levels, would be necessary, and this is impossible because the applet supports only four levels.

You can insert the most items by deliberately inserting them into nodes that lie on paths with no full nodes, so that no splits are necessary. Of course this is not a reasonable procedure with real data. For random data you probably can't insert more than about 50 items into the applet. The Fill button allows only 45, to minimize the possibility of overflow.

Summary

In this hour, you've learned the following:

- Nodes in a multiway tree have more keys and children than nodes in a binary tree.
- A 2-3-4 tree is a multiway tree with up to three keys and four children per node.
- In a multiway tree, the keys in a node are arranged in ascending order.

- In a 2-3-4 tree, all insertions are made in leaf nodes, and all leaf nodes are on the same level.

- Three kinds of nodes are possible in a 2-3-4 tree: A 2-node has one key and two children, a 3-node has two keys and three children, and a 4-node has three keys and four children.

- There is no 1-node in a 2-3-4 tree.

- In a search in a 2-3-4 tree, at each node the keys are examined. If the search key is not found, the next node will be child 0 if the search key is less than key 0; child 1 if the search key is between key 0 and key 1; child 2 if the search key is between key 1 and key 2; and child 3 if the search key is greater than key 2.

- Insertion into a 2-3-4 tree requires that any full node be split on the way down the tree, during the search for the insertion point.

- Splitting the root creates two new nodes; splitting any other node creates one new node.

- The height of a 2-3-4 tree can increase only when the root is split.

Q&A

Q When would I use a 2-3-4 tree as opposed to a red-black tree?

A If you're using prewritten software, you'll find that red-black trees are the most commonly available tree. If for some reason you need to write your own tree software, the 2-3-4 tree is probably easier to program.

Q Are there other reasons to know about 2-3-4 trees?

A Yes. 2-3-4 trees are a special form of a multiway tree, and a special kind of multiway tree called a B-tree is important for storing data on disk drives. We'll comment on this at the end of the next hour.

19

Workshop

The Workshop helps you solidify what you learned in this hour. See Appendix A for quiz answers.

Quiz

1. True or false: In a multiway tree, each node can have more than two children.

2. What is the maximum number of data items per node in a 2-3-4 tree?

3. When should a node be split?

4. What happens when a node (other than the root) is split?

5. If a node is split (assuming it's not the root) what is the increase in the number of levels in the tree?

6. What happens when the root is split?

7. True or false: Sometimes a node split results in additional node splits in nodes farther up the tree.

8. What keeps a 2-3-4 tree balanced?

Exercise

Write down a series of 30 random numbers in the range 1 to 99. Use the Tree234 Workshop applet to create a tree containing these numbers as data items. Start with an empty tree using the Fill button with a value of 0.

HOUR 20

Implementing 2-3-4 Trees

In this hour we'll continue our exploration of 2-3-4 trees. We'll examine

- C++ code for a 2-3-4 tree
- The equivalence of 2-3-4 trees and red-black trees
- The efficiency of 2-3-4 trees

The second point might seem surprising, but it turns out a red-black tree can be transformed into a 2-3-4 tree by following some simple rules. First, though, we'll focus on programming.

Implementing a 2-3-4 Tree in C++

In this section we'll examine a C++ program that models a 2-3-4 tree. We'll show the complete tree234.cpp program at the end of the section. This is a relatively large and complex program, and the classes are extensively inter-related, so you'll need to peruse the entire listing to see how it works.

There are three classes: DataItem, Node, and Tree234, as well as the main() function. We'll discuss them in turn.

The `DataItem` Class

Objects of this class represent the data items stored in nodes. In a real-world program each object would contain an entire personnel or inventory record, but here there's only one piece of data, of type `double`, associated with each `DataItem` object.

The only actions that objects of this class can perform are to initialize themselves and display themselves. The display is the data value preceded by a slash: /27. (The display routine in the `Node` class will call this routine to display all the items in a node.)

The `Node` Class

The `Node` class contains two arrays: `childArray` and `itemArray`. The first array is four cells long and holds pointers to whatever children the node might have. The second array is three cells long and holds pointers to objects of type `DataItem` contained in the node.

Note that the data items in `itemArray` comprise an ordered array. New items are added, or existing ones removed, in the same way they would be in any ordered array (as described in Hour 3, "Ordered Arrays"). Items might need to be shifted to make room to insert a new item in order, or to close an empty cell when an item is removed.

We've chosen to store the number of items currently in the node (`numItems`) and the node's parent (`pParent`) as data members in this class. Neither of these is strictly necessary, and could be eliminated to make the nodes smaller. However, including them clarifies the programming, and only a small price is paid in increased node size.

Various small utility routines are provided in the `Node` class to manage the connections to child and parent and to check whether the node is full and whether it is a leaf. However, the major work is done by the `findItem()`, `insertItem()`, and `removeItem()` member functions. These handle individual items within the node. They search through the node for a data item with a particular key; insert a new item into the node, moving existing items if necessary; and remove an item, again moving existing items if necessary. Don't confuse these member functions with the `find()` and `insert()` routines in the `Tree234` class, which we'll look at next.

A display routine displays a node with slashes separating the data items, like /27/56/89/, /14/66/, or /45/. It calls the `displayItem()` routine in the `DataItem` class to display each item's key.

The `Tree234` Class

An object of the `Tree234` class represents the entire tree. The class has only one data member: `pRoot`, of type `Node*`. All operations start at the root, so that's all a tree needs to remember.

The two important tasks carried out by the Tree234 class are searching and insertion. Insertion requires another task: splitting nodes. Let's look at these three activities.

Searching

Searching for a data item with a specified key is carried out by the find() routine. It starts at the root, and at each node calls that node's findItem() routine to see whether the item is there. If so, it returns the index of the item within the node's item array.

If find() is at a leaf and can't find the item, the search has failed, so it returns -1. If it can't find the item in the current node, and the current node isn't a leaf, find() calls the getNextChild() member function, which figures out which of a node's children the routine should go to next.

Inserting

The insert() member function starts with code similar to find(), except that if insert() finds a full node it splits it. Also, insert() assumes it can't fail; it keeps looking, going to deeper and deeper levels, until it finds a leaf node. At this point it inserts the new data item into the leaf. (There is always room in the leaf, otherwise the leaf would have been split.)

Splitting

The split() member function is the most complicated in this program. It is passed the node that will be split as an argument. First, the two rightmost data items are removed from the node and stored. Then the two rightmost children are disconnected; their pointers are also stored.

A new node, pointed to by pNewRight, is created. It will be placed to the right of the node being split. If the node being split is the root, an additional new node is created: a new root.

Next, appropriate connections are made to the parent of the node being split. It might be a pre-existing parent, or if the root is being split it will be the newly created root node. Assume the three data items in the node being split are called A, B, and C. Item B is inserted in this parent node. If necessary, the parent's existing children are disconnected and reconnected one position to the right to make room for the new data item and new connections. The pNewRight node is connected to this parent. (Refer to Figures 19.5 and 19.6 in the last hour.)

Now the focus shifts to the pNewRight node. Data item C is inserted in it, and child 2 and child 3, which were previously disconnected from the node being split, are connected to it. The split is now complete, and the split() routine returns.

20

Now let's see how `main()` uses the `Tree234` class to store and access data.

The `main()` Function

The `main()` routine inserts a few data items into the tree. It then presents a character-based interface for the user, who can enter s to see the tree, i to insert a new data item, and f to find an existing item. Here's some sample interaction:

```
Enter first letter of show, insert, or find: s
level=0 child=0 /50/
level=1 child=0 /30/40/
level=1 child=1 /60/70/

Enter first letter of show, insert, or find: f
Enter value to find: 40
Found 40

Enter first letter of show, insert, or find: i
Enter value to insert: 20
Enter first letter of show, insert, or find: s
level=0 child=0 /50/
level=1 child=0 /20/30/40/
level=1 child=1 /60/70/

Enter first letter of show, insert, or find: i
Enter value to insert: 10
Enter first letter of show, insert, or find: s
level=0 child=0 /30/50/
level=1 child=0 /10/20/
level=1 child=1 /40/
level=1 child=2 /60/70/
```

The output is not very intuitive, but there's enough information to draw the tree on paper if you want. The level is shown, starting with 0 at the root, as well as the child number. The display algorithm is depth-first, so the root is shown first, then its first child and the subtree of which the first child is the root, then the second child and its subtree, and so on.

The output shows two items being inserted, 20 and 10. The second of these caused a node (the root's child 0) to split. Figure 20.1 depicts the tree that results from these insertions, following the final press of the S key.

Listing for `tree234.cpp`

Listing 20.1 shows the complete `tree234.cpp` program, including the classes just discussed. As with most object-oriented programs, it's probably easiest to start by examining the big picture first and then working down to the detail-oriented classes. In this program this order is `main()`, `Tree234`, `Node`, and `DataItem`.

FIGURE 20.1

Sample output of the
`tree234.cpp` *program.*

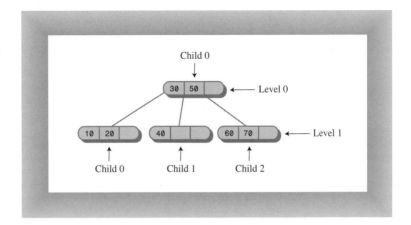

```cpp
//tree234.cpp
//demonstrates 234 tree
#include <iostream>
using namespace std;
//////////////////////////////////////////////////////////////
class DataItem
   {
   public:
      double dData;               //one piece of data
//-----------------------------------------------------------
   DataItem() : dData(0.0)        //default constructor
      {  }
//-----------------------------------------------------------
   DataItem(double dd) : dData(dd)  //1-arg constructor
      {  }
//-----------------------------------------------------------
   void displayItem()             //format "/27"
      { cout << "/" << dData; }
   };  //end class DataItem
//////////////////////////////////////////////////////////////
class Node
   {
   private:
      enum {ORDER=4};
      int numItems;
      Node* pParent;
      Node* childArray[ORDER];       //array of ptrs to nodes
      DataItem* itemArray[ORDER-1];  //array of ptrs to data
   public:
```

continues

20

LISTING 20.1   CONTINUED

```
//-------------------------------------------------------------
   Node() : numItems(0)
      {
      for(int j=0; j<ORDER; j++)     //initialize arrays
         childArray[j] = NULL;
      for(int k=0; k<ORDER-1; k++)
         itemArray[k] = NULL;
      }
//-------------------------------------------------------------
   //connect child to this node
   void connectChild(int childNum, Node* pChild)
      {
      childArray[childNum] = pChild;
      if(pChild != NULL)
         pChild->pParent = this;
      }
//-------------------------------------------------------------
   //disconnect child from this node, return it
   Node* disconnectChild(int childNum)
      {
      Node* pTempNode = childArray[childNum];
      childArray[childNum] = NULL;
      return pTempNode;
      }
//-------------------------------------------------------------
   Node* getChild(int childNum)
      { return childArray[childNum]; }
//-------------------------------------------------------------
   Node* getParent()
      { return pParent; }
//-------------------------------------------------------------
   bool isLeaf()
      { return (childArray[0]==NULL) ? true : false; }
//-------------------------------------------------------------
   int getNumItems()
      { return numItems; }
//-------------------------------------------------------------
   DataItem getItem(int index)      //get DataItem at index
      { return *( itemArray[index] ); }
//-------------------------------------------------------------
   bool isFull()
      { return (numItems==ORDER-1) ? true : false; }
//-------------------------------------------------------------
   int findItem(double key)         //return index of
      {                             //item (within node)
      for(int j=0; j<ORDER-1; j++)  //if found,
         {                          //otherwise,
         if(itemArray[j] == NULL)   //return -1
```

```
            break;
         else if(itemArray[j]->dData == key)
            return j;
         }
      return -1;
      } //end findItem
//-----------------------------------------------------------
   int insertItem(DataItem* pNewItem)
      {
      //assumes node is not full
      numItems++;                         //will add new item
      double newKey = pNewItem->dData;    //key of new item

      for(int j=ORDER-2; j>=0; j--)       //start on right,
         {                                //    examine items
         if(itemArray[j] == NULL)         //if item null,
            continue;                     //go left one cell
         else                             //not null,
            {                             //get its key
            double itsKey = itemArray[j]->dData;
            if(newKey < itsKey)           //if it's bigger
               itemArray[j+1] = itemArray[j]; //shift it right
            else
               {
               itemArray[j+1] = pNewItem; //insert new item
               return j+1;                //return index to
               }                          //    new item
            } //end else (not null)
         } //end for                      //shifted all items,
      itemArray[0] = pNewItem;            //insert new item
      return 0;
      } //end insertItem()
//-----------------------------------------------------------
   DataItem* removeItem()                 //remove largest item
      {
      //assumes node not empty
      DataItem* pTemp = itemArray[numItems-1]; //save item
      itemArray[numItems-1] = NULL;       //disconnect it
      numItems--;                         //one less item
      return pTemp;                       //return item
      }
//-----------------------------------------------------------
   void displayNode()                     //format "/24/56/74/"
      {
      for(int j=0; j<numItems; j++)
         itemArray[j]->displayItem();     //format "/56"
      cout << "/";                        //final "/"
      }
//-----------------------------------------------------------
```

20

continues

LISTING 20.1 CONTINUED

```
    };  //end class Node
//////////////////////////////////////////////////////////////
class Tree234
    {
    private:
        Node* pRoot;                        //root node
    public:
//------------------------------------------------------------
    Tree234()
        { pRoot = new Node; }
//------------------------------------------------------------
    int find(double key)
        {
        Node* pCurNode = pRoot;             //start at root
        int childNumber;
        while(true)
            {
            if(( childNumber=pCurNode->findItem(key) ) != -1)
                return childNumber;         //found it
            else if( pCurNode->isLeaf() )
                return -1;                  //can't find it
            else                            //search deeper
                pCurNode = getNextChild(pCurNode, key);
            }  //end while
        }
//------------------------------------------------------------
    void insert(double dValue)      //insert a DataItem
        {
        Node* pCurNode = pRoot;
        DataItem* pTempItem = new DataItem(dValue);

        while(true)
            {
            if( pCurNode->isFull() )        //if node full,
                {
                split(pCurNode);            //split it
                pCurNode = pCurNode->getParent(); //back up
                                                  //search once
                pCurNode = getNextChild(pCurNode, dValue);
                }  //end if(node is full)

            else if( pCurNode->isLeaf() )   //if node is leaf,
                break;                      //go insert
            //node is not full, not a leaf; so go to lower level
            else
                pCurNode = getNextChild(pCurNode, dValue);
            }  //end while
```

```
        pCurNode->insertItem(pTempItem);     //insert new item
        }  //end insert()
//--------------------------------------------------------------
    void split(Node* pThisNode)        //split the node
        {
        //assumes node is full
        DataItem *pItemB, *pItemC;
        Node *pParent, *pChild2, *pChild3;
        int itemIndex;

        pItemC = pThisNode->removeItem();    //remove items from
        pItemB = pThisNode->removeItem();    //this node
        pChild2 = pThisNode->disconnectChild(2); //remove children
        pChild3 = pThisNode->disconnectChild(3); //from this node

        Node* pNewRight = new Node;           //make new node

        if(pThisNode==pRoot)                  //if this is the root,
            {
            pRoot = new Node();               //make new root
            pParent = pRoot;                  //root is our parent
            pRoot->connectChild(0, pThisNode); //connect to parent
            }
        else                                  //this node not the root
            pParent = pThisNode->getParent(); //get parent

        //deal with parent
        itemIndex = pParent->insertItem(pItemB); //item B to parent
        int n = pParent->getNumItems();       //total items?

        for(int j=n-1; j>itemIndex; j--)      //move parent's
            {                                 //connections
            Node* pTemp = pParent->disconnectChild(j); //one child
            pParent->connectChild(j+1, pTemp); //to the right
            }
                                             //connect newRight to parent
        pParent->connectChild(itemIndex+1, pNewRight);

        //deal with newRight
        pNewRight->insertItem(pItemC);        //item C to newRight
        pNewRight->connectChild(0, pChild2); //connect to 0 and 1
        pNewRight->connectChild(1, pChild3); //on newRight
        }  //end split()
//--------------------------------------------------------------
    //gets appropriate child of node during search for value
    Node* getNextChild(Node* pNode, double theValue)
        {
        int j;
        //assumes node is not empty, not full, not a leaf
```

continues

20

LISTING 20.1 CONTINUED

```
        int numItems = pNode->getNumItems();
        for(j=0; j<numItems; j++)          //for each item in node
            {                              //are we less?
          if( theValue < pNode->getItem(j).dData )
              return pNode->getChild(j);   //return left child
            } //end for                    //we're greater, so
        return pNode->getChild(j);         //return right child
        }
//------------------------------------------------------------
    void displayTree()
        {
        recDisplayTree(pRoot, 0, 0);
        }
//------------------------------------------------------------
    void recDisplayTree(Node* pThisNode, int level,
                                              int childNumber)
        {
        cout << "level=" << level
             << " child=" << childNumber << " ";
        pThisNode->displayNode();          //display this node
        cout << endl;

        //call ourselves for each child of this node
        int numItems = pThisNode->getNumItems();
        for(int j=0; j<numItems+1; j++)
            {
            Node* pNextNode = pThisNode->getChild(j);
            if(pNextNode != NULL)
                recDisplayTree(pNextNode, level+1, j);
            else
                return;
            }
        } //end recDisplayTree()
//------------------------------------------------------------
    }; //end class Tree234
//////////////////////////////////////////////////////////////
int main()
    {
    double value;
    Tree234* pTree = new Tree234;
    pTree->insert(50);
    pTree->insert(40);
    pTree->insert(60);
    pTree->insert(30);
    pTree->insert(70);

    while(true)
        {
```

```
    int found;

    cout << "Enter first letter of show, insert, or find: ";
    char choice;
    cin >> choice;
    switch(choice)
        {
        case 's':
            pTree->displayTree();
            break;
        case 'i':
            cout << "Enter value to insert: ";
            cin >> value;
            pTree->insert(value);
            break;
        case 'f':
            cout << "Enter value to find: ";
            cin >> value;
            found = pTree->find(value);
            if(found != -1)
                cout << "Found " << value << endl;
            else
                cout << "Could not find " << value << endl;
            break;
        default:
            cout << "Invalid entry\n";
        } //end switch
    } //end while
return 0;
delete pTree;
} //end main()
```

In a commercial program we would need to include code to delete the memory allocated for all the data items and nodes. This code could go in the 234Tree class destructor. However, this code is quite complicated and adds little to understanding the fundamental operations of 2-3-4 trees, so we don't show it here.

You can exit the program by typing the Ctrl+C key combination.

This completes our examination of 2-3-4 trees. Now we'll move on to a somewhat unusual topic: the relationship between 2-3-4 trees and red-black trees.

20

2-3-4 Trees and Red-Black Trees

NEW TERM   At this point 2-3-4 trees and red-black trees (described in Hours 17, "Red-Black Trees," and 18, "Red-Black Tree Insertions") probably seem like entirely different entities. However, it turns out that in a certain sense they are completely equivalent. One can be transformed into the other by the application of a few simple rules, and even the operations needed to keep them balanced are equivalent. Mathematicians would say they were *isomorphic*, which means there is a one-to-one correspondence between the parts or operations of two different things.

You probably won't ever need to transform a 2-3-4 tree into a red-black tree, but the equivalence of these structures casts additional light on their operation and is useful in analyzing their efficiency. Historically the 2-3-4 tree was developed first; the red-black tree evolved from it.

Transformation from 2-3-4 to Red-Black

A 2-3-4 tree can be transformed into a red-black tree by applying the following rules:

- Transform any 2-node in the 2-3-4 tree into a black node in the red-black tree.
- Transform any 3-node into a child C (with two children of its own) and a parent P (with children C and one other child). It doesn't matter which item becomes the child and which the parent. C is colored red and P is colored black.
- Transform any 4-node into a parent P and two children C1 and C2, both with two children of their own. C1 and C2 are colored red and P is black.

Figure 20.2 shows these transformations. The child nodes in these subtrees are colored red; all other nodes are colored black.

Figure 20.3 shows a 2-3-4 tree and the corresponding red-black tree obtained by applying these transformations. Dotted lines surround the subtrees that were made from 3-nodes and 4-nodes. The red-black rules are automatically satisfied by the transformation. Check that this is so: Two red nodes are never connected, and there is the same number of black nodes on every path from root to leaf (or null child).

You can say that a 3-node in a 2-3-4 tree is equivalent to a parent with a red child in a red-black tree, and a 4-node is equivalent to a parent with two red children. It follows that a black parent with a black child in a red-black tree does *not* represent a 3-node in a 2-3-4 tree; it simply represents a 2-node with another 2-node child. Similarly, a black parent with two black children does not represent a 4-node.

Operational Equivalence

Not only does the structure of a red-black tree correspond to a 2-3-4 tree, but the operations applied to these two kinds of trees are also equivalent. In a 2-3-4 tree the tree is kept balanced using node splits. In a red-black tree the two balancing methods are color flips and rotations. Let's examine the equivalence of 4-node splits and color flips first, and then the equivalence of 3-node splits and rotations.

FIGURE 20.2

Transformations: 2-3-4 to red-black.

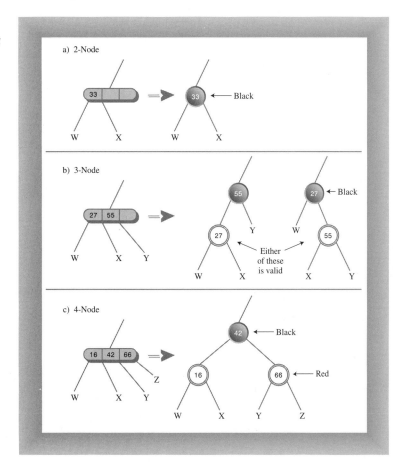

a) 2-Node

b) 3-Node

c) 4-Node

4-Node Splits and Color Flips

As you descend a 2-3-4 tree searching for the insertion point for a new node, you split each 4-node into two 2-nodes. In a red-black tree you perform color flips. How are these operations equivalent?

In Figure 20.4a we show a 4-node in a 2-3-4 tree before it is split; Figure 20.4b shows the situation after the split. The 2-node that was the parent of the 4-node becomes a 3-node.

FIGURE 20.3

A 2-3-4 tree and its red-black equivalent.

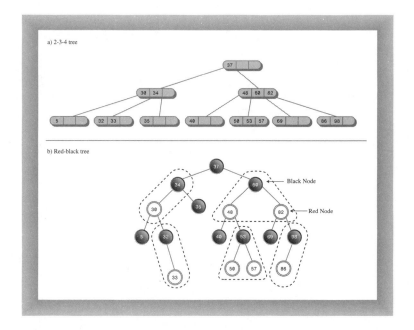

FIGURE 20.4

4-node split and color flip.

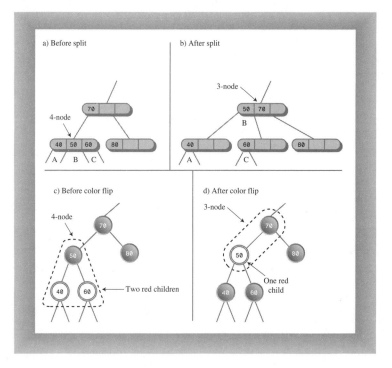

In Figure 20.4c we show the red-black equivalent to the 2-3-4 tree in Figure 20.4a. The dotted line surrounds the equivalent of the 4-node. A color flip results in the red-black tree of Figure 20.4d. Now nodes 40 and 60 are black and 50 is red. Thus 50 and its parent form the equivalent of a 3-node, as shown by the dotted line. This is the same 3-node formed by the node split in Figure 20.4b.

Thus we see that splitting a 4-node during the insertion process in a 2-3-4 tree is equivalent to performing color flips during the insertion process in a red-black tree.

3-Node Splits and Rotations

When a 3-node in a 2-3-4 tree is transformed into its red-black equivalent, two arrangements are possible, as we showed earlier in Figure 20.2b. Either of the two data items can become the parent. Depending on which one is chosen, the child will be either a left child or a right child, and the slant of the line connecting parent and child will be either left or right.

Both arrangements are valid; however, they might not contribute equally to balancing the tree. Let's look at the situation in a slightly larger context.

Figure 20.5a shows a 2-3-4 tree, and Figures 20.5b and 20.5c show two equivalent red-black trees derived from the 2-3-4 tree by applying the transformation rules. The difference between them is the choice of which of the two data items in the 3-node to make the parent—in Figure 20.5b, 80 is the parent; in Figure 20.5c, it's 70.

Although these arrangements are equally valid, you can see that the tree in Figure 20.5b is not balanced, whereas that in Figure 20.5c is balanced. Given the red-black tree in Figure 20.5b, we would want to rotate it to the right (and perform two color changes) to balance it. Amazingly, this rotation results in the exact same tree shown in Figure 20.5c.

Thus we see an equivalence between rotations in red-black trees and the choice of which node to make the parent when transforming 2-3-4 trees to red-black trees. Although we don't show it, a similar equivalence can be seen for the double rotation necessary for inside grandchildren.

Efficiency of 2-3-4 Trees

It's harder to analyze the efficiency of a 2-3-4 tree than a red-black tree, but the equivalence of red-black trees and 2-3-4 trees gives us a starting point. We'll look at efficiency in terms of both speed and storage requirements.

20

FIGURE 20.5

3-node and rotation.

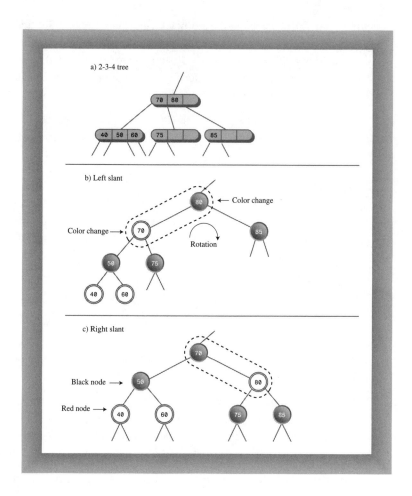

Speed

As we saw in Hour 15, "Binary Trees," in a red-black tree one node on each level must be visited during a search, whether to find an existing node or insert a new one. The number of levels in a red-black tree (a balanced binary tree) is about $\log_2(N+1)$, so search times are proportional to this.

One node must be visited at each level in a 2-3-4 tree as well, but the 2-3-4 tree is shorter (has fewer levels) than a red-black tree with the same number of data items. Refer back to Figure 20.3, where the 2-3-4 tree has three levels and the red-black tree has five.

More specifically, in 2-3-4 trees there are up to 4 children per node. If every node were full, the height of the tree would be proportional to $\log_4 N$. Logarithms to the base 2 and to the base 4 differ by a constant factor of 2. Thus the height of a 2-3-4 tree would be about half that of a red-black tree, provided that all the nodes were full. Because they aren't all full, the height of a 2-3-4 tree is somewhere between $\log_2(N+1)$ and $\log_2(N+1)/2$.

Thus the reduced height of the 2-3-4 tree decreases search times slightly compared with red-black trees.

On the other hand, there are more items to examine in each node, which increases the search time. Because the data items in the node are examined using a linear search, this multiplies the search times by an amount proportional to M, the average number of items per node. The result is a search time proportional to $M*\log_4 N$.

Some nodes contain one item, some two, and some three. If we estimate that the average is two, search times will be proportional to $2*\log_4 N$. This is a small constant number that can be ignored in Big O notation.

Thus for 2-3-4 trees the increased number of items per node tends to cancel out the decreased height of the tree. The search times for a 2-3-4 tree and for a balanced binary tree such as a red-black tree are approximately equal, and are both O(log N).

Storage Requirements

Each node in a 2-3-4 tree contains storage for three pointers to data items and four pointers to its children. This space may be in the form of arrays as shown in tree234.cpp, or of individual variables. Not all this storage is used. A node with only one data item will waste two-thirds of the space for data and one-half the space for children. A node with two data items will waste one-third of the space for data and one-quarter of the space for children; or to put it another way, it will use 5/7 of the available space.

If we take two data items per node as the average utilization, about 2/7 of the available storage is wasted.

One might imagine using linked lists instead of arrays to hold the child and data pointers, but for only three or four items, the overhead of the linked list compared with an array would probably not make this a worthwhile approach.

Because they're balanced, red-black trees contain few nodes that have only one child, so almost all the storage for child pointers is used. Also, every node contains the maximum number of data items, which is one. This makes red-black trees more efficient than 2-3-4 trees in terms of memory usage.

20

If we store pointers to objects instead of the objects themselves, this difference in storage between 2-3-4 trees and red-black trees might not be important, and the programming is certainly simpler for 2-3-4 trees. However, if we store the objects themselves, the difference in storage efficiency between red-black trees and 2-3-4 trees might be significant.

Let's wrap up our discussion of 2-3-4 trees by mentioning how they relate to storing data on disk drives.

B-Trees and External Storage

An important reason for learning about 2-3-4 trees is that they are a simple form of multiway tree. They are multiway trees of order 4 (where the order is the number of possible children). It turns out that multiway trees called B-trees, which have a much larger order, are very useful for external storage.

External storage means data storage devices outside of main memory, such as disk drives. Such devices require a different approach than does storing data in memory. This results from the physical properties of the device. In memory, every byte can be accessed in the same amount of time. On a disk drive, it takes a long time to access the first byte in a sequence, but after the first byte is found, subsequent bytes can be accessed more quickly.

In a B-tree, a sequence of data (a block) on a disk drive is made to correspond to a node in a B-tree. For efficiency, the nodes hold a large number of data items, and have a correspondingly large number of children. However, aside from this disparity in node size, the principles of B-tree operation are much the same as those of 2-3-4 trees.

Summary

In this hour, you've learned the following:

- There is a one-to-one correspondence between a 2-3-4 tree and a red-black tree.
- To transform a 2-3-4 tree into a red-black tree, make each 2-node into a black node, make each 3-node into a black parent with a red child, and make each 4-node into a black parent with two red children.
- When a 3-node is transformed into a parent and child, either node can become the parent.
- Splitting a node in a 2-3-4 tree is the same as performing a color flip in a red-black tree.
- A rotation in a red-black tree corresponds to changing between the two possible orientations (slants) when transforming a 3-node.

- The height of a 2-3-4 tree is less than $\log_2 N$.
- Search times are proportional to the height.
- The 2-3-4 tree wastes space because many nodes are not even half full.

Q&A

Q Can I use the code in the `tree234.cpp` program in a production job?

A Not without modification. As it stands, it has a memory leak because the data items and nodes aren't deleted at the end of the program. There's also no way to remove data items from the tree, which you would probably want in a serious program.

Q What's the practical importance of the correspondence between red-black trees and 2-3-4 trees?

A In terms of using an existing tree class, probably not much. However, it does cast an interesting light on how both kinds of trees work to understand that they are essentially the same.

Workshop

The Workshop helps you solidify what you learned in this hour. See Appendix A for quiz answers.

Quiz

1. In the `tree234.cpp` program, what C++ feature corresponds to a connection from one node to another?

2. What is the equivalent in a red-black tree to a 2-node in a 2-3-4 tree?

3. True or false: There are two equivalent ways to transform a 4-node in a 2-3-4 tree into a red-black equivalent.

4. When a 3-node is transformed into its equivalent in a red-black tree, does it matter whether the child is red or black?

5. What operation in a 2-3-4 tree corresponds to a rotation in a red-black tree?

6. What does a color flip in a red-black tree correspond to in a 2-3-4 tree?

7. Does a 2-3-4 tree operate at the same Big O speed as a red-black tree?

20

Exercise

Write 10 random numbers on a piece of paper. Use them to create a 2-3-4 tree. You can use the Tree234 Workshop applet if you want. Now, using pencil and paper, transform this 2-3-4 tree into a red-black tree using the rules discussed in this hour and shown in Figure 20.2. Finally, insert the resulting tree into the RBTree Workshop applet to make sure it is red-black correct.

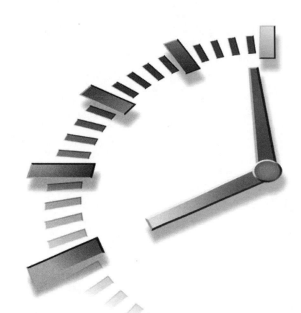

PART V
Hash Tables

Hour

Hour 21

Hash Tables

A hash table is a data structure that offers very fast insertion and searching, but with disadvantages in some circumstances. In this hour you'll learn

- The basic idea behind hash tables
- The simplest hashing scheme: linear probing
- How to write C++ code for linear probing

We'll discuss hashing in this and the next two hours. In Hour 22, "Quadratic Probing," we'll show several alternatives to linear probing. In Hour 23, "Separate Chaining," we'll show a different conceptual approach to hashing. These schemes all attempt to solve some of the problems inherent in simple linear probing.

Introduction to Hashing

When you first hear about them, hash tables sound almost too good to be true. No matter how many data items there are, insertion and searching (and sometimes deletion) can take close to constant time: $O(1)$ in Big O notation. In practice this is just a few machine instructions.

For a human user of a hash table this is essentially instantaneous. It's so fast that computer programs typically use hash tables when they need to look up tens of thousands of items in less than a second (as in spelling checkers). Hash tables are significantly faster than trees, which, as we learned in the preceding hours, operate in relatively fast O(log N) time. Not only are they fast, hash tables are relatively easy to program.

Hash tables do have several disadvantages. They're based on arrays, and arrays are difficult to expand after they've been created. Also, for some kinds of hash tables, performance might degrade catastrophically when the table becomes too full, so the programmer needs to have a fairly accurate idea of how many data items will need to be stored (or be prepared to periodically transfer data to a larger hash table, a time-consuming process).

Also, there's no convenient way to visit the items in a hash table in any kind of order (such as from smallest to largest). If you need this capability, you'll need to look elsewhere.

However, if you don't need to visit items in order, and you can predict in advance the size of your database, hash tables are unparalleled in speed and convenience.

In this section we'll introduce hash tables and hashing. One important concept is how a range of key values is transformed into a range of array index values. In a hash table this is accomplished with a hash function. However, for certain kinds of keys, no hash function is necessary; the key values can be used directly as array indices. We'll look at this simpler situation first, and then go on to show how hash functions can be used when keys aren't distributed in such an orderly fashion.

Employee Numbers as Keys

Suppose you're writing a program to access employee records for a small company with, say, 1,000 employees. Each employee record requires 1,000 bytes of storage. Thus you can store the entire database in only 1 megabyte, which will easily fit in your computer's memory.

The company's personnel director has specified that she wants the fastest possible access to any individual record. Also, every employee has been given a number from 1 (for the founder) to 1,000 (for the most recently hired worker). These employee numbers can be used as keys to access the records; in fact access by other keys (such as last names) is deemed unnecessary. Employees are seldom laid off, but even when they are, their records remain in the database for reference (concerning retirement benefits and so on). What sort of data structure should you use in this situation?

Keys Are Index Numbers

One possibility is a simple array. Each employee record occupies one cell of the array, and the index number of the cell is the employee number for that record. This is shown in Figure 21.1.

FIGURE 21.1

*Employee numbers as
array indices.*

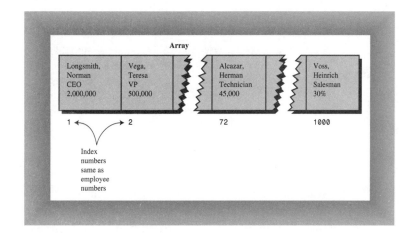

As you know, accessing a specified array element is very fast if you know its index number. The clerk looking up Herman Alcazar knows that he is employee number 72, so he enters that number, and the program goes instantly to index number 72 in the array. A single program statement is all that's necessary:

```
empRecord rec = databaseArray[72];
```

It's also very quick to add a new item: You insert it just past the last occupied element. The next new record—for Jim Chan, the newly hired employee number 1,001—would go in cell 1,001. Again, a single statement inserts the new record:

```
databaseArray[totalEmployees++] = newRecord;
```

Presumably the array is originally made somewhat larger than the maximum possible number of employees, so it doesn't need to be expanded.

Not Always So Orderly

The speed and simplicity of data access using this array-based database make it very attractive. However, it works in our example only because the keys are unusually well organized. They run sequentially from 1 to a known maximum, and this maximum is a reasonable size for an array. There are no deletions, so memory-wasting gaps don't develop in the sequence. New items can be added sequentially at the end of the array.

21

A Dictionary

In many situations the keys are not so well behaved as in the employee database just described. The classic example is a dictionary. If you want to put every word of an English-language dictionary, from *a* to *zyzzyva* (yes, it's a word) into your computer's memory so they can be accessed quickly, a hash table is a good choice.

 A similar, widely used application for hash tables is in computer-language compilers, which typically maintain a symbol table in a hash table. The symbol table holds all the variable and function names made up by the programmer, along with the address where they can be found in memory. The program needs to access these names very quickly, so a hash table is the preferred data structure.

Let's say we want to store a 50,000-word English-language dictionary in main memory. You would like every word to occupy its own cell in a 50,000-cell array, so you can access the word using an index number. This will make access very fast. But what's the relationship of these index numbers to the words? Given the word *morphosis*, for example, how do we find its index number?

Converting Words to Numbers

What we need is a system for turning a word into an appropriate index number. To begin, we know that computers use various schemes for representing individual characters as numbers. One such scheme is the ASCII code, in which *a* is 97, *b* is 98, and so on, up to 122 for *z*.

However, the ASCII code runs from 0 to 255, to accommodate capitals, punctuation, and so on. There are really only 26 letters in English words, so let's devise our own code; a simpler one that can potentially save memory space. Let's say *a* is 1, *b* is 2, *c* is 3, and so on up to 26 for *z*. We'll also say a blank is 0, so we have 27 characters. (Uppercase letters aren't used in this dictionary.)

How do we combine the digits from individual letters into a number that represents an entire word? There are all sorts of approaches. We'll look at two representative ones. We'll see that ultimately they both have serious disadvantages, and this will motivate an understanding of why hash tables are so attractive.

Add the Digits

A simple approach to converting a word to a number might be to simply add the code numbers for each character. Say we want to convert the word *cats* to a number. First we convert the characters to digits using our homemade code:

```
c = 3
a = 1
t = 20
s = 19
```

Then we add them:

```
3 + 1 + 20 + 19 = 43
```

Thus in our dictionary the word *cats* would be stored in the array cell with index 43. All the other English words would likewise be assigned an array index calculated by this process.

How well would this work? For the sake of argument, let's restrict ourselves to 10-letter words. Then (remembering that a blank is 0), the first word in the dictionary, *a*, would be coded by

```
0 + 0 + 0 + 0 + 0 + 0 + 0 + 0 + 0 + 1 = 1
```

The last potential word in the dictionary would be *zzzzzzzzzz* (ten Zs). Our code obtained by adding its letters would be

```
26 + 26 + 26 + 26 + 26 + 26 + 26 + 26 + 26 + 26 = 260
```

Thus the total range of word codes is from 1 to 260. Unfortunately, there are 50,000 words in the dictionary, so there aren't enough index numbers to go around. Each array element will need to hold about 192 words (50,000 divided by 260).

Clearly this presents problems if we're thinking in terms of our one-word-per-array element scheme. Maybe we could put a subarray or linked list of words at each array element. However, this would seriously degrade the access speed. It would be quick to access the array element, but slow to search through the 192 words to find the one we wanted.

So our first attempt at converting words to numbers leaves something to be desired. Too many words have the same index. (For example, *was*, *tin*, *give*, *tend*, *moan*, *tick*, *bails*, *dredge*, and hundreds of other words add to 43, as *cats* does.) We conclude that this approach doesn't discriminate enough, so the resulting array has too few elements. We need to spread out the range of possible indices.

21

Multiply by Powers

Let's try a different way to map words to numbers. If our array was too small before, let's make sure it's big enough. What would happen if we created an array in which every word, in fact every potential word, from *a* to *zzzzzzzzzz*, was guaranteed to occupy its own unique array element?

To do this, we need to be sure that every character in a word contributes in a unique way to the final number.

We'll begin by thinking about an analogous situation with numbers instead of words. Recall that in an ordinary multi-digit number, each digit-position represents a value 10 times as big as the position to its right. Thus 7,546 really means

```
7*1000 + 5*100 + 4*10 + 6*1
```

Or, writing the multipliers as powers of 10

$$7*10^3 + 5*10^2 + 4*10^1 + 6*10^0$$

> An input routine in a computer program performs a similar series of multiplications and additions to convert a sequence of digits, entered at the keyboard, into a number stored in memory.

In this system we break a number into its digits, multiply them by appropriate powers of 10 (because there are 10 possible digits), and add the products.

In a similar way we can decompose a word into its letters, convert the letters to their numerical equivalents, multiply them by appropriate powers of 27 (because there are 27 possible characters, including the blank), and add the results. This gives a unique number for every word.

Say we want to convert the word *cats* to a number. We convert the digits to numbers as shown earlier. Then we multiply each number by the appropriate power of 27, and add the results:

$$3*27^3 + 1*27^2 + 20*27^1 + 19*27^0$$

Calculating the powers gives

```
3*19,683 + 1*729 + 20*27 + 19*1
```

and multiplying the letter codes times the powers yields the following, which sums to 60,337:

```
59,049 + 729 + 540 + 19
```

This process does indeed generate a unique number for every potential word. We just calculated a four-letter word. What happens with larger words? Unfortunately the range of numbers becomes rather large. The largest 10-letter combination, *zzzzzzzzzz*, translates into

$$26*27^9 + 26*27^8 + 26*27^7 + 26*27^6 + 26*27^5 + 26*27^4 + 26*27^3 + 26*27^2 + 26*27^1 + 26*27^0$$

Just by itself, 27^9 is more than 7,000,000,000,000, so you can see that the sum will be huge. An array stored in memory can't possibly have this many elements.

The problem is that this scheme assigns an array element to every potential word, whether it's an actual English word or not. Thus there are cells for *aaaaaaaaaa*, *aaaaaaaaab*, *aaaaaaaaac*, and so on, up to *zzzzzzzzzz*. Only a small fraction of these are necessary for real words, so most array cells are empty. This is shown in Figure 21.2.

FIGURE 21.2

Index for every potential word.

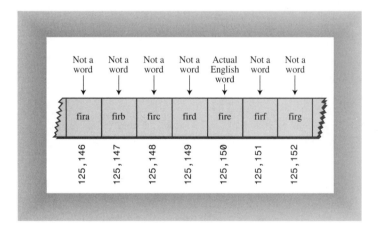

Our first scheme—adding the numbers—generated too few indices. This latest scheme—adding the numbers times powers of 27—generates too many.

Hashing

What we need is a way to compress the huge range of numbers we obtain from the numbers-multiplied-by-powers system into a range that matches a reasonably sized array.

21

How big an array are we talking about for our English dictionary? If we only have 50,000 words, you might assume our array should have approximately this many elements. However, it turns out we're going to need an array with about twice this many cells. (It will become clear later why this is so.) So we need an array with 100,000 elements.

Thus we look for a way to squeeze a range of 0 to more than 7,000,000,000,000 into the range 0 to 100,000. A simple approach is to use the modulo operator (%), which finds the remainder when one number is divided by another.

To see how this works, let's look at a smaller and more comprehensible range. Suppose we squeeze numbers in the range 0 to 199 (we'll represent them by the variable largeNumber) into the range 0 to 9 (the variable smallNumber). There are 10 numbers in the range of small numbers, so we'll say that a variable smallRange has the value 10. It doesn't really matter what the large range is (unless it overflows the program's variable size). The C++ program statement for the conversion is

```
smallNumber = largeNumber % smallRange;
```

The remainders when any number is divided by 10 are always in the range 0 to 9; for example, 13%10 gives 3, and 157%10 is 7. This is shown in Figure 21.3. We've squeezed the range 0–199 into the range 0–9, a 20-to-1 compression ratio.

A similar C++ statement can be used to compress the really huge numbers which uniquely represent every English word into index numbers that fit in our dictionary array.

```
arrayIndex = hugeNumber % arraySize;
```

NEW TERM   This is an example of a *hash function*. It hashes (converts) a number in a large range into a number in a smaller range. This smaller range corresponds to the index numbers in an array. An array into which data is inserted using a hash function is called a *hash table*. (We'll talk more about the design of hash functions in Hour 23.)

To review: We convert a word into a huge number by multiplying each character in the word by an appropriate power of 27.

```
hugeNumber = ch0*27⁹ + ch1*27⁸ + ch2*27⁷ + ch3*27⁶ + ch4*27⁵ +
ch5*27⁴ + ch6*27³ + ch7*27² + ch8*27¹ + ch9*27⁰
```

Then, using the modulo (%) operator, we squeeze the resulting huge range of numbers into a range about twice as big as the number of items we want to store. This is an example of a hash function.

```
arraySize = numberWords * 2;
arrayIndex = hugeNumber % arraySize;
```

In the huge range, each number represents a potential data item (an arrangement of let-ters), but few of these numbers represent actual data items (English words). A hash func-tion transforms these large numbers into the index numbers of a much smaller array. In this array we expect that on the average, there will be one word for every two cells. However, some cells will have no words, and some more than one.

FIGURE 21.3

Range conversion.

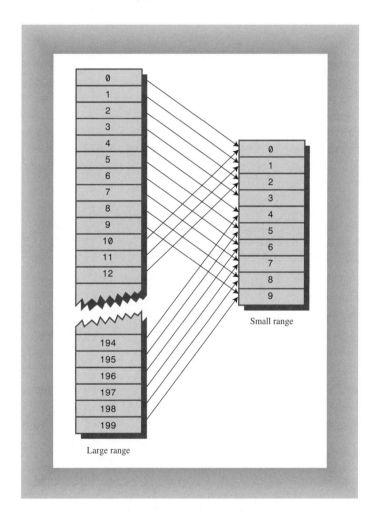

A practical implementation of this scheme runs into trouble because hugeNumber will probably overflow its variable size, even for type long. We'll see how to deal with this later.

21

Collisions

We pay a price for squeezing a large range into a small one. There's no longer a guarantee that two words won't hash to the same array index.

This is similar to what happened when we added the letter codes, but the situation is nowhere near as bad. When we added the letters, there were only 260 possible results (for words up to 10 letters). Now we're spreading this out into 50,000 possible results.

Even so, it's impossible to avoid hashing several different words into the same array location, at least occasionally. We hoped that we could have one data item per index number, but this turns out to be impossible. The best we can do is hope that not too many words will hash to the same index.

NEW TERM Perhaps you want to insert the word melioration into the array. You hash the word to obtain its index number, but find that the cell at that number is already occupied by the word *demystify*, which happens to hash to the exact same number (for a certain size array). This situation, shown in Figure 21.4, is called a *collision*.

FIGURE 21.4

Collision.

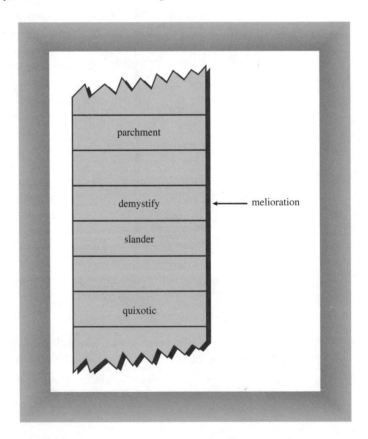

It might appear that the possibility of collisions renders the hashing scheme impractical, but in fact we can work around the problem in a variety of ways.

NEW TERM   Remember that we've specified an array with twice as many cells as data items. Thus perhaps half the cells are empty. One approach, when a collision occurs, is to search the array in some systematic way for an empty cell, and insert the new item there, instead of at the index specified by the hash function. This approach is called *open addressing*. If the word *cats* hashes to 5,421, but this location is already occupied by *parsnip*, we might try to insert *cats* in 5,422 or 6,000, for example.

NEW TERM   An alternative to open addressing is to create an array that consists of linked lists of words instead of the words themselves. Then when a collision occurs, the new item is simply inserted in the list at that index. This is called *separate chaining,* which we'll look at in Hour 23.

In open addressing, when a data item can't be placed at the index calculated by the hash function, another location in the array is sought. We'll explore three methods of open addressing, which vary in the method used to find the next vacant cell. In this hour we'll examine linear probing, which is the simplest approach. In Hour 22 we'll investigate quadratic probing and double hashing, which are more complicated but avoid certain problems with linear probing.

Linear Probing

NEW TERM   In linear probing we search sequentially for vacant cells when a collision occurs. If 5,421 is occupied when we try to insert *cats* there, we go to 5,422, then 5,423, and so on, incrementing the index until we find an empty cell. This is called *linear probing* because it steps sequentially along the line of cells, probing for an empty cell.

The Hash Workshop Applet

The Hash Workshop applet demonstrates linear probing. When you start this applet you'll see a screen similar to Figure 21.5.

In this applet the range of keys runs from 0 to 999. The initial size of the array is 60. The hash function has to squeeze the range of keys down to match the array size. It does this with the modulo (%) operator, as we've seen before:

```
arrayIndex = key % arraySize;
```

For the initial array size of 60, this is

```
arrayIndex = key % 60;
```

21

FIGURE 21.5

The Hash Workshop applet.

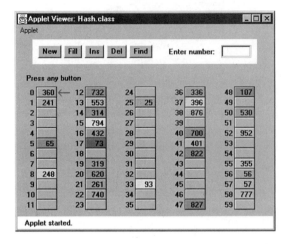

This hash function is simple enough that you can solve it mentally. For a given key, keep subtracting multiples of 60 until you get a number under 60. For example, to hash 143, subtract 60, giving 83, and then subtract 60 again, giving 23. This is the index number where the algorithm will place 143. Thus you can easily check that the algorithm has hashed a key to the correct address. (An array size of 10 is even easier to figure out, as a key's last digit is the index it will hash to.)

> As with other applets, operations are carried out by repeatedly clicking the same button. For example, to find a data item with a specified number, click the Find button repeatedly. Remember, finish a sequence with one button before using another button. For example, don't switch from clicking Fill to some other button until the Press any key message is displayed.

All the operations require you to type a numerical value at the beginning of the sequence. The Find button requires you to type a key value, for example, whereas New requires the size of the new table.

The New Button

You can create a new hash table of a size you specify by using the New button. The maximum size is 60; this limitation results from the number of cells that can be viewed in the applet window. The initial size is also 60. We use this number because it makes it easy to check whether the hash values are correct, but as we'll see later, in a general-purpose hash table, the array size should be a prime number, so 59 would be a better choice.

The Fill Button

Initially the hash table contains 30 items, so it's half full. However, you can also fill it with a specified number of data items using the Fill button. Keep clicking Fill, and when prompted, type the number of items to fill. Hash tables work best when they are not more than 1/2 or at the most 2/3 full (40 items in a 60-cell table).

You'll see that the filled cells aren't evenly distributed in the cells. Sometimes there's a sequence of several empty cells, and sometimes a sequence of filled cells.

New Term   Let's call a sequence of filled cells in a hash table a *filled sequence*. As you add more and more items, the filled sequences become longer. This is called *clustering*, and is shown in Figure 21.6.

FIGURE 21.6

Clustering.

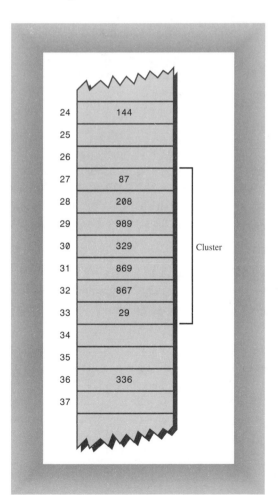

21

> When you use the applet, note that it might take a long time to fill a hash
> table if you try to fill it too full (for example, if you try to put 59 items in a
> 60-cell table). You might think the program has stopped, but be patient. It's
> extremely inefficient at filling an almost-full array.
>
> Also, note that if the hash table becomes completely full the algorithms all
> stop working; in this applet they assume that the table has at least one
> empty cell.

The Find Button

The Find button starts by applying the hash function to the key value you type into the
number box. This results in an array index. The cell at this index might be the key you're
looking for; this is the optimum situation, and success will be reported immediately.

New Term   However, it's also possible that this cell is already occupied by a data item with
some other key. This is a collision; you'll see the red arrow pointing to an occupied cell. Following a collision, the search algorithm will look at the next cell in
sequence. The process of finding an appropriate cell following a collision is called a
probe.

Following a collision, the Find algorithm simply steps along the array looking at each
cell in sequence; this is linear probing. If it encounters an empty cell before finding the
key it's looking for, it knows the search has failed. There's no use looking further
because the insertion algorithm would have inserted the item at this cell (if not earlier).
Figure 21.7 shows successful and unsuccessful linear probes.

The Ins Button

The Ins button inserts a data item, with a key value that you type into the number box,
into the hash table. It uses the same algorithm as the Find button to locate the appropriate
cell. If the original cell is occupied, it will probe linearly for a vacant cell. When it finds
one, it inserts the item.

New Term   Try inserting some new data items. Type a 3-digit number and watch what happens. Most items will go into the first cell they try, but some will suffer collisions, and need to step along to find an empty cell. The number of steps they take is the
probe length. Most probe lengths are only a few cells long. Sometimes, however, you
might see probe lengths of 4 or 5 cells, or even longer as the array becomes excessively
full.

FIGURE 21.7

Linear probes.

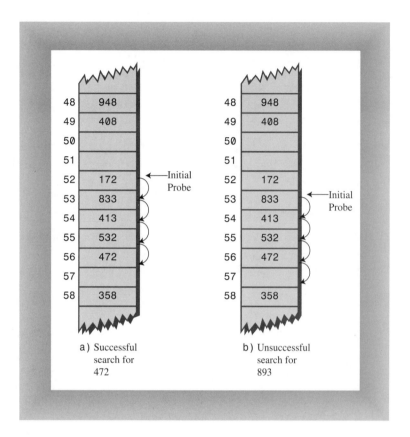

a) Successful
search for
472

b) Unsuccessful
search for
893

Notice which keys hash to the same index. If the array size is 60, the keys 7, 67, 127, 187, 247 and so on up to 967 all hash to index 7. Try inserting this sequence or a similar one. This will demonstrate the linear probe.

The Del Button

The Del button deletes an item whose key is typed by the user. Deletion isn't accomplished by simply removing a data item from a cell, leaving it empty. Why not? Remember that during insertion the probe process steps along a series of cells, looking for a vacant one. If a cell is made empty in the middle of this sequence of full cells, the Find routine will give up when it sees the empty cell, even if the desired cell can eventually be reached.

21

For this reason a deleted item is replaced by an item with a special key value that identifies it as deleted. In this applet we assume all legitimate key values are positive, so the deleted value is chosen as –1. Deleted items are marked with the special key `*Del*`.

The Insert button will insert a new item at the first available empty cell or in a `*Del*` item. The Find button will treat a `*Del*` item as an existing item for the purposes of searching for another item further along.

If there are many deletions, the hash table fills up with these ersatz `*Del*` data items, which makes it less efficient. For this reason many hash table implementations don't allow deletion. If it is implemented, it should be used sparingly.

Duplicates Allowed?

Can you allow data items with duplicate keys to be used in hash tables? The fill routine in the Hash applet doesn't allow duplicates, but you can insert them with the Insert button if you like. Then you'll see that only the first one can be accessed. The only way to access a second item with the same key is to delete the first one. This isn't too convenient.

You could rewrite the `Find` algorithm to look for all items with the same key instead of just the first one. However, it would then need to search through all the cells of every linear sequence it encountered. This wastes time for all table accesses, even when no duplicates are involved. In the majority of cases you probably want to forbid duplicates.

Clustering

Try inserting more items into the hash table in the Hash Workshop applet. As it gets more full, clusters grow larger. Clustering can result in very long probe lengths. This means that it's very slow to access cells at the end of the sequence.

The more full the array is, the worse clustering becomes. It's not a problem when the array is half full, and still not too bad when it's two-thirds full. Beyond this, however, performance degrades seriously as the clusters grow larger and larger. For this reason it's critical when designing a hash table to ensure that it never becomes more than one-half, or at the most two-thirds, full. (We'll discuss the mathematical relationship between how full the hash table is and probe lengths in Hour 22.)

C++ Code for a Linear Probe Hash Table

Our sample program implements a hash table with linear probing. You can display the hash table, and find, insert, and delete data items. Listing 21.1 shows the complete `hash.cpp` program.

```
//hash.cpp
//demonstrates hash table with linear probing
#include <iostream>
#include <vector>
#include <cstdlib>                      //for random numbers
#include <ctime>                        //for random numbers

using namespace std;
////////////////////////////////////////////////////////////////
class DataItem
   {                                    //(could have more data)
   public:
      int iData;                        //data item (key)
//--------------------------------------------------------------
   DataItem(int ii) : iData(ii)         //constructor
      {  }
//--------------------------------------------------------------
   };   //end class DataItem
////////////////////////////////////////////////////////////////
class HashTable
   {
   private:
      vector<DataItem*> hashArray;      //vector holds hash table
      int arraySize;
      DataItem* pNonItem;               //for deleted items
   public:
//--------------------------------------------------------------
   HashTable(int size) : arraySize(size)  //constructor
      {
      arraySize = size;
      hashArray.resize(arraySize);      //size the vector
      for(int j=0; j<arraySize; j++)   //initialize elements
         hashArray[j] = NULL;
      pNonItem = new DataItem(-1);      //deleted item key is -1
      }
//--------------------------------------------------------------
   void displayTable()
      {
      cout << "Table: ";
      for(int j=0; j<arraySize; j++)
         {
         if(hashArray[j] != NULL)
            cout << hashArray[j]->iData << " ";
         else
            cout << "** ";
         }
      cout << endl;
```

21

continues

LISTING 21.1 CONTINUED

```
        }
//------------------------------------------------------------
    int hashFunc(int key)
        {
        return key % arraySize;        //hash function
        }
//------------------------------------------------------------
    void insert(DataItem* pItem)       //insert a DataItem
    //(assumes table not full)
        {
        int key = pItem->iData;        //extract key
        int hashVal = hashFunc(key);   //hash the key
                                       //until empty cell or -1,
        while(hashArray[hashVal] != NULL &&
                          hashArray[hashVal]->iData != -1)
            {
            ++hashVal;                 //go to next cell
            hashVal %= arraySize;      //wraparound if necessary
            }
        hashArray[hashVal] = pItem;    //insert item
        }  //end insert()
//------------------------------------------------------------
    DataItem* remove(int key)          //remove a DataItem
        {
        int hashVal = hashFunc(key);   //hash the key

        while(hashArray[hashVal] != NULL)  //until empty cell,
            {                              //found the key?
            if(hashArray[hashVal]->iData == key)
                {
                DataItem* pTemp = hashArray[hashVal]; //save item
                hashArray[hashVal] = pNonItem;        //delete item
                return pTemp;                         //return item
                }
            ++hashVal;                 //go to next cell
            hashVal %= arraySize;      //wraparound if necessary
            }
        return NULL;                   //can't find item
        }  //end remove()
//------------------------------------------------------------
    DataItem* find(int key)            //find item with key
        {
        int hashVal = hashFunc(key);   //hash the key

        while(hashArray[hashVal] != NULL)  //until empty cell,
            {                              //found the key?
            if(hashArray[hashVal]->iData == key)
                return hashArray[hashVal];  //yes, return item
```

```
            ++hashVal;                   //go to next cell
            hashVal %= arraySize;        //wraparound if necessary
            }
        return NULL;                     //can't find item
        }
//------------------------------------------------------------
    };  //end class HashTable
//////////////////////////////////////////////////////////////
int main()
    {
    DataItem* pDataItem;
    int aKey, size, n, keysPerCell;
    time_t aTime;
    char choice = 'b';
                                    //get sizes
    cout << "Enter size of hash table: ";
    cin >> size;
    cout << "Enter initial number of items: ";
    cin >> n;
    keysPerCell = 10;
                                    //make table
    HashTable theHashTable(size);
    srand( static_cast<unsigned>(time(&aTime)) );
    for(int j=0; j<n; j++)          //insert data
        {
        aKey = rand() % (keysPerCell*size);

        pDataItem = new DataItem(aKey);
        theHashTable.insert(pDataItem);
        }

    while(choice != 'x')            //interact with user
        {
        cout << "Enter first letter of "
             << "show, insert, delete, or find: ";
        char choice;
        cin >> choice;
        switch(choice)
            {
            case 's':
               theHashTable.displayTable();
               break;
            case 'i':
               cout << "Enter key value to insert: ";
               cin >> aKey;
               pDataItem = new DataItem(aKey);
               theHashTable.insert(pDataItem);
```

continues

21

LISTING 21.1   CONTINUED

```
            break;
         case 'd':
            cout << "Enter key value to delete: ";
            cin >> aKey;
            theHashTable.remove(aKey);
            break;
         case 'f':
            cout << "Enter key value to find: ";
            cin >> aKey;
            pDataItem = theHashTable.find(aKey);
            if(pDataItem != NULL)
               cout << "Found " << aKey << endl;
            else
               cout << "Could not find " << aKey << endl;
            break;
         default:
            cout << "Invalid entry\n";
      }  //end switch
   }  //end while
   return 0;
}  //end main()
```

Classes in `hash.cpp`

A `DataItem` object contains just one data member, an integer that is its key. As in other data structures we've discussed, these objects could contain more data, or a pointer to an object of another class (such as `employee` or `partNumber`).

The major data member in class `HashTable` is an array (actually an STL vector) called `hashArray`. Other data members are the size of the array and a pointer `pNonItem` used for deletions. In the constructor this pointer is set to an item with the value –1.

The `find()` Member Function

The `find()` member function of `HashTable` first calls `hashFunc()` to hash the search key to obtain the index number `hashVal`. The `hashFunc()` member function applies the `%` operator to the search key and the array size, as we've seen before.

Next, in a `while` condition, `find()` checks whether the item at this index is empty (`NULL`). If not, `find()` checks whether the item contains the search key. If the item does contain the search key, `find()` returns the item. If it doesn't, `find()` increments `hashVal` and goes back to the top of the `while` loop to check whether the next cell is occupied.

As hashVal steps through the array, it eventually reaches the end. When this happens we want it to wrap around to the beginning. We could check for this with an if statement, setting hashVal to 0 whenever it equaled the array size. However, we can accomplish the same thing by applying the % operator to hashVal and the array size.

Cautious programmers might not want to assume the table is not full, as is done here. The table should not be allowed to become full, but if it did, this member function would loop forever. For simplicity we don't check for this situation.

The insert() Member Function

The insert() member function uses about the same algorithm as find() to locate where a data item should go. However, it's looking for an empty cell, or a deleted item (key –1), rather than a specific item. After this empty cell has been located, insert() places the new item into it.

The remove() Member Function

The remove() member function finds an existing item using code similar to find(). After the item is found, remove() writes over it with the special data item that is predefined with a key of –1 and pointed to by pNonItem.

The main() Routine

The main() routine contains a user interface that allows the user to show the contents of the hash table (enter s), insert an item (i) delete an item (d), or find an item (f). You can quit the program by typing the Ctrl+C key combination.

Initially, the program asks the user to input the size of the hash table and the number of items in it. You can make it almost any size, from a few items to 10,000. (It might take a little time to build larger tables than this.) Don't use the s (for show) option on tables of more than a few hundred items; they scroll off the screen and it takes a long time to display them.

A variable in main(), keysPerCell, specifies the ratio of the range of keys to the size of the array. In the listing, it's set to 10. This means that if you specify a table size of 20, the keys will range from 0 to 200.

To see what's going on, it's best to create tables with fewer than about 20 items, so all the items can be displayed on one line. Here's some sample interaction with hash.cpp:

```
Enter size of hash table: 12
Enter initial number of items: 8
```

21

```
Enter first letter of show, insert, delete, or find: s
Table: 108 13 0 ** ** 113 5 66 ** 117 ** 47

Enter first letter of show, insert, delete, or find: f
Enter key value to find: 66
Found 66

Enter first letter of show, insert, delete, or find: i
Enter key value to insert: 100
Enter first letter of show, insert, delete, or find: s
Table: 108 13 0 ** 100 113 5 66 ** 117 ** 47

Enter first letter of show, insert, delete, or find: d
Enter key value to delete: 100
Enter first letter of show, insert, delete, or find: s
Table: 108 13 0 ** -1 113 5 66 ** 117 ** 47
```

Key values run from 0 to 119 (12 times 10, minus 1). The ** symbol indicates that a cell is empty. The item with key 100 is inserted at location 4 (the first item is numbered 0) because 100%12 is 4. Notice how 100 changes to −1 when this item is deleted.

In this hour we've focused on linear probing. In the next hour we'll examine more sophisticated methods of open addressing.

Summary

In this hour, you've learned the following:

- Hash tables are based on arrays.

- The range of key values is usually greater than the size of the array.

- A key value is hashed to an array index by a hash function.

- An English-language dictionary is a typical example of data that can be efficiently handled with a hash table.

- The hashing of a key to an already-filled array cell is called a collision.

- Collisions can be handled in two major ways: open addressing and separate chaining.

- Three kinds of open addressing are linear probing, quadratic probing, and double hashing.

- In open addressing, data items that hash to an occupied array cell are placed in another cell in the array.

Q&A

Q I'm confused by the discussion of dictionaries and trying to convert words to numbers at the beginning of this hour.

A That section attempts to explain why hash functions are necessary. The heart of the matter is that somehow you must find a way to convert each item's key to an array index, where the array is a reasonable size. This is handled with a hash function.

Q Collisions seem to cause a lot of trouble. Can't they be avoided?

A Collisions are an inevitable part of the hashing process. Hashing the key to find the array index is easy; it's handling collisions that can be complicated.

Workshop

The Workshop helps you solidify what you learned in this hour. See Appendix A for quiz answers.

Quiz

1. What is hashing?

2. What is a collision?

3. What is open addressing?

4. What is linear probing?

5. What is clustering?

6. True or false: Clustering is a problem with linear probing.

7. True or false: When using linear probing, it's common to fill an array almost full.

Exercise

Write down 10 random numbers between 1 and 999 on a piece of paper. Use the Hash Workshop applet to create an array with 10 cells. Insert the random numbers one by one. For each insertion, count how long the probe length is. Assume a probe length of 1 if there are no collisions. The first item will have a probe length of 1, but as the table gets fuller the probe lengths will get longer. Write down all the probe lengths.

Repeat this process several times and average your results. You should see the probe lengths rise gradually from 1 when there are no items in the array to about 5 when there is only one empty cell.

21

Hour **22**

Quadratic Probing

There are problems with the simple linear probing technique discussed in the last hour. More sophisticated approaches can help. In this hour we'll examine

- The problems with linear probing
- A first alternative: quadratic probing
- A second alternative: double hashing
- The C++ code for double hashing
- The efficiency of the various open addressing methods

We've seen that clusters can occur in the linear probe approach to open addressing. After a cluster forms, it tends to grow larger. Items that hash to any value in the range of the cluster will step along and insert themselves at the end of the cluster, thus making it even bigger. The bigger the cluster gets, the faster it grows.

It's like the crowd that gathers when someone faints at the shopping mall. The first arrivals come because they saw the victim fall; later arrivals gather because they wondered what everyone else was looking at. The larger the crowd grows, the more people are attracted to it.

NEW TERM The ratio of the number of items in a table to the table's size is called the *load factor*. A table with 10,000 cells and 6,667 items has a load factor of 2/3.

```
loadFactor = nItems / arraySize;
```

In general, the greater the load factor the more clusters there will be. However, clusters can form even when the load factor isn't high. Parts of the hash table might consist of big clusters, whereas others are sparsely inhabited. Clusters reduce performance.

Two approaches to avoiding clustering are quadratic probing and double hashing. In this hour we'll look briefly at quadratic probing and in more detail at double hashing.

Quadratic Probing

Quadratic probing is an attempt to keep clusters from forming. The idea is to probe more widely separated cells, instead of those adjacent to the initial hash site. In this section we'll explain quadratic probing and show how it looks with a Workshop applet.

The Step Is the Square of the Step Number

In a linear probe, if the primary hash index is x, subsequent probes go to x+1, x+2, x+3, and so on. In quadratic probing, probes go to x+1, x+4, x+9, x+16, x+25, and so on. The distance from the initial site is the square of the step number, so the probes fall at $x+1^2$, $x+2^2$, $x+3^2$, $x+4^2$, $x+5^2$, and so on.

Figure 22.1 shows some quadratic probes.

It's as if a quadratic probe became increasingly desperate as its search lengthened. At first it calmly picks the adjacent cell. If that's occupied, it thinks it might be in a small cluster so it tries something 4 cells away. If that's occupied the probe becomes a little concerned, thinking it might be in a larger cluster, and tries 9 cells away. If that's occupied the probe feels the first tinges of panic and jumps 16 cells away. Pretty soon it's flying hysterically all over the place, as you can see if you try searching with the HashDouble Workshop applet when the table is almost full.

The HashDouble Applet with Quadratic Probes

The HashDouble Workshop applet allows two different kinds of collision handling: quadratic probes and double hashing. This applet generates a display much like that of the Hash Workshop applet, except that it includes radio buttons to select quadratic probing or double hashing. Let's see what a quadratic probe looks like using the Workshop applet.

FIGURE 22.1

Quadratic probes.

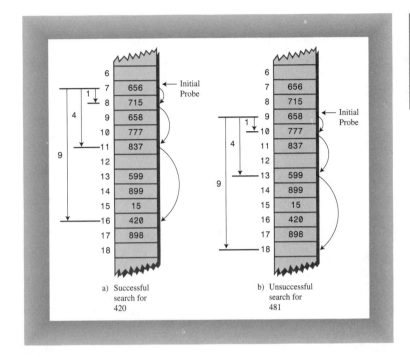

a) Successful
   search for
   420

b) Unsuccessful
   search for
   481

To Do: Generate a Quadratic Probe

1. Start up the applet and create a new hash table of 59 items using the New button.

2. When you're asked to select double or quadratic probe, click the Quad button.

3. After the new table is created, fill it 4/5 full using the Fill button (47 items in a 59-cell array). This is too full, but it will generate longer probes so you can study the probe algorithm.

4. Select an existing key value and use the Find key to see whether the algorithm can find it.

If you try to fill the hash table too full, you might see the message Can't complete fill. This occurs when the probe sequences get very long. Every additional step in the probe sequence makes a bigger step size. If the sequence is too long, the step size will eventually exceed the capacity of its integer variable, so the applet shuts down the fill process before this happens.

Often the item you're trying to find is located at the initial cell or the cell adjacent to it. If you're patient, however, you'll find a key that requires three or four steps, and you'll see the step size lengthen for each step. You can also use Find to search for a nonexistent key; this search continues until an empty cell is encountered.

> Always make the array size a prime number. Use 59 instead of 60, for example. (Other primes less than 60 are 53, 47, 43, 41, 37, 31, 29, 23, 19, 17, 13, 11, 7, 5, 3, and 2.) If the array size is not prime, an endless sequence of steps might occur during a probe. If this happens during a Fill operation, the applet will be paralyzed.

The Problem with Quadratic Probes

NEW TERM Quadratic probes eliminate the clustering problem we saw with the linear probe, which is called *primary clustering*. However, quadratic probes suffer from a different and more subtle clustering problem. This occurs because all the keys that hash to a particular cell follow the same sequence in trying to find a vacant space.

NEW TERM Let's say 184, 302, 420, and 544 all hash to 7 and are inserted in this order. Then 302 will require a one-step probe, 420 will require a 2-step probe, and 544 will require a 3-step probe. Each additional item with a key that hashes to 7 will require a longer probe. This phenomenon is called *secondary clustering*.

Secondary clustering is not a serious problem, but quadratic probing is not often used because there's a slightly better solution. For this reason we don't show any C++ code to implement quadratic probing. Instead let's look at double hashing.

Double Hashing

NEW TERM To eliminate secondary clustering as well as primary clustering, another approach can be used: *double hashing* (sometimes called rehashing). Secondary clustering occurs because the algorithm that generates the sequence of steps in the quadratic probe always generates the same steps: 1, 4, 9, 16, and so on.

What we need is a way to generate probe sequences that depend on the key instead of being the same for every key. Then numbers with different keys that hash to the same index will use different probe sequences.

The solution is to hash the key a second time, using a different hash function, and use the result as the step size. For a given key the step size remains constant throughout a probe, but it's different for different keys.

Experience has shown that this secondary hash function must have certain characteristics. These are as follows:

- It must not be the same as the primary hash function.
- It must never output a 0 (otherwise there would be no step; every probe would land on the same cell, and the algorithm would go into an endless loop).

Experts have discovered that functions of the following form work well:

```
stepSize = constant - (key % constant);
```

where `constant` is prime and smaller than the array size. For example,

```
stepSize = 5 - (key % 5);
```

This is the secondary hash function used in the Workshop applet. For any given key all the steps will be the same size, but different keys generate different step sizes. With this hash function the step sizes are all in the range 1 to 5. This is shown in Figure 22.2.

FIGURE 22.2

Double hashing.

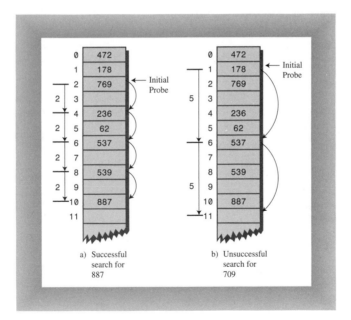

a) Successful search for 887

b) Unsuccessful search for 709

The HashDouble Applet with Double Hashing

You can use the HashDouble Workshop applet to see how double hashing works. It starts up automatically in double-hashing mode, but if it's in quadratic mode you can switch to double by creating a new table with the New button and clicking the Double button when prompted. To best see probes at work you'll need to fill the table rather full; say to about 9/10ths capacity or more. Even with such high load factors, most data items will be found in the cell by the first hash value; only a few will require extended probe sequences.

Try finding existing keys. When one needs a probe sequence, you'll see how all the steps are the same size for a given key, but that the step size is different—between 1 and 5— for different keys.

C++ Code for Double Hashing

The hashDouble.cpp program demonstrates double hashing. It's similar to the hash.cpp program in Hour 21, "Hash Tables," but uses two hash functions, one for finding the initial index, and the second for generating the step size. As before, the user can show the table contents, insert an item, delete an item, and find an item. Listing 22.1 shows the hashDouble.cpp program.

INPUT   **LISTING 22.1**   THE hashDouble.cpp PROGRAM

```
//hashDouble.cpp
//demonstrates hash table with double hashing
#include <iostream>
#include <vector>
#include <cstdlib>                     //for random numbers
#include <ctime>                       //for random numbers
using namespace std;
////////////////////////////////////////////////////////////////
class DataItem
   {                                   //(could have more items)
   public:
      int iData;                       //data item (key)
//--------------------------------------------------------------
   DataItem(int ii) : iData(ii)        //constructor
      {  }
//--------------------------------------------------------------
   };  //end class DataItem
////////////////////////////////////////////////////////////////
class HashTable
   {
   private:
      vector<DataItem*> hashArray;     //vctor holds hash table
      int arraySize;
      DataItem* pNonItem;              //for deleted items
   public:
//--------------------------------------------------------------
   HashTable(int size) : arraySize(size)  //constructor
      {
```

22

```
        hashArray.resize(arraySize);    //size the vector
        for(int j=0; j<arraySize; j++) //initialize elements
            hashArray[j] = NULL;
        pNonItem = new DataItem(-1);
        }
//-------------------------------------------------------------
    void displayTable()
        {
        cout << "Table: ";
        for(int j=0; j<arraySize; j++)
            {
            if(hashArray[j] != NULL)
                cout << hashArray[j]->iData << " ";
            else
                cout << "** ";
            }
        cout << endl;
        }
//-------------------------------------------------------------
    int hashFunc1(int key)
        {
        return key % arraySize;
        }
//-------------------------------------------------------------
    int hashFunc2(int key)
        {
        //non-zero, less than array size, different from hF1
        //array size must be relatively prime to 5, 4, 3, and 2
        return 5 - key % 5;
        }
//-------------------------------------------------------------
                                      //insert a DataItem
    void insert(int key, DataItem* pItem)
    //(assumes table not full)
        {
        int hashVal = hashFunc1(key);  //hash the key
        int stepSize = hashFunc2(key); //get step size
                                       //until empty cell or -1
        while(hashArray[hashVal] != NULL &&
                        hashArray[hashVal]->iData != -1)
            {
            hashVal += stepSize;        //add the step
            hashVal %= arraySize;       //for wraparound
            }
        hashArray[hashVal] = pItem;    //insert item
        } //end insert()
//-------------------------------------------------------------
    DataItem* remove(int key)    //delete a DataItem
        {
```

continues

LISTING 22.1   CONTINUED

```cpp
   int hashVal = hashFunc1(key);   //hash the key

   while(hashArray[hashVal] != NULL)  //until empty cell,
      {                               //is correct hashVal?
      if(hashArray[hashVal]->iData == key)
         {
         DataItem* pTemp = hashArray[hashVal]; //save item
         hashArray[hashVal] = pNonItem;        //delete item
         return pTemp;                         //return item
         }
      hashVal += stepSize;       //add the step
      hashVal %= arraySize;      //for wraparound
      }
   return NULL;                  //can't find item
   }  //end remove()
//-------------------------------------------------------------
   DataItem* find(int key)          //find item with key
   //(assumes table not full)
      {
      int hashVal = hashFunc1(key);   //hash the key
      int stepSize = hashFunc2(key); //get step size

      while(hashArray[hashVal] != NULL)  //until empty cell,
         {                               //is correct hashVal?
         if(hashArray[hashVal]->iData == key)
            return hashArray[hashVal];   //yes, return item
         hashVal += stepSize;            //add the step
         hashVal %= arraySize;           //for wraparound
         }
      return NULL;                  //can't find item
      };
//-------------------------------------------------------------
   };  //end class HashTable
//////////////////////////////////////////////////////////////
int main()
   {
   int aKey;
   DataItem* pDataItem;
   int size, n;
   char choice = 'b';
   time_t aTime;
                                   //get sizes
   cout << "Enter size of hash table (use prime number): ";
   cin >> size;
   cout << "Enter initial number of items: ";
   cin >> n;
```

```
                                 //make table
HashTable theHashTable(size);      //seed random numbers
srand( static_cast<unsigned>(time(&aTime)) );

for(int j=0; j<n; j++)            //insert data
   {
   aKey = rand()  % (2 * size);
   pDataItem = new DataItem(aKey);
   theHashTable.insert(aKey, pDataItem);
   }

while(true)                       //interact with user
   {
   cout << "Enter first letter of ";
   cout << "show, insert, delete, or find: ";
   cin >> choice;
   switch(choice)
      {
      case 's':
         theHashTable.displayTable();
         break;
      case 'i':
         cout << "Enter key value to insert: ";
         cin >> aKey;
         pDataItem = new DataItem(aKey);
         theHashTable.insert(aKey, pDataItem);
         break;
      case 'd':
         cout << "Enter key value to delete: ";
         cin >> aKey;
         theHashTable.remove(aKey);
         break;
      case 'f':
         cout << "Enter key value to find: ";
         cin >> aKey;
         pDataItem = theHashTable.find(aKey);
         if(pDataItem != NULL)
            cout << "Found " << aKey << endl;
         else
            cout << "Could not find " << aKey << endl;
         break;
      default:
         cout << "Invalid entry\n";
      }  //end switch
   }  //end while
return 0;
}  //end main()
```

22

ANALYSIS   The operation of this program is similar to that of the `hash.cpp` program in Hour 21. The difference is that the `find()`, `remove()`, and `insert()` member functions now call a new function, `hashFunc2()`, to determine the step size to use following a collision.

Table 22.1 shows what happens when 21 items are inserted into a 23-cell hash table using double hashing. The step sizes run from 1 to 5.

TABLE 22.1   FILLING A 23-CELL TABLE USING DOUBLE HASHING

Item Number	Key	Hash Value	Step Size	Cells in Probe Sequence
1	1	1	4	
2	38	15	2	
3	37	14	3	
4	16	16	4	
5	20	20	5	
6	3	3	2	
7	11	11	4	
8	24	1	1	2
9	5	5	5	
10	16	16	4	20 1 5 9
11	10	10	5	
12	31	8	4	
13	18	18	2	
14	12	12	3	
15	30	7	5	
16	1	1	4	5 9 13
17	19	19	1	
18	36	13	4	17
19	41	18	4	22
20	15	15	5	20 2 7 12 17 22 4
21	25	2	5	7 12 17 22 4 9 14 19 1 6

The first 15 keys mostly hash to a vacant cell (the 10th one is an anomaly). After that, as the array fills up, the probe sequences become quite long. Here's the resulting array of keys, as displayed by the program:

```
** 1 24 3 15 5 25 30 31 16 10 11 12 1 37 38 16 36 18 19 20 ** 41
```

Make the Table Size a Prime Number

Double hashing requires that the size of the hash table is a prime number. To see why, imagine a situation where the table size is not a prime number. For example, suppose the array size is 15 (indices from 0 to 14), and that a particular key hashes to an initial index of 0 and a step size of 5. The probe sequence will be 0, 5, 10, 0, 5, 10, and so on, repeating endlessly. Only these three cells are ever examined, so if they're full the algorithm will never find the empty cells that might be waiting at 1, 2, 3, and so on. The algorithm will crash and burn.

If the array size were 13, which is prime, the probe sequence would eventually visit every cell. It's 0, 5, 10, 2, 7, 12, 4, 9, 1, 6, 11, 3, and so on and on. If there is even one empty cell, the probe will find it. Using a prime number as the array size makes it impossible for any number to divide it evenly, so the probe sequence will eventually check every cell.

A similar effect occurs using the quadratic probe. In that case, however, the step size gets larger with each step, and will eventually overflow the variable holding it, preventing an endless loop but crashing anyway.

In general, double hashing is the probe sequence of choice when open addressing is used.

Efficiency of Open Addressing

We've noted that insertion and searching in hash tables can approach $O(1)$ time. If no collision occurs, only a call to the hash function and a single array reference are necessary to insert a new item or find an existing item. This is the minimum access time.

If collisions occur, access times become dependent on the resulting probe lengths. Each cell accessed during a probe adds another time increment to the search for a vacant cell (for insertion) or for an existing cell. During an access, a cell must be checked to see whether it's empty, and—in the case of searching or deletion—whether it contains the desired item.

Thus an individual search or insertion time is proportional to the length of the probe. This is in addition to a constant time for the hash function.

The average probe length (and therefore the average access time) is dependent on the load factor (the ratio of items in the table to the size of the table). As the load factor increases, probe lengths grow longer.

In open addressing, unsuccessful searches generally take longer than successful searches. During a probe sequence, the algorithm can stop as soon as it finds the desired item, which is, on the average, halfway through the probe sequence. On the other hand, it must go all the way to the end of the sequence before it's sure it can't find an item.

Now let's look in more detail at the relationship between probe lengths and load factors for the various kinds of open addressing techniques we've studied.

Linear Probing

The following equations show the relationship between probe length (P) and load factor (L) for linear probing. For a successful search it's

```
P = ( 1 + 1 / (1-L)² ) / 2
```

and for an unsuccessful search it's

```
P = ( 1 + 1 / (1-L) ) / 2
```

These formulas are from Knuth (see Appendix C, "Further Reading"), and their derivation is quite complicated. Figure 22.3 shows the result of graphing these equations.

At a load factor of 1/2, a successful search takes 1.5 comparisons and an unsuccessful search takes 2.5. At a load factor of 2/3, the numbers are 2.0 and 5.0. At higher load factors the numbers become very large.

The moral, as you can see, is that the load factor must be kept under 2/3 and preferably under 1/2. On the other hand, the lower the load factor, the more memory is needed for a given amount of data. The optimum load factor in a particular situation depends on the tradeoff between memory efficiency, which decreases with lower load factors, and speed, which increases.

Quadratic Probing and Double Hashing

Quadratic probing and double hashing share their performance equations. These indicate a modest superiority over linear probing. For a successful search, the formula (again from Knuth) is

FIGURE 22.3

Linear probe performance.

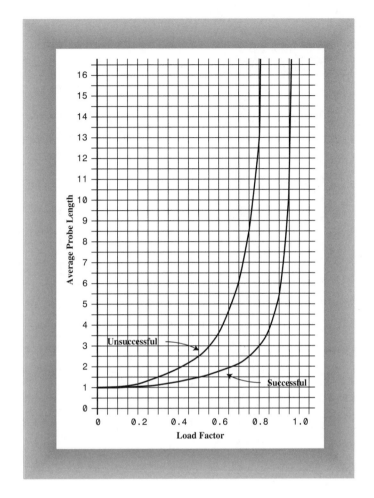

-log$_2$(1-loadFactor) / loadFactor

For an unsuccessful search it is

1 / (1-loadFactor)

Figure 22.4 shows graphs of these formulas. At a load factor of 0.5, successful and unsuccessful searches both require an average of two probes. At a 2/3 load factor, the numbers are 2.37 and 3.0, and at 0.8 they're 2.90 and 5.0. Thus somewhat higher load factors can be tolerated for quadratic probing and double hashing than for linear probing.

FIGURE 22.4

*Quadratic-probe and
double-hashing perfor-
mance.*

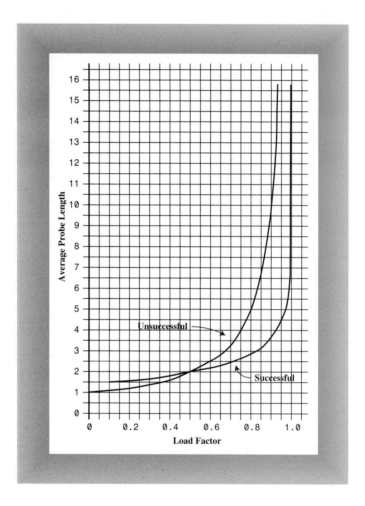

Expanding the Array

One option when a hash table becomes too full is to expand its array. Classic C++ arrays
have a fixed size and can't be expanded. Your program could create a new, larger array,
and then rehash the contents of the old small array into the new, large one.

You can't simply copy the data into the larger array. Remember that the hash function
calculates the location of a given data item based on the array size, so the locations in the
large array won't be the same as those in a small array. You'll need to go through the old
array in sequence, inserting each item into the new array with the insert() member
function. This is a time-consuming process.

22

You can use a vector instead of an array. As we've seen, vectors can be expanded with the `resize()` member function. However, this is not much help because of the need to rehash all data items when the table changes size. Expanding arrays or vectors is only practical when there's plenty of time available for rehashing all the contents.

In the next hour we'll look at an alternative to open addressing.

Summary

In this hour, you've learned the following:

- In quadratic probing the offset from x is the square of the step number, so the probe goes to x, x+1, x+4, x+9, x+16, and so on.

- Quadratic probing eliminates primary clustering, but suffers from the less severe secondary clustering.

- Secondary clustering occurs because all the keys that hash to the same value follow the same sequence of steps during a probe.

- In double hashing the step size depends on the key, and is obtained from a secondary hash function.

- If the secondary hash function returns a value s in double hashing, the probe goes to x, x+s, x+2s, x+3s, x+4s, and so on, where s depends on the key, but remains constant during the probe.

- The load factor is the ratio of data items in a hash table to the array size.

- The maximum load factor in open addressing should be around 0.5. For double hashing at this load factor, searches will have an average probe length of 2.

- Search times go to infinity as load factors approach 1.0 in open addressing.

- Hash table sizes should generally be prime numbers.

Q&A

Q It seems like there must be all kinds of schemes for hashing with open addressing. I bet I could think of a new one, like using random numbers.

A You probably could. All you need is some way to generate a sequence of step lengths. But you need a system that's as simple as possible so it will be fast. Random numbers take time to generate. The techniques we've discussed are the fastest discovered so far.

Q Why worry about quadratic probing if it's inferior to double hashing?

A It's a little easier to understand than double hashing, and might be easier to program and marginally faster for small load factors.

Workshop

The Workshop helps you solidify what you learned in this hour. See Appendix A for quiz answers.

Quiz

1. Why do we need quadratic probing and double hashing?
2. What determines the step size in quadratic probing?
3. What determines the step size in double hashing?
4. What's the disadvantage of quadratic probing (compared with double hashing)?
5. Why should the table size be a prime number when double hashing is used?
6. What is the load factor of a hash table?
7. What are the main disadvantages of all the open addressing schemes?

Exercise

Rewrite the hashDouble.cpp program to use the C++ random number generator to generate the step sizes. The find(), remove(), and insert() member functions should seed the generator with the C++ srand() function when they are first called. Then each time they need a new step size they should call the rand() function to generate it. Measure the efficiency of this approach against the original hashDouble.cpp program.

HOUR 23

Separate Chaining

In Hours 21, "Hash Tables," and 22, "Quadratic Probing," we saw how collisions can be resolved with various schemes based on open addressing. In this hour we'll examine a different approach to handling collisions: separate chaining. We'll learn

- How separate chaining works
- How to write C++ code for separate chaining
- The efficiency of separate chaining
- What constitutes a good hash function

In open addressing, collisions are resolved by looking for an open cell in the hash table. In separate chaining a linked list is installed at each index in the hash table. A data item's key is hashed to the index in the usual way, and the item is inserted into the linked list at that index. Other items that hash to the same index (collisions) are simply inserted in the same linked list; there's no need to search for empty cells in the primary array. Figure 23.1 shows how separate chaining looks.

FIGURE 23.1

Separate chaining.

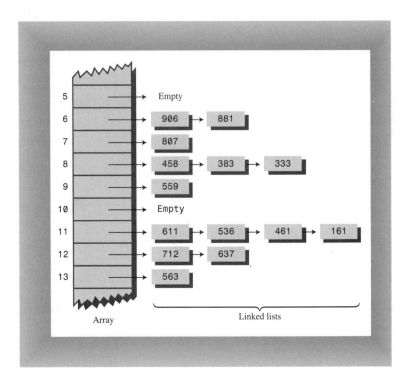

Separate chaining is conceptually somewhat simpler than the various probe schemes used in open addressing. However, the code is longer because it must include the mechanism for the linked lists, usually in the form of an additional class.

The HashChain Workshop Applet

To see how separate chaining works, start the HashChain Workshop applet. It displays an array of linked lists, as shown in Figure 23.2.

Each element of the array occupies one line of the display, and the linked lists extend from left to right. Initially there are 25 cells in the array (25 lists). This is more than fits on the screen; you can move the display up and down with the scrollbar to see the entire array. The display shows up to six items per list. You can create a hash table with up to 100 lists, and use load factors up to 2.0. Higher load factors may cause the linked lists to exceed six items and run off the right edge of the screen, making it impossible to see all the items. (This can happen very occasionally even at the 2.0 load factor.)

FIGURE 23.2

*The HashChain
Workshop applet.*

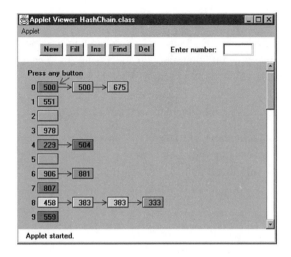

Insertion

Experiment with the HashChain applet by inserting some new items.

To Do: Insert Items

1. Click the Ins button. You'll be asked for the key of the item to be inserted. Type a number between 1 and 999.

2. After a few more clicks you'll see the red arrow jump to the appropriate list and the message `Will insert in list 16`. (Of course, the actual number depends on the key.)

3. Next the item will be inserted in the list.

4. If the list was previously empty, the item will be inserted in the blank space marking the list position.

▲ 5. If the list was not empty, the item will be inserted at the beginning of the list.

The lists in the HashChain applet are not sorted, so insertion does not require searching through the list. (The C++ sample program will demonstrate sorted lists.)

Try to find specified items using the Find button. During a find operation, if there are several items on the list, the red arrow must step through the items looking for the correct one. For a successful search, half the items in the list must be examined on the average, as we discussed in Hour 8, "Linked Lists." For an unsuccessful search all the items must be examined.

Load Factors

The load factor (the ratio of the number of items in a hash table to its size) is typically different in separate chaining than in open addressing. In open addressing the load factor should not be much above 0.5. In separate chaining it's normal to put N or more items into an N-cell array; thus the load factor can be 1 or greater. There's no problem with this; some locations will simply contain two or more items in their lists.

Let's call the average number of items on the linked lists M. If M is large, access time is reduced because access to a specified item requires searching through an average of M/2 items. Finding the initial cell takes fast O(1) time, but searching through the list takes time proportional to the number of items on the list—O(M) time. Thus we don't want the lists to become too full.

A load factor of 1, as shown in the Workshop applet, is common. With this load factor, roughly 1/3 of the cells will be empty, 1/3 will hold one item, and 1/3 will hold two or more items.

In open addressing, performance degrades badly as the load factor increases above 1/2 or 2/3. In separate chaining the load factor can rise above 1 without hurting performance very much. This makes separate chaining a more robust mechanism, especially when it's hard to predict in advance how much data will be placed in the hash table.

Duplicates

Duplicates are allowed and may be generated in the Fill process. All items with the same key will be inserted in the same list, so if you need to discover all of them, you must search the entire list in both successful and unsuccessful searches. This lowers performance. The Find operation in the Workshop applet only finds the first of several duplicates.

Deletion

In separate chaining, deletion poses no special problems as it does in open addressing. The algorithm hashes to the proper list, and then deletes the item from the list. Because probes aren't used, it doesn't matter if the list at a particular cell becomes empty. We've included a Del button in the Workshop applet to show how deletion works.

Table Size

With separate chaining it's not so important to make the table size a prime number, as it is with quadratic probes and double hashing. There are no probes in separate chaining, so there's no need to worry that a probe will go into an endless sequence because the step size divides evenly into the array size.

On the other hand, certain kinds of key distributions can cause data to cluster when the array size is not a prime number. We'll have more to say about this when we discuss hash functions later in this hour.

Buckets

NEW TERM   Another approach similar to separate chaining is to use an array at each location in the hash table, instead of a linked list. Such arrays are called *buckets*. This approach is not as efficient as the linked list approach, however, because of the problem of choosing the size of the buckets. If they're too small they might overflow, and if they're too large they waste memory. Linked lists, which allocate memory dynamically, don't have this problem.

Now let's see how we might implement separate chaining in C++.

C++ Code for Separate Chaining

The hashChain.cpp program includes a SortedList class and an associated Link class. Sorted lists don't speed up a successful search, but they do cut the time of an unsuccessful search in half. (As soon as an item larger than the search key is reached, which on average is half the items in a list, the search is declared a failure.)

Sorted lists also cut deletion times in half; however, insertion times are lengthened because the new item can't just be inserted at the beginning of the list. The new item's proper place in the ordered list must be located before it's inserted. However, if the lists are short, the increase in insertion times might not be important.

In situations where many unsuccessful searches are anticipated, it might be worthwhile to use the slightly more complicated sorted list, rather than an unsorted list. However, an unsorted list is preferred if insertion speed is more important.

The hashChain.cpp program, shown in Listing 23.1, begins by constructing a hash table with a table size and number of items entered by the user. The user can then insert, find, and delete items, and display the list. For the entire hash table to be viewed on the screen, the size of the table must be no greater than 16 or so.

```cpp
//hashChain.cpp
//demonstrates hash table with separate chaining
#include <iostream>
#include <vector>
#include <cstdlib>                         //for random numbers
#include <ctime>                           //for random numbers
using namespace std;
//////////////////////////////////////////////////////////////
class Link
    {                                      //(could be other items)
    public:
        int iData;                         //data item
        Link* pNext;                       //next link in list
//-----------------------------------------------------------------
    Link(int it) : iData(it)               //constructor
        {  }
//-----------------------------------------------------------------
    void displayLink()                     //display this link
        { cout << iData << " "; }
//-----------------------------------------------------------------
    };  //end class Link
//////////////////////////////////////////////////////////////
class SortedList
    {
    private:
        Link* pFirst;                      //ref to first list item
    public:
//-----------------------------------------------------------------
    SortedList()                           //constructor
        { pFirst = NULL; }
//-----------------------------------------------------------------
    void insert(Link* pLink)               //insert link, in order
        {
        int key = pLink->iData;
        Link* pPrevious = NULL;            //start at first
        Link* pCurrent = pFirst;
                                           //until end of list,
        while(pCurrent != NULL && key > pCurrent->iData)
            {                              //or pCurrent > key,
            pPrevious = pCurrent;
            pCurrent = pCurrent->pNext;    //go to next item
            }
        if(pPrevious==NULL)                //if beginning of list,
            pFirst = pLink;                //   first -> new link
        else                               //not at beginning,
            pPrevious->pNext = pLink;      //   prev -> new link
        pLink->pNext = pCurrent;           //new link -> current
        }  //end insert()
```

```
//--------------------------------------------------------------
   void remove(int key)         //delete link
      {                                //(assumes non-empty list)
      Link* pPrevious = NULL;          //start at first
      Link* pCurrent = pFirst;
                                       //until end of list,
      while(pCurrent != NULL && key != pCurrent->iData)
         {                             //or key == current,
         pPrevious = pCurrent;
         pCurrent = pCurrent->pNext;   //go to next link
         }
                                       //disconnect link
      if(pPrevious==NULL)              //  if beginning of list
         pFirst = pFirst->pNext;       //     delete first link
      else                             //  not at beginning
                                       //delete current link
         pPrevious->pNext = pCurrent->pNext;
      }  //end remove()
//--------------------------------------------------------------
   Link* find(int key)               //find link
      {
      Link* pCurrent = pFirst;        //start at first
                                      //until end of list,
      while(pCurrent != NULL &&  pCurrent->iData <= key)
         {                            //or key too small,
         if(pCurrent->iData == key)   //is this the link?
            return pCurrent;          //found it, return link
         pCurrent = pCurrent->pNext;  //go to next item
         }
      return NULL;                    //didn't find it
      }  //end find()
//--------------------------------------------------------------
   void displayList()
      {
      cout << "List (first->last): ";
      Link* pCurrent = pFirst;       //start at beginning of list
      while(pCurrent != NULL)        //until end of list,
         {
         pCurrent->displayLink();    //print data
         pCurrent = pCurrent->pNext; //move to next link
         }
      cout << endl;
      }
//--------------------------------------------------------------
   };  //end class SortedList
//////////////////////////////////////////////////////////////
class HashTable
   {
   private:
      vector<SortedList*> hashArray;  //vector of lists
```

continues

LISTING 23.1 CONTINUED

```cpp
      int arraySize;
   public:
//--------------------------------------------------------------
   HashTable(int size)                    //constructor
      {
      arraySize = size;
      hashArray.resize(arraySize);   //set vector size
      for(int j=0; j<arraySize; j++)  //fill vector
         hashArray[j] = new SortedList; //with lists
      }
//--------------------------------------------------------------
   void displayTable()
      {
      for(int j=0; j<arraySize; j++)  //for each cell,
         {
         cout << j << ". ";           //display cell number
         hashArray[j]->displayList(); //display list
         }
      }
//--------------------------------------------------------------
   int hashFunc(int key)                  //hash function
      {
      return key % arraySize;
      }
//--------------------------------------------------------------
   void insert(Link* pLink)              //insert a link
      {
      int key = pLink->iData;
      int hashVal = hashFunc(key);    //hash the key
      hashArray[hashVal]->insert(pLink); //insert at hashVal
      }  //end insert()
//--------------------------------------------------------------
   void remove(int key)                  //delete a link
      {
      int hashVal = hashFunc(key);    //hash the key
      hashArray[hashVal]->remove(key); //delete link
      }  //end remove()
//--------------------------------------------------------------
   Link* find(int key)                   //find link
      {
      int hashVal = hashFunc(key);    //hash the key
      Link* pLink = hashArray[hashVal]->find(key);  //get link
      return pLink;                     //return link
      }
//--------------------------------------------------------------
   };  //end class HashTable
////////////////////////////////////////////////////////////////
int main()
```

```
{
int aKey;
Link* pDataItem;
int size, n, keysPerCell = 100;
time_t aTime;
char choice = 'b';
                                    //get sizes
cout << "Enter size of hash table: ";
cin >> size;
cout << "Enter initial number of items: ";
cin >> n;
HashTable theHashTable(size);   //make table
                                //initialize random numbers
srand( static_cast<unsigned>(time(&aTime)) );

for(int j=0; j<n; j++)              //insert data
   {
   aKey = rand() % (keysPerCell * size);
   pDataItem = new Link(aKey);
   theHashTable.insert(pDataItem);
   }
while(choice != 'x')               //interact with user
   {
   cout << "Enter first letter of ";
   cout << "show, insert, delete, or find: ";
   cin >> choice;
   switch(choice)
      {
      case 's':
         theHashTable.displayTable();
         break;
      case 'i':
         cout << "Enter key value to insert: ";
         cin >> aKey;
         pDataItem = new Link(aKey);
         theHashTable.insert(pDataItem);
         break;
      case 'd':
         cout << "Enter key value to delete: ";
         cin >> aKey;
         theHashTable.remove(aKey);
         break;
      case 'f':
         cout << "Enter key value to find: ";
         cin >> aKey;
         pDataItem = theHashTable.find(aKey);
         if(pDataItem != NULL)
            cout << "Found " << aKey << endl;
         else
            cout << "Could not find " << aKey << endl;
         break;
```

continues

23

LISTING 23.1   CONTINUED

```
        default:
            cout << "Invalid entry\n";
        } //end switch
    } //end while
return 0;
}  //end main()
```

OUTPUT   Here's the output when the user creates a table with 20 lists, inserts 20 items into it, and displays it with the *s* option.

```
Enter size of hash table: 20
Enter initial number of items: 20
Enter first letter of show, insert, delete, or find: s
0. List (first->last): 240 1160
1. List (first->last):
2. List (first->last):
3. List (first->last): 143
4. List (first->last): 1004
5. List (first->last): 1485 1585
6. List (first->last):
7. List (first->last): 87 1407
8. List (first->last):
9. List (first->last): 309
10. List (first->last): 490
11. List (first->last):
12. List (first->last): 872
13. List (first->last): 1073
14. List (first->last): 594 954
15. List (first->last): 335
16. List (first->last): 1216
17. List (first->last): 1057 1357
18. List (first->last): 938 1818
19. List (first->last):
```

If you insert more items into this table you'll see the lists grow longer, but maintain their sorted order. You can delete items as well.

Efficiency of Separate Chaining

The efficiency analysis for separate chaining is different, and generally easier, than for open addressing.

We want to know how long it takes to search for or insert an item into a separate-chaining hash table. We'll assume that the most time-consuming part of these operations is comparing the search key of the item with the keys of other items in the list. We'll also assume that the time required to hash to the appropriate list, and to determine when the end of a list has been reached, is equivalent to one key comparison. Thus all operations require 1+nComps time, where nComps is the number of key comparisons.

Let's say that the hash table consists of arraySize elements, each of which holds a list, and that N data items have been inserted in the table. Then, on the average, each list will hold N divided by arraySize items:

```
AverageListLength = N / arraySize
```

This is the same as the definition of the load factor:

```
loadFactor = N / arraySize
```

So the average list length equals the load factor.

Searching

In a successful search, the algorithm hashes to the appropriate list, and then searches along the list for the item. On the average, half the items must be examined before the correct one is located. Thus the search time is

```
1 + loadFactor / 2
```

This is true whether the lists are ordered or not. In an unsuccessful search, if the lists are unordered, all the items must be searched, so the time is

```
1 + loadFactor
```

These formulas are graphed in Figure 23.3.

For an ordered list, only half the items must be examined in an unsuccessful search, so the time is the same as for a successful search.

In separate chaining it's typical to use a load factor of about 1.0 (the number of data items equals the array size). Smaller load factors don't improve performance significantly, but the time for all operations increases linearly with load factor, so going beyond 2 or so is generally a bad idea.

Insertion

If the lists are not ordered, insertion is always immediate, in the sense that no comparisons are necessary. The hash function must still be computed, so let's call the insertion time 1.

FIGURE 23.3

Separate-chaining performance.

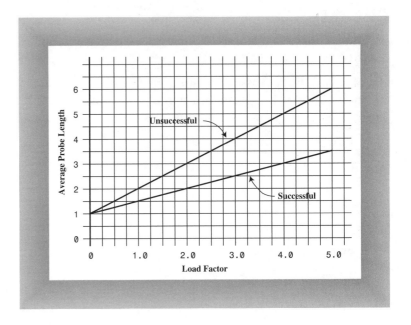

If the lists are ordered, then, as with an unsuccessful search, an average of half the items in each list must be examined, so the insertion time is 1 + loadFactor / 2.

That completes our discussion of separate chaining. How does separate chaining compare with the open addressing approach seen in Hours 21 and 22?

Open Addressing Versus Separate Chaining

If open addressing is to be used, double hashing seems to be the preferred system by a small margin over quadratic probing. The exception is the situation where plenty of memory is available and the data won't expand after the table is created; in this case linear probing is somewhat simpler to implement and, if load factors below 0.5 are used, causes little performance penalty.

If the number of items that will be inserted in a hash table isn't known when the table is created, separate chaining is preferable to open addressing. Increasing the load factor causes major performance penalties in open addressing, but performance degrades only linearly in separate chaining.

When in doubt, use separate chaining. Its drawback is the need for a linked list class, but the payoff is that adding more data than you anticipated won't cause performance to slow to a crawl.

Hash Functions

In this section we'll explore the issue of what makes a good hash function, and see if we can improve the approach to hashing strings mentioned at the beginning of Hour 21.

Quick Computation

A good hash function is simple, so it can be computed quickly. The major advantage of hash tables is their speed. If the hash function is slow, this speed will be degraded. A hash function with many multiplications and divisions is not a good idea. (The bit-manipulation facilities of C++, such as shifting bits right to divide a number by a multiple of 2, can sometimes be used to good advantage.)

The purpose of a hash function is to take a range of key values and transform them into index values in such a way that the key values are distributed randomly across all the indices of the hash table. The scheme should work with keys that are completely random as well as not so random.

Random Keys

NEW TERM A so-called *perfect* hash function maps every key into a different table location. This is only possible for keys that are unusually well behaved, and whose range is small enough to be used directly as array indices (as in the employee-number example discussed in Hour 21).

In most cases neither of these situations exist, and the hash function will need to compress a larger range of keys into a smaller range of index numbers.

The distribution of key values in a particular set of data determines what the hash function needs to do. So far we've assumed that the data was randomly distributed over its entire range. In this situation the following hash function is satisfactory:

```
index = key % arraySize;
```

It involves only one mathematical operation, and if the keys are truly random the resulting indices will be random too, and therefore well distributed.

Non-Random Keys

However, data is often distributed non-randomly. Imagine a set of data that uses car part numbers as keys. Perhaps these numbers are of the form

```
033-400-03-94-05-0-535
```

This is interpreted as follows:

- Digits 0–2: Supplier number (1 to 999, currently up to 70)
- Digits 3–5: Category code (100, 150, 200, 250, up to 850)
- Digits 6–7: Month of introduction (1 to 12)
- Digits 8–9: Year of introduction (00 to 99)
- Digits 10–11: Serial number (1 to 99, but never exceeds 100)
- Digit 12: Toxic risk flag (0 or 1)
- Digits 13–15: Checksum (sum of other fields, modulo 100)

The key used for the part number shown would be 0,334,000,394,050,535. However, such keys are not randomly distributed. The majority of numbers from 0 to 9,999,999,999,999,999 can't actually occur. (For example, supplier numbers above 70, category codes that aren't multiples of 50, and months from 13 to 99.) Also, the checksum is not independent of the other numbers. Some work should be done to these part numbers to ensure that they form a range of more truly random numbers.

Don't Use Non-Data

The key fields should be squeezed down until every bit counts. For example, the category codes should be changed to run from 0 to 15. Also, the checksum should be removed because it doesn't add any additional information; it's deliberately redundant. Various bit-twiddling techniques are appropriate for compressing the various fields in the key.

Use All the Data

Every part of the key (except non-data, as described above) should contribute to the hash function. Don't just use the first four digits or some such expurgation. The more data that contributes to the key, the more likely it is that the keys will hash evenly into the entire range of indices.

Sometimes the range of keys is so large it overflows type `int` or type `long` variables. We'll see how to handle overflow when we talk about hashing strings in a moment.

> The trick is to find a hash function that's simple and fast, yet excludes the non-data parts of the key and uses all the data.

Use a Prime Number for the Modulo Base

Often the hash function involves using the modulo operator (%) with the table size. We've already seen that it's important for the table size to be prime number when using a quadratic probe or double hashing. However, if the keys themselves might not be randomly distributed, it's important for the table size to be a prime number no matter what hashing system is used.

This is because if many keys share a divisor with the array size, they might tend to hash to the same location, causing clustering. Using a prime table size eliminates this possibility. For example, if the table size is a multiple of 50 in our car part example, the category codes will all hash to index numbers that are multiples of 50. However, with a prime number such as 53, you are guaranteed that no keys will divide into the table size.

The moral is to examine your keys carefully, and tailor your hash algorithm to remove any irregularity in the distribution of the keys.

Hashing Strings

Let's see how to apply hash functions to hashing strings. We'll show three versions of such a hash function, each more refined than the last.

Hash Function Version 1

We saw in Hour 21 how to convert short strings to key numbers by multiplying digit codes by powers of a constant. In particular, we saw that the four-letter word *cats* could turned into a number by calculating

```
key = 3*27³ + 1*27² + 20*27¹ + 19*27⁰
```

This approach has the desirable attribute of involving all the characters in the input string. The calculated key value can then be hashed into an array index in the usual way:

```
index = (key) % arraySize;
```

Here's a C++ hash function that finds the key value of a word:

```
int hashFunc1(string key)
   {
   int hashVal = 0;
   int pow27 = 1;                         //1, 27, 27*27, etc

   for(int j=key.length()-1; j>=0; j-) //right to left
      {
```

```
        int letter = key[j] - 96;        //get char code
        hashVal += pow27 * letter;       //times power of 27
        pow27 *= 27;                     //next power of 27
        }
    return hashVal % arraySize;
    }  // end hashFunc1()
```

ANALYSIS The loop starts at the rightmost letter in the word. If there are N letters, this is N–1. The numerical equivalent of the letter, according to the code we devised in Hour 21 (a=1 and so on), is placed in `letter`. This is then multiplied by a power of 27, which is 1 for the letter at N–1, 27 for the letter at N–2, and so on.

Hash Function Version 2

The `hashFunc1()` function is not as efficient as it might be. Aside from the character conversion, there are two multiplications and an addition inside the loop. We can eliminate a multiplication by taking advantage of a mathematical identity called Horner's method. (Horner was an English mathematician, 1773–1827.) This states that an expression like

```
var4*n⁴ + var3*n³ + var2*n² + var1*n¹ + var0*n⁰
```

can be written as

```
(((var4*n + var3)*n + var2)*n + var1)*n + var0
```

To evaluate this, we can start inside the innermost parentheses and work outward. If we translate this to a C++ function we have the following code:

```
int hashFunc2(string key)
    {
    int hashVal = 0;
    for(int j=0; j<key.length(); j++)     //left to right
        {
        int letter = key[j] - 96;         //get char code
        hashVal = hashVal * 27 + letter;  //multiply and add
        }
    return hashVal % arraySize;           //mod
    }  // end hashFunc2()
```

ANALYSIS Here we start with the leftmost letter of the word (which is somewhat more natural than starting on the right), and we have only one multiplication and one addition each time through the loop (aside from extracting the character from the string).

Hash Function Version 3

The `hashFunc2()` function unfortunately can't handle strings longer than about 7 letters. Longer strings cause the value of `hashVal` to exceed the size of type `int`. (This assumes you're using a 32-bit system, in which a variable of type `int` occupies 4 bytes of memory.)

Can we modify this basic approach so we don't overflow any variables? Notice that the key we eventually end up with is always less than the array size, because we apply the modulo operator. It's not the final index that's too big, it's the intermediate key values.

ANALYSIS   It turns out that with Horner's formulation we can apply the modulo (%) operator at each step in the calculation. This gives the same result as applying the modulo operator once at the end, but avoids overflow. (It does add an operation inside the loop.) The hashFunc3() function shows how this looks.

```
int hashFunc3(string key)
   {
   int hashVal = 0;
   for(int j=0; j<key.length(); j++)      //left to right
      {
      int letter = key[j] - 96;           //get char code
      hashVal = (hashVal * 27 + letter) % arraySize;  //mod
      }
   return hashVal;                        //no mod
   } // end hashFunc3()
```

This approach or something like it is normally taken to hash a string. Various bit-manipulation tricks can be played as well, such as using a base of 32 (or a larger power of 2) instead of 27, so that multiplication can be effected using the shift (>>) operator, which is faster than the modulo (%) operator.

You can use an approach similar to this to convert any kind of string to a number suitable for hashing. The strings can be words, names, or any other concatenation of characters.

Summary

In this hour, you've learned the following:

- In separate chaining, each table location contains a linked list. Data items that hash to the same location are simply inserted in the list.

- A load factor of 1.0 is appropriate for separate chaining.

- At this load factor a successful search has an average probe length of 1.5, and an unsuccessful search, 2.0.

- Probe lengths in separate chaining increase linearly with load factor.

- A string can be hashed by multiplying each character by a different power of a constant, adding the products, and using the modulo (%) operator to reduce the result to the size of the hash table.

- To avoid overflow, the modulo operator can be applied at each step in the process, if the polynomial is expressed using Horner's method.

Q&A

Q **I didn't get the point of all that discussion about complicated part numbers. Can you explain a bit more?**

A The point is that you should pay attention to what numbers you use for keys. If you don't squeeze out redundant or constant information, your hash table won't be as efficient as it could be.

Q **In the car part numbers, isn't there a Y2K problem because only two digits are used for the year?**

A That depends how the software handles this field. There's no problem if the assumption is that numbers from 00 to (say) 49 refer to 2000 to 2049, whereas 50 to 99 refer to 1950 to 1999.

Q **When should I use a hash table as opposed to a tree?**

A We'll get to that in the next chapter.

Workshop

The Workshop helps you solidify what you learned in this hour. See Appendix A, "Quiz Answers," for quiz answers.

Quiz

1. When a collision occurs in separate chaining, how is an open array cell located?

2. In separate chaining, how do you access an item with a given key?

3. True or false: Unsorted lists must be used in separate chaining.

4. If there are N items in a hash table that uses separate chaining, and an average of M items on each list, how long does it take, on average, to find a particular item?

5. What is a bucket?

6. In separate chaining with unsorted lists, which is faster, a successful search or an unsuccessful search?

7. True or false: The efficiency of separate chaining degrades rapidly as the load factor approaches 1.

Exercise

Rewrite the hashChain.cpp program to use an UnsortedList class instead of a SortedList class. Run both versions of the program with large amounts of data and time which one is faster for insertion, deletion, and searching.

HOUR 24

When to Use What

In this hour we briefly summarize what we've learned so far in this book, with an eye toward deciding what data structure or algorithm to use in a particular situation. You'll lean

- How to decide which general-purpose data structure—array, linked list, tree, or hash table—to use
- How to decide which specialized data structure—stack, queue, or priority queue—to use
- How to decide which sorting algorithm to use

For detailed information on these topics, refer to the individual hours in this book.

The summary in this hour comes with the usual caveats. Of necessity it's very general. Every real-world situation is unique, so what we say here might not be the right answer to your problem.

General-Purpose Data Structures

If you need to store real-world data such as personnel records, inventories, contact lists, or sales data, you need a general-purpose data structure. The structures of this type that we've discussed in this book are arrays, linked lists, trees, and hash tables. We call these general-purpose data structures because they are used to store and retrieve data using key values. They provide convenient access to any data item (as opposed to specialized structures such as stacks, which allow access to only certain data items).

Which of these general-purpose data structures is appropriate for a given problem? Figure 24.1 shows a first approximation to this question. However, there are many factors besides those shown in the figure. For more detail, we'll explore some general considerations first, and then zero in on the individual structures.

FIGURE 24.1

The relationship of general-purpose data structures.

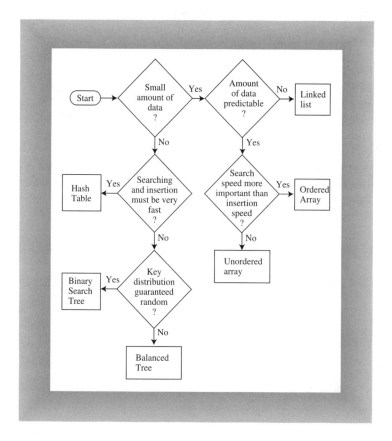

Speed and Algorithms

The general-purpose data structures can be roughly arranged in terms of speed: Arrays and linked lists are slow, trees are fairly fast, and hash tables are very fast.

However, don't draw the conclusion from this figure that it's always best to use the fastest structures. There's a penalty for using them. First, they are—in varying degrees—more complex to program than the array and linked list. Also, hash tables require you to know in advance about how much data can be stored, and they don't use memory very efficiently. Ordinary binary trees will revert to slow O(N) operation for ordered data, and balanced trees, which avoid this problem, are difficult to program.

Computers Grow Faster Every Year

The fast structures come with penalties, and another development makes the slow structures more attractive. Every year there's an increase in the CPU and memory-access speed of the latest computers. Moore's Law (postulated by Gordon Moore in 1965) specifies that CPU performance will double every 18 months. This adds up to an astonishing difference in performance between the earliest computers and those available today, and there's no reason to think this increase will slow down any time soon.

Suppose a computer a few years ago handled an array of 100 objects in acceptable time. Now, computers are 100 times faster, so an array with 10,000 objects can run at the same speed. Many writers of computer science texts provide estimates of the maximum size you can make a data structure before it becomes too slow. Don't trust these estimates (including those in this book). Today's estimate doesn't apply to tomorrow.

Instead, start by considering the simple data structures. Unless it's obvious they'll be too slow, code a test version of an array or linked list and see what happens. If it runs in acceptable time, look no further. Why slave away on a balanced tree, when no one would ever notice that you used an array instead? Even if you must deal with thousands or tens of thousands of items, it's still worthwhile to see how well an array or linked list will handle them. Only when experimentation shows their performance to be too slow should you revert to more sophisticated data structures.

Pointers Are Faster

C++ has an advantage over some languages in the speed with which objects can be manipulated because, in many data structures, C++ stores only pointers, not actual objects. Therefore most algorithms will run faster than if actual objects occupy space in a data structure. In analyzing the algorithms it's not the case, as when objects themselves are stored, that the time to "move" an object depends on the size of the object. Because only a pointer is moved, it doesn't matter how large the object is.

Libraries

Libraries of data structures are available commercially for all major programming languages. Languages themselves may have some structures built in. C++, as we've noted in previous hours, includes vector, stack, and various other container classes as part of the Standard Template Library (STL).

Using a ready-made library might eliminate or at least reduce the programming necessary to create the data structures described in this book. When that's the case, using a complex structure such as a balanced tree, or a delicate algorithm such as quicksort, becomes a more attractive possibility. However, you must ensure that the class can be adapted to your particular situation.

Arrays

In many situations the array is the first kind of structure you should consider when storing and manipulating data. Arrays are useful when

1. The amount of data is reasonably small.
2. The amount of data is predictable in advance.

If you have plenty of memory, you can relax the second condition; just make the array big enough to handle any foreseeable influx of data.

If insertion speed is important, use an unordered array. If search speed is important, use an ordered array with a binary search. Deletion is always slow in arrays because an average of half the items must be moved to fill in the newly vacated cell. Traversal is fast in an ordered array but not supported in an unordered array.

Vectors, such as the vector class supplied with the C++ STL, are arrays that expand themselves when they become too full. Vectors might work well when the amount of data isn't known in advance. They should probably be considered before a normal array. However, there might periodically be a significant pause while they enlarge themselves by copying the old data into a new space. This might make vectors inappropriate for some programming situations, such as real-time systems.

Linked Lists

Consider a linked list whenever the amount of data to be stored cannot be predicted in advance or when data will frequently be inserted and deleted. The linked list obtains whatever storage it needs as new items are added, so it can expand to fill all of the available memory; there is no need to fill "holes" during deletion, as there is in arrays.

Insertion is fast in an unordered list. Searching and deletion are slow (although deletion is faster than in an array), so, like arrays, linked lists are best used when the amount of data is comparatively small.

A linked list is somewhat more complicated to program than an array, but is simple compared with a tree or hash table.

Binary Search Trees

A binary tree is the first structure to consider when arrays and linked lists prove too slow. A tree provides fast O(log N) insertion, searching, and deletion. Traversal is O(N), which is the maximum for any data structure (by definition, you must visit every item). You can also find the minimum and maximum quickly, and traverse a range of items.

An unbalanced binary tree is much easier to program than a balanced tree, but unfortunately ordered data can reduce its performance to O(N) time, no better than a linked list. However, if you're sure the data will arrive in random order, there's less necessity to using a balanced tree.

Balanced Trees

Of the various kinds of balanced trees, we discussed red-black trees and 2-3-4 trees. They are both balanced trees, and thus guarantee O(log N) performance whether the input data is ordered or not. However, these balanced trees are challenging to program, with the red-black tree being the more difficult. They also impose additional memory overhead, which might or might not be significant. The problem of complex programming is reduced if a commercial class can be used for a tree.

In some cases a hash table might be a better choice than a balanced tree. Hash table performance doesn't degrade when the data is ordered.

There are other kinds of balanced trees, including AVL trees, splay trees, 2-3 trees, and so on, but they are not as commonly used as the red-black tree.

Hash Tables

Hash tables are the fastest data storage structure. This makes them a necessity for situations where a computer program, rather than a human, is interacting with large amounts of data. Hash tables are typically used in spelling checkers and as symbol tables in computer language compilers, where a program must check thousands of words or symbols in a fraction of a second.

24

Hash tables might also be useful when a person, as opposed to a computer, initiates data-access operations. As noted above, hash tables are not sensitive to the order in which data is inserted, and so can take the place of a balanced tree. Programming is much simpler than for balanced trees.

Hash tables require additional memory, especially for open addressing. Also, the amount of data to be stored must be known fairly accurately in advance because an array is used as the underlying structure.

A hash table with separate chaining is the most robust implementation, unless the amount of data is known accurately in advance, in which case open addressing offers simpler programming because no linked list class is required.

Hash tables don't support any kind of ordered traversal, or access to the minimum or maximum items. If these capabilities are important, the binary search tree is a better choice.

Comparing the General-Purpose Storage Structures

Table 24.1 summarizes the speeds of the various general-purpose data storage structures using Big O notation.

TABLE 24.1 GENERAL-PURPOSE DATA STORAGE STRUCTURES

Data Structure	Search	Insertion	Deletion	Traversal
Array	O(N)	O(1)	O(N)	—
Ordered array	O(log N)	O(N)	O(N)	O(N)
Linked list	O(N)	O(1)	O(N)	—
Ordered linked list	O(N)	O(N)	O(N)	O(N)
Binary tree (average)	O(log N)	O(log N)	O(log N)	O(N)
Binary tree (worst case)	O(N)	O(N)	O(N)	O(N)
Balanced tree (average and worst case)	O(log N)	O(log N)	O(log N)	O(N)
Hash table	O(1)	O(1)	O(1)	—

In this table, insertion in an ordinary (unordered) array is assumed to be at the end of the array. The ordered array uses a binary search, which is fast, but insertion and deletion require moving half the items on the average, which is slow. Traversal implies visiting the data items in order of ascending or descending keys. A dash (—) means the indicated operation is not supported.

Let's move on from general-purpose data structures to structures that are more applicable in specialized situations.

Special-Purpose Data Structures

The special-purpose data structures discussed in this book are the stack, the queue, and the priority queue. These structures, rather than supporting a database of user-accessible data, are more often used by a computer program to aid in carrying out some algorithm.

Stacks, queues, and priority queues are abstract data types (ADTs) that are implemented by a more fundamental structure such as an array or linked list. These ADTs present a simple interface to the user, typically allowing only insertion and the ability to access or delete only one data item. These items are

- For stacks: the last item inserted
- For queues: the first item inserted
- For priority queues: the item with the highest priority

These ADTs can be seen as conceptual aids. Their functionality could be obtained using the underlying structure (such as an array) directly, but the reduced interface they offer simplifies many problems.

These ADTs can't be conveniently searched for an item by key value, or traversed.

Stack

A stack is used when you want access only to the last data item inserted; it's a last-in-first-out (LIFO) structure.

A stack is often implemented as an array or a linked list. The array implementation is efficient because the most recently inserted item is placed at the end of the array, where it's also easy to delete it. Stack overflow can occur, but is not likely if the array is reasonably sized, because stacks seldom contain huge amounts of data.

If the stack will contain a lot of data and the amount can't be predicted accurately in advance (as when recursion is implemented as a stack) a linked list is a better choice than an array. A linked list is efficient because items can be inserted and deleted quickly from the head of the list. Stack overflow can't occur (unless the entire memory is full). A linked list is slightly slower than an array because memory allocation is necessary to create a new link for insertion, and deallocation of the link is necessary at some point, usually following removal of an item from the list.

Queue

A queue is used when you want access only to the first data item inserted; it's a first-in-first-out (FIFO) structure.

Like stacks, queues can be implemented as arrays or linked lists. Both are efficient. The array requires additional programming to handle the situation where the queue wraps around at the end of the array. A linked list must be double-ended, to allow insertions at one end and deletions at the other.

As with stacks, the choice between an array implementation and a linked list implementation is determined by how well the amount of data can be predicted. Use the array if you know about how much data there will be; otherwise, use a linked list.

Priority Queue

A priority queue is used when the only access desired is to the data item with the highest priority. This is the item with the largest (or sometimes the smallest) key.

Priority queues can be implemented as ordered arrays or ordered linked lists. Insertion in these structures is slow, but deletion is fast. The array works when the amount of data to be stored can be predicted in advance; the linked list when the amount of data is unknown. A vector can be substituted for the array.

NEW TERM   A priority queue can also be implemented as a heap, a data structure that we don't discuss in this book. A *heap* is a tree-like structure, usually based on an array, that provides fast access to the largest (or smallest) data item. As the basis for a priority queue, the heap allows insertion in O(log N) time; unfortunately, deletion is also O(log N), not as fast as an ordered array. The heap is more complicated than the array or linked list. However it's the structure of choice when insertion speed is vital.

Comparison of Special-Purpose Structures

Table 24.2 shows the Big O times for stacks, queues, and priority queues. These structures don't support searching or traversal.

TABLE 24.2   SPECIAL-PURPOSE DATA-STORAGE STRUCTURES

Data Structure	Insertion	Deletion	Comment
Stack (array or linked list)	O(1)	O(1)	Deletes most recently inserted item
Queue (array or linked list)	O(1)	O(1)	Deletes least recently inserted item
Priority queue (ordered array)	O(N)	O(1)	Deletes highest-priority item
Priority queue (heap)	O(log N)	O(log N)	Deletes highest-priority item

We've summarized two kinds of data structures. We'll conclude with a review of the most common complex algorithm: sorting.

Sorting

As with the choice of data structures, it's worthwhile initially to try a slow but simple sort, such as the insertion sort. It might be that the fast processing speeds available in modern computers will allow sorting of your data in reasonable time. (As a wild guess, the slow sort might be appropriate for under 1,000 items.)

Insertion sort is also good for almost-sorted files, operating in about O(N) time if not too many items are out of place. This is typically the case where a few new items are added to an already-sorted file.

If the insertion sort proves too slow you can use one of the more complex but faster sorts: mergesort or quicksort. Mergesort requires extra memory and is somewhat slower than quicksort, so quicksort is the usual choice when the fastest sorting time is necessary.

24

However, quicksort is suspect if there's a danger that the data may not be random, in which case it may deteriorate to $O(N^2)$ performance in some implementations. For potentially non-random data, heapsort is better. Quicksort is also prone to subtle errors if it is not implemented correctly. Small mistakes in coding can make it work poorly for certain arrangements of data, a situation that might be hard to diagnose.

Several sorts we did not discuss in this book might be worth considering. The shellsort is intermediate in speed between the slow sorts like the insertion sort and the fast sorts like mergesort and quicksort. It's considerably easier to program than the faster sorts, and might therefore be useful in situations when there's too much data for a slow sort but not enough to justify a fast sort.

The heapsort is based on the heap structure, just mentioned in connection with priority queues. The heapsort rivals the mergesort in its ability to handle non-random data.

Table 24.3 summarizes the running time for various sorting algorithms. The column labeled Comparison attempts to estimate the minor speed differences between algorithms with the same average Big O times. (There's no entry for shellsort because there are no other algorithms with the same Big O performance.)

TABLE 24.3   COMPARISON OF SORTING ALGORITHMS

Sort1	Average	Worst	Comparison	Extra Memory
Bubble	$O(N^2)$	$O(N^2)$	Fair	No
Insertion	$O(N^2)$	$O(N^2)$	Good	No
Shellsort	$O(N^{3/2})$	$O(N^{3/2})$		No
Quicksort	$O(N*\log N)$	$O(N^2)$	Good	No
Mergesort	$O(N*\log N)$	$O(N*\log N)$	Fair	Yes
Heapsort	$O(N*\log N)$	$O(N*\log N)$	Fair	No

Onward

We've come to the end of our survey of data structures and algorithms. The subject is large and complex, so no one book can make you an expert, but we hope this book has made it easy for you to learn the fundamentals. Appendix C, "Further Reading," contains suggestions for further study.

Because this chapter is itself a summary, we don't include the usual end-of-chapter material such as the summary and workshop.

24

Part VI
Appendixes

APPENDIX A

Quiz Answers

Hour 1, "Overview of Data Structures and Alogrithms"

1. What is a data structure?

   An arrangement of data in a computer's memory (or hard disk).

2. What is an algorithm?

   A procedure or set of instructions for carrying out some operation.

3. Name two things you can use data structures for.

   Pick two from: data storage, programmer's tools, and modeling.

4. Name an algorithm commonly applied to stored data.

   Pick one from: insertion, searching, deletion.

5. True or false: There is only one record in a data file.

   False, there are many similar records.

6. What is one of the problems with procedural languages?

   Pick one from: protects data poorly, does not model the real world well.

7. True or false: There is only one object of each class.

False. There are (usually) many objects of a class.

8. What is the most common use for the dot operator?

It associates a particular object with one of its member functions.

Hour 2, "Arrays"

1. On average, how many items must be moved to insert a new item into an unsorted array with N items?

None.

2. On average, how many items must be moved to delete an item from an unsorted array with N items?

N/2

3. On average, how many items must be examined to find a particular item in an unsorted array with N items?

N/2

4. What is a class interface?

The public member functions (and occasionally data) that are accessible outside the class.

5. Why is it important to make things easier for the class user than for the class designer?

The class is written only once, but it may be used many times.

6. What are the advantages of wrapping an array in a class?

Its data is less likely to be corrupted, and it can be easier to use.

7. What's an example of an operation that's easier to perform on an array that's in a class than on a simple array?

Displaying all the array contents requires only a single statement (calling a member function) if the array is in a class.

8. What is abstraction?

Abstraction is the focus on how to use something rather than on how it works.

Hour 3, "Ordered Arrays"

1. Why is an ordered array better than an unordered array?

Searches can be carried out much faster.

2. In one sentence, how does a binary search work?

   By repeatedly dividing in half the range to be searched.

3. What is the maximum number of comparisons necessary when performing a binary search of 100,000 items?

   17

4. What is the equation that tells you how many steps a binary search will take if you already know the size of the range to be searched?

   $s = \log_2(r)$

5. True or false: Only simple variables like int can be stored in a data structure.

   False. Objects are commonly stored in data structures.

6. What is the purpose of Big O notation?

   It provides a concise way to specify how fast an algorithm is.

7. Big O notation specifies a relationship between two variables. What are these variables?

   The size of a data structure and the speed of an algorithm applied to the data structure.

A

Hour 4, "The Bubble Sort"

1. Describe the algorithm for carrying out the bubble sort.

   Start on the left. (1) Compare two items. (2) Swap them if the one on the left is larger. (3) Move one space left. (4) Stop going left when you reach a sorted item. (5) Continue until all items are sorted.

2. How many statements does a C++ program need to carry out the bubble sort?

   About four (not counting declarations and a swap function).

3. What's an invariant?

   A condition that remains unchanged throughout an algorithm's operation (or sometimes part of the operation).

4. Why is the bubble sort so slow?

   One loop nested within another is a sign an algorithm may run in $O(N^2)$ time. The inner loop does something N times, and the outer loop executes the inner loop N times. N times N is N^2.

5. How many comparisons does a bubble sort perform in sorting N items?

   N*(N-1)/2

6. In the bubbleSort.cpp program, why is the bubbleSort() function a member function of a class?

It's an operation that can be carried out on an object of the array class, just as displaying the array or inserting a new item are.

Hour 5, "The Insertion Sort"

1. What does *partially sorted* mean?

If a group of items are sorted among themselves, but not yet sorted when compared with items not in the group, they are said to be partially sorted.

2. During the insertion sort, where is the marked item placed?

In the appropriate place in the partially sorted group.

3. What is one reason the insertion sort is more efficient than the sorted group?

It performs copies (as it shifts items) rather than swaps.

4. True or false: When using the insertion sort on N items, memory space for N*2 items is required.

False. Only one additional variable is required, so we need space for only N+1 items.

5. True or false: The insertion sort runs in $O(N^2)$ time, the same as the bubble sort.

True, although it is more than twice as fast on random data, and much faster for data that is only slightly out of order.

6. Define the term *stable* as applied to sorting.

A sorting algorithm is stable if items with the same key remain in the same order after the sort.

7. When would you use a bubble sort as opposed to an insertion sort?

Only if the amount of data was very small, so that speed was less important than the simplicity of the algorithm.

Hour 6, "Stacks"

1. True or false: A stack works on the first-in-first-out (FIFO) principle.

False. A stack works on the last-in-first-out (LIFO) principle.

2. Name two ways stacks and queues differ from arrays.

Pick one from the following: (1) Stacks and queues are more often used as programmers' tools. (2) Stacks and queues restrict access to certain data. (3) Stacks and queues are more abstract, being defined by their interface.

3. True or false: A good analogy for a stack is the line of people waiting at the bank teller's window.

False. The line at a bank is a first-in-first-out situation.

4. Define *push* and *pop*.

Push means to insert at the top of a stack, and *pop* means to remove from the top of a stack.

5. True or false: If there's only one item in a stack, the bottom of the stack is the same as the top.

True.

6. In the C++ code that pushes an item onto a stack, should you insert the item first or increment the top first?

Increment the top first.

Hour 7, "Queues and Priority Queues"

1. Give a one-sentence description of how a queue works.

Items are inserted at one end of a queue and removed at the other.

2. In the C++ code for a queue, when you insert an item, which do you do first: insert the item, increment Rear, or check whether Rear is at the end of the array.

Check whether Rear is at the end of the array (in which case wraparound is necessary).

3. Why is wraparound necessary for (at least some implementations of) queues but not for stacks?

Stacks grow and shrink from the same end of an array, while queues grow from one end and shrink from the other, causing them to move through the array like a caterpillar.

4. What does it mean when we say the remove() member function for a queue "assumes" the queue is not empty?

It means the function will operate incorrectly if the queue is empty. Thus the entity calling the function should ensure the queue's emptiness before making the call.

5. What's the difference between a queue and a priority queue?

In a queue the first item inserted is the one removed. In a priority queue the highest-priority item is the one removed.

6. Why is wraparound necessary in priority queues?

Trick question. Wraparound is used in queues but not in priority queues.

A

7. True or false: Assuming array implementations, insertion and deletion in queues and priority queues operate in O(1) time.

False. Insertion in a priority queue takes O(N) time.

Hour 8, "Linked Lists"

1. What one piece of data must be included in a link class?

A pointer to the next link.

2. What one piece of data must be included in a linked list class?

A pointer to the first link.

3. Deleting a link from a linked list involves only one change in the list's structure. What is it?

Changing the pointer in the preceding link so it points to the link that follows the one being deleted.

4. How do you get from the current link to the next link?

Go to the link pointed to by pNext in the current link.

5. What task must be carried out by both the find(int key) and remove(int key) member functions?

They must both search for a given key.

6. How many objects of the linked list class are normally used to implement a linked list?

One.

7. What task should be carried out by the destructor of a linked list class in a C++ program?

It should delete any links currently in the list. Failure to do this might cause memory to fill up with unused links.

Hour 9, "Abstract Data Types"

1. When you implement a stack using a linked list rather than an array, what is the chief difference noticed by a user of the stack class?

There should be no difference. That's the point of considering the stack as an ADT.

2. True or false: An abstract C++ class is one whose interface is not yet clearly defined.

False. The interface is defined but the implementation might not be.

3. What does *implementation* mean?

   Implementation is the actual code a class uses to carry out its tasks.

4. What is an ADT?

   An abstract data type is a class (perhaps a data storage structure) where we focus on the interface rather than the implementation.

5. Is a stack an example of an ADT?

   Yes, a stack is an ADT because what defines a stack is the push() and pop() operations, not how they're implemented.

6. Would it make sense to implement an array using a stack?

   Not really. A stack has such a limited interface it would be difficult to use it to implement a stack.

7. Is a linked list an example of an ADT?

   A linked list is not an ADT because we think of it as being implemented in a certain way (with pointers from one link to the next).

Hour 10, "Specialized Lists"

1. What is the advantage of a sorted list over an unsorted list?

   You can access the item with the largest (or smallest) key much more quickly in a sorted list.

2. What is the advantage of a sorted list over a sorted array?

   You can insert and delete items more quickly in a list than an array because no items need to be moved.

3. True or false: It takes O(N) time to insert an item in a sorted list.

   True. You must examine an average of N/2 items to find the insertion point.

4. How does the insertion sort work?

   You copy the contents of an unsorted array to the sorted list, then copy the list contents back into the array.

5. Besides its use in the insertion sort, what's another application for the sorted list?

   It can implement a priority queue.

6. What is the advantage of a doubly linked list over a singly linked list?

   You can traverse in either direction in a doubly linked list.

7. What is the main disadvantage of a doubly linked list?

   The algorithms must keep track of twice as many pointers.

Hour 11, "Recursion"

1. Complete the sentence: A recursive function is one that...

   calls itself.

2. The value of the eighth triangular number is

   36

3. True or false: Recursion is used because it is more efficient.

   False. It's usually used because it simplifies a problem conceptually.

4. What is a base case?

   The situation in which a recursive function returns rather than calls itself.

5. Describe briefly how to anagram a word.

   Rotate the word, then anagram all but the first letter. Continue until all letters have occupied the first position.

6. What's the advantage of the recursive approach to binary searches, as opposed to the loop approach?

   It's easier to program.

7. True or false: A recursive approach can be replaced with a stack-based approach.

   True.

8. In a recursive approach to a binary search, what two things does the recursive function call itself to do?

   There are two calls to itself in the recursive function, one for each half of the range it's searching. However, only one of these calls is actually executed.

Hour 12, "Applied Recursion"

1. Define the term *subtree* as used in our discussion of the Towers of Hanoi puzzle.

   A stack of disks used in the solution of the puzzle.

2. Briefly describe the recursive solution to the Towers of Hanoi puzzle.

   Move a subtree of all but the bottom disk to an intermediate post. Move the bottom disk to the destination post. Move the subtree to the destination post.

3. True or false: The mergesort is faster than the insertion sort.

   True.

4. What does it mean to merge two arrays?

The contents of two sorted arrays are copied to a larger array in such a way that the result is sorted.

5. Briefly describe the mergesort.

An array is divided in half and each half is sorted separately. Then the halves are merged. The process is carried out recursively for smaller and smaller arrays.

6. What is the base case for the mergesort?

When the array size is reduced to 1.

7. What is the Big O efficiency of the mergesort?

O(N*logN).

Hour 13, "Quicksort"

1. What does it mean to partition a number of data items?

To put those with a key greater than a certain value in one group, and those with a key less than the value in another.

2. What is the name given to the value used to separate the two groups into when partitioning?

The pivot value.

3. Describe briefly how the C++ code that carries out the partitioning algorithm works.

Pointers start at opposite ends of the array and move toward each other. Each one stops when it finds a data item that should be swapped. When both have stopped, they swap the items and continue on.

4. True or false: The partitioning algorithm runs in O(N) time.

True.

5. Briefly describe the operation of the quicksort algorithm.

A recursive function does three things: It partitions the array into two groups, calls itself to sort the left group, and calls itself to sort the right group.

6. What is the name of the data item whose key is the same as the pivot value?

The pivot.

7. How do we pick the pivot in the quicksort examples in this hour?

It's the rightmost item in the array being partitioned.

A

Hour 14, "Improving Quicksort"

1. Is there a particular arrangement of data that the naive version of quickSort (where the pivot is always on the right) might have trouble sorting?

   Yes, it's very inefficient when applied to inversely sorted data.

2. Why is the naive quicksort so slow for inversely sorted data?

   Because if the pivot is always chosen on the right, the subarray will be divided into very unequal parts. Partitioning is most efficient with equal parts.

3. What is median-of-three partitioning?

   Choosing the pivot for each partition by picking the median of the first, last, and middle items of the subarray.

4. Name three ways, besides quicksort, to sort small partitions.

   1. Three items or fewer can be sorted "by hand" with a few lines of code.

   2. The insertion sort can be applied to each small partition.

   3. Quicksort can leave small partitions unsorted, and the insertion sort can then sort the entire almost-sorted array.

5. Which is the best system?

   Probably either 1 or 2.

6. If you use median-of-three partitioning, why can't you use quicksort to sort very small partitions?

   The median-of-three process itself requires four cells, so you can't apply quicksort to partitions this size or smaller.

7. What is an easy but tedious way to measure the efficiency of the quicksort algorithm, using the Workshop applet?

   Measure the length of all the dotted lines the applet draws on the screen during the sorting process.

Hour 15, "Binary Trees"

1. The tree class stores the location of only one node. Which node is it?

   The root node.

2. What is the name for a node with no children?

   A leaf node.

3. True or false: In a binary tree, each node can have a maximum of two children.

   True.

4. What does it mean to traverse a tree?

   To visit all the nodes in some order.

5. What defines a binary search tree (as opposed to a binary tree)?

   The left child of a node P has a key value less than P, while the right child has a key value greater than (or perhaps equal to) P.

6. In a tree with N nodes, how many nodes must be examined to find a given node?

   Approximately $\log_2 N$ nodes.

7. What are the advantages of using a binary search tree to store data?

   It performs searches, insertions, and deletions in O(log N) time, making it the most versatile of the data structures.

Hour 16, "Traversing Binary Trees"

1. What three tasks should a recursive function execute to perform an inorder traversal?

   Call itself to traverse a node's left subtree, visit the node, and call itself to traverse the node's right subtree.

2. What is the base case in such traversals?

   When the node is NULL.

3. Here's an expression in postfix notation: AB+C-. Express this in infix notation.

   A+B-C.

4. Describe how to find the node with the maximum key value in a binary search tree.

   Start at the root, and continually go to each node's right child. The first node with no right child is the maximum.

5. The number of steps involved in searching and insertion in a binary tree is proportional to what aspect of the tree?

   The number of levels in the tree.

6. The efficiency of binary search trees in Big O notation is

   O(logN)

7. In C++, what two data members must the Node class contain?

   Pointers to the node's left and right children.

A

Hour 17, "Red-Black Trees"

1. Why is a balanced tree desirable?

   It keeps certain arrangements of data from causing very slow operation.

2. How is the tree kept balanced?

   Rotations are performed on the tree or its subtrees.

3. How do the red-black algorithms know what rotations to perform?

   By noticing when the red-black rules are violated.

4. What is black height?

   The number of black nodes on a path from the root to a leaf (or to a null child).

5. Name the red-black rules.

   - Every node is red or black.
   - The root is always black.
   - If a node is red, its children must be black.
   - Every path from the root to a leaf must have the same black height.

6. What actions can the red-black algorithms perform to keep a tree balanced?

   The colors of nodes can be changed, and rotations can be performed.

7. In what ways can the colors of nodes be changed?

   Color flips can switch the colors of a parent and its children. The colors of individual nodes can be changed.

8. True or false: During a rotation, an entire subtree can be unattached from its parent and reattached to another node.

   True.

Hour 18, "Red-Black Tree Insertions"

1. During what operations are color changes and rotations applied?

   During insertion of a new node and deletion of an existing node.

2. What is the principle way a red-black tree is balanced?

   By performing rotations.

3. What is the purpose of the color rules?

   By making sure the color rules aren't violated, an insertion routine is directed when to perform rotations to keep the tree balanced.

4. What is a color flip?

   Swapping the colors of a parent node and its two children.

5. What is a rotation?

   A reorganization of the tree in which a node's left children move up and its right children move down, or vice versa.

6. What's an inside grandchild?

   A node X is an inside grandchild if it's on the opposite side of its parent P than P is of its parent G (X's grandparent).

7. Briefly describe the insertion process in red-black trees.

   During the following steps, ensure the color rules are not violated. First, perform color flips and rotations, when necessary, on the way down the tree to the insertion point. Then, if necessary, perform rotations after the node is inserted.

8. What do you do when rule 3, (a parent and its child can't both be red) is violated?

   Perform the appropriate rotation.

9. How do you know whether to perform a single rotation or a double rotation?

   A single rotation is used when X is an outside grandchild, a double rotation when it is an inside grandchild.

Hour 19, "2-3-4 Trees"

1. True or false: In a multiway tree, each node can have more than two children.

   True.

2. What is the maximum number of data items per node in a 2-3-4 tree?

   Three.

3. When should a node be split?

   When a full node is encountered during the insertion process.

4. What happens when a node (other than the root) is split?

   Assume the full node X contains items A, B, and C. A new node is created as the right-hand sibling of X. Item A remains in X. Item B moves into X's parent. Item C moves into the new node.

5. If a node is split (assuming it's not the root) what is the increase in the number of levels in the tree?

   None.

A

6. What happens when the root is split?

    Assume the root X contains items A, B, and C. A new node P is created that becomes X's parent (and the new root). A second new node S is created as the right-hand sibling of X. Item A remains in X. Item B moves into P. Item C moves into S.

7. True or false: Sometimes a node split results in additional node splits in nodes farther up the tree.

    False.

8. What keeps a 2-3-4 tree balanced?

    Roughly speaking, the fact that node splits expand the tree horizontally.

Hour 20, "Implementing 2-3-4 Trees"

1. In the `tree234.cpp` program, what C++ feature corresponds to a connection from one node to another?

    A pointer.

2. What is the equivalent in a red-black tree to a 2-node in a 2-3-4 tree?

    A black node with two children.

3. True or false: There are two equivalent ways to transform a 4-node in a 2-3-4 tree into a red-black equivalent.

    False. There are two equivalent forms for the 3-node, not the 4-node.

4. When a 3-node is transformed into its equivalent in a red-black tree, does it matter whether the child is red or black?

    Yes. The child must be red.

5. What operation in a 2-3-4 tree corresponds to a rotation in a red-black tree?

    The choice of which orientation to use when transforming a 3-node into a black parent with a red child.

6. What does a color flip in a red-black tree correspond to in a 2-3-4 tree?

    Splitting a 4-node.

7. Does a 2-3-4 tree operate at the same Big O speed as a red-black tree?

    Yes.

Hour 21, "Hash Tables"

1. What is hashing?

   Hashing is the process of transforming a data item's key into an array address. The keys should be distributed more or less uniformly across the array.

2. What is a collision?

   A collision occurs when two keys hash to the same array index.

3. What is open addressing?

   In open addressing, collisions are resolved by finding an open cell at some other location in the array.

4. What is linear probing?

   Linear probing resolves collisions by stepping along the array one index at a time, looking for the first empty cell.

5. What is clustering?

   Clustering is the tendency for groups of contiguously filled cells to grow larger and larger.

6. True or false: Clustering is a problem with linear probing.

   True.

7. True or false: When using linear probing, it's common to fill an array almost full.

   False. It should be filled only about half full.

Hour 22, "Quadratic Probing"

1. Why do we need quadratic probing and double hashing?

   Because clustering slows down collision resolution in linear probing.

2. What determines the step size in quadratic probing?

   The number of steps that have been taken so far.

3. What determines the step size in double hashing?

   The key of the item.

4. What's the disadvantage of quadratic probing (compared with double hashing)?

   Quadratic probing causes secondary clustering.

5. Why should the table size be a prime number when double hashing is used?

   If it isn't, the fixed step size might divide evenly into the array size, which would cause the probe to fail to visit some cells.

A

6. What is the load factor of a hash table?

   The load factor is the ratio of the number of items to the array size.

7. What are the main disadvantages of all the open addressing schemes?

   The are all very sensitive to the load factor. If the array becomes too full, they slow down to an unacceptable degree.

Hour 23, "Separate Chaining"

1. When a collision occurs in separate chaining, how is an open array cell located?

   An array cell isn't used. Instead, the new item is inserted in a list at the original array location.

2. In separate chaining, how do you access an item with a given key?

   Hash to the appropriate array address, then search the linked list at that location.

3. True or false: Unsorted lists must be used in separate chaining.

   False. Sorted lists can be used as well.

4. If there are N items in a hash table that uses separate chaining, and an average of M items on each list, how long does it take, on average, to find a particular item?

   $1 + M/2$

5. What is a bucket?

   It's an array used instead of a linked list in a modified version of separate chaining.

6. In separate chaining with unsorted lists, which is faster, a successful search or an unsuccessful search?

   A successful search is faster because an average of only half the items on a list must be examined.

7. True or false: The efficiency of separate chaining degrades rapidly as the load factor approaches 1.

   False. Efficiency degrades slowly (linearly) as the load factor exceeds 1.

APPENDIX B

How to Run the Workshop Applets and Sample Programs

In this appendix we discuss the details of running the Workshop applets and the sample programs. The Workshop applets are graphics-based demonstration programs, written in Java, that show what trees and other data structures look like. You can run the applets with a Web browser. The sample programs, whose source files are shown in the text, present runnable C++ code.

The readme.txt file in the CD-ROM that accompanies this book contains further information on the topics discussed in this appendix. Be sure to read this file for the latest information on working with the Workshop applets and example programs.

The Workshop Applets

An *applet* is a special kind of Java program that is easy to send over the Internet's World Wide Web. Because Java applets are designed for the Internet, they can run on any computer platform that has an appropriate applet viewer or Web browser.

In this book, the Workshop applets provide dynamic graphics-based demonstrations of the concepts discussed in the text. For example, the discussion of binary trees (Hour 15, "Binary Trees" and Hour 16, "Traversing Binary Trees") includes a Workshop applet that shows a tree in the applet window. Clicking buttons will show the steps involved in inserting a new node into the tree, deleting an existing node, traversing the tree, and so on. Other hours include appropriate Workshop applets. Screen shots (figures) in the book show what the applets look like.

Opening the Workshop Applets

The Workshop applets will be found on the CD-ROM that accompanies this book. Each applet consists of an `.html` file and several `.class` files. These are grouped in a subdirectory that has approximately the same name as the applet itself. This subdirectory is placed within the directory for the appropriate hour. Don't confuse the directory that holds the applets (JavaApps) with the directory that holds the sample programs (C++Progs).

To run the Workshop applets, use your browser to navigate to the appropriate directory by selecting Open from the File menu and then going to the appropriate directory. Then open the appropriate .HTML file.

The applet should start running. (Sometimes they take a while to load, so be patient.) The applet's appearance should be close to the screen shots shown in the text. (It won't look exactly the same because every browser and applet viewer interprets HTML and Java format somewhat differently.)

Operating the Workshop Applets

Each hour gives instructions for operating specific Workshop applets. Remember that in most cases you'll need to repeatedly click a single button to carry out an operation. Each press of the Ins button in the Array Workshop applet, for example, causes one step of the insertion process to be carried out. Generally a message is displayed telling what's happening at each step.

You should complete each operation—that is, each sequence of button clicks—before clicking a different button to start a different operation. When an operation is complete, you'll see the message `Press any Button`. For example, keep clicking the Find button until the item with the specified key is located, and you see the message Press any button. Only then should you switch to another operation involving another button, such as inserting a new item with the Ins button.

The sorting applets from Hours 4, "The Bubble Sort," 5, "The Insertion Sort," 13, "Quicksort," and 14, "Improving Quicksort" have a Step button with which you can view the sorting process one step at a time. They also have a Run mode in which the sort runs at high speed without additional button clicks. Just click the Run button once and watch the bars sort themselves. To pause, you can click the Step button at any time. Running can be resumed by clicking the Run button again.

The sorting applets also include a Draw button. Sometimes during the run process the display becomes corrupted. If this happens, pressing the Draw button restores the display. It also stops the run, so you'll need to press the Run button again to continue.

It's not intended that readers study the code for the Workshop applets, which is mostly concerned with the graphic presentation. Hence source listings are not provided.

Multiple Class Files

Often several Workshop applets will use .class files with the same names. Note, however, that these files might not be identical. The applet or sample program might not work if the wrong class file is used with it, even if the file has the correct name.

This should not normally be a problem because all the files for a given program are placed in the same subdirectory. However, if you move files by hand you might inadvertently copy a file to the wrong directory. Doing this might cause problems that are hard to trace.

B

The Sample Programs

The sample programs are intended to show as simply as possible how the data structures and algorithms discussed in this book can be implemented in C++.

For simplicity, our sample programs run in console mode, which means that output is displayed as text and input is performed by the user typing at the keyboard. In the Windows environment the console mode runs in an MS-DOS box. There is no graphics display in console mode.

The source code for the sample programs is presented in the text of the book. Source files, consisting of the same text as in the book, are included on the CD-ROM. These have the .cpp file extension. There are also compiled versions of the sample programs that can be executed directly. These have the .exe extension.

Running the Sample Programs

You can run executable versions of the sample programs from within MS-DOS. You can invoke MS-DOS from Windows by selecting Programs from the Start menu, and then selecting MS-DOS Prompt.

From an MS-DOS prompt, go to the appropriate subdirectory (using the `cd` command) and find the `.exe` file. For example, for the `insertSort` program, go to the C++Progs directory and then to the `insertSort` subdirectory in Hour 5. (Don't confuse C++Progs, the directory holding the sample programs, with JavaApps, which holds the Workshop applets.) You should see the insertSort.exe file when you type dir (for directory). To execute the program, simply enter the filename:

```
C:\C++Progs\Chap05\insertSort>insertSort
```

Don't type a file extension. The `insertSort` program should run, and you'll see a text display of unsorted and sorted data. In some sample programs you'll see a prompt inviting you to enter input, which you type at the keyboard.

Compiling the Sample Programs

If you have a C++ compiler, you can experiment with the sample programs by modifying them and then compiling and running the modified versions. You can also write your own applications from scratch, compile them, and run them. We don't provide a C++ compiler, but capable basic compilers are available from manufacturers such as Microsoft and Borland for under $100.

Terminating the Sample Programs

You can terminate any running console-mode program, including any of the sample programs, by pressing the Ctrl+C key combination (the control key and the C key pressed at the same time). Some sample programs have a termination procedure that's mentioned in the text, such as pressing Enter at the beginning of a line, but for the others you must press Ctrl+C.

APPENDIX C

Further Reading

This appendix mentions some relevant books on data structures and algorithms and other components of software development. This is a subjective, noninclusive list; there are many other excellent titles on all the topics mentioned.

Data Structures and Algorithms

The definitive reference for any study of data structures and algorithms is *The Art of Computer Programming* by Donald E. Knuth, of Stanford University (Addison Wesley, 1997). This seminal work, originally published in the 1970s, is now in its third edition. It consists of three volumes: *Volume 1: Fundamental Algorithms*, *Volume 2: Seminumerical Algorithms*, and *Volume 3: Sorting and Searching*. Of these, the last is the most relevant to the topics in this book. This work is highly mathematical and does not make for easy reading, but it is the bible for anyone contemplating serious research in the field.

A somewhat more accessible text is Robert Sedgewick's *Algorithms in C++* (Addison Wesley, 1992). This book is adapted from the earlier *Algorithms* (Addison Wesley, 1988) in which the code examples were written in Pascal. It is comprehensive and authoritative. The text and code examples are quite compact and require close reading, but this is an excellent second book on DS&A. The first volume of an improved and expanded version of this work has recently been added: *Algorithms in C++, Pts 1-4*, (1999). (The "Pts" in the title means "Parts.")

A good text for an undergraduate course in data structures and algorithms is *Data Abstraction and Problem Solving with C++: Walls and Mirrors* by Frank M. Carrano (Benjamin Cummings, 1997). There are many illustrations, and the chapters end with exercises and projects.

Practical Algorithms in C++, by Bryan Flamig (John Wiley and Sons, 1995), covers many of the usual topics in addition to some topics not frequently covered by other books, such as algorithm generators and string searching.

If you want to learn about data structures and algorithms with sample programs written in the Java programming language instead of C++, try *Mitchell Waite Signature Series: Data Structures and Algorithms in Java*, by Robert Lafore (Waite Group Press, 1998). That book, extensively modified, forms the basis of the present book.

Some other worthwhile texts on data structures and algorithms are *Classic Data Structures in C++* by Timothy A. Budd (Addison Wesley, 1994); *Algorithms, Data Structures, and Problem Solving with C++* by Mark Allen Weiss (Addison Wesley, 1996); and *Data Structures Using C and C++* by Y. Langsam, et al. (Prentice Hall, 1996).

Object-Oriented Programming Languages

An introduction to C++ and object-oriented programming by the same author as this book is *Object-Oriented Programming in C++, Third Edition*, by Robert Lafore (Sams Publishing, 1999). It's aimed at newcomers to programming and covers ANSI Standard C++.

The most authoritative work on C++ is *The C++ Programming Language* by Bjarne Stroustrup, the creator of C++ (Addison Wesley, 1997). This isn't a book for beginners, but it's necessary if you want to understand the nuances of how the language should be used.

C++ Distilled, by Ira Pohl (Addison Wesley, 1997) is a short book that summarizes C++ syntax. It's handy if you've forgotten how to use some language feature and need to look it up in a hurry.

After you've mastered the fundamentals of C++ syntax, you can learn a great deal about how to use the language from *Effective C++* by Scott Meyers (Addison Wesley, 1997) and the sequel *More Effective C++* (1996).

The Java programming language is similar to C++. One important difference is that it dispenses with pointers, which makes it easier to learn (but not quite as flexible). If you're interested in Java programming, *Java How to Program* by H. M. Deitel and P. J. Deitel (Prentice Hall, 1997) is a good textbook, complete with many exercises.

Core Java 1.2 by Cay S. Horstmann and Gary Cornell (Prentice Hall, 1998) is a multi-volume series that covers advanced Java topics in depth.

Object-Oriented Design and Software Engineering

For an easy, non-academic introduction- to software engineering, try *The Object Primer: The Application Developer's Guide to Object-Orientation* by Scott W. Ambler (Sigs Books, 1998). This short book explains in plain language how to design a large software application. The title is a bit of a misnomer; it goes way beyond mere OO concepts.

A classic in the field of OOD is *Object-Oriented Analysis and Design with Applications* by Grady Booch (Addison Wesley, 1994). The author is one of the pioneers in this field and the creator of the Booch notation for depicting class relationships. This book isn't easy for beginners, but is essential for more advanced readers.

An early book on OOD is *The Mythical Man-Month* by Frederick- P. Brooks, Jr. (Addison Wesley, 1975, reprinted in 1995), which explains in a very clear and literate way some of the reasons why good software design is necessary. It is said to have sold more copies than any other computer book.

Mitchell Waite Signature Series: Object-Oriented Design in Java by Stephen Gilbert and Bill McCarty (Waite Group Press, 1998) is an unusually accessible introduction to OOD and software engineering.

Other good texts on OOD are *An Introduction to Object-Oriented Programming*, by Timothy Budd (Addison Wesley, 1996); *Object-Oriented Design Heuristics*, by Arthur J. Riel, (Addison Wesley, 1996); and *Design Patterns: Elements of Reusable Object-Oriented Software*, by Erich Gamma, et al. (Addison Wesley, 1995).

C

Programming Style

Books on other aspects of good programming:

Programming Pearls by Jon- Bentley (Addison Wesley, 1986) was written before OOP but is nevertheless stuffed full of great advice for the programmer. Much of the material deals with data structures and algorithms.

Writing Solid Code, by Steve Maguire (Microsoft Press, 1993) and *Code Complete* by Steve McConnell (Microsoft Press, 1993) contain good ideas for software development and coding and will help you develop good programming practices.

INDEX

mcp.com
The Authoritative Encyclopedia of Computing

Resource Centers
Books & Software
Personal Bookshelf
WWW Yellow Pages
Online Learning
Special Offers
Site Search
Industry News

▶ Choose the online ebooks that you can view from your personal workspace on our site.

About MCP   Site Map   Product Support

Get the best information and learn about latest developments in:

- ■ Design
- ■ Graphics and Multimedia
- ■ Enterprise Computing and DBMS
- ■ General Internet Information
- ■ Operating Systems
- ■ Networking and Hardware
- ■ PC and Video Gaming
- ■ Productivity Applications
- ■ Programming
- ■ Web Programming and Administration
- ■ Web Publishing

Turn to the *Authoritative* Encyclopedia of Computing

You'll find over 150 full text books online, hundreds of shareware/freeware applications, online computing classes and 10 computing resource centers full of expert advice from the editors and publishers of:

- Adobe Press
- BradyGAMES
- Cisco Press
- Hayden Books
- Lycos Press
- New Riders

- Que
- Que Education & Training
- Sams Publishing
- Waite Group Press
- Ziff-Davis Press

mcp.com
The Authoritative Encyclopedia of Computing

When you're looking for computing information, consult the authority. The Authoritative Encyclopedia of Computing at mcp.com.

Get FREE books and more...when you register this book online for our Personal Bookshelf Program

http://register.samspublishing.com/

SAMS

 Register online and you can sign up for our *FREE Personal Bookshelf Program*—immediate and unlimited access to the electronic version of more than 200 complete computer books! That means you'll have 100,000 pages of valuable information onscreen, at your fingertips!

 Plus, you can access product support, including complimentary downloads, technical support files, book-focused links, companion Web sites, author sites, and more!

 And, don't miss out on the opportunity to sign up for a *FREE subscription to a weekly email newsletter* to help you stay current with news, announcements, sample book chapters, and special events, including sweepstakes, contests, and various product giveaways.

 We value your comments! Best of all, the entire registration process takes only a few minutes to complete, so go online and get the greatest value going—absolutely FREE!

Don't Miss Out On This Great Opportunity!

Sams® is a brand of Macmillan Computer Publishing USA. For more information, visit *www.mcp.com*

Copyright ©1999 Macmillan Computer Publishing USA

SAMS
Teach Yourself
in 24 Hours

When you only have time for the answers™

Sams Teach Yourself in 24 Hours *gets you the results you want—fast! Work through 24 proven 1-hour lessons and learn everything you need to know to get up to speed quickly. It has the answers you need at the price you can afford.*

Sams Teach Yourself Database Programming with Visual Basic 6 in 24 Hours

Dan Rahmel
ISBN: 0-672-31409-6
$19.99 US/$29.95 CAN

Other Sams Teach Yourself in 24 Hours Titles

Visual C++ 6
Mickey Williams
ISBN: 0-672-31303-0
$24.99 US/$37.95 CAN

Palm Programming
Gavin Maxwell
ISBN: 0-672-31611-0
$24.99 US/$37.95 CAN

GIMP
Joshua Pruitt
ISBN: 0-672-31509-2
$24.99 US/$37.95 CAN

MFC
Michael Morrison
ISBN: 0-672-31553-x
$24.99 US/$37.95 CAN

Shell Programming
Sriranga Veeraraghavan
ISBN: 0-672-31481-9
$19.99 US/$29.95 CAN

Linux Programming
Warren W. Gay
ISBN: 0-672-31582-3
$24.99 US/$37.95 CAN

C++ Starter Kit
Jesse Liberty
ISBN: 0-672-31067-8
$24.99 US/$37.95 CAN

Linux
Bill Ball
ISBN: 0-672-31526-2
$24.99 US/$37.95 CAN

All prices are subject to change.

SAMS

www.samspublishing.com

Other Related Titles

Using C++
Rob McGregor
ISBN: 0-7897-1667-4
$29.99 US/$44.95 CAN

The Waite Group's COM/DCOM Primer Plus
John Cadman
ISBN: 0-672-31492-4
$39.99 US/$59.95 CAN

CORBA Programming Unleashed
Suhail Ahmed
ISBN: 0-672-31026-0
$39.99 US/$59.95 CAN

HPL: Volume IV: Functional and Logic Programming Languages
Peter Salus
ISBN: 0-57870-011-6
$49.99 US/$74.95 CAN

Smart Card Developer's Kit
Scott Guthery, Tim Jurgensen
ISBN: 1-57870-027-2
$79.99 US/$119.95 CAN

Mitch Waite Signature Series: C++ Primer Plus
Stepen Prata
ISBN: 1-57169-131-6
$49.99 US/$74.95 CAN

C++ Interactive Course
Robert LaFore
ISBN: 1-57169-063-8
$49.99 US/$74.95 CAN

Turbo C++ Programming in 12 Easy Lessons
Borland International Inc.
ISBN: 0-672-30523-2
$39.99 US/$59.95 CAN

Mastering Turbo Assembler
Tom Swan
ISBN: 0-672-30526-7
$45.00 US/$67.95 CAN

HPL: Volume II: Imperative Programming Languages
Peter Salus
1-57870-009-4
$49.99 US/$74.95 CAN

Java by Example
Clay Walnum
ISBN: 0-7897-0814-0
$34.99 US/$52.95 CAN

SAMS

www.samspublishing.com

All prices are subject to change.

What's on the Disc

The companion CD-ROM contains all the author's source code, samples from the book, and some third-party software products.

Windows 95, Windows 98, and Windows NT 4 Installation Instructions

1. Insert the CD-ROM disc into your CD-ROM drive.
2. From the desktop, double-click the My Computer icon.
3. Double-click the icon representing your CD-ROM drive.
4. Double-click the icon titled START.EXE to run the installation program.
5. Follow the onscreen instructions to finish the installation.

If Windows 95, Windows 98, or Windows NT 4 is installed on your computer and you have the AutoPlay feature enabled, the START.EXE program starts automatically whenever you insert the disc into your CD-ROM drive.

GNU GENERAL PUBLIC LICENSE

Version 2, June 1991

Copyright (C) 1989, 1991 Free Software Foundation, Inc.

675 Mass Ave, Cambridge, MA 02139, USA

Everyone is permitted to copy and distribute verbatim copies of this license document, but changing it is not allowed.

Preamble

The licenses for most software are designed to take away your freedom to share and change it. By contrast, the GNU General Public License is intended to guarantee your freedom to share and change free software—to make sure the software is free for all its users. This General Public License applies to most of the Free Software Foundation's software and to any other program whose authors commit to using it. (Some other Free Software Foundation software is covered by the GNU Library General Public License instead.) You can apply it to your programs, too.

When we speak of free software, we are referring to freedom, not price. Our General Public Licenses are designed to make sure that you have the freedom to distribute copies of free software (and charge for this service if you wish), that you receive source code or can get it if you want it, that you can change the software or use pieces of it in new free programs; and that you know you can do these things.

To protect your rights, we need to make restrictions that forbid anyone to deny you these rights or to ask you to surrender the rights. These restrictions translate to certain responsibilities for you if you distribute copies of the software, or if you modify it.

For example, if you distribute copies of such a program, whether gratis or for a fee, you must give the recipients all the rights that you have. You must make sure that they, too, receive or can get the source code. And you must show them these terms so they know their rights.

We protect your rights with two steps: (1) copyright the software, and (2) offer you this license which gives you legal permission to copy, distribute and/or modify the software.

Also, for each author's protection and ours, we want to make certain that everyone understands that there is no warranty for this free software. If the software is modified by someone else and passed on, we want its recipients to know that what they have is not the original, so that any problems introduced by others will not reflect on the original authors' reputations.

Finally, any free program is threatened constantly by software patents. We wish to avoid the danger that redistributors of a free program will individually obtain patent licenses, in effect making the program proprietary. To prevent this, we have made it clear that any patent must be licensed for everyone's free use or not licensed at all.

The precise terms and conditions for copying, distribution and modification follow.

GNU GENERAL PUBLIC LICENSE

TERMS AND CONDITIONS FOR COPYING, DISTRIBUTION
AND MODIFICATION

0. This License applies to any program or other work which contains a notice placed by the copyright holder saying it may be distributed under the terms of this General Public License. The "Program", below, refers to any such program or work, and a "work based on the Program" means either the Program or any derivative work under copyright law: that is to say, a work containing the Program or a portion of it, either verbatim or with modifications and/or translated into another language. (Hereinafter, translation is included without limitation in the term "modification".) Each licensee is addressed as "you".

Activities other than copying, distribution and modification are not covered by this License; they are outside its scope. The act of running the Program is not restricted, and the output from the Program is covered only if its contents constitute a work based on the Program (independent of having been made by running the Program). Whether that is true depends on what the Program does.

1. You may copy and distribute verbatim copies of the Program's source code as you receive it, in any medium, provided that you conspicuously and appropriately publish on each copy an appropriate copyright notice and disclaimer of warranty; keep intact all the notices that refer to this License and to the absence of any warranty; and give any other recipients of the Program a copy of this License along with the Program.

You may charge a fee for the physical act of transferring a copy, and you may at your option offer warranty protection in exchange for a fee.

2. You may modify your copy or copies of the Program or any portion of it, thus forming a work based on the Program, and copy and distribute such modifications or work under the terms of Section 1 above, provided that you also meet all of these conditions:

a) You must cause the modified files to carry prominent notices stating that you changed the files and the date of any change.

b) You must cause any work that you distribute or publish, that in whole or in part contains or is derived from the Program or any part thereof, to be licensed as a whole at no charge to all third parties under the terms of this License.

c) If the modified program normally reads commands interactively when run, you must cause it, when started running for such interactive use in the most ordinary way, to print or display an announcement including an appropriate copyright notice and a notice that there is no warranty (or else, saying that you provide a warranty) and that users may redistribute the program under these conditions, and telling the user how to view a copy of this License. (Exception: if the Program itself is interactive but does not normally print such an announcement, your work based on the Program is not required to print an announcement.)

These requirements apply to the modified work as a whole. If identifiable sections of that work are not derived from the Program, and can be reasonably considered independent and separate works in themselves, then this License, and its terms, do not apply to those sections when you distribute them as separate works. But when you distribute the same sections as part of a whole which is a work based on the Program, the distribution of the whole must be on the terms of this License, whose permissions for other licensees extend to the entire whole, and thus to each and every part regardless of who wrote it.

Thus, it is not the intent of this section to claim rights or contest your rights to work written entirely by you; rather, the intent is to exercise the right to control the distribution of derivative or collective works based on the Program.

In addition, mere aggregation of another work not based on the Program with the Program (or with a work based on the Program) on a volume of a storage or distribution medium does not bring the other work under the scope of this License.

3. You may copy and distribute the Program (or a work based on it, under Section 2) in object code or executable form under the terms of Sections 1 and 2 above provided that you also do one of the following:

a) Accompany it with the complete corresponding machine-readable source code, which must be distributed under the terms of Sections 1 and 2 above on a medium customarily used for software interchange; or,

b) Accompany it with a written offer, valid for at least three years, to give any third party, for a charge no more than your cost of physically performing source distribution, a complete machine-readable copy of the corresponding source code, to be distributed under the terms of Sections 1 and 2 above on a medium customarily used for software interchange; or,

c) Accompany it with the information you received as to the offer to distribute corresponding source code. (This alternative is allowed only for noncommercial distribution and only if you received the program in object code or executable form with such an offer, in accord with Subsection b above.)

The source code for a work means the preferred form of the work for making modifications to it. For an executable work, complete source code means all the source code for all modules it contains, plus any associated interface definition files, plus the scripts used to control compilation and installation of the executable. However, as a special exception, the source code distributed need not include anything that is normally distributed (in either source or binary form) with the major components (compiler, kernel, and so on) of the operating system on which the executable runs, unless that component itself accompanies the executable.

If distribution of executable or object code is made by offering access to copy from a designated place, then offering equivalent access to copy the source code from the same place counts as distribution of the source code, even though third parties are not compelled to copy the source along with the object code.

4. You may not copy, modify, sublicense, or distribute the Program except as expressly provided under this License. Any attempt otherwise to copy, modify, sublicense or distribute the Program is void, and will automatically terminate your rights under this License. However, parties who have received copies, or rights, from you under this License will not have their licenses terminated so long as such parties remain in full compliance.

5. You are not required to accept this License, since you have not signed it. However, nothing else grants you permission to modify or distribute the Program or its derivative works. These actions are prohibited by law if you do not accept this License. Therefore, by modifying or distributing the Program (or any work based on the Program), you indicate your acceptance of this License to do so, and all its terms and conditions for copying, distributing or modifying the Program or works based on it.

6. Each time you redistribute the Program (or any work based on the Program), the recipient automatically receives a license from the original licensor to copy, distribute or modify the Program subject to these terms and conditions. You may not impose any further restrictions on the recipients' exercise of the rights granted herein. You are not responsible for enforcing compliance by third parties to this License.

7. If, as a consequence of a court judgment or allegation of patent infringement or for any other reason (not limited to patent issues), conditions are imposed on you (whether by court order, agreement or otherwise) that contradict the conditions of this License,

they do not excuse you from the conditions of this License. If you cannot distribute so as to satisfy simultaneously your obligations under this License and any other pertinent obligations, then as a consequence you may not distribute the Program at all. For example, if a patent license would not permit royalty-free redistribution of the Program by all those who receive copies directly or indirectly through you, then the only way you could satisfy both it and this License would be to refrain entirely from distribution of the Program.

If any portion of this section is held invalid or unenforceable under any particular circumstance, the balance of the section is intended to apply and the section as a whole is intended to apply in other circumstances.

It is not the purpose of this section to induce you to infringe any patents or other property right claims or to contest validity of any such claims; this section has the sole purpose of protecting the integrity of the free software distribution system, which is implemented by public license practices. Many people have made generous contributions to the wide range of software distributed through that system in reliance on consistent application of that system; it is up to the author/donor to decide if he or she is willing to distribute software through any other system and a licensee cannot impose that choice.

This section is intended to make thoroughly clear what is believed to be a consequence of the rest of this License.

8. If the distribution and/or use of the Program is restricted in certain countries either by patents or by copyrighted interfaces, the original copyright holder who places the Program under this License may add an explicit geographical distribution limitation excluding those countries, so that distribution is permitted only in or among countries not thus excluded. In such case, this License incorporates the limitation as if written in the body of this License.

9. The Free Software Foundation may publish revised and/or new versions of the General Public License from time to time. Such new versions will be similar in spirit to the present version, but may differ in detail to address new problems or concerns.

Each version is given a distinguishing version number. If the Program specifies a version number of this License which applies to it and "any later version", you have the option of following the terms and conditions either of that version or of any later version published by the Free Software Foundation. If the Program does not specify a version number of this License, you may choose any version ever published by the Free Software Foundation.

10. If you wish to incorporate parts of the Program into other free programs whose distribution conditions are different, write to the author to ask for permission. For software

which is copyrighted by the Free Software Foundation, write to the Free Software Foundation; we sometimes make exceptions for this. Our decision will be guided by the two goals of preserving the free status of all derivatives of our free software and of promoting the sharing and reuse of software generally.

NO WARRANTY

11. BECAUSE THE PROGRAM IS LICENSED FREE OF CHARGE, THERE IS NO WARRANTY FOR THE PROGRAM, TO THE EXTENT PERMITTED BY APPLICABLE LAW. EXCEPT WHEN OTHERWISE STATED IN WRITING THE COPYRIGHT HOLDERS AND/OR OTHER PARTIES PROVIDE THE PROGRAM "AS IS" WITHOUT WARRANTY OF ANY KIND, EITHER EXPRESSED OR IMPLIED, INCLUDING, BUT NOT LIMITED TO, THE IMPLIED WARRANTIES OF MERCHANTABILITY AND FITNESS FOR A PARTICULAR PURPOSE. THE ENTIRE RISK AS TO THE QUALITY AND PERFORMANCE OF THE PROGRAM IS WITH YOU. SHOULD THE PROGRAM PROVE DEFECTIVE, YOU ASSUME THE COST OF ALL NECESSARY SERVICING, REPAIR OR CORRECTION.

12. IN NO EVENT UNLESS REQUIRED BY APPLICABLE LAW OR AGREED TO IN WRITING WILL ANY COPYRIGHT HOLDER, OR ANY OTHER PARTY WHO MAY MODIFY AND/OR REDISTRIBUTE THE PROGRAM AS PERMITTED ABOVE, BE LIABLE TO YOU FOR DAMAGES, INCLUDING ANY GENERAL, SPECIAL, INCIDENTAL OR CONSEQUENTIAL DAMAGES ARISING OUT OF THE USE OR INABILITY TO USE THE PROGRAM (INCLUDING BUT NOT LIMITED TO LOSS OF DATA OR DATA BEING RENDERED INACCURATE OR LOSSES SUSTAINED BY YOU OR THIRD PARTIES OR A FAILURE OF THE PROGRAM TO OPERATE WITH ANY OTHER PROGRAMS), EVEN IF SUCH HOLDER OR OTHER PARTY HAS BEEN ADVISED OF THE POSSIBILITY OF SUCH DAMAGES.

END OF TERMS AND CONDITIONS